Sentimental Men

Sentimental Men

*Masculinity and the Politics of Affect
in American Culture*

Mary Chapman and Glenn Hendler

EDITORS

UNIVERSITY OF CALIFORNIA PRESS

Berkeley   Los Angeles   London

Earlier versions of chapters appearing herein were previously published as follows: chapter 1 in *American Literature* (December 1996): 707–737; chapter 4 in *Journal of the History of Sexuality* 5, no. 3 (January 1995): 403–428; chapter 7 in Henry B. Wonham, ed., *Critics and the Color Line* (New Brunswick, N.J.: Rutgers University Press, 1996), 191–204; chapter 9 in a forthcoming book by Scott A. Sandage (Cambridge: Harvard University Press), reprinted by permission of Harvard University Press; chapter 10 in *Arizona Quarterly* 52, no. 1 (1996): 1–25.

University of California Press
Berkeley and Los Angeles, California

University of California Press, Ltd.
London, England

Library of Congress Cataloging-in-Publication Data

Sentimental men : masculinity and the politics of affect in American
culture / Mary Chapman and Glenn Hendler, editors.
    p.   cm.
    Includes bibliographical references.
    ISBN 0-520-21621-0 — ISBN 0-520-21622-9 (pbk.)
    1. American literature—Male authors—History and criticism.
2. Men—United States—Psychology. 3. Sentimentalism in literature.
4. Masculinity in literature. 5. Sex role in literature.
6. Emotions in literature. 7. Men in literature. I. Chapman,
Mary, 1962–   . II. Hendler, Glenn, 1962–   .
PS153.M3S46   1999
810.9′353—dc21   99-21585
                                       CIP

Printed in the United States of America
9 8 7 6 5 4 3 2 1

CONTENTS

ILLUSTRATIONS

ACKNOWLEDGMENTS

Many people helped make this book happen. First of all, we are extremely grateful to the many scholars who responded to our initial call for papers, and to others whose interest in work that theorized the intersections of masculinity and sentimentality in nineteenth-century American culture convinced us of the value of this project.

A special thanks is extended to our anonymous readers at the University of California Press; to Heather Zwicker and Mark Simpson, who commented on a draft of the introduction; to Robert W. Gray, for thorough research and indexing; and to Damion Searls, for crack copyediting. Because of their efforts and the willingness of our contributors to follow their guidance, we are convinced that *Sentimental Men* is a better book than it might have been.

In addition, we are indebted to a number of agencies whose financial support enabled us to pursue intercontinental scholarly collaboration: The Social Sciences and Humanities Research Council of Canada, the University of Notre Dame's Institute for Scholarship in the Liberal Arts, and the University of Alberta's Humanities and Fine Arts Research Grants.

Introduction

Mary Chapman and Glenn Hendler

ANNALS OF BLUBBERING: PRESIDENTIAL TEARS
FROM GEORGE WASHINGTON TO GEORGE BUSH

In the fall of 1994, *Time* magazine published a list of occasions on which George Bush shed tears while president. Sardonically headlined "Annals of Blubbering," the article deems it "surprising" that Bush is "a frequent weeper," quoting Barbara Bush's admission that "touching, poignant things" bring "tears to the eyes" of her husband.[1] The article is symptomatic in a number of ways of the politics of affect in contemporary American culture. First, it is clear that Bush's tears are "surprising" because sentimentality and the public display of emotion are conventionally seen as feminine characteristics. At the same time, however, the list demonstrates that there is space in American public life for sentimental men: big boys do cry, even when they become president. Finally, it is noteworthy that Bush's tears were deliberately publicized and that a major national magazine deemed them newsworthy. Masculine affect, in contemporary American culture, can be deployed as a form of public display and political rhetoric.

Tracing the public, political, and cultural precedents of such deployments of sentiment is one of the projects of *Sentimental Men*. Two incidents on *Time*'s list clearly locate Bush's tears in that history. For instance, the sight of "Millie's first litter—five females and a male—brought a tear" to Bush's eyes, staging perhaps the most familiar of sentimental scenarios: a mother in loving proximity to her offspring. Another lachrymal event reported by the magazine portrays the object of sympathy, also conventionally, as the body of a suffering woman: "Tailhook victim Paula Coughlin testified that President Bush 'started to cry' when she told him about her ordeal" of being harassed and assaulted by military men. The last two decades and more of critical and historical work on domestic ideology have provided us with many conceptual tools for reading these two scenes. The scenes' deployment of maternal discourse and domesticity, as well as their location of the source of sentiment in female bodies even when the sympathizer is male, make them seem uncannily familiar to scholars of American sentimental culture.

However, two of the events sketched in *Time*'s story stage Bush's emotionality in less familiar terms, conjoining lachrymose sentimentality with military, public, national, and cultural discourses conventionally coded as masculine. For example, *Time* recounts that in 1990, Dixie Carter's performance of the national anthem made the president cry, and in 1992, Bush "quietly wept" in the "private quarters of Air Force One" as the Oak Ridge Boys "got going on some gospel songs" (18). Popular assumptions about proper gender roles, like current critical understandings of sentimentality as relegated to a feminine domestic sphere, make the image of tears on Air Force One seem anomalous, oxymoronic, contradictory, "surprising." One purpose of *Sentimental Men* is to revise and complicate any understanding of sentimentality that occludes the meaning of such performances of masculine affect—to make the history and cultural significance of an American president's tears more legible.

Presidential blubbering is not, after all, a new phenomenon. Two centuries ago another president named George staged two scenes of tearful masculine sentimentality that solidified his position in the hearts of Americans and quickly became canonical images of masculine self-fashioning and national self-understanding. Washington's address to mutinous officers in 1783 and his resignation from his military command later that year were both self-defining performances, characterized by those in attendance and by later chroniclers as scenes of collective male sentimentality. The latter speech has become more indexical of Washington's foundational authority, perhaps because in the former Washington did not visibly share in his listeners' emotions, while in the latter "his voice faultered [*sic*] and sunk, and the whole house felt his agitations."[2] In both cases, Washington's words and manner evoked tears expressing sympathy, identification, and admiration, but only in the latter was this exchange reciprocal, with audience and speaker alike visibly displaying their emotions. Walt Whitman perfectly captures the affective reciprocity of this exchange in "The Sleepers," describing how Washington "cannot repress the weeping drops" while he "encircles [his officers'] necks with his arm and kisses them on the cheek, / He kisses lightly the wet cheeks one after another. . . ."[3] In other words, one of America's foundational national moments, reproduced in one of its canonical literary texts, involves a fluid affective exchange between men. It is both "surprising" and historically revealing to recognize this exchange—and its recurrent representation in both history and literature—as an example of sentimentality, one of "a set of cultural practices designed to evoke a certain form of emotional response, usually empathy, in the reader or viewer."[4]

THE FEMINIZATION OF AMERICAN SENTIMENTALISM

To explain the cultural and historical trajectory from one George's tears to the other's requires a theoretical and historical revision of the now canonical association of sen-

timentality with femininity. At its eighteenth-century inception, the cult of sentiment—or sensibility, as it was then known—constructed the figure of the "man of
feeling" as a male body feminized by affect, a sort of emotional cross-dresser. In its
early years as a literary and philosophical movement, the cult of sentiment was pro-
pelled by male writers such as Laurence Sterne, Samuel Richardson, J. W. Goethe,
and Henry MacKenzie, and by characters who epitomized the "man of feeling"
such as Goethe's Werther and MacKenzie's Harley. Among its most prominent theorists was Adam Smith, who famously described the affective dynamic underpinning
the politics of sympathy in 1759 in *The Theory of Moral Sentiments:* "It is by the imagination only that we can form any conception of what are [the] sensations [of our
brother on the rack]. . . . By the imagination we place ourselves in his situation, we
conceive ourselves enduring all the same torments, we enter as it were into his body
and become in some measure the same person with him."[5] For Smith and his
eighteenth-century contemporaries, sensibility was an ideology motivated by a logic
of affective androgyny, encompassing the republican discourses of both manly virtue
and benevolent motherhood. Rousseau's paradigmatic sentimental scenario in his
Discourse on the Origin and Foundations of Inequality among Men evinces a similarly complex
gender ideology, imagining the emotions of an imprisoned man watching a beast
violently murder and disembowel a child it has just torn from a mother's arms.[6]

By the middle of the nineteenth century, however, American sentimentality
seemed to have become ensconced solely in a feminine "world of love and ritual,"
in "the empire of the mother."[7] According to this history, as the ideology of separate spheres took hold in the early nineteenth century, the domestic realm came to
be considered the locus of feeling. In the process, the culture of sentiment became
less directly identified with public virtue and benevolence and more associated
with women's moral, nurturing role in the private sphere of the bourgeois family.
Within domestic ideology, in its classic nineteenth-century formulations such as
Catharine Beecher's *Treatise on Domestic Economy*, the home was a feminine realm,
where a woman's influence reigned over the affections of her children and husband.[8] For the man, domesticity offered a "haven in a heartless world," where he
could seek comfort after a day in the marketplace.[9] The public sphere was a cor-
respondingly masculine realm, a site of rational political discourse and economic
production characterized by competition rather than sentiment, by inscrutable
business practices rather than transparent moral tenets. That this binary was
more a class, race, and national ideology than a universal social practice made it
no less effective in shaping discourse on gender, affect, and cultural space.

As the gendered binary of public and domestic became more deeply inscribed,
nineteenth-century cultural forms registered this shift, which might be referred to
in shorthand as a transition from republican ideology to domestic ideology. As
Leslie A. Fiedler, Herbert Ross Brown, and other literary historians noted as early
as the 1940s, the most popular literary formulae replaced virtuous maidens threatened with seduction in the streets of a large city with virtuous children threatened
with death inside the family home. Characters such as the eighteenth-century

"man of feeling" were, according to standard literary histories, replaced by the crying mothers and dying daughters of nineteenth-century fiction, in a sentimental formula Jane Tompkins has more recently described as "the story of salvation through motherly love."[10] By this account, sentiment, sympathy, and sensibility became thoroughly feminized.

The earliest twentieth-century scholarly work on American sentimentality used overtly gendered rhetoric to dismiss sentimental culture, describing it as "escapis[t]," "overly emotional," "sterile . . . anti-intellectual . . . [and] simple-minded."[11] In *The Sentimental Novel in America* (1940), Herbert Ross Brown derided sentimentality for "not facing squarely the realities of American life without losing its high ideals," and for "shrouding the actualities of American life in the flattering mists of sentimental optimism." Although he did not develop an explicitly gendered critique of sentimental literary production, he mourned the "unmistakably feminine treble which dominated the opening chorus of American fiction," and contrasted "authentic artists like Hawthorne" with followers of "sentimental formulas."[12] While E. Douglas Branch's *The Sentimental Years* (1934) noted significant contributions to sentimental literature by male writers like George Lippard, Donald Grant Mitchell ("Ik Marvel"), and Timothy Shay Arthur, it dismissed the productions of "lady novelists" as "flabby," "precious," "unlabored expression[s]" coming from "talent . . . spread widely if thinly."[13]

These repudiations of sentimental culture were repeated and extended in the androcentric canons of American literature drafted by F. O. Matthiessen in *The American Renaissance* (1941) and R. W. B. Lewis in *The American Adam* (1955). Matthiessen's valorizations of Hawthorne for his "psychology," Melville for his "force," and Whitman as the quintessential "man in the open air" were all contrasted with the supposedly sentimental, weak, and domestic writings of women.[14] The contrast was generally made only implicitly, for most critics disdained even a mention of popular texts by women. For instance, Matthiessen's passionate argument, over six hundred pages long, that the American Renaissance produced a "literature for democracy" is famous for referring only once to the most popular and influential novel of the period, *Uncle Tom's Cabin*.[15] Lewis contrasted his canon with the sentimental and the domestic far more explicitly, as he constructed a master plot of American literature centered on an anti-domestic Adam who escapes the apron-strings of wife and family to seek self-sufficient manhood on the frontier.[16]

Leslie A. Fiedler's *Love and Death in the American Novel* (1966) came closer than any other analysis of classic American literature to loosening the conceptual link between sentimentality and femininity, though in the end his argument forcefully reaffirmed the connection. While Fiedler recognized Richardson as a prototype of the sentimental novelist and acknowledged traces of the sentimental tradition in Cooper, Melville and Hawthorne, he argued that "when women became the chief authors as well as the chief characters of the novel," the result was "a blight, a universal influence which was also a universal calamity."[17] Fiedler also claimed that the homoerotic male bond present in classic American literature such as *The Last of the Mohicans* and *The Adventures of Huckleberry Finn* was a defense against the feminization and sentimentality of American culture. According to Fiedler, the "sentimental novel in the United States must end with the downfall of the male" (90). Thus, in the end, masculinity and sentimentality were placed in irreconcilable binary opposition.

The critical demonization of sentimental culture culminated in the 1977 publication of *The Feminization of American Culture*, in which Ann Douglas criticized sentimentality for its "debased religiosity [and] sentimental peddling of Christian belief for its nostalgic value," its "dishonesty," and its conservative anti-intellectualism, as well as blaming it for the disappearance or even "vanquish[ing]" of masculinity and the rise of modern mass culture.[18] Although Douglas's study gives more attention to such genteel "male sentimentalists" as Mitchell and Arthur than anyone before or since, she does so only to deny that canonical writers like Melville and Hawthorne are imbricated in the sentimental literary production she genders female.

Critics and historians have since problematized the opposition Douglas sets up between canonical writers and the writers Hawthorne labeled a "d——d mob of scribbling women."[19] The former Douglas judges as "serious non-commercial writers [who] wrote principally about men . . . engaged in economically and ecologically significant activities [and who] attempted to re-educate, defy and ignore a public addicted to the absorption of sentimental fare"; in this category she includes Melville, Hawthorne, Emerson, Thoreau, and Whitman. The latter were, according to Douglas, occupied with the anti-intellectual, domestically oriented "lighter productions of the press."[20] In responding to Douglas as well as to Matthiessen and Lewis, feminist criticism has initiated a re-examination of the politics of canon formation, exposing the patriarchal principles that underwrote key literary critical concepts such as the American Adam and the self-made man. Patriarchal values have not only excluded women writers from the canon, they have also distorted the ways in which we read the canon: by constructing American masculine types such as the anti-domestic American Adam or the individual loner / revolutionary, critical master narratives like Matthiessen's and Lewis's have masked the continued presence of sentimental men in American culture and letters.[21]

Another response to Douglas's polemic has been what Eve Kosofsky Sedgwick calls "a project . . . of rehabilitating the sentimental."[22] This rehabilitation takes a number of forms. The first, undertaken by feminist historians such as Mary P. Ryan, Linda K. Kerber and Nancy Cott, as well as by literary historians and critics such as Mary Kelley and Lauren Berlant, involves challenging the absolute binary represented by the ideology of separate spheres. Unsettling the alignment of femininity with domesticity in nineteenth-century women's lives, such work has brought "female subjects and the representation of gender into the center of a social history of the public," and provided evidence of women's involvement in the public sphere as political, commercial, and moral agents.[23]

Other critical works, especially Jane Tompkins's *Sensational Designs* (1985) and Philip Fisher's *Hard Facts* (1985), have focused on the political value of sentimentality, drawing out its reformist implications. Tompkins's influential study interprets sentimental novels as radical texts of "power and ambition" that attempt to "redefine the social order."[24] Similarly, Fisher calls sentimentality "a politically radical technique" that "trains and explicates new forms of feeling" by modeling the extension of subjectivity to marginalized groups and individuals.[25] Some feminist scholars have built on this foundation, arguing that sentimentality can be interpreted as part of a popular feminist counter-politics. Hazel V. Carby's *Reconstructing Womanhood* (1987), Jean Fagin Yellin's *Women and Sisters* (1989), Lori D. Ginzberg's *Women and the Work of Benevolence* (1990) and Dana Nelson's *The Word in Black and White* (1993) have all explored the politics of sentiment as a set of important though problematic identificatory strategies between white women and racial Others, seeing sentiment as an index of women's political engagement in reform movements such as abolition and protests against Indian removal.[26] For these critics, the sentimental doctrine of womanly influence found its logical extension in white women's involvement in the national domestic sphere as reformers, philanthropists, and lobbyists. At the other end of the spectrum from an argument like Fisher's—but still analyzing sentimentality's link with the discourses and politics of antebellum reform—is Saidiya V. Hartman's argument in *Scenes of Subjection* (1997) that "rather than bespeaking the mutuality of social relations or the expressive and affective capacity of the subject, sentiment . . . facilitated subjection, domination, and terror precisely by preying upon the flesh, the heart, and the soul."[27]

Recent critics who have traced sentimentalism's development from the seduction novels of the early republic to the bestsellers of the antebellum period have continued the debate over the politics of sympathy. Julia A. Stern's *The Plight of Feeling* (1997) argues that the excessive sentimentality of the early republican novel articulates "collective mourning over . . . the preemption of liberty in the wake of the post-Revolution settlement." She sees these novels as counternarratives, voicing the passions and concerns of "invisible Americans" denied subjectivity and citizenship by the constitution and other discourses of national legitimation.[28] In contrast, Elizabeth Barnes's *States of Sympathy* (1997) is closer to Hartman's argument. Barnes resists assuming the political radicalism of sentimentalism, demonstrating how sympathetic identification, a key trope of the early American novel and its successors, reinforced rather than challenged the patriarchal family model of politics, by mystifying patriarchal discipline as sympathetic coincidence of desires.[29] Similarly, in *Romances of the Republic* (1996), Shirley Samuels analyzes early American fiction as the "prehistory of the separate spheres concept," a division of the social field into "male and female, world and home." For Samuels as for Barnes, the valorization and mystification of familialized emotional bonds work towards making the privatized family into "an instrument of governmental measures of social control even as the separateness of the family from these measures is insisted on."[30]

Nevertheless, throughout these debates about the political value of sentimental culture, work on sentimentality since 1985 has largely accepted the gendering of sentiment as feminine. Critical works responding to Douglas and sentimentality's other detractors have continued to assume that sentimentality is a fundamentally feminine affective structure. Sentimental literature is presumed to be centered on an identification with a suffering female protagonist, a sympathy extended to other subordinated groups in novels such as *Uncle Tom's Cabin*. Contemporary feminist literary criticism has continued to perpetuate this gendering of sentiment by constructing what amounts to an alternative canon of popular but critically marginalized texts written for, by, and about women, thereby ignoring the ways in which canonical male writers, such as Brockden Brown, Cooper, Melville, Hawthorne, Whitman, Holmes, Norris, and Dreiser, all deploy the discourse of sentiment in their works. In the midst of these recuperations, critics have tended to reinforce rather than question the gender binary, to such an extent that the origins of American sentimentality in the "man of feeling"—as well as his traces in nineteenth- and even twentieth-century culture—have been all but lost.[31]

Histories and critical analyses of eighteenth- and especially nineteenth-century sentimentalism, in particular, have provided powerful descriptions of the binary structure of domestic ideology, and have found it repeated in every cultural form and social practice they study. The fit between ideology and cultural form is rarely so tight, however. Assuming that sentimental cultural forms duplicate the doctrine of separate spheres risks replicating the binary structure that one intends to describe and critique. In that replication, the ideology's exclusions and normativity can be reinscribed so that, for instance, the middle-class, white, and heterosexual biases of the doctrine of separate spheres are left unexamined and unchallenged, and male-authored texts like *Reveries of a Bachelor* or *Clara Howard*—both unquestionably traversed by sentimental discourse—are left out of histories of sentimental literature, just as they were left out of earlier canons.

As a result, studies of gender in American sentimental culture have focused almost exclusively on women. For instance, Shirley Samuels's otherwise excellent volume of essays entitled *The Culture of Sentiment: Race, Gender and Sentimentality in Nineteenth-Century America* (1992) reads sentimentality as a "national project about imagining the nation's bodies and the national body," but, with the exception of Ann Fabian's essay on an antebellum gambling man, the volume measures the impact of sentimentality exclusively on women's bodies, women's texts, and women's lives.[32] The continuing lack of attention to male writers', artists', and philosophers' engagement with American sentimental culture suggests, even now, a critical unwillingness to imagine the American man of sentiment, as if this subject position is too paradoxical, too unstable, too threatening to discuss; as if critics fear the results of deconstructing the alignments of reason, commerce, and the public sphere with men, and feelings, domesticity and the private sphere with women. But if, as Douglas claims, American men have been disempowered by the feminizing effects of sentimental culture, why would they not participate in a discourse that, according to Annette Kolodny, has represented a "genuine tool for [those] otherwise disenfranchised?"[33]

THE CULTURAL WORK OF SENTIMENTAL MEN

The essays in *Sentimental Men: Masculinity and the Politics of Affect in American Culture* demonstrate that men did in fact participate in sentimental discourse. The goal of this volume is to build on the important work mentioned above by recognizing and analyzing the importance of masculine sentimentality in American cultural history. The contributors to *Sentimental Men* question any uncomplicated gendering of sentiment as feminine, demonstrating that the ideology of separate spheres was suffused by contested discourses of race, class, ethnicity, and sexuality. They also extend the work done by feminist scholars on the identificatory politics of sentiment by examining the affinities—or lack of affinities—which might motivate a male sentimental discourse. Could a man of privilege identify with a male object of suffering in the same way that white women are believed to have identified with racial Others? Would that identification have the same political force—and the same limitations—as white women's politics of sympathetic identification?

Sentimental Men also joins and supplements the recent explosion of work on American masculinity. Until recently, much of what has been written about American manhood has focused on elite white men's participation in the public sphere, rather than on the lives of men across class and racial lines.[34] For instance, although Peter Filene's *Him / Her / Self* (1976), Joe L. Dubbert's *A Man's Place: Masculinity in Transition* (1979), E. Anthony Rotundo's *American Manhood* (1993), and Michael S. Kimmel's *Manhood in America: A Cultural History* (1996) do much to advance the study of American masculinity, all focus primarily on "the most influential group of Americans in the nineteenth century: white, middle-class, Yankee Northerners."[35] Mark C. Carnes and Clyde Griffen's important collection *Meanings for Manhood: Constructions of Masculinity in Victorian America* (1990) is also, as the editors themselves note, limited by its primary focus on white middle-class straight masculinity. Other valuable work on masculinity in American culture has followed Douglas's lead in characterizing men's relationship to the culture of sentiment in largely oppositional terms.[36]

In contrast, *Sentimental Men* complicates understandings of the American man as self-reliant frontiersman, examining men who inhabit the spaces denied them by earlier accounts of the cult of sentiment. It treats African-Americans and Native Americans, working-class men and downwardly mobile men, businessmen and poets, gay men and family men. It is also concerned with spatializing male sentiment, locating it as readily at the Seaside as at the Fireside (to borrow Longfellow's title), as easily in the halls of commerce as in the parlor. Rather than see American "men of feeling" as oxymorons—exceptions to the hard and fast gender rules of sentimental culture—we consider them exemplary of the competing definitions of masculinity available in the pre-twentieth-century United

States. Although some recent research suggests that a crisis in masculinity occurred in America in the late nineteenth century because women's expanding involvement in the public sphere increasingly deprived men of their "traditional roles,"[37] the essays collected in this volume imply a different hypothesis: as early as the founding of the nation, when George Washington and his officers shed tears in public, American masculinity was in flux. American masculinity has always been in crisis, in the sense of being constantly engaged in its own redefinition. Most particularly, pre-twentieth-century American masculinity engaged with the popular culture of the day, a culture in which sentimentality was central to the definitions of both genders' characters and subjectivities. If, as Samuels claims, "sentimentality is literally at the heart of nineteenth-century American culture,"[38] *Sentimental Men* reveals the hidden hearts of sentimental men: crying over their drunken depravities, emotionally begging for financial support, grieving the deaths of their children.

The essays in this volume analyze sentimentality not just as a literary genre or a rhetorical mode but as a practical consciousness—what Raymond Williams calls a "structure of feeling"—that traverses many cultural forms, including begging letters, temperance testimonials, portraits and photographs, philanthropy, and advice manuals.[39] They revise understandings of the American literary canon by revealing the ways in which canonical figures such as Brockden Brown, Emerson, Melville, Longfellow, and Norris can be read as "sentimental men."[40] Many of the essays see the same cluster of tropes normally associated with female sentimentality present in the male cult of sentiment: the dying child; the destruction of families by death, slavery, poverty, and intemperance; and the unnecessary suffering of marginalized figures. They supplement feminist work done on sentimentality by treating men as producers and consumers of sentimental culture, rather than merely protagonists of "melodramas of beset manhood."[41] Like the women Mary Kelley examines in *Private Woman, Public Stage,* sentimental men straddle the ideological boundaries between public and private spheres.

Like many collections of essays, this volume represents the interdisciplinary coincidence of critical work on a single topic. The overwhelming response to a call for papers for a 1994 Modern Language Association panel on "Men and Sentiment in Nineteenth-Century American Literature," and the strong attendance at the resulting event, encouraged us to pursue the topic further by expanding its chronological boundaries to include the early republic, and by extending its disciplinary focus beyond literature to include art history, history, politics, sociology, and economics.

The volume is divided into three sections, each organized chronologically to trace historical shifts and continuities in the topic at hand. The realization that masculinity and sentimentality are mutually constitutive discursive formations will change our understanding of both, as well as of the categories referred to in our section headings—domesticity, the public sphere, and canonicity. The first two sections in the collection confound the binary spatializations of criticism influenced by the ideology of separate spheres by examining the ways in which men have participated in what is known as the domestic sphere, while demonstrating that male involvement in the public sphere, traditionally characterized as a locus of competition rather than compassion, evinces some of the emotion and intimacy critics usually restrict to the home.

Contrary to the argument, mentioned above, that masculine domesticity was not available before 1900, the essays in the section called "Domestic Men" trace the origins of masculine domesticity to an earlier period, and show how even men who were not fathers or husbands could have "feelings for the fireside" in their meditations on family, love and grief. Both Vincent J. Bertolini's and Kirsten Silva Gruesz's essays focus on the hearth, a location symbolically associated in sentimental culture with maternal nurture and moral guidance. Drawing on male advice manuals and bachelor texts like Mitchell's *Reveries of a Bachelor*, as well as selected fiction by Melville, Bertolini argues that the "revery" is at once a site for a bachelor's fantasies about his future wife and a euphemism for masturbation, simultaneously promising the future pleasures of heteronormative family life and threatening a disruption of the bourgeois social and sexual ideology through the possibilities of queer masculinity.

In "Feeling for the Fireside: Longfellow, Lynch, and the Topography of Poetic Power," Gruesz takes to task recent studies of nineteenth-century sentimental poetry, demonstrating that dead-child elegies and other sentimental verse forms were not the exclusive property of popular poetesses, but were also written by canonical male authors such as Longfellow. Gruesz promotes a doubled view of Longfellow as both acolyte of domestic bliss and heroic pioneer and patriarch of a male verse tradition, whose works pair "tears . . . with manly action" (49), borrowing cultural authority from the domestic sphere while reclaiming a particularly masculine dominion over that sphere. Finally, though, Longfellow asserts the male poet's ability to assimilate "female feeling" into a myth of the male authorial self, rewriting the hearth as a site of paternal regulation. Gruesz reads the hearth not only as literary trope but also as physical location in the developing forms of home architecture she analyzes, a remapped domestic space where the now-canonical Longfellow might have been read aloud alongside the popular poetess Anne Lynch (Botta).

Karen Sánchez-Eppler's essay concerns male responses to the deaths of children. Like the figure of the sentimental man, the consolation poem and the mortuary photograph of the dead child confound notions of separate public and private spheres since they are both deeply privatized and endlessly circulated and reproduced. By juxtaposing such photographs and poems with a comparison between Stowe's and Emerson's sentimental meditations on the deaths of their respective sons, Sánchez-Eppler examines the relation between male loss and representation in an age of mechanical reproduction.

If men's presence in the domestic sphere has been largely ignored in criticism and historical writing, the degree to which the public sphere trades on sentimental attachments has been afforded still less critical attention. The essays in "Public Sentiment" assert that the private discourse of sentiment was never a separate sphere divorced from men's public lives. Rather, the public and the private were intimately linked: in abolitionist representations of the relations between black and white men as simultaneously erotic and political; in public philanthropic pleas and temperance testimonies mobilizing sympathetic identification in order to accomplish reform; and in depictions of national leaders and captains of industry as benevolent paternal figures. John Saillant's "The Black Body Erotic and the Republican Body Politic, 1790–1820" examines how a view popularized by prominent sentimentalists such as Jefferson—that blacks and whites could not share bonds of affection because of their irreconcilable differences—was countered by antislavery stories of interracial male friendships published in the early republic. Joseph LaVallée's *The Negro Equalled By Few Europeans*, translated from the French and first published in America in 1791, is one of Saillant's examples of an early antislavery text that refashioned the classical ideal of public martial virtue into an ideal of private affection, benevolence, sentiment and sympathy shared among men. Contesting the dominant argument that sympathy functioned to produce emotional identifications between women and racial others, Saillant argues that these abolitionist stories figured relations between black and white men sexually, whether as the same-sex rape of a slave by his owner or the homoerotic fraternity of a slave and his advocate.

Philip Gould's "Remembering Metacom: Historical Writing and the Cultures of Masculinity in Early Republican America" explores how the Native American military leader Metacom, vilified by Puritan historians for causing colonial war, was sentimentally eulogized by early national history writers as a model of republican virtue through an emphasis on his paternal tenderness, benevolent heart, and sentimental appreciation of friendship. By discussing early historiography, drama, and fiction, Gould outlines how the ascription of republican virtue to the Native American leader could suggest the inclusion of racial Others in America; the early republic's model of sentimental manhood at once humanizes and erases the racial Other.

Glenn Hendler's "Bloated Bodies and Sober Sentiments: Masculinity in 1840s Temperance Narratives" challenges analyses of nineteenth-century sentiment which too quickly categorize it as a form of feminization and a force of privatization, by arguing that the tearful male sentiment represented in temperance novels and eyewitness accounts of temperance meetings refigured and buttressed the homosocial bonds underlying the masculine character of the public sphere. Each man's transformation from "bloated" drunkard to respectable man affirmed the masculinity, middle-classness, and racial whiteness of the narratives' characters and readers, as well as of the participants in Washingtonian "experience meetings."

P. Gabrielle Foreman's "Sentimental Abolition in Douglass's Decade: Revision, Erotic Conversion, and the Politics of Witnessing in *The Heroic Slave* and *My*

Bondage and My Freedom" argues that even when Douglass explicitly abandoned William Lloyd Garrison's "sentimental" abolition, which emphasized "the affectional over the authoritative" (150), he continued to embrace sentimental language and concepts rhetorically in his writing, most particularly in his use of interracial male friendship as a means of moral suasion. Unlike Stowe, who represented white women's conversion to abolition through sympathetic listening to the stories of enslaved women, Douglass uses the language of domestic affection to represent eroticized bonds between men, representing them as more sympathetic listeners than women, even in the domestic sphere, and thereby masculinizing home and family.

Cassandra Cleghorn's essay discusses the dynamics of identification and power on which sentimentality and philanthropy both depend. "Chivalric Sentimentalism: The Case of Dr. Howe and Laura Bridgman" examines the public deployment of sentiment in Dr. Samuel Gridley Howe's well-publicized exhibitions of Bridgman, his model deaf and blind student, to raise money for schools for children with disabilities. Howe's belief that he could teach Bridgman to communicate through sign language was based on a central tenet of sentimentality: that the body is legible. In this case study, Cleghorn elucidates the paternalist potential of philanthropy, an exchange that is always both affective and economic, private and public.

Scott A. Sandage's "The Gaze of Success: Failed Men and the Sentimental Marketplace, 1873–1893" reveals the operation of male sentiment within the competitive sphere of market capitalism at a moment when traditionally defined American manhood was under siege. Sandage analyzes the discourses of sentimentality and masculinity in the thousands of "begging letters" that failed men wrote to celebrated tycoons between the panics of 1873 and 1893. He argues that the sentimental rhetoric deployed in these letters challenges assumptions about the rationalization of business practices in nineteenth-century America; in fact, emotions were among the forms of currency exchanged in the business world.

In the final section of the volume, "Canonical Sentiments," Bruce Burgett, Tara Penry, Martin A. Berger, and Francesca Sawaya explore the implications of the volume's argument for the pervasiveness of male sentiment by offering essays on sentimentalism and antisentimentalism in fiction, art history, and literary criticism. Burgett's "Masochism and Male Sentimentalism: Charles Brockden Brown's *Clara Howard*" counters the canonical critical tradition that reads masochism as a diagnostic figure which pathologizes male sentimentality as a feminization. Burgett's analysis of "the male complaint" implicit in *Clara Howard* brings to light the "paradoxical figure of the sentimental male in a cultural context that increasingly aligned masculinity with rational authority and femininity with moral sentiment."

Like Burgett's essay, Tara Penry's "Sentimental and Romantic Masculinities in *Moby-Dick* and *Pierre*" rereads canonical literary texts while resisting a binarism persistent in American literary criticism and reproduced in Ann Douglas's influential

Feminization of American Culture. Penry contests the characterization of these two novels as the romantic and sentimental extremes of Melville's oeuvre. Whereas Douglas, like many others, has read Melville's conception of masculinity as "essentially
. . . resistan[t] to sentimentalism,"[42] Penry argues instead that, in both of these novels, Melville valorizes sentimental masculinity and its valuation of familial and communal bonds while indicting romantic masculinity's narcissistic self-absorption.

Berger's "Sentimental Realism in Thomas Eakins's Late Portraits" similarly
deconstructs the critical opposition between realism and sentimentalism in
nineteenth-century American art by arguing that Eakins's late portraits draw on
such sentimental traditions as attention to emotion and physiognomy. Art history,
like literary history, has produced a canon by treating sentimentality as its
abjected Other, in this case by treating Eakins's focus on realist science and photography as antithetical to the sentimentalism of more popular artists.

Finally, in "Sentimental Tentacles: Frank Norris's *The Octopus*," Sawaya argues
that naturalism insisted on its masculinity and opposed itself to femininity and the
feminine genre of sentimentalism, but simultaneously deployed sentimental
tropes and themes. While Norris, in particular, criticizes sentimentality for its
inherent domestication of or disconnection from social reality, Sawaya detects an
unacknowledged mesalliance between sentimentality and naturalism.

᛭

Sentimental Men includes within its purview a wide variety of cultural forms and
social practices—popular politics and culture, several literary genres, historiography, the visual arts, economic discourses, and philanthropy. A range of theoretical
approaches is also represented, including feminism and gender studies, queer theory, new historicism, psychoanalysis, and Marxist-inflected cultural studies. But,
much more remains to be said about the intimate and active links between masculinity and sentimentality in pre-twentieth-century American culture. We hope
this volume will initiate a discussion that could also include analysis of other literary genres—for instance, men's contribution to sentimental genres like the gift-
book, or Cuban revolutionary José Martí's use of his time in the United States to
translate into Spanish Helen Hunt Jackson's sentimental novel *Ramona*.[43] Attention
to the problematic conjunction of sentimentality and masculinity could also illuminate the politics of affect in twentieth-century American literature and culture,
from Ernest Hemingway's almost hysterical antisentimentality to the popularity of
Forrest Gump in the 1990s. And perhaps it could help explain the electoral popularity of a president who, despite George Bush's tears, defeated him while repeating
what could be the mantra of the politics of sympathy: "I feel your pain."

NOTES

1. "Annals of Blubbering." *Time*, 17 October 1994, 18.
2. James McHenry to Miss Margaret Caldwell, 23 December 1783, *Letters of Members of
the Continental Congress*, 8 vols., ed. Edmund C. Burnett (Washington: Carnegie Institute of

Washington, 1934): 7:394–6, quotation from 394. Sandra Gustafson discusses this scene in "Deborah Sampson Gannett was a Woman Warrior . . . and so was George Washington: The Framing of Gender Identity and Difference in Early Republican Politics" (paper presented at the American Studies Association conference, Pittsburgh, Pa., November 1995).

3. Walt Whitman, "The Sleepers," in *Complete Poetry and Selected Prose* (New York: Library of America, 1982), 546–7.

4. Shirley Samuels, introduction to *The Culture of Sentiment: Race, Gender, and Sentimentality in Nineteenth-Century America* (New York: Oxford University Press, 1992), 3–84, quotation from 4.

5. Adam Smith, *The Theory of Moral Sentiments,* ed. D. D. Raphael and A. L. Macfie (Oxford: Clarendon Press, 1976), 9.

6. Jean-Jacques Rousseau, "Discourse on the Origin and Foundations of Inequality Among Men," in *The First and Second Discourses,* Roger D. Masters, ed., Roger D. Masters and Judith R. Masters, trans. (New York: St. Martins Press, 1964): 104–20. Philip Fisher analyzes this passage from Rousseau in his *Hard Facts: Setting and Form in the American Novel* (New York: Oxford University Press, 1985), 104–7.

7. These phrases are drawn from the titles of Carroll Smith Rosenberg's essay "The Female World of Love and Ritual," *Signs* 1 (1975): 1–29, and Mary P. Ryan's *The Empire of the Mother: American Writing about Domesticity, 1830–1860* (New York: Harrington Park, 1985).

8. Catharine Beecher, *A Treatise on Domestic Economy, for the Use of Young Ladies at Home and at School* (Boston: Marsh, Capen, 1841), revised and expanded in 1869 in collaboration with Harriet Beecher Stowe as *The American Woman's Home* (Hartford: The Stowe-Day Foundation, 1975).

9. This phrase is drawn from the title of Christopher Lasch's latter-day lament for the passing of domestic ideology, *Haven in a Heartless World: The Family Besieged* (New York: Basic Books, 1977).

10. Jane Tompkins, *Sensational Designs: The Cultural Work of American Fiction, 1790–1860* (New York: Oxford University Press, 1985), 125.

11. Herbert Ross Brown, *The Sentimental Novel in America* (Durham, N.C.: Duke University Press, 1940), 360; Fred Pattee, *The Feminine Fifties* (Port Washington, N.Y.: Kennikat Press, 1966), 92; Leslie A. Fiedler, *Love and Death in the American Novel* (New York: Anchor, 1992), 76, 79, 105.

12. Brown, *Sentimental Novel in America,* 370, 360, 100, 322.

13. E. Douglas Branch, *The Sentimental Years* (New York: D. Appleton-Century Company, 1934), 138, 136, 132, 135.

14. F. O. Matthiessen, *The American Renaissance: Art and Expression in the Age of Emerson and Whitman* (New York: Oxford University Press, 1941), 5.

15. Matthiessen, *American Renaissance,* xv. Tompkins points out Matthiessen's single reference to Stowe in *Sensational Designs,* 200.

16. R. W. B. Lewis, *The American Adam: Innocence, Tragedy, and Tradition in the Nineteenth Century* (Chicago: University of Chicago Press, 1955).

17. Fiedler, *Love and Death,* 82, 75.

18. Ann Douglas, *The Feminization of American Culture* (New York: Doubleday, 1988), 6, 289, 19.

19. Nathaniel Hawthorne to William Ticknor, 19 January 1855, in *Centenary Edition of Nathaniel Hawthorne,* vol. 17 (Columbus: Ohio State University Press, 1987), 304.

20. Douglas, *Feminization of American Culture,* 6, 10, 8.

21. Extending this argument into the twentieth century, Suzanne Clark's *Sentimental Modernism: Women Writers and the Revolution of the Word* (Bloomington: Indiana University Press, 1991) argues persuasively that "modernism rejected the sentimentalism, because modernism was sentimental" (7).

22. Eve Kosofsky Sedgwick, *Epistemology of the Closet* (Berkeley and Los Angeles: University of California Press, 1990), 154.

23. Mary P. Ryan, *Women in Public: Between Banners and Ballots, 1825–1880* (Baltimore: Johns Hopkins University Press, 1990), ix. See also Linda K. Kerber, "Separate Spheres, Female Worlds, Woman's Place: The Rhetoric of Women's History," *The Journal of American History* 75, no. 1 (June 1988: 9–39; Nancy Cott, "On Men's History and Women's History," in *Meanings for Manhood: Constructions of Masculinity in Victorian America*, ed. Mark C. Carnes and Clyde Griffen (Chicago: University of Chicago Press, 1990), 205–11; Mary Kelley, *Private Woman, Public Stage: Literary Domesticity in Nineteenth-Century America* (New York: Oxford University Press, 1984); and Lauren Berlant, "The Female Complaint," *Social Text* 19/20 (Fall 1988): 237–59.

24. Tompkins, *Sensational Designs,* xiv, xi.

25. Fisher, *Hard Facts,* 17, 18.

26. Hazel V. Carby, *Reconstructing Womanhood: The Emergence of the Afro-American Woman Novelist* (New York: Oxford University Press, 1987); Jean Fagin Yellin, *Women and Sisters: The Antislavery Feminists in American Culture* (New Haven: Yale University Press, 1989); Lori D. Ginzberg, *Women and the Work of Benevolence* (New Haven: Yale University Press, 1990); Dana Nelson, *The World in Black and White: Reading 'Race' in American Literature, 1638–1867* (New York: Oxford University Press, 1993).

27. Saidiya V. Hartman, *Scenes of Subjection: Terror, Slavery, and Self Making in Nineteenth-Century America* (New York: Oxford University Press, 1997), 5.

28. Julia A. Stern, *The Plight of Feeling: Sympathy and Dissent in the Early American Novel* (Chicago: University of Chicago Press, 1997), 2.

29. Elizabeth Barnes, *States of Sympathy: Seduction and Democracy in the American Novel* (New York: Columbia University Press, 1997), passim.

30. Shirley Samuels, *Romances of the Republic: Women, the Family, and Violence in the Literature of the Early American Nation* (New York: Oxford University Press, 1996), 20, 18.

31. Literature on the sentimental seems divided both geographically and chronologically into studies of eighteenth-century English "sensibility," which acknowledge the centrality of the man of feeling and the importance of male writers and philosophers to the cult of sensibility, and studies of nineteenth-century American sentimentality, which often gender sentiment female. For works on British sensibility, see Anne Jessie Van Sant, *Eighteenth-Century Sensibility and the Novel: The Senses in Social Context* (Cambridge: Cambridge University Press, 1993); Claudia L. Johnson, *Equivocal Beings: Politics, Gender, and Sentimentality in the 1790s* (Chicago: University of Chicago Press, 1995); and John Mullan, *Sentiment and Sociability: The Language of Feeling in the Eighteenth Century* (Oxford: Clarendon Press, 1988). One critic who has made the link between British sensibility and American sentimentality is Philip Fisher, but few critics have taken up his suggestive comment that "Sensibility . . . cannot be easily differentiated from what I am calling Sentimentality," or his comparison between the affective structure of Richardson, Sterne, and Rousseau's works and that of Stowe's *Uncle Tom's Cabin* (*Hard Facts,* 91–9, quotation from 94). The recent tendency to link nineteenth-century American sentimentality to the early American seduction novel and to

Scottish Common Sense philosophical writings is beginning to correct this omission. See Stern, *Plight of Feeling;* Barnes, *States of Sympathy;* and Gregg Camfield, *Sentimental Twain: Samuel Clemens in the Maze of Moral Philosophy* (Philadelphia: University of Pennsylvania Press, 1994).

32. Samuels, introduction to *Culture of Sentiment,* 3. See Ann Fabian, "Unseemly Sentiments: The Cultural Problem of Gambling," in Samuels, *Culture of Sentiment,* 143–56.

33. Annette Kolodny, *The Land Before Her: Fantasy and Experience of the American Frontiers, 1630–1860* (Chapel Hill: University of North Carolina Press, 1984), 163.

34. As works that fit this description, see Michael Paul Rogin, *Fathers and Children: Andrew Jackson and the Subjugation of the American Indian* (New York: A. Knopf, 1975), and George B. Forgie, *Patricide in the House Divided: A Psychological Interpretation of Lincoln and His Age* (New York: Norton, 1979).

35. E. Anthony Rotundo, *American Manhood: Transformations in Masculinity from the Revolution to the Modern Era* (New York: Basic Books, 1993), ix. See also Joe L. Dubbert, *A Man's Place: Masculinity in Transition* (Englewood Cliffs, N.J.: Prentice Hall, 1979); Peter Filene, *Him / Her / Self* (New York: New American Library, 1975); and Michael S. Kimmel, *Manhood in America: A Cultural History* (New York: Free Press, 1996).

36. See for instance David Pugh's *Sons of Liberty: The Masculine Mind in 19th-Century America* (Westport, Conn.: Greenwood Press, 1983). Carnes and Griffen's admission is in *Meanings for Manhood,* 6.

37. See Margaret Marsh, "Suburban Men and Masculine Domesticity, 1870–1915," in Carnes and Griffen, 111–127.

38. Samuels, introduction to *Culture of Sentiment,* 4.

39. Raymond Williams, *Marxism and Literature* (New York: Oxford University Press, 1978), 128–35. For another argument for the analysis of affect as a "structure of feeling," see Joel Pfister, "On Conceptualizing the Cultural History of Emotional and Psychological Life in America," in *Inventing the Psychological: Toward a Cultural History of Emotional Life in America,* ed. Joel Pfister and Nancy Schnog (New Haven: Yale University Press, 1997), 17–59.

40. Because of his engagement—however anxious—with what he saw as the feminized world of popular literary magazines and children's fiction, the one canonical writer whose connection to sentimentalism has been fairly widely acknowledged is Nathaniel Hawthorne. One study of Hawthorne that makes this connection is T. Walter Herbert, *Dearest Beloved: The Hawthornes and the Making of the Middle-Class Family* (Berkeley: University of California Press, 1993). As a result, the present volume contains no essay on Hawthorne; instead we have chosen to print two essays that treat Herman Melville at length, since Melville is so often held up as the canonical masculine alternative to feminine sentimentalism. See for instance Ann Douglas's final chapter, "Herman Melville and the Revolt Against the Reader"—a reader who has clearly been characterized as feminine and / or feminized throughout her study—the first section of which is subtitled "The Masculine Inheritance" (*Feminization of American Culture,* 349–395).

41. Nina Baym, "Melodramas of Beset Manhood: How Theories of American Literature Exclude Women," in *Feminism and American Literary History: Essays* (New Brunswick, N.J.: Rutgers University Press, 1992), 3–18.

42. Douglas, *Feminization of American Culture,* 294.

43. Thanks to José David Saldívar for pointing out this intriguing conjunction of sentimentalism and anti-imperialism.

PART ONE

Domestic Men

CHAPTER ONE

Fireside Chastity

The Erotics of Sentimental Bachelorhood in the 1850s

Vincent J. Bertolini

> I dreamed pleasant dreams that night;—
> for I dreamed that my Reverie was real.
>
> IK MARVEL
> (DONALD GRANT MITCHELL)

Bachelors and fireplaces go together in the antebellum period. The scene of the solitary lounging bachelor dreaming before the glowing embers, lost in that mood of feelingful reminiscence and imaginative projection that the nineteenth century called "revery," is common in the narrative literature of the period. Not merely a literary motif or familiar setting, the bachelor's fireside revery is a widely diffused cultural topos, emerging not only in such canonical high-literary texts as Melville's *Pierre* and Hawthorne's *The Blithedale Romance*, but also in the pages of *Godey's Lady's Book* and—in especially crystallized form—in Donald Grant Mitchell's *Reveries of a Bachelor*, a hugely popular book published in 1850. Indeed, bachelorhood was an obsessive preoccupation of antebellum American culture, and the bachelor, a highly problematized social identity, was the frequent topic of stories, plays, magazine pieces, poetry, and songs, as a rapid check of publication records from the period immediately reveals.

What then was the antebellum bachelor doing by his fire? He was sitting and thinking: sitting before the lonely bachelor hearth, a crude approximation of the warm center of official domesticity, the sentimentalized heart of the nineteenth-century home; and thinking, thinking in the bachelor's dreamy, longing way, primarily of what it would be like *not* to be a bachelor. This combination of physical passivity and feelingful imaginative activity, enacted in the resonantly symbolic site of normative familyhood, marks the bachelor's fireside revery as a moment of discursive pressure, intrasubjective conflict, and emergent identity.

By the middle of the nineteenth century, the bachelor in America had—as the proliferation of popular references to bachelorhood attests—fully entered the national consciousness; he had become a well-known, primarily urban social type specified by a determinate set of features. At the same time, bachelor identity was wholly defined in relation to the terms of normative white masculinity, the discursive contours of which by now are quite well-known—heterosexual, generally desensualized, (eventually) married, and (ultimately) procreative. That is, though the bachelor was a fact of the American social scene, he represented one of the worst threats to nineteenth-century bourgeois social and sexual ideology: the appearance of a codified male subject position that could respectably host non-normative sexual subjectivity and alternative erotic practice. Such an identity did in fact come fully into place by the end of the century.[1] But in the discursive environment of antebellum America, the bachelor was still a fluid category. To the northeastern writers of reform theory—those educators, divines, and medical men who produced advice books for young men and women, educational reform treatises, and scientific tracts on everything from diet to "sexual hygiene"—the bachelor could be easily associated with the anarchic sexual possibilities of solo masculinity. He embodied the potential for deviance from the reformers' strict domesticating and desensualizing regimes. In his solitary and unmonitorable status as an autonomous unmarried adult male, the bachelor represented the transgressive triple threat of masturbation, whoremongering, and that nameless horror—homosexual sex.

But threat to what? The history of American sexuality shows that sexual reform discourse, from the 1830s onward, reflected and attempted to manage bourgeois anxieties about the social fragmentation of American society resulting from rapid urbanization, industrialization, and the expanding Western frontier.[2] Reform theory emerged in full flower in the context of the breakup of the small, local socioeconomic units (the agricultural, mercantile town) and intimate social institutions (primarily the family) which regulated and normalized everyday life. The ascetic regimens of the reformers were intended to institute a kind of nostalgic rural discipline within the flesh of actual subjects, so that, for example, the rootless young men who inhabited the bustling city or the lone prairie would bring the forms of pre-industrial social life with them as a system of beliefs and values that determined their sexual practice. By transforming young white males into self-interpellating subjects of sexual ideology, the reformers aimed to keep them out of prostitutes', their own, and each other's hands, and oriented towards infrequent, productive, and what was thought of as socially stabilizing sexuality. Reform theory attempted to execute this monumental task of social construction by appealing to foundational ethico-religious as well as physiological principles: not only the truth of scriptural precept and the unequivocal social good of normative procreativity, but also the scientific fact that any erotic activity (auto-, hetero-, or homo-) was physically and psychically destructive to the health of men, women, children, and unborn generations, hence to society and the nation at large.[3]

The weight of the world, it seemed, rested on the bachelor's shoulders. And the conflicts and stresses registered in certain bachelor texts derive from the peculiar situation of bachelor identity in the antebellum phase of its emergence. The bachelor occupies an ambiguous position within the mid-Victorian system of sex, gender, and body ideologies. Not yet the subject of etiquette books such as *The Complete Bachelor* (1896),[4] no longer an addressee of the young men's guides of the thirties and forties (in which the word "bachelor" can barely be mentioned),[5] nowhere to be found in the treatises on domestic life and marital sexuality, the bachelor's sociosexual identity is undefined and unregulated. Located in a kind of negative conceptual space, on the threshold between domestication and transgression, the bachelor is a liminal concept in antebellum culture and a transitional state within proper masculine development.[6]

Within the antebellum sex / gender system, bachelorhood is a liminal concept since it is negatively defined by its total lack of explicit sexual content, all practices, single or reciprocal, being proscribed (hence the double meaning, which persists as a Latin trace in modern romance languages, of *celibate* as "unmarried male" and "sexually abstinent"). With no socially validated practices to call his own, the bachelor exists as a purely conceptual entity in relation to sexualized nonbachelorhood, and not as a practical (that is, activity-oriented) sexual identity. The bachelor is precisely he who must fend off his association with the socially abject sexualities—the self-abuser, whoremonger, or sodomite—as well as he who struggles to define himself in imaginative relation to what he is not yet—a lover, husband, and father. Bachelorhood is a transitional state because the bachelor has left properly constituted boyhood, in which the young man's sexuality is monitored, chastened, and directed towards proper objects by the mother, but not yet entered properly constituted manhood, in which the wife extends the maternal regime within the bounds of a limited, procreative conjugal sexuality.[7] From both a synchronic and a diachronic perspective, the antebellum bachelor finds himself in erotic limbo.[8]

It is no wonder then that the bachelor in antebellum culture is so often domesticated. Some cultural artifacts merely rail against the bachelor or leave him on the cusp of husbandhood.[9] Other texts convert him outright in moralistic parables intended to illustrate the loneliness and pain of the unmarried condition and the pleasures and virtues of transcending it. Such texts can be thought of as constituting a specific literary mode—*bachelor sentimentalism*—strategically related to a female-authored sentimentalism that functioned in complex ways within nineteenth-century ideology. Sentimentalism in the nineteenth century was not merely a literary genre but a widespread mode of cultural signification or, as Shirley Samuels calls it, "a set of cultural practices designed to evoke a certain form of emotional response, usually empathy, in the reader or viewer." In her introduction to *The Culture of Sentiment,* Samuels writes that sentimentalism, by embodying a "double logic of power and powerlessness," offered an "affective alternative" to politics, one which "gave political actions their emotional significance" and "intimately linked individual bodies to the national body."[10] Samuels has in mind primarily female-authored sentimentalism in a wide variety of cultural products, and the thrust of the essays in her volume is towards a dialectical reading of sentimentalism that sets sentimentalism's reiteration of the hegemonic against the oppositional political values resulting from its ability to cross boundaries of race, class, and gender. This double cultural work of sentimentalism also finds expression in Mitchell's *Reveries of a Bachelor* and, more consciously and critically, in Melville's parodic bachelor sentimentalism from the 1850s.

"BACHELOR'S DISEASE"

Let every young man who reads these pages resolve, in his own mind and heart, to do all in his power to effect on society, a most important and most thorough work of reform. Shall he not, at least, take the first step—that which must, forever, be the first step—shall he not reform himself?

WILLIAM A. ALCOTT, *THE PHYSIOLOGY OF MARRIAGE*

Samuels's analysis illuminates the literature of domesticated bachelorhood, for much bachelor sentimentalism works toward normalizing reformist ends. Bachelor sentimentalism employs not only the representational and plot conventions of sentimental fiction, but also its affective strategies. It is precisely through the representation of bachelor subjectivity—and the male reader's empathetic identification with those representations—that bachelor discourse does its regulatory work. By producing a subject who finds in himself the painful affects represented as belonging to bachelorhood (and who then desires to remake himself in the national image of ideal masculinity), bachelor sentimentalism mimics the operations of antebellum sex and gender ideology. Conversely, antebellum ideology works sentimentally: it tries to train subjects to desire and to "freely obey" the Law by cultivating in them the pleasurable feeling of a properly ordered subjectivity, rather than through potentially provocative and antidemocratic interdiction.[11] Within the domestic sphere, as G. M. Goshgarian argues, pleasure and law were conjoined through the ideological "open secret" of maternally supervised filial masturbation, a dynamic of prohibition / permission that had incestuous qualities.[12] But in their postfilial state, away from the surveillance of mothers and not yet under the watchful eyes of wives, men had to be trained out of bachelorhood through reading effects: through the pain-avoidance and pleasure-maximization that bachelor sentimentalism signaled. In the most normalizing narratives of bachelor domestication, the bachelor is represented as lonely and depressed, at loose ends but at the same time tightly bound, incapable of releasing the natural upwelling feeling that orients proper men towards the opposite sex and marriage.

The descriptions of the bachelor's situation and affect—and the metaphors used to characterize both—reveal bachelorhood to be a cultural pathology that parallels the most worrisome male medical problem in the nineteenth century: spermatorrhea. The affective strategies of bachelor sentimentalism operate according to the diagnostic logic of the disease; as the spermatorrheic is cured of his condition by nineteenth-century medicine, so the bachelor is cured of his by sentimental reading.

The etiology and pathology of spermatorrhea, or involuntary loss of semen (through wet dreams or premature ejaculation, or during urination or defecation), show the disease to be the medicalized expression of two of the period's primary sociosexual anxieties: excessive male sexuality and decreased procreativity. The disease was thought to be caused by masturbation or early sexual overindulgence, and the ultimate effect of untreated spermatorrhea was impotence.[13] In the interim, the subject suffered psychic as well as physical symptoms, including nervousness, shyness, a " 'disrelish for society,' " wandering attention, bad memory, moroseness, sadness, and the "substituting [of] 'shadowy dreams' and 'erratic phantasms' for intellectual labor." The physical symptoms of the disease were various, and reinforced the separation in post-1830 sexual ideology between vigorous and pleasurable sexuality and the reproductive function.[14] Behavioral incontinence, in particular early masturbation, was correlated with physical incontinence ("seminal leakage"); at the same time, the affected body was also constipated, less fluid and loose than in its healthy state. The erotic sensations that catalyzed the disease gave way to discomfort and pain or dullness and deadness.[15] The pathology of spermatorrhea, in other words, combined a desensualizing fear of excessive and perverse male sexuality with a re-sensualizing desire to harness a more naturalized conception of male eros for normative sociophysiological ends. The historical evidence suggests that sexual reform theory had the desired effect, and that generations of men were affected by the terror tactics of medicine allied with ideology.[16] The only fully effective cure for "bachelor's disease," men learned, was coitus within the bounds of matrimony.[17] Impotence would come to an end; full erections and moderate sexual pleasure would follow.

Just as marriage cured the bachelor's traumatized body, it also promised the only pleasurable relief from the traumatic interstitial situation of bachelor identity. "The Old Bachelor," a two-part story in *Godey's* of 1850, shows the logic of spermatorrhea at work in the sentimental domestication of antebellum bachelors.[18] The "hero" of the story—"for Dr. Hinton *is* our hero" (232)—is troped by the alternating metaphors of hardness / boundness and fluidity / looseness conventionally used to describe subjects who resist feeling (such as bachelors and spinsters): he is a "colossal" and "terrific iceberg . . . inwardly consumed by a fierce volcano, which boils, and spits, and rages, and tries frantically to let off steam, while it is held in durance vile by the strong, consolidated ice of ages" (231). This image of emotional constipation, with its sense of a repressed ejaculatory sexuality, is repeated, after the doctor meets his "innamorata" (233), in the description of his feelings for her: he is "no ordinary lover" but loves "with the concentrated and accumulated love which had been lying dormant in his system for full thirty years" (269). A clear case of developmental delay, the doctor is undergoing a crisis he should have suffered ("strange animal" (231) that he is) as a young man: the danger of this suggested affective / seminal backup is that our hero's passions will find an outlet in transgressive behavior. He needs to be melted, but also prevented from overflowing, by conjugal love.

The onset of the unnerved, insomniac bachelor's crisis is cast in the domesticating formula of True Womanhood's relation to True Manhood: "she [was] that good angel, come at last, for whom, through boyhood, manhood, and old-bachelorhood, he now, upon his lonely bed, acknowledged he had in secret sighed" (231). This bachelor realizes he has existed only as the pathetic shadow of what he could be. The negativity of his bachelor identity registers temporally: "He looked back into the past, and found it all a blank compared to this moment. He looked forward into the future, and the coming days and years actually menaced him" (232). This bachelor, on the verge of transformation along normative sociosexual lines, experiences his liminal identity qua bachelor as empty of prior content and at the same time—if it continues unchanged—as threatening. That his is an ordeal of identity also registers—on the sleep-deprived morning after he meets Clara—in his alienation from his physical self: he "consult[s] his mirror with eager and unusual anxiety," and as never before finds himself "hopelessly ugly"; he is "disgusted with himself" (231). Thoughts of his unmarried state make him desire the obliteration of his incomplete self:

> "It is not good for man to live alone. . . . I despise myself! I wish I was dead and decently interred this very minute!"
> Thus he sat and mused, all solitary and alone, and was on the verge of suicide. Had a gentle wife but ran her fingers through his hair, or a prattling boy but climbed upon his knee, there would have been none of this. No murmurs against fate—no wish for oblivion. (233)

This desire to commit suicide, without the will to execute it, is another symptom of spermatorrhea.[19] In this sexual ideology, the spermatorrheic's desire to commit suicide encodes a warning against the transgressive practices that bring on the often fatal disease. In the terms of bachelor discourse, however, the desire for suicide seems to be the affective expression of the bachelor's inability to live out his impossible identity; suicide also tropes bachelorhood as the self-inflicted destruction of a proper masculine identity, immanent in all men, that can be realized if they will only *act* appropriately.

It is the absence of action, however, that shakily preserves bachelorhood; that absence is nowhere more present than at the bachelor's hearth, in the moment of fireside chastity. As our suffering hero sits by the fire, his imagination calls up the physical attractions of Clara in minute detail and in language resonant with the claims she makes upon his desire. She is "coy," "spicy," "piquant," "imperious," and "witching." These mental images and the movements of feeling they stimulate totally define the practical erotic life of this obedient bachelor; they are both alive and (as nonpractice) dead: "he embalmed them in his good, pure heart, and there they lay as all he had ever known of beauty and of love" (233).

In the gap between desire and praxis that opens in the moment of the fireside revery, pain is introjected as the bachelor measures his situation (in the blithe, gloating voice of the married male narrator) against the practical delights of normative hearth life:

> Life became now a burden to our bachelor friend. Time did not even kindly strike a trot, but groped along heavily, slowly, and oppressively. Oh, the long, long hours of that dreary, hopeless winter! Who can measure them?—who can tell how painfully they passed away? I cannot, I am sure; for I love old Winter, with its heavy frosts and bridal snows, its long evenings and cosy nights, and roaring, cheering fires. I have heard old bachelors talk about the horrors of these; and my imagination will sometimes sketch them as they yawn, and smoke, and twirl their fingers, and poke the fire, and consult their creeping watches, and *wish in vain for something on earth to do.* (233, emphasis added.)

The sentimental effect of a passage like this is embodied both in its narrative form and in the dynamic of readerly identification and counter-identification it constructs. In his breezy, even offhanded way, the married narrator both engages bachelor subjectivity and disengages himself from it: he is "sure" he cannot feel the bachelor's pain, because he inhabits an identity which so totally excludes its Other that the phenomenology of the Other's identity is unimaginable; at the same time, he presents the matter in a rhetorical form ("who can tell . . . ?") which invites a bachelor reader's affective identification ("my imagination will sometimes sketch them"). Careful, however, not to let the reader wallow in self-pity, and quick to present the alternative to bachelorhood in a vivid way that would motivate action, the narrator shows that the conjugal hearth and home is where the bachelor really wants to be:

> I do not like to dwell upon [bachelors'] miseries. Not I. I had rather marshal up the married man, who returns from his office, after the busy day, to meet the baby's eager greeting and his wife's glad kiss at the door—who finds his paper ready aired, his slippers and his gown all waiting, the fire briskly burning, and a welcome everywhere—who in sorrow finds a comforter, and in joy finds others happy through him. (233)

The conjugal hearth is the scene not of lonely reminiscence but of bustling activity characterized in affective terms (eagerness, gladness, comfort, joyfulness, happiness), domestic activity which, unlike the oppressive non-activity associated with bachelorhood, pleasurably complements male endeavors in the economic sphere. In contrast to the spermatorrheic's "disrelish for society," this scene of normative domesticity displays the achievement of happiness through society and points towards its socially stabilizing benefits. As the well-known reform writer and doctor William Alcott says in *The Physiology of Marriage*, matrimony is "the golden chain that binds society together. Remove it, and you set the world ajar, if you do not drive it back to its original chaos."[20]

What makes "The Old Bachelor" a domesticating tale is, of course, the bachelor's achievement of happiness through marriage. At the end of the tale, Dr. Hinton himself adopts the domesticating role of the narrator, illustrating for the "four-and-twenty sheepish bachelors" who attend his wedding how they too can "be of good cheer." At this point the narrator pipes up with a final wish that "all the old bachelors under the sun" may also come to the Doctor's "wise conclusion" (273).

SWEET SIN AND STIRRING WEAKNESS

I wonder, thought I, as I dropped asleep, if the married man with his sentiment made actual, is, after all, as happy as we poor fellows in our dreams?

IK MARVEL (DONALD GRANT MITCHELL)

What happens if the bachelor refuses to obey, chafes against domesticity? What are the psychic, affective, and practical ramifications of resistance for bachelorhood as a sociosexual identity? The answer lies in the dynamic of co-constitution between the transgressive (that is, active, embodied, and erotic) and the normalizing (that is, passive, abstract, and chaste) aspects of bachelor identity; it lies also in the paradoxical way sentimentalism works on embodied subjects. It is at the moment of the bachelor's fireside revery that we find the active and passive, transgressive and normalizing, sides of bachelor identity contending against one another. At the moment of sentimental revery, domestic ideologies of sex and gender, which bear on the bachelor not only cognitively but as variously valued structures of feeling, contend with the antidomestic thoughts, desires, and identifications available to bachelors as the (only) potential stuff of practical identity. If bachelors, in the process of sentimental domestication, are trained to inhabit other subjectivities imaginatively and to desire to adopt them, these affective operations always take place in the hidden context of prohibited practices and abject identities. Hence, if the bleak moods and obvious suffering of the obedient bachelor spring from his vain wish "for something on earth to do," the unspoken content of his wish draws as much from prohibited as from permitted conduct. Indeed, the pull of the transgressive-practical can seem almost as strong as the desire (whatever its cause) to remain single: the bachelor can erotically practice outside of matrimony (even if he is stigmatized) and still in some sense remain a "bachelor."

It is at the moment of the bachelor's fireside revery, the moment of discursive convergence and conflict within the bachelor's imagining / feeling subjectivity, that sentimentalism does its double cultural work. During the revery, the moment of feelingful imagination that both constitutes bachelor identity and opens bachelor subjectivity to the operation of dominant ideology, the boundaries between the head and the heart, the mind and the body, sentiment and sexuality, begin to blur. At such moments, distinctions between affective objects can muddle: warm regard for the goodness of women, intended to produce an ethicized longing that moves men toward the prospect of lifelong instruction within the conjugal relation, can spill over into more eroticized forms of desire. With this enlarged affect, the cognitive content of the revery can diversify in such a way that the bachelor begins to imagine specific kinds of erotic resolutions that remain "nonthematizable" with respect to the overt purposes of sentimental subjectivization.[21] Within the representational practices of texts that host such reveries, objects and values can cross in a way that challenges dominant concepts of proper male desire, praxis, and identity. That is, at the moment in the revery of the access of sentiment, the bachelor experiences his own sexual subjectivity as excessive—as "extravagant" (to use Thoreau's term)—with respect to the conceptual boundaries of normative masculinity. And as this sociocultural phenomenon achieves concrete (counter-)discursive form, bachelor sentimentalism begins to function as a literary medium through which a fraught social category opens itself up to reveal the faint outlines of alternative sexual subjectivity, the seed of some alternative sexual identity.

Nowhere in the antebellum period is this process more evident than in *Reveries of a Bachelor*.[22] Mitchell's book was reprinted throughout the nineteenth century, and its enormous popularity certainly had to do with its overt thematizing of normative domesticity and explicit affirmations of dominant values. Here was an exemplary bachelor, or so it must have seemed to many, if not all, readers. F. W. Shelton, in his essay "On Old Bachelors," is "disposed to show no quarter to the sentimental bachelor," one of the four types of bachelor he discusses.[23] By this type he means bachelors in the Mitchell tradition: "By my ancient friendship for Isaac Marvel, I declare that no apology can be found for any of the set. Do not believe a single word which they say." The problem with the sentimental bachelor lies in the seeming incongruity between inside and outside, in the fact that he talks a good game but does not follow through, and in what this discrepancy suggests about what he is holding back and why. The reveries of the sentimental bachelor "are no unhealthy, night-mare visions, crude, vague, undigested phantasies. They are delicate, airy, sweet pictures, which can be gazed at with pleasure by one who is wide awake." They seem to be "just the ones to be over head and ears in love the whole time." Sentimental bachelors say the proper sentimental things in just the right accents and with the right affect, "discours[ing] in such amiable, set phrase, all about the tender affections, with tears in their eyes, and their cheeks flushing with emotion" (225). But neither the evoked feelings nor the sweet speeches are ever translated into action, and the reason for this "remains a mystery" (226).

The elusiveness of the sentimental bachelor, this sense that all his fine emotional expression masks hidden motivations, emerges in the fireside fantasies of domestic life of Mitchell's fictional alter ego, "Ik Marvel." Indeed, the moods represented in Ik's first revery are volatile, ranging from enthusiasm to anger, proceeding (as Mitchell's chapter titles suggest) through "doubt," "cheer," and "desolation." The structure of the first revery correlates these last three moods with stages in the life of the fire (smoke, flame, and ashes), and with stages of the domestic fantasy (opposition to marriage and family, happy husband- and fatherhood, and the husband / father's bereavement). The volatility of affect hints at the psychic costs of toeing the normative line, and the resolutions that he fantasizes finely balance reiteration and resistance.

Marvel begins the first revery before his smoky, cold hearth with the negative aspects of "unchanging, relentless, marriage" (21)—pesky children, nosy relatives, and wives who are too rich or too poor, too henpecking or too literary. At the moment of the fire's hopeful blaze, he delivers a paean to the normative family, to the beauties of prattling lively children and a soul-communion with his sister / angel wife, whose loving and correcting influence increases joy and makes "love master self" (35). At the end of the revery, as the fire turns to ash, Marvel imagines death taking off his loved ones one by one. Significantly, sentiment increases and is enriched by the fantasy deaths of this fantasy family. As soon as the bachelor comes into being as he who (only) dreams of wife and family, he imagines being restored, through no agency of his own, to his bachelor state. In obsessive and lovingly rendered detail, the bachelor describes the progress of his wife's disease, her paling, weakening, fading descent into the well-made coffin that sits on the staunch table: " 'It is a nice coffin, a very nice coffin. Pass your hand over it; how smooth!' " (47). In passages like these, the sentimental inhabitation of the role of loving husband and father brings the bachelor into being through mutual constitution with dominant masculinity; at the same time, sentimentalism provides the bachelor with a language and a structure of feeling that allow him to respectably fend off the grubby realities of actual family life with which the book begins.

In the second revery, Marvel's thoughts turn away from domestic matters towards courtship, the rituals preceding marriage, and the fantasies they provoke. In these passages Mitchell renders women as objects of the bachelor's erotic interest, and the revery registers the bachelor's frustrations at having to inhabit a liminal, transitional identity defined by what he is not and characterized by inactivity. The fantasies of this section reveal how the gateways of feeling, once open, can swing wide, flooding the bachelor subject with very undomestic thoughts and with the painful internal conflict that results from acknowledging a structure of desires which cannot be satisfied through socially validated forms of practical life. At this point, the bachelor dreams not in front of his country fireplace but before his city grate, warmed into revery not by solid oak and hickory but by flickering sea-coal and long-burning anthracite. This movement between the country and the city reflects the bachelor's peculiar position between the reformers' nostalgic rural vision of normative sociosexuality and the evolving reality of the Jacksonian city as a democratizing place of transgressive practices and emergent identities.

And here by his city grate the bachelor's revery of the allurements of a courted "coquette" threatens to spill over into what looks like masturbatory fantasy. By inviting an interpretive link between masturbation and revery, in a context in which neither is stigmatized, Mitchell makes a bold cultural gesture. As we saw, "shadowy dreams" and "erratic phantasms" were one of the hallmarks of male sexual disease; F. W. Shelton also emphasized—in his remark about "unhealthy, night-mare visions, crude, vague, undigested phantasies"—the ethico-biological dimension of certain dreams that bachelors may be subject to (though sentimental bachelors, he says, are not). When John Todd, the famous "male purity" reformer whom I will discuss in more detail below, inveighed against the "rovings of the imagination" and the "habit of reverie" in *The Student's Manual* (1835), he directly connected these states of mind to the horrific results of "permitting the thoughts to wander when alone—evils which want a name, to convey any conception of their enormity." (These evils so want a name, in fact, that Todd gives the subsequent two-page disquisition on the destructiveness of *Onanis scelus* [heinous onanism] in chaste Latin.)[24] In the context of such discursively driven paranoia, the "coquette" passage, which ends the "Sea-coal" chapter, reads as the bachelor's fairly brazen assertion of a solo sexual fantasy, if not (or not obviously) an actual act of masturbation:

> And so, with my eye clinging to the flickering blaze I see in my reverie a bright one dancing before me with sparkling, coquettish smile, teasing me with the prettiest graces in the world; and I grow maddened between hope and fear, and still watch with my whole soul in my eyes; and see her features by-and-by relax to pity, as a gleam of sensibility comes stealing over her spirit; and then to a kindly, feeling regard: presently she approaches,—a coy and doubtful approach,—and throws back the ringlets that lie over her cheek, and lays her hand—a little bit of white hand—timidly upon my strong fingers, and turns her head daintily to one side, and looks up in my eyes as they rest on the playing blaze; and my fingers close fast and passionately over that little hand, like a swift night-cloud shrouding the pale tips of Dian; and my eyes draw nearer and nearer to those blue, laughing, pitying, teasing eyes, and my arm clasps round that shadowy form,—and my lips feel a warm breath—growing warmer and warmer—
>
> Just here the maid comes in, and throws upon the fire a panful of Anthracite, and my sparkling sea-coal reverie is ended. (76)

It is the rhythm of the passage as well as its content—its repeated short phrases and the accelerating pace that builds towards a climax—that mark this as a scene of possible *masturbatio,* decidedly *interruptus.* The style of the passage—with its images of energy and passion, its description of warm, sensate, proximate bodies, and its trope of Dian eclipsed—suggests that sentimental expression functions here as an erotic vehicle: by casting his eroticized imaginings in the respectable contexts of a "whole soul['s]" appreciation, and of "pity," "sensibility," and "kindly, feeling regard," the bachelor is allowed to verge imaginatively toward proscribed practices.

The arrested fantasy / activity that ends the chapter spurs Marvel to social polemic and to a kind of oxymoronic language that tries to unite pleasure and law, activity and thought, within bachelor identity. The companion passage to Marvel's masturbatory fantasy complicates the relations of content and value structured by antebellum sexual ideology, and may be read as a plea for the right to a respectable solo sexual praxis:

> I know not justly, if it be a weakness or a sin to create these phantoms that we love, and to group them into a paradise—soul-created. But if it is a sin, it is a sweet and enchanting sin; and if it is a weakness, it is a strong and stirring weakness. If this heart is sick of the falsities that meet it at every hand, and is eager to spend that power which nature has ribbed it with on some object worthy of its fulness and depth, shall it not feel a rich relief, nay more, an exercise in keeping with its end, if it flow out, strong as a tempest, wild as a rushing river, upon those ideal creations which imagination invents, and which are tempered by our best sense of beauty, purity, and grace? (77–78)

As sexual ideology always does, the passage relies upon a concept of nature as the ontological ground for its ethics of male sexuality. But here wildness, fluidity, and power are proposed as ethically good; the disease-ridden body of the masturbator is nowhere to be found. Instead, Mitchell joins affective terms denoting male pleasure with traditional moral concepts, shifting (almost fully reversing) their meanings. Sexualized revery and the act it can lead to may be "weakness" and "sin" (concepts drawn from the medico-moral and religious reformism of the day), but if giving in to one's heart's desire—allowing it to "spend that power which nature has ribbed it with"—is weakness, it is, oxymoronically, a "strong and stirring weakness." Such desires, as these terms suggest, powerfully animate not just the heart but the sexualized male body. Indeed, the image of the expending, ribbed, full, deep, flowing, and relieving heart does not need to be teased into a trope for the erect and ejaculating penis. Rather, the fact that heart and penis are related in more than a merely tropic sense is what is at issue in the passage. Marvel is pleading to be allowed to bring his unmarried and excited penis into contact with his feeling and properly ordered heart, to unify sentiment and sexuality in a socially validated practical identity informed by his culture's "best sense of beauty, purity, and grace." That is, this bachelor desires—through reconstructed social values—to free from the "falsities that meet it at every hand" not just his heart but his desiring male body.

LIGHTNING IN THE CLOSET

In thunder as in sunshine, I stand at ease in the hands of my God.
HERMAN MELVILLE, "THE LIGHTNING-ROD MAN"

The rhetorical structure of Marvel's polemic reveals the suffering that the narrator endures as a result of living with the tension between bodily desire and social actuality. He "know[s] not justly" how to judge his erotic life, cannot—save oxy-moronically—think himself out of his culture's ethical terms; he leaves his rhetor-ical question—"if this heart is sick . . . shall it not feel a rich relief . . . ?"—unan-swered. Marvel never tests his alternate bachelor identity beyond the bounds of the fireside revery, in social circumstances fraught with real risk and transforma-tive possibility. While Mitchell's sentimental bachelor evades the social world to inhabit the world of his sexual fantasies, Melville represents bachelors and hus-bands who engage bachelor discourse in the context of specific social relation-ships. In *Pierre*, "I and My Chimney," and "The Lightning-Rod Man," Melville deploys the topos of fireside chastity in plots that diagnose the ideological produc-tion of domesticated bachelorhood and imagine tentative forms of practical resistance to heteroerotic and procreative norms.[25]

In *Pierre*, the bachelor revery is variously linked with a fictitious domestic order established through Pierre's design, with an act of self-writing in Pierre's thinly disguised fictional autobiography, and with a type of utopian reformism shot through with the desensualizing practices of antebellum sexual ideology. In the midst of the clashing racial identities, sexual license, and drunken pandemonium Pierre encounters in the Jacksonian city, he takes refuge in a flesh-mortifying male reform community and an unconsummated, fake heterosexual marriage which realizes, in its structure and desensualizing effect, the equation of sisters and wives in domestic ideology. Pierre is in one sense neither a married nor a single man but a sad, neutered combination of both. But Pierre is, of course, still a bachelor, and Melville introduces the topos of fireside chastity to show the discursive filiations between male domesticity and midcentury bachelor identity. The bachelor hearth by which Ik Marvel affirms his single manhood by symbolically killing his wife and children becomes the pathetic stove-warmed bricks and flagging that Delly puts under Pierre's feet while he writes. The warm city grate by which Marvel fantasizes his coquettes becomes the crook of stovepipe that enters Pierre's cold writer's garret, only "to elbow right out of it, as some coquettish maidens enter the heart."[26] At the moment of revery, when Mitchell's bachelor at least imagina-tively projects himself into a scene of sexual exchange, Pierre thinks of his fictional alter-ego Vivia, whose problems his creator cannot resolve, making Pierre's literary effort look like the liminal bachelor's activity of ideological self-interpellation.

Indeed, the novel's rhetoric of an ahistorical and decorporealized propagation of identity—the self as "self-reciprocally efficient hermaphrodite" (259)—reads as an idealizing fantasy of transcending the ideology that produces a conflicted structure of feeling within the bachelor's traumatized body. Melville links bache-lorhood and idealism through the ragtag community of Transcendentalist reformers (" 'The great men are all bachelors, you know' " [281]), in order to exhibit how both philosophical and medico-moral idealism have the same effects on the embodied subjectivities of unmarried men. As *Pierre* shows, even utopian alternatives to dominant forms of socioeconomic life do not easily escape the desensualizing logic of normative masculinity.[27] Pierre is unable, finally, either to inhabit an eroticized domesticity or to enjoy a pleasurable solo sexuality. He sits, we are told, on his "indigent bachelor's pallet . . . entirely idle, apparently; there was nothing in his hands" (270). Neither he nor any of the flesh-chastening bachelor reformers he lives among can translate same-sex desire into action.[28] *Pierre* stands as a testament to the painful impasse of midcentury bachelor identity and the effects of nineteenth-century sexual ideology on male erotic subjectivity.

Melville's story "I and My Chimney" avoids this ahistorical fantasy of a place of freedom beyond discourse. Instead, the story engages bachelor discourse from within the institution of marriage and carves out a tiny space of freedom within marriage's normalizing constraints. We find the story's narrator, a husband and father, striking the attitude of sentimental bachelorhood, sitting by the fire smoking his pipe in melancholy meditation on the beauties and transience of human life. He is often in a mood of nostalgic contemplation and, like bachelors, enjoys the compensatory pleasures of the table. But this male subject, narrating in a bluffly comic tone a skittish and elusive tale, is enmeshed in a life-or-death cultural struggle for domestic power. The motive for the narration is the conflict between the narrator and his wife over whether the massive phallic chimney in their house, which extends from the basement through the roof, should be torn out. Through plot and trope, Melville writes the conflicts about evolving forms of American political thought and social life onto the relations between husband and wife. The narrator identifies with Old-World monarchical government, and, nearer to home, with an old-fashioned and stable federalism; he values aristocratic social relations of dominance and subservience, playing the ministering subject to the king, his chimney. His wife, a restless projector, builder, and transformer, incarnates the energy and diversity of Jacksonian America: she embraces dietary reform, Swedenborgianism, spirit rapping, and ladies' magazines, living in a future-directed state of constant flux. Their battle over the chimney symbolizes the contest over the patriarchal foundations of American social life. With the growth of the ideology of "separate spheres," which reconfigured gender roles and entrusted women with the supervision of their sons' and husbands' sexuality, and within the tradition of postrevolutionary democratic antipatriarchalism, paternal power in the domestic sphere had been significantly diminished and redistributed. The narrator's ongoing battle to save his lordly chimney from his wife's destructive schemes tropes an attitude of embattled conservatism, a desire to preserve patriarchal institutions and forms of social organization.

But within the narrator's patriarchalism—as within the bachelor identity itself—the dominant is shown to hide its opposite: the possibility of antidomestic male sexuality. Unlike Ik Marvel, whose potent sexuality craves an outlet simultaneously physical, emotional, and societal, the narrator of Melville's story, though a father, is almost wholly de-eroticized. His wife, on the other hand, is hilariously, punningly, eroticized, suggesting not only the sexual energies being released within the new forms of nineteenth-century life but also the norms—perhaps constrictive for the narrator—of heterosexual activity within the procreative family.[29] The narrator wants simply to be left alone with his chimney, in a relation of political submission which, in an absurdly extended trope of behindness and rearness, seems also a relation of sexual submission. He goes about "with [his] hands behind [his] back," belongs to "the rear guard," and "bring[s] up the rear of [his] chimney," his "superior," whom he "ministers" to by "bowing over" (160). This hint of homoerotic identification is paralleled near the end of the story by the rumors of a secret "closet" built into the chimney by the narrator's bachelor relative, who remained a mysterious and eccentric stranger to the townsfolk among whom he lived until his death. This closet, as the architect (a "Mr. Scribe") in league with the projecting wife speculates, may hide the relative's never-discovered fortune or may have served some "other purpose, [which] may be left to those better acquainted with the history of the house to guess" (180).[30] The narrator thinks the rumored closet may be a "secret ash-hole" linked to the "queer hole" in which he and his wife already put ashes (183). Subsequently, the narrator slips, referring to "this secret oven; I mean secret closet of yours, wife" (184), a moment linked lexically and thematically to another "mysterious closet" maintained by the narrator himself, one in which he keeps "mysterious cordials, of a choice, mysterious flavor," but won't keep his wife's eggs, "on account of hatching" (168).

Ovens and eggs on the one hand, queer secret holes on the other: the closet becomes a site of cultural conflict between the domestic regime and excessive male subjectivity. It also functions as a psychic space within which nineteenth-century males can assert the one prerogative of bachelorhood—that of preserving the privacy of desire—in a culture in which marital sexuality was increasingly a matter of public discussion and regulation. It is in this context that the narrator defends the inviolable privacy of his bachelor kinsman's closet, at the same time expressing his related desire that his own closet and its mysterious, sensual, anti-domestic contents remain inviolate:

> even if there were a secret closet, secret it should remain, and secret it shall. Yes, wife, here, for once, I must say my say. Infinite sad mischief has resulted from the profane bursting open of secret recesses. Though standing in the heart of this house, though hitherto we have all nestled about it, unsuspicious of aught hidden within, this chimney may or may not have a secret closet. But if it have, it is my kinsman's. To break into that wall would be to break into his breast. (188)

In "I and My Chimney," Melville leaves his married narrator hunkered down in the heart of the normative family, guarding the last corner of an already purely negative bachelor freedom within which the dim hope of an alternative erotic subjectivity can still flicker.[31]

If in "I and My Chimney" Melville imagines the trials of excessive masculinity within the confines of the bourgeois home, in "The Lightning-Rod Man" he represents the impulse towards an alternative eroticized homo-domesticity and an exuberant rejection of reform discipline. In this story the closet expands to the walls of the house and, instead of shutting out the normative social world, opens up to receive it, invites it to shelter there, to accept and be accepted by its Other. The tale begins with a reformulation of sentimental bachelorhood—with an image of the bachelor standing on his hearthstone and meditating not on melancholy bachelor topics, but on the thrilling power of grand and glorious nature as represented by the raging storm outside his house. The lightning-rod man arrives, selling his long copper and wood device affixed to two glass balls and terminating in three devilish tines at the top. The narrator invites the salesman to join him on his hearth, but the terrified salesman refuses. Again he is offered a chair placed "invitingly on the broad hearth," and again he refuses, ordering the narrator to " 'quit the hearth . . . the most dangerous part of a house' " (152). The fear-inducing words of the salesman make the narrator "involuntarily" step off the hearth, but at the stranger's "unpleasant air of successful admonition" he "involuntarily" steps back on again, revealing a proud instinct to resist such smugly paranoid counsel. The "strange mixture of alarm and intimidation" and the salesman's "conjur[ing]" and "command[ing]" anger the narrator, who is "not accustomed to be commanded in [his] own house" (153).

The hearth (most parts of the house, it seems) conducts electricity, the dangerous power of nature, which the salesman's coldly mechanical phallic product can carry safely away from the house and harmlessly into the earth. Not only will the salesman not share the narrator's hearth with him, he won't touch the narrator, because " 'a man is a good conductor.' " " 'Are not lonely Kentuckians, ploughing, smit in the unfinished furrow?' " the salesman says. " 'Of all things, I avoid tall men' " (157). But the narrator is not frightened by nature's power and indeed lives in a house that attracts it: his floors are made of " 'heart-of-oak' " (an image that connotes both sentiment and hardness / strength / durability), and oak, as the stranger tells him, " 'draws lightning more than other timber' " (154). In fact, one manifestation of natural power, " 'instead of alarming [the narrator], has strangely inspired confidence.' " He learns that lightning can strike backwards, " 'when the earth, being overcharged with the fluid, flashes its surplus upward.' " He is cheered: " 'The returning-stroke; that is, from earth to sky. Better and better. But come here on the hearth,' " he says to the stranger, " 'and dry yourself' " (156).

This interchange, and the story as a whole, can be read as a coded dialogue between reform theory (represented by the lightning-rod man) and the possibilities of excessive masculinity (represented by the bachelor), about the containment or free expression of male sexuality. The reformer wants to attach a kind of ideological prosthetic to this domestic sphere, a phallus which conducts the forces of sexuality away from men and their penises; he does this by an appeal to powerful voices of authority within nineteenth-century culture, those of science and religion, as they reach American subjects through discursive products: " 'I will publish your infidel notions,' " the salesman rants at the narrator, who instead

" 'reads' " in the blue sky and the " 'scroll' " of the storm the essential benevolence of nature (158). The narrator celebrates the potential of warm homoerotic domesticity and the pleasures of an ejaculatory and excessive manhood—of coming on the hearth and flashing your surplus at the sky.

The salesman, whom the narrator jokingly calls "Jupiter Tonans," has been identified as the Reverend John Todd, the real object of the story's satire, an identification that supports my reading of the story as a critique of reform ideology and a fantasy of a newly sexualized male domesticity.[32] Todd was the pastor of the Congregational Church of Pittsfield throughout Melville's tenure at Arrowhead (1850 to 1863), where he wrote "The Lightning-Rod Man"; a copy of Todd's *The Student's Manual* was to be found at Melville's boyhood home from 1839 on. (Also, Todd's church assembly room was struck by lightning during a prayer meeting in 1835.) However, it is not Todd the peddler of Calvinist fear or bad moral philosophy that Melville satirizes in the story but Todd the peddler of repressive sexual ideology, and with him all other commodifiers and popularizers of disciplinary systems that constrain and neuter male sexuality. The end of the story can be read as a victory for a resistant solo masculinity and as an exhortation to male defiance of the domesticators' regimes. When the lightning-king thrusts the lightning-rod at the narrator's heart, the seat of all the trouble in the first place, the narrator smashes the rod and flings his nemesis out of his house. The narrator ultimately remains alone, and "the Lightning-rod man still dwells in the land . . . driv[ing] a brave trade with the fears of man" (158). Nevertheless, the transgressive tone of the story and its representation of a proud and fearless bachelor opening his home to embodied activity both single and reciprocal—not just longing revery—make it perhaps the limit-text of Melville's social imaginary: "The Lightning-Rod Man" comes closer than any of his other fictions to imagining lee shore versions of both Ishmael and Queequeg's homosocial domesticity and the homoerotic fellowship of "A Squeeze of the Hand."

⁂

Recent work on American bachelorhood paints late-nineteenth- and early-twentieth-century bachelors as inhabiting more socially integrated and more conceptually diversified identities than their predecessors. As Peter Laipson points out, by the last third of the nineteenth century bachelors had recourse to a quite viable form of alternative homo-domesticity: the bachelor's club. These were available both as déclassé (but quite civilized and comfortable) communal living arrangements and as fancier, more "formal organizations of men united around some common interest or identity (from politics to a shared alma mater) which supplied most domestic amenities, including, in some cases, lodging for those who desired it." Against the charge that club denizens were "reckless and rootless sybarites" isolated from the kinds of proper domestic experience that would make them selfless, fully productive men, members deployed an "explicit rhetoric of domesticity and kinship, arguing that clubs not only replicated the structure of the family but ennobled the relationships between members." This kind of counterargument "was not only polemical but performative, reflecting the desire of club members to create the very relationships they claimed already existed."[33] Thus, by the end of the century the meanings of single-male identity had shifted with respect to the defining categories of father-, husband-, and familyhood: both single and married men could participate in a richly articulated communal domesticity different from the limited scenarios available in the antebellum period.

Similarly, the sexual content of late-nineteenth-century bachelor identity expanded and diversified. Katherine Snyder argues that though the representations of bachelorhood remain fairly consistent from the middle of the century on, "nevertheless the stereotyped traits, motifs, and plots associated with bachelors do shift in their meanings, particularly because bachelorhood maintains a dialectical relationship to normative (bourgeois / professional / married / paternal / patriarchal) masculinities which themselves were undergoing changes over this period, changes which contributed and responded to shifts in the ideologies, institutions, and practices of marriage, domesticity, and sexuality, among others." The sexual doubleness in Mitchell's and Melville's representations of sentimental bachelors—particularly in the ways they portray bodiliness, affect, revery, domestic space, and intersubjective relations—can thus be seen to prefigure the enlarged possibilities for the bachelor's erotic practice that later cultural changes were to make possible. Indeed, as Snyder points out, the fact that bachelorhood existed as a social category before the emergence of the heterosexual / homosexual binarism means not only that bachelor identity was marked by the new binary regime, but also that "bachelor discourse—both in representations and in lives— . . . contributed to the bi-formation of heterosexuality and homosexuality; bachelor figures contributed to the formation of categories of sexual identity that were both repressive / disciplinary and also emotionally and politically enabling."[34] As "the bachelor" acquired structured associations in the social imaginary of the nation, actual embodied bachelors could then order extravagant affect, identification, and activity within evolving practical identities that could be lived more publicly and communally. Though this process produced a determinate type of sexual identity, the homosexual man, who could then be subject to both personal and social forms of discrimination and violence, it also provided, in the variety of fluidly signifying social traits that characterized bachelorhood, the rudimentary materials for a distinctively gay culture.[35]

Bachelor discourse did similarly liberating cultural work in its constitutive impact on the formation of heterosexual masculinity. For while the norms of proper masculinity remained largely heteroerotic, matrimonial, and procreative (as to an extent they still do), respectable forms of eroticized, unmarried, and anti-sentimental (hence not subject to the feeling of Law) heteromasculinity became available in the period. In a 1905 article on "Men Who Marry and Men Who Do Not," Lyndon Orr describes a kind of man who is at once the delight and the despair of women. He is their delight because they secretly respect him for not giving in to them and because he has the charm of the unattainable; and he is their despair, because they feel so utterly baffled and helpless when they encounter his perfectly invincible admiration, his urbane and deferential indifference. Moreover, the man who will not marry is really more attractive than the man who can be made to walk into a trap with his eyes wide open. He is one who has a sense of relativity. He looks at life in a scientific way, and while he wants to enjoy all of its pleasures and opportunities, he is very much averse to tying himself by the leg in letting any single pleasure master him. He likes women so much that he cannot concentrate his whole interest upon just one of them. He is a connoisseur, finding a special charm in each individual type, but no overmastering, compelling charm in one more than in another. Holding himself in the innermost sanctuary of his heart, a little bit aloof, he is able to enjoy to the full the esoteric attractions of womankind—the sympathetic intelligence, the grace, the wit, and all those softer feminine attributes which are so delightful to a man of mind and taste.[36]

Not even (or perhaps especially not) the polemical midcentury defense of bachelorhood in *Single Blessedness* pictures a bachelor who radiates this kind of fascinating and powerful detachment. While Orr does not explicitly mention sex, his frank talk about a cool bachelor taking advantage of "all of [life's] pleasures and opportunities" deftly keeps all erotic implications in play. Though a rationalizing motivation may lurk behind this male writer's description, and though the kind of self-serving behavior here described does not exactly look like male liberation from the sex / gender system, a passage like this nevertheless could not have been imagined fifty years earlier. This bachelor utterly and blithely disregards the affective connections through which domestic ideology was often propagated and which often led to husband- and fatherhood: he is a "man *who does not feel, in that compelling way,* who does not care, in the sense that he is bound by his concern" (emphasis added). His "fundamental unconcern," which makes him (unlike a Marvel or a Pierre) "at ease and free from all self-consciousness," and the sense that he has an actual, practical erotic life represent a new phenomenon of heteromasculinity. This turn-of-the-century bachelor seems unbound by either the constraints on excessive sexual subjectivity or the injunction to procreative norms that so shaped and defined midcentury bachelorhood. And this seems to be the case in part because of the ease with which the new bachelor can revel in either solitude or masculine company, a freedom that makes the boundaries of his "straight" identity slip suggestively.[37]

Surely not every bachelor at the turn of the century, queer or otherwise, experienced the relativistic pleasures of the "scientific" life, the life lived in thrall to no dominating enjoyment or idea. Still, Orr's model bachelor represents a breaking free from the cultural and conceptual binds that produced the antebellum topos of fireside chastity, and from its associated moods and manners. Mitchell's and Melville's bachelor types, represented within the paradigmatic scene of the fireside revery, anticipate the reconstruction of bachelor identity and the re-eroticization of

American manhood generally. Mitchell's alter ego semireflectively registers the stresses inherent in the metaphysics of antebellum bachelorhood, while Melville's critical bachelors parodically foreground, allusively reveal, or exuberantly reject features of the conflictual bachelor subjectivity. In these different ways, both authors' literary creations begin the cultural spade work that was to bring the bachelor away from his lonely fireside and passive meditations into a world where he could live a newly sensualized practical identity.

NOTES

1. See Eve Kosofsky Sedgwick's discussion of the cultural work of late-Victorian bachelor identity, especially vis-à-vis the emergence of homosexuality, in *Epistemology of the Closet* (Berkeley: University of California Press, 1990), 188–212.

2. On the relations between antebellum history, normative masculinity, and sexual ideology, see John D'Emilio and Estelle B. Freedman, *Intimate Matters: A History of Sexuality in America* (New York: Harper & Row, 1988); Carroll Smith-Rosenberg, *Disorderly Conduct: Visions of Gender in Victorian America* (New York: Alfred A. Knopf, 1985); Stephen Nissenbaum, *Sex, Diet, and Debility in Jacksonian America: Sylvester Graham and Health Reform* (Westport, Conn.: Greenwood Press, 1980); G. J. Barker-Benfield, *The Horrors of the Half-Known Life: Male Attitudes Toward Women and Sexuality in Nineteenth-Century America* (New York: Harper & Row, 1976); Michael Moon, *Disseminating Whitman: Revision and Corporeality in "Leaves of Grass"* (Cambridge: Harvard University Press, 1991); G. M. Goshgarian, *To Kiss the Chastening Rod: Domestic Fiction and Sexual Ideology in the American Renaissance* (Ithaca: Cornell University Press, 1992).

3. The dire micro-and macro-consequences of "onanism," "sodomy," "libertinism," and "marital profligacy" are elaborately spelled out in the sexual advice literature (such as treatises on marital sexuality) and "moral purity" tracts (such as "young men's guides") that flooded American print culture from 1830 on. See especially Nissenbaum, *Sex, Diet, and Debility.*

4. *The Complete Bachelor* (New York: D. Appleton & Co., 1896).

5. There is one exception that I have found: the subtitle of William Cobbett's *Advice to Young Men* (New York: J. Doyle, 1831) addresses his disquisition to "a Youth, a Bachelor, a Lover, a Husband, and a Citizen or a Subject." The word "bachelor," however, never appears in his text, and I believe that the curious status of antebellum bachelor identity explains why.

6. Anne Norton, following Victor Turner, discusses liminality as a spatial metaphor denoting relations of "exclusion or withdrawal from the political order" (*Alternative Americas: A Reading of Antebellum Political Culture* [Chicago: University of Chicago Press, 1986], 12 and passim).

7. On the continuity between maternal and wifely surveillance of male sexuality, see Goshgarian, *To Kiss the Chastening Rod,* 45–55.

8. This of course does not mean that there was not plenty of illicit behavior in mid-century America, and among various classes. According to Dr. William Sanger's estimates, by the 1850s there were six thousand prostitutes in New York, one for every sixty-four men

(D'Emilio and Freedman, *Intimate Matters*, 130–8 and passim). As I have suggested, the explosion of sexual reform literature occurred as a result of the kinds of socioeconomic transformations which made illicit sex easy to come by in urban environments. And it is certainly easy to imagine that members of certain social groups—itinerant urban laborers, for example—could remain generally isolated from discursive culture. But insofar as given subjects lived certain experiences in view of the sex and gender ideologies which, by mid-century, had been powerfully projected upon the national imagination, those subjects would more or less feel the kinds of conceptual conflict which dominant discourses of identity conditioned. Such mentalistic conflict, I would argue, has everything to do with the subject's experience of embodiment in the first instance.

9. "Bachelor's Hall," a song published in *Godey's* 27 (1843) wastes no time establishing its moral point of view on the domestic life of bachelors: "Bachelor's hall, what a quare looking place it is! / Kape me from sich, all the days of my life! / Sure but I think what a burnin' disgrace it is, / Niver at all to be gettin' a wife" (91–2). "The Bachelor's Dilemma," a poem, and "An Old Bachelor's Soliloquy," a sketch (*Godey's* 46 [1853]: 555 and 50 [1855]: 76, respectively), introduce their protagonists to the women who will end their bachelor conditions, bring them to the verge of action, and then leave them there. The poem ends with the "QUERY.—'Did he propose?' " while the sketch will only provide "The *denouement* . . . when we get it." These texts seem as loath, or as unable, to resolve the conundrum of bachelor identity as the bachelor himself.

10. Shirley Samuels, ed., *The Culture of Sentiment: Race, Gender, and Sentimentality in Nineteenth-Century America* (New York: Oxford University Press, 1992), 4.

11. This mode of subjectivization springs from an ideological tradition combining ideals of democratic voluntarism, Enlightenment theories of education through moral feeling, and a post-Calvinist emphasis on individual agency in salvation; see Goshgarian, *To Kiss the Chastening Rod*, 37–45. On the political dimension of sentimental nurture in Revolutionary America, see Jay Fliegelman, *Prodigals and Pilgrims: The American Revolution Against Patriarchal Authority, 1750–1800* (Cambridge: Cambridge University Press, 1982).

12. Goshgarian, *To Kiss the Chastening Rod*, 49–52.

13. John S. Haller, "Bachelor's Disease: Etiology, pathology, and treatment of spermatorrhea in the nineteenth century," *New York State Journal of Medicine* (15 August 1973): 2076–82, quotation from 2077. See also Gail Pat Parsons, "Equal Treatment for All: American Medical Remedies for Male Sexual Problems: 1850–1900," *Journal of the History of Medicine* 32 (January 1977): 55–71; and Kevin J. Mumford, " 'Lost Manhood' Found: Male Sexual Impotence and Victorian Culture in the United States," *Journal of the History of Sexuality* 3 (July 1992): 33–57.

14. On this point, see Nissenbaum, *Sex, Diet, and Debility.*

15. Haller, "Bachelor's Disease," 2077.

16. The profusion of guilt-ridden confessions to doctors and the rise of itinerant quackery, patent medicines, and nostrums intended to cure the condition illustrate how the fear of spermatorrhea reached near panic levels. Not to mention some of the terror-inducing treatments: the anally inserted "egg," the four-pointed urethral ring, lead sheets, purgings, "electric baths," urethral cauterization, and the bleeding and blistering of the perineum. Within the broad specifications of the disease's pathology, nearly every physical symptom or sign of psychic distress could be attributed to it. See Haller, "Bachelor's Disease," 2078, 2080–1.

17. Haller, "Bachelor's Disease," 2080.

18. Page references to "The Old Bachelor," *Godey's* 41 (1850): 250–7, 269–73, will be cited parenthetically in the text. The presence of sentimental bachelor discourse in the nineteenth-century's preeminent women's magazine demonstrates the theoretical interdependence of normative female and normative male domestic ideology. But the question remains: who was the intended addressee of sentimental bachelor tales published in the pages of women's magazines, and how would these tales participate in the affective construction of normative masculinity? The few instances of direct address in the story clearly imply a female reader. But familiarity with the plight of bachelors—especially good-hearted, eligible ones—might induce single women to work their own healing matrimonial cures in real life. It might also induce them to circulate such stories among likely bachelor friends. The stories of T. S. Arthur (whose temperance fiction is discussed by Glenn Hendler's essay in this volume) frequently appeared in *Godey's,* and seem clearly addressed to the harried and domestically neglectful businessman who picks up his wife's magazine in the evening. *Godey's* was also popular reading fare among Civil War soldiers, many of whom were bachelors; see John Tebbel and Mary Ellen Zuckerman, *The Magazine in America, 1741–1990* (New York: Oxford University Press, 1991), 35–6. At the very least, stories like "The Old Bachelor" function as an exemplary expression of what the nineteenth-century viewed as a cultural pathology, one which needed to and could be reformed through the operations of literature. As one writer acerbically puts it: "Our country swarms with bachelors, the most useless of all bipeds, and, apparently only born to eat up the corn. This book shows how to bring this race of drones upon their knees, while they are glad to put on the wreath of wedlock" (preface to Timothy Flint's *The Bachelor Reclaimed, or Celibacy Vanquished* [Philadelphia: Key, 1834]). But had stories such as this found their way into the hands of bachelors, they could very well have provoked the kinds of ideological effects upon male subjectivity that I will go on to elaborate.

19. See G. N. Dangerfield, "The symptoms, pathology, causes and treatment of spermatorrhea," *Lancet* 1 (1843): 211; cited in Haller, "Bachelor's Disease," 2077. The language of bachelor suicide is also interestingly used in an anonymous story called "The Bachelor Beset," in the *Southern Literary Messenger* 5 (1839): 751–7. In a "magnanimous act of self-immolation," a bachelor proposes to a homely spinster who has been embarrassingly discovered snooping in his room. His own act so threatens the bachelor's fragile identity, however, that he is cast into the sphere of his own thought, in search of the only kind of ontological security bachelors are allowed: " 'Am I in my senses? . . . Do I really exist? Yes,' he added, reasoning with Descartes, 'I think, therefore, I exist' " (756). In contrast to Dr. Hinton, this bachelor escapes domestication, but only barely, by fleeing to the margins of the nation, to Texas.

20. William A. Alcott, *The Physiology of Marriage* (Boston: John P. Jewett & Company, 1857), 14.

21. The term "nonthematizable" is Judith Butler's; see *Bodies that Matter: On the Discursive Limits of "Sex"* (New York: Routledge, 1993).

22. Donald Grant Mitchell, *Reveries of a Bachelor* (New York: Scribner's, 1850). Page references to this work will be cited parenthetically in the body of this essay.

23. F. W. Shelton, "On Old Bachelors," *Southern Literary Messenger* 19 (April 1853): 223–8.

24. John Todd, *The Student's Manual* (Northampton, Miss: J. H. Butler, 1835), 88, 146–7, 321.

25. This analysis omits Melville's more canonical story, "The Paradise of Bachelors and The Tartarus of Maids." Like other of Melville's tales of the 1850s, this story works

analytically: the trope of the paper mill pictures a female sexuality economically enslaved within a discursive technology of reproduction, which is the ideological flip side of patriarchally structured homosocial bonds between bachelors. See Robyn Wiegman, "Melville's Geography of Gender," *American Literary History* 1 (1989): 735–53. But because this story represents a specifically English bachelor culture, already highly articulated and characterized by a relative lack of social agon, it does not do the same kind of constructive fantasy work concerning American bachelor identity that the texts I treat in this essay do.

26. *Pierre, or The Ambiguities* (Evanston: Northwestern University Press, 1971), 297. Further references to this work will be cited parenthetically in the body of this essay.

27. The "frosty bachelor" Miles Coverdale in *The Blithedale Romance* (New York: New American Library, 1980), Hawthorne's novel about the Brook Farm utopian experiment, is particularly germane to this point (quotation from 5). Coverdale's preference for the meditative passivity of the fireside, and his inability to acknowledge, much less act upon, his desire for Zenobia, show the extent to which ideological norms expressed at the level of embodied subjectivity can form the necessary deep structure of schematic social alternatives. The writer of an anonymous defense of bachelor- and spinsterhood acknowledges this point in reverse when s / he argues that in order for institutions like marriage or utopian communitarianism to work, subjects must entirely suppress the natural vicissitudes of feeling within a "human heart" that would bring subjectivity into conflict with an idealizing conceptual regime; see *"Single Blessedness"; or, Single Ladies and Gentlemen, Against the Slanders of the Pulpit, the Press, and the Lecture-room* (New York: C. S. Francis & Co., 1852), 92–3.

28. The narrator, in contrast, would have the Apostles leave aside their Kantian Categories and Graham crackers and lead an ecstatic corporeal existence: "attach the screw of your hose pipe to some fine old butt of Madeira! pump us some sparkling wine into the world!" (301).

29. The narrator's wife has "unsuitable young hankerings" and "itches," likes "young company" and "offers to ride young colts," and "sets out young suckers in the orchard" (*Selected Tales and Poems by Herman Melville*, ed. Richard Chase [New York: Holt, Rinehart and Winston, 1950], 171). Further references to this story and to "The Lightning-Rod Man" are from this edition, and will be cited parenthetically in the body of this essay.

30. The plans for model houses in *Godey's* show the reformation of nineteenth-century architecture to be part and parcel of the general propagation of domestic ideology, and the career of Orson Fowler, another "scribe," demonstrates that an "architectural reformer" (as the subsequent architect who consults with the wife is called [189]) can be a sexual reformer as well.

31. This homoerotic reading of a central image of the story flirts of course with anachronism. The trope of the closet, as George Chauncey points out, seems "nowhere" to have been used, by homosexuals or others, with respect to homosexual identity until after the 1960s. But, as Chauncey admits in a note, *"Nowhere* is a strong word, and it is more difficult to find conclusive evidence of an absence than a presence" (*Gay New York: Gender, Urban Culture, and the Makings of the Gay Male World, 1890–1940* [New York: Basic Books, 1994], 374). Chauncey's fascinating analysis of the myth of pre-Stonewall gay "invisibility," and the closet consciousness it produced, does not in any way compromise the aptness of the trope of the closet as one way of characterizing gay-identified subjectivity in "prehomosexual" American culture. I have no trouble imagining that Melville could have exploited the socially symbolic utility of an appropriate trope (positively connoting intimacy and safekeeping, as well as paranoia and hiddenness) well before its codification in general or sub-

cultural speech. My embrace of anachronism here also parallels the epistemological project underlying James Creech's queer reading of *Pierre*. See *Closet Writing / Gay Reading: The
Case of Melville's "Pierre"* (Chicago: University of Chicago Press, 1993), 69 and passim.

32. The initial identification, as Philip Young points out, was made in 1948, by Egbert
Oliver, but it is Young who marks out Todd's anti-onanism, and not solely his dour Calvin-
ism, as the target of Melville's satire: see Young, "Melville in the Berkshire Bishopric: 'The
Lightning-Rod Man,' " *College Literature* 16 (Fall 1989): 201–10.

33. Peter Laipson, "The Social Geographies of Bachelorhood," in *"I have No Genius for
Marriage": Bachelorhood in Urban America, 1870–1930* (forthcoming).

34. Katherine Snyder, *Bachelors, Manhood, and the Novel, 1850–1925* (Cambridge and
New York: Cambridge University Press, 1999).

35. On the associations between bachelor subculture and nascent gay subculture, see
Chauncey, *Gay New York*.

36. Lyndon Orr, "Men Who Marry and Men Who Do Not," *The Cosmopolitan* 38
(March 1905): 543–6, quotation from 545. I am grateful to Peter Laipson for bringing this
piece to my attention.

37. "There is something mentally enervating in feminine companionship after a while;
and so, after having been both delighted and delightful in the society of women, the genuine man feels that he must go off and be alone or with other men, out in the open air, as it
were, roughing it among the rough, as a mental tonic" (545). The latter half of this remark
recalls that exemplary excessive bachelor Walt Whitman, who made tremendous efforts—
from the first edition of *Leaves of Grass* on through the "deathbed edition"—to clear the
ground for new conceptions of sexualized American manhood. On the "body politics" of
Whitman's revisionary strategies through the various editions of *Leaves of Grass*, see Moon,
Disseminating Whitman.

CHAPTER TWO

Feeling for the Fireside

Longfellow, Lynch, and the Topography of Poetic Power

Kirsten Silva Gruesz

In a recent essay, Ron Rosenbaum tells of an unexpected insight into the banality of evil, triggered by his pilgrimage to the South Carolina lake where Susan Smith drowned her two young sons in 1994. An outpouring of public sympathy followed the sensational murders, turning the lakeshore into an impromptu shrine littered with offerings of teddy bears, flowers, and photographs of other dead children whose loss must have seemed similarly inexplicable and tragic. Rosenbaum's eye was caught by an anonymous, handwritten poem stapled onto a wooden stake, for it repeated, with slight variations, the text of another poem he had noticed a short distance away. "The gist of the poem was this: God looked around heaven one day and found it a bit dreary. . . . He looked down at Earth and saw two lovely little 'rosebuds' He fancied—the unblemished souls of Susan Smith's two boys," and so directed the Angel of Death to pluck them and carry them off to heaven. It strikes him that "this cute little poem, amid the flowers and the heart-shaped balloons and the stuffed animals, posing as just another fluffy piece of sentimentality," depicts a weirdly *wicked* God, "an irritable, demonic esthete so easily bored with His décor that He arranges the murder of two young children in order to add a dash of color to His abode. It's meant to be consoling, but in fact it's one of the most terrifying depictions of the deity I can imagine." To this, Rosenbaum compares the Hallmarked language of Susan Smith's written confession: "I love my children with all my ♥. . . . My children deserve to have the best, and now they will." "What could be better," he asks caustically, "than an honored place in God's little garden?" Thus, he suggests, the conventions of sentimental consolation by which those anonymous mourners protested Smith's act are the same ones that enabled her to rationalize it in the first place.[1]

Rosenbaum's argument—that the cheerful mask of sentimental piety belies a far more sinister lapse in our collective conscience—reveals how powerfully the modernist quarrel with Victorianism continues to inform contemporary debates about the national character. He takes offense at the poem's lazy theodicy, its "well-meaning but pitifully inadequate efforts to explain or understand the evil deed and the deaths," blaming this inadequacy on the flaccid form of Protestantism practiced by the nameless mourners (presumably not regular readers of the *New York Times Magazine*, where the piece appeared), who had taken the tragedy so much to heart. Following the strain in American thought that runs at least from George Santayana through Ann Douglas, Rosenbaum ridicules the consolation genre for its lack of intellectual rigor, even as he registers a deeper unease with the considerable cultural influence it continues to exercise. Like those predecessors, Rosenbaum associates sentimentalism with the feminine sphere in general and the immature moral consciousness in particular: the poem is copied in a "schoolmarmish" hand; Smith writes in a "childish scrawl." The menace of sentimentalism lies in its hidden manipulative power: behind every iconic heart and angel there is a budding Susan Smith, a monstrous mother waiting to emerge.

As is well known, feminist literary history of the past two decades has made the recuperation of "the female world of love and ritual" one of its central concerns: the antebellum emergence of the Cult of True Womanhood, and its dominance for the remainder of the century, has become a pivotal moment for theorists of American subjectivity, one to which current debates about the state of women return as regularly as pundits to Emerson. We now read sentimental literature for what it reveals about ideologies of domesticity, and about women writers' circumscription within, or resistance to, those ideologies. Thus the recovery of that literature initially focused on the more obviously mimetic genres—fiction, memoirs, diaries—rather than on lyric or narrative poetry. Although recent years have witnessed a new pull toward poetry, critics continue to privilege subgenres like the dead-child elegy, which seem to offer the most intense access to common yet intimate circumstances of nineteenth-century women's lives. In their survey of maternal consolation literature, Wendy Simonds and Barbara Katz Rothman assert that these poems reflect "a realm of experience not touched upon in men's writing," arguing that the consolation lyric forces the female speaker to question her own worth in a system that made motherhood a virtual requirement for complete womanliness.[2]

Critics also tend to read those poetic subgenres that are more evasive of such historicist readings primarily through the lens of domestic ideology. Following the model that portrays sentimental fiction as a self-enclosed and agoraphobic reflection of actual women's restricted material and psychic spaces, Cheryl Walker and Emily Stipes Watts have characterized sentimental poetry as a series of meditations on the themes of restriction and containment, of the protective retreat of the female self. Walker's pioneering study begins from the assumption that women turned to writing to counteract the frustration of their own powerlessness, and constructs a typology of women's poetry according to the driving themes of restriction and impotence.[3] Other scholars have reiterated her paradigm, finding the defining features of these nineteenth-century texts to be a tendency toward collective conformity and an unease about the consequences of individual speech. Annie Finch, for instance, writes that the female poet, conditioned to mistrust female individuality and therefore reluctant to engage in the agonistic struggle to assert the lyric poet's subjective "I," would eschew the "privileged central self" of the Romantic tradition in favor of poetic modes that foregrounded the difficulty of self-expression.[4]

From the historical conditions of women's literary production, then, critics have extrapolated a sentimental aesthetic that verges on the transhistorical, on the "essentially" feminine. Simonds and Katz Rothman, for example, introduce their survey with Lydia Sigourney, claiming a continuity between her and the sentimentalists and consolation writers of the present day, which returns us to the problem of Rosenbaum's anonymous—but strongly female-identified—poem at the lakeshore shrine. Yet the poetic artifact that Rosenbaum describes bears an unmistakable resemblance to Henry Wadsworth Longfellow's "The Reaper and the Flowers," first published in 1839 and a staple of consolation literature ever since.[5] Longfellow transforms Death into a figure as gentle, and as integral to the life of a community, as the village blacksmith. The friendly Reaper is just doing his job: he explains to the grieving mother, "My Lord has need of these flowerets gay," as they remind God of his own time on earth.

And the mother gave, in tears and pain,
The flowers she most did love;
She knew she should find them all again
In the fields of light above.

Oh, not in cruelty, not in wrath,
The Reaper came that day;
'T was an angel visited the green earth,
And took the flowers away.[6]

Longfellow noted in his journal that he wrote "The Reaper and the Flowers" spontaneously, "not without tears in my eyes," and he uncharacteristically rejected a later revision, "leaving the piece as it came from my mind yesterday in a gush."[7] Such tearful spontaneity was, of course, highly prized by the cult of sensibility, and equally denigrated by its critics. In terms of its conventional imagery and unimaginative rhymes (atypical of Longfellow, who was generally an inventive prosodist), "The Reaper and the Flowers" seems indistinguishable from any of the maternal consolation poems scattered in *Godey's*, *Graham's*, or other middle-brow periodicals. Like female sentimentalists, Longfellow was not unwilling to position himself publicly within a critical economy of tears: upon hearing that the wife of a Harvard colleague wept upon reading "Footsteps of Angels," a similar lyric published in the same year, he wrote, "I want no more favorable criticism than this."[8] Moreover, his consolation poems achieved a canonical place within what Lydia Sigourney had famously described as "the whole sweet circle of the domestic affections,—the hallowed ministries of woman, at the cradle, the

hearthstone, and the death-bed": one historian recounts the rather macabre anecdote of a little girl who memorized "The Reaper and the Flowers" and recited it
as a prayer before bedtime.[9] If our critical apparatus for reading such work relies
upon the notion of the disempowered individual, the retreating woman writer,
what are we to make of similar work coming from the most publicly empowered
American poet of the century?

The very vehicles by which maternal consolation poems were disseminated
serve to upset Walker's contention, in the introduction to her invaluable anthology *American Women Poets of the Nineteenth Century,* that "the realm in which women's
poetry flourished was for most of the century considered a distinctly separate
sphere": "there were poets and there were *women* poets." Her primary source for
this claim is Rufus Griswold, who, in his gender-segregated anthologies of American poetry, made the famous distinction that poetesses wrote about—and in the
manner of—"dews and flowers" rather than "glaciers and rocks."[10] But did that
distinction really possess the prescriptive and prohibitive power that critics have
attributed to it, or was it simply a necessary by-product of Griswold's effort to
market both books? Griswold's earlier collection, *The Cypress Wreath: A Book of Consolation for Those Who Mourn,* contains a nearly equal distribution of works by male
and female poets; a similar consolation book, *Echoes of Infant Voices,* uses two
Longfellow poems as bookends, leading off with "The Reaper and the Flowers"
and ending with "Resignation," and although Felicia Hemans is, predictably, the
best-represented author, Emerson's "Threnody" occupies a central place.[11]

The genre of consolation lyric, then, resists any easy segregation into masculine and feminine forms of affect. As the vestigial presence of Longfellow's poem
in the mourning rituals of a recent murder case suggests, male grief may look
identical, on the page, to female grief. Antebellum readers, of course, would have
imposed different assumptions upon a text (and particularly a lyric poem) according to the gender of the author: in an age preoccupied both by literary biography
as character study and by the hopeful search for a native American genius, assessing the contiguity between a writer's life and work was not a scholarly luxury but
in some sense a matter of communal and national import. Yet even if a given literary convention was prevalently associated with one gender, writers were not
powerless to manipulate that association to their own benefit. In particular, they
often sought to influence the material conditions under which poems should be
read alone or read aloud by imagining the familiar topographies of the nineteenth-century home as places variously charged with the expression of sentiment. By returning some specificity to the misleadingly transparent category of
"Fireside" poetry, I want to think about the lyric experience as one that signifies
differently in public, familial contexts as opposed to private ones—before a parlor
hearth, or within a solitary library. Ultimately, this venture leads back to what I
have described as an originary point in feminist literary history, the question of
differing access to cultural power, which I will address through the figure of Anne
Charlotte Lynch (Botta), a midcentury writer whose attunement to Longfellow's

mapping of the domains of fireside, parlor, and library as discrete poetic domains is reflected in her conscious rewritings of his lyrics.

As his authorship of "The Reaper and the Flowers" suggests, Longfellow confounds the notion of separate spheres of literary production. To account for the poet's rise and thudding fall from the American canon, literary history has frequently reiterated the notion that there were two mutually irreconcilable Longfellows: one domestic, sentimental, cannily commercial—the grandfatherly muse of "The Children's Hour"; the other cosmopolitan, intellectual, virilely master of poetic tradition—the translator of Dante.[12] Rebutting this binary division, Eric Haralson has recently speculated that the "cultural logic of his popularity" had to do with Longfellow's "advocacy of a cross-gendered sensibility—and, crucially, of a 'sentimental' masculinity—that answered to the experiential trials and affective needs of his audience" by merging the 'feminine' values of self-abnegation to a higher authority with the 'masculine' capacity for strength and endurance.[13] It might be said that Longfellow, like a number of his contemporaries, was playing the margins of a literary vocation that was by popular consensus neither wholly masculine nor purely feminine, to paraphrase Margaret Fuller. But if we can isolate a practice of sentimental masculinity brought to one of its fullest expressions by Longfellow, does that practice conform to female sentimentalism, as Haralson suggests, or strategically appropriate it in order to challenge women's dominance of the domestic order? Might it have provided (as Vincent J. Bertolini suggests with regard to bachelor literature elsewhere in this volume) a kind of sanctuary from domesticity, subversively located *within* the domestic sphere?

Like Hawthorne, with whom he shared a long and mutually supportive fellowship, Longfellow was often described by his contemporaries as a kind of literary cross-dresser: a writer in whom were combined the probing intellect of a man and a woman's intuitive sensibility. James Russell Lowell's *A Fable for Critics* (1849) playfully imagines that when Nature formed Hawthorne there was insufficient "clay" to shape a "full-sized man," so "a little was spared / From some finer-grained stuff for a woman prepared."[14] Longfellow is a similarly hybrid vessel, who patiently suffers the "mud-balls" (i.e., accusations of plagiarism) flung at him by Poe, in whom "the heart somehow seems all squeezed out by the mind." In defense of Longfellow, Lowell's Critic asks, "Does it make a man worse that his character's such / As to make his friends love him, as you think, too much?" That pure love, he goes on to say, is his era's closest connection to the Greek golden age: works like *Evangeline* will endure as long as Homer because they represent "a shrine of retreat from Earth's hubbub and strife / as quiet and chaste as the author's own life."[15] Lowell's prediction is interesting not only because it proved so thoroughly mistaken, but because it allows Longfellow's writing to usurp the role of the True Woman, providing a chaste "shrine" to beauty and a place of "retreat" for the world-weary Critic. *A Fable for Critics* might be seen as a fable of family that details the troubled yet loving relationships among America's literary men: stripped of the complications of female presence, the authorial characters in the *Fable* are free to play as they wish, to expose the tender "heart" of a less than "full-sized" man or fling mud-balls at one another.

Longfellow, like Hawthorne, had to fight to define writing in masculine terms against a skeptical father, who urged him toward the law. While teaching modern languages at Bowdoin, he published a Sidneyesque "Defence of Poetry" in the *North American Review* in 1832 that articulates, and politicizes, the relationship between manliness and writing, calling for a national literature "as original, characteristic, and national as possible": a strong nativist statement that the Young America movement would seize upon and cite for its own ends, and one that Longfellow himself would later parody in *Kavanagh*. The essay seems bent on defending not poetry per se, but rather the virility of those who write it: "With us," Longfellow complains in anticipation of Whitman, "the spirit of the age is clamorous for utility,—for visible, tangible utility,—for bare, brawny, muscular utility." Americans

> hold the appellation of scholar and man of letters in as little repute, as did our Gothic ancestors that of Roman; associating it with about the same ideas of effeminacy and inefficiency. They think, that the learning of books is not wisdom; that study unfits a man for action; that poetry and nonsense are convertible terms; that literature begets an effeminate and craven spirit; in a word, that the dust and cobwebs of a library are a kind of armor, which will not stand long against the hard knocks of "the bone and muscle of the State," and the "huge two-fisted sway" of the stump orator.

In answer to the Goths of the literary world, Longfellow suggests that poetic expression is a natural bodily urge, and scoffs at their fear that poetry will "enervate the mind, corrupt the heart, [and] incapacitate us for performing the private and public duties of life." Echoing the sexual reform discourse of the period, he argues that the acts of reading and writing poetry are unmanly only when performed in the wrong context—that is, outside of the public arena, outside the national family. Instead of producing the great "soldier-poets" of Sidney's time, the American literary scene has allowed its resources to be hopelessly scattered: each small village has "its little Byron, its self-tormenting scoffer at morality, its gloomy misanthropist in song." Those local poets are misguided not because of what they write, but because they write it solo: like masturbatory "self-tormenters," they spread their seed randomly and fruitlessly, rather than dedicating their energies toward the common good of bringing a national literature into being. The native literati—young, untutored, and lacking in self-control—publish their writing too soon, which "tends to give an effeminate and unmanly character to our literature. . . . Premature exhibitions of talent are an unstable foundation to build a national literature upon."[16] Longfellow's point is that literary energy needs to be husbanded, not thoughtlessly expended for individual pleasure alone; he proposes that American poets need to learn a kind of poetic continence and rein in their tendency toward Byronic bursts, to control their embarrassingly "premature" literary ejaculations.[17]

Longfellow here assumes, in the spirit of Goethe and Schiller,[18] a masculine civic poetry that offers up authentic interiority in the Romantic tradition, but does so in the service of a collective aim: to engender a family feeling among dangerously isolated subjectivities. The process is dialectical, for it requires an alternating assertion and effacement of the lyrical "I." William Charvat long ago identified this "public poetic stance" as the primary mode of the Fireside Poets,[19] but it resonates as well with the ambivalent self-abnegation of the speaking subject that Walker, Watts, and other feminist critics identify as the defining feature of nineteenth-century women's poetry. However, readers of *Voices of the Night*, Longfellow's first collection of original poetry (following his own advice, he waited until 1839 to expose it to public view), identified this publicly private form of expression as explicitly masculine. One reviewer praised the "dignity of sentiment and the lessons of high-toned resolve and manly resolution" of the lyrics; another, their "quality of generous, genial manhood."[20] Longfellow's brother Alexander wrote that *Voices of the Night* "gives to these Western shores a new species of poetry—the *mental* in contradiction to the *sentimental*—the healthy, in opposition to the morbid."[21] Given that *Voices* contained a number of consolation poems— "The Reaper and the Flowers," "The Light of Stars" and "Footsteps of Angels"—this claim to have transcended the sentimental and "morbid" sounds exaggerated, wishful at best. Yet the opposition he describes is grounded in the material presence of the book itself.

Read within the context of a popular mourner's book like Griswold's, "Reaper" serves two aims: to provoke an unrestrained flow of sympathetic tears, and to reaffirm the theological order that promises eventual recompense for those tears. But placed within the material context of the whole of Longfellow's volume, the excesses of the consolation poem are balanced—disciplined—by corresponding lyrics of manly action, which pursued the martial theme Longfellow had sounded in "Defence of Poetry." "Reaper" was originally subtitled "A Psalm of Death," and was followed in the book by "A Psalm of Life": the very source of the motto of the age, "Let us, then, be up and doing."[22] The two poems are closely paired: "Psalm of Life" begins from a negation of grieving ("Tell me not, in mournful numbers . . ."), then urges the reader to move beyond it ("Let the dead Past bury its dead!") into virile action ("Let us, then, be up and doing").[23] Likewise, the famous lines that close "The Light of Stars," another meditation on loss, marry sensitivity of feeling with manly endurance: "Know how sublime a thing it is / To suffer *and* be strong" (emphasis added). The dual phases through which the volume repeatedly passes demonstrate first a venting of emotional energy, then a careful husbanding of it, a redirection of feeling toward productive ends.[24]

Such a strategy casts new light upon Charvat's claim that Longfellow was able to become the first American poet to make a living from writing only because he took *control* of the stereotype plates of his works and was thus able to republish them in book form, earning far more than he could have made from a single periodical appearance.[25] Despite his swipe in the "Defence" at the American tendency to identify masculinity with mercantile success, Longfellow took a number of cues in this regard from Nathaniel Parker Willis, the reigning genius of the literary marketplace. Willis wrote him, "I see perfectly the line you are striking out for renown, and it will succeed. Your severe, chaste, lofty-thoughted style of poetry will live a good deal longer than that which would be more salable and more popular now; and if you preferred the money and the hurrah, I should be . . . sorry as I am obliged to do so myself. Still, I think you are not quite *merchant* enough with your poems after they are written."[26] Willis counterposes a "chaste" manner of self-publicizing against a salesman's urge to disseminate his work widely; later, Longfellow would complain to his friend Sam Ward that Willis "says he has made ten thousand dollars the last year by his writings. I wish I had made ten hundred."[27] With his next collection, Longfellow would advance that wish: plotting the "new field" of *Ballads* (1841), he writes, "I have a great notion of working upon the *people's feelings*."[28] Here he resolves the problem of the "Defence": to see the writing of poetry as a form of "work" that is not subjugated to "utility."

Longfellow structures this second volume, as well, to provide a counterpoint between the free flow of feeling and manly continence. Later he would remark, "People like books of poems which they can read at one sitting. The publishers insist on quantity, but I have always aimed to have my books small."[29] Here he rejects alleged market forces that would encourage "Byronic excess," while building in an important degree of control over the way individual poems are read— that is, in meaningful relation to each other. The most popular piece in *Ballads*, "Excelsior!" seems an exception, in that it builds the dynamic of expansion and consolation into the structure of a single poem. Its hero abandons the "household fires" of "happy homes" to follow a voice that chants the hypnotic mantra of "Excelsior!" as it directs him up a treacherous mountain passage. His body is later found, "lifeless, but beautiful," ennobled and aestheticized for his heroic attempt to reach "higher, ever higher!" As the poet's brother and editor Samuel Longfellow would note approvingly, the youth attains his glory *because* he detaches himself from the domestic realm: "refusing to listen to the pleadings of home affections, of woman's love, or of formal religion, [he] presses on to a higher goal."[30] At the same time, the poem indulges the sentimental death-cult, rewriting the consolation poem in the sublime setting of the Alps. Here, Longfellow complicates the schematic pairing of psalms of life and death with a topographical contrast between the intimate light of home fires and the sublime expanse of bracing snow to provide an allegory of the rough work of life.[31]

These two realms again appear in equipoise in a further volume, *The Seaside and the Fireside* (1849), which divides into the separate sections suggested by the title. The voice offering the introductory "Dedication" tenders his companionship on "your seaside walk, / saddened, and mostly silent, with emotion / Not interrupting with intrusive talk / The grand, majestic symphonies of ocean." As in "Excelsior!" he lays claim to the Romantic sublime, with its melancholy natural silences; at the same time, he makes himself—literally—at home in the reader's family circle: "I hope, as no unwelcome guest, / At your warm fireside, when the lamps are lighted, / To have my place reserved among the rest."[32] Both this poem and the book itself move from the wild heath to the tame hearth in a way that divides the labor of lyric: the encounters with History and Nature described in the "seaside" poems are steeped in the domestic virtues; and the "fireside" lyrics place their narrowly circumscribed emotional themes into larger frames of historical reference. For instance, "By the Seaside" begins with "The Building of the Ship," which allegorizes national union through a domestic event, the young captain's marriage to the daughter of the builder of the "ship of state." "By the Fireside" opens with a consolation poem, "Resignation," which envisions the home as a vulnerable polity ("There is no fireside, howsoe'er defended, / But has one vacant chair!").[33] "The Fire of Drift-Wood," the hinge between the two sections, exemplifies this mutual inscription. Gathered in a beach house around a driftwood fire "[b]uilt of the wreck of stranded ships," a group of friends ponders the transience of those glorious endeavors described in "The Building of the Ship"—the national allegory leading off the "Seaside" section. Each crackle of the fire conjures up visions of "ships dismasted, that were hailed / And sent no answer back again." This meditation on history provokes an inward turn of sentiment, as each guest contemplates "The long-lost ventures of the heart / That send no answers back again."[34] Here, as throughout, readers are directed to carry their "fireside" feelings into the larger public topographies suggested in the "seaside" poems.

But what, exactly, does the imagined space of the fireside *mean*, to readers of not only Longfellow but also Lowell, Whittier, and Bryant, who have been traditionally grouped together beneath this uninterrogated rubric? "Fireside" hints at a spatial reading practice that it does not actually specify or locate. Like the adjectival "parlor," it suggests to twentieth-century readers the physical and intellectual constraints imposed upon the individual by the Victorian family structure and reinforced in its architectural and decorative tastes. Reimposing distinction and historicity upon such terms may allow us to see these topographies as inviting—or prohibiting—a particular range of lyric experience.

Historian Clifford Edward Clark, Jr., has charted the process by which the literal importance of the fireside became subsumed into the symbolic one, as innovations in heating systems enabled average home builders, by the 1830s, to replace many of the heating and cooking functions of the open fire with furnaces and stoves: the hearth became most significant as the center around which the family gathered.[35] At the same time, architectural reformers as diverse as Andrew Jackson Downing, Gervase Wheeler, Orson Fowler, and Catharine Beecher were arguing forcefully for new middle-class home designs that would reflect the idealized unity of the family: "each room in the house, like each member of the family, should have a clearly defined role and function."[36] Generally speaking, their reformist house plans isolated bedchambers upstairs, grouped workspaces of the kitchen and pantry toward the back of the house, and divided space on the ground floor into a front parlor (or sitting room) and a back parlor (or library, or drawing room) dedicated to private family use.[37] Despite their broad enthusiasm for technology's potential to improve the material and spiritual conditions of American homes, these reformers remained nostalgically attached to the fireplace: as Downing wrote, "We must have a little of the living soul—the glow of the hearth—there."[38] Beecher went further, advising the construction of one central fireplace that would heat kitchen and parlor at once, while improving the quality of air circulating within the home.[39]

Ultimately, however, the new meaning of the fireside was more closely linked to the circulation of *ideas* within the home. Although private reading certainly went on there, the fireside of the family parlor seems to be identified as the locus of performative reading: the place in which an individual was most powerfully encouraged to imagine herself as part of a larger readerly community, whether familial, religious, or national. Communal reading was one of the few amusements Beecher's domestic manuals endorsed; although the parlor was part of "woman's sphere," she assigned responsibility for family reading to Christian fathers, who were enjoined to "subtract time from their business, to spend at home, in reading with their wives and children" and to "keep a supervision of the current literature of the day, as guardians, to warn others of danger."[40] Yet the notion that *women* exercised principal moral influence in the family by way of the tears, sighs, and prayers provoked by literary texts is a central premise of scholarship on sentimentalism and domestic ideology.[41] If images of women and men guiding the family in fireside reading were both available to antebellum readers, how might we distinguish between the forms of experience each scene conjures up? What sort of authority—parental or otherwise—is the lyric voice in Longfellow's poem seeking when he says, "I hope, as no unwelcome guest, / At your warm fireside, when the lamps are lighted, / To have my place reserved among the rest"? Tentative, intimate, and just a bit insistent, the speaker imagines and dictates the very conditions by which the page will mediate his voice. He calls attention to the materiality of the book and its culture: the "I" here might refer to a person inviting himself or herself to warm up at the parlor fire, or it may play upon the conceit of the talking book, as the volume asks to have a "place reserved" for it upon the shelves of the reader's library.

It is this image—the book on the home library shelves—that suggests how we might particularize the "fireside" within various scenes of, and ideologies about, domestic reading. The plan books of the architectural reformers included, if the house was of a suitable size, a library or study, "usually located near the back in a more quiet part of the house," for "the gentleman who 'has either professional occupations, or literary taste.' It had its own side entrance so that his comings and goings would not disturb the rest of the family."[42] The idealized library would thus constitute the most private of the semiprivate rooms downstairs, serving as a kind of paternal retreat: a haven *from* the haven from a heartless world. Granting that such model-home plans were adapted and reconfigured in actual domestic life, it nonetheless seems important to imagine, in our gallery of scenes of ante-bellum reading, the place from which a reader might have approached the fireside circle. The act of choosing the reading, of bringing a book across the threshold, suggests the ability to control access between these two spaces.

If the Firesiders have often been referred to as a self-proclaimed "high priest-hood" of literary culture in America, the nature of their priestly mediation is fundamentally parental: to select, to distill, and finally to offer for communal consumption a canon newly organized in meaningful ways. That work is often analogous to that of an anthologist. Griswold's volumes on American poetry informed, and sought to exert influence over, the national family; Longfellow designed *Poets and Poetry of Europe* (1845), more than a decade after his "Defence of Poetry," to redress what he had come to see as the provincialism of a nation of readers overly hungry to see themselves, and only themselves, on the page.[43] On a somewhat less elevated plane, yet evincing the same sense of tender paternal supervision, came the ubiquitous "fireside collections": Henry T. Coates's *Fireside Encyclopedia of Poetry*, which went through 34 editions, claims it "will be a welcome companion at every FIRESIDE; and . . . while representing all that is best and brightest in our poetic literature, should contain nothing that would tend to undermine any one's faith or destroy a single virtuous impulse."[44] To some degree, this mission to canonize and censor in the name of familial "safety" dove-tails with that of all the significant American periodical editors of the century, from Sigourney to Stowe to Stedman. Yet an anthology, unlike a periodical, has a library scene as its necessary pre-text: a scene of the anthologist retreating into the library's sacrosanct masculine quiet and finally emerging, compilation in hand, to supervise the literary experience of the family parlor—which is in turn set apart from the public area at the front of the house. Thus male uses of domestic, famil-ial space to exert the power of sympathy do not simply replicate women's domain but rather augment it, investing the private realm of the library with the ultimate sentimental authority.

If the bedside and the fireside are commonly imagined in nineteenth-century women's poems, this inner sanctum of the library appears only rarely. One exception can be found in the work of Anne Charlotte Lynch, whose career offers suggestive analogies to Longfellow's despite her comparatively thin literary output. She locates lyric experience in an array of household settings, from the open front parlor to the family hearth to the private intimacy of the library, and thematizes these spaces as analogous to kinds of literary influence. For Lynch as for Longfellow, the library comes to represent the equipoise of the "mental" and "sentimental" that had brought such success to *Voices of the Night*.

Born in 1815 (eight years after Longfellow), Lynch was a promising scholarship student from a family of modest income just out of the Albany Female Seminary when her poems caught the eye of Lydia Sigourney. Sigourney bought one of her poems for the *Religious Souvenir for 1839,* and Lynch moved to New York in 1845 to follow her vocation, supporting herself as a teacher and inviting players in the literary and musical scenes into her home for the next decade. It was in her parlor that the alleged rivalry between Poe and Griswold for the attentions of Frances Osgood was played out; over the course of the decade, her frequent visitors were said to include Emerson, Fuller, Bryant, Willis, Howe, Catharine Sedgwick, Horace Greeley, the Cary sisters, Elizabeth Ellet, Elizabeth Oakes-Smith, and Grace Greenwood (Sara Lippincott).[45] Longfellow, unlike Bryant and Whittier, did not take a particular interest in encouraging the careers of female writers as such: indeed, he wrote his closest confidante, Samuel Ward, that the poetic ambitions of Ward's sister, Julia Ward Howe, might be met with resistance because she was "carrying almost too many guns for any man, who does not want to be *firing salutes* all the time."[46] Howe was a close friend of Anne Charlotte Lynch; their connection to this brother and sister stands in lieu of any closer relationship between her and Longfellow.[47] In the midst of all her activity, Lynch published the misleadingly titled "Diary of a Recluse" in 1845, along with a number of stray lyrics, travel pieces, and criticism. Her collection, *Poems,* was published in 1849; it went through expanded editions in 1852 and 1881.[48]

Poems, like *Voices of the Night,* is ambitiously eclectic: Lynch tries her hand at the ballad, the patriotic ode, the descriptive panorama of the Mississippi, the "Battle of Life" theme, and translations from the French, as well as a meditation "On the Death of an Infant." Nina Baym, following Watts, sees this eclecticism as typical of the "women's miscellany," a collection of poems that, when taken as a whole, "exhibits an identity specific to the writer that, given the events through which she defines herself, is ineluctably female."[49] Such an interpretation assumes that despite the subject matter of the poems themselves, which range across the boundaries of supposedly gendered experience, readers would unfailingly identify the lyric speaker as female. A letter that N. P. Willis sent "Lynchie" in 1845 seems to reinforce the idea that readerly expectations of female subjectivity were impossible for a poet to evade. Its contrast with his earlier letter of advice to Longfellow is tellingly stark:

> This much I may say, as a literary godfather . . . that the intense passionateness of your nature is all ready for utterance in undying language; and that if you do not breathe your heart soon upon an absorbent object, you will either be corroded by the stifled intensity of undeveloped feeling, or you will overflow with poetry and (like other volcanoes that find a vent) blacken the verdure around you with the cinders of exposed agonies. In short, you must *love or be famous!* Wretched dilemma![50]

With ominous imagery of volcanic repression and destruction, the "godfather" insists that women's poetic energy is principally erotic: it can be directed toward a man or the Muse, but not both. Willis implies that whether Lynch chooses to "love or be famous," she will be incapable of controlling her "volcano."

Lynch's "Lines to One Who Wished to Read a Poem I Had Written" seems to corroborate both Willis's glib assumptions and the feminist claim that women's poetry reveals a gender-specific anxiety about writing. Within the context of Walker's anthology, surrounded by that critical apparatus, the poem does seem to thematize the propriety of self-expression. Exposing the work of the title to the public eye is portrayed as a betrayal of the speaker's modesty, as well as her private pact with an intimate partner: "My lyre is skillful to repress / Each deep, impassioned tone; / Its gushing springs of tenderness / Would flow for one alone."[51] Since the poem was of course published, the hint of a "gushing spring" of passion seeking its perfect recipient could be read as a coy device to entice readerly pursuit: Poe and Osgood both made use of this device, as Joanne Dobson's account of their literary relationship suggests.[52] Yet that model subordinates writing to passion, just as Willis's letter, with its unsatisfactory choice of extremes, suggests. His association between literary and sexual energies was neither unusual nor, as Longfellow's "Defence" demonstrates, reserved for women. When Willis made his barbed comment linking Longfellow's "chaste" poetic style to his unmanly failure to be "*merchant* enough with your poems," Longfellow was able to respond by husbanding his energies: finding a publication method that gave him control over the material conditions by which readers would encounter the poems, and inventing the authorial persona of the fatherly figure who would bring selections from his library into the intimate space of the fireside. Lynch's attention in the *Poems* seems focused not on refuting Willis's association, but on locating a similar strategy of carefully managed poetic-erotic continence.

That strategy is strikingly expressed in Lynch's rewriting of "Excelsior!" entitled simply "An Imitation." Shifting into the first person Longfellow's narrative of a youth's mysterious, orphic calling, Lynch has her speaker hear the "one charméd word, 'Excelsior!' " echoing down from a mountain. It "called me up that dazzling height / I could not choose but heed its tone / And climb that dreary path alone." Unlike the youth of "Excelsior!" however, Lynch's speaker stops midway, torn between the upward pull of "aspiring thought" that rings in her ears and the claims of emotion that remind her of loved ones and home fires:

> The heavy heart in vain would soar
> The heart hears not "Excelsior!"
> The heart's home is the vale below,
> Where kind words greet, where fond eyes glow;
> It withers 'neath those frozen skies
> Where the aspiring thought would rise.

The domestic sphere "below" and the public sphere of aspiration and achievement "above" seem riven, incommensurable. But, as in Longfellow's original, the seeker's faltering doubts are overcome—not by the disembodied sound of a voice urging the youth ever higher, but by the intervention of a man "whose brow

Thought's kingly impress bore, / Whose soul thrilled to 'Excelsior!' ": in other words, a fellow reader. Once this masterly figure appears, the speaker again climbs up the mountain, which seems "no longer dread . . . for thou wert there," and successfully penetrates into the "upper air."[53] The "Imitation" revises Longfellow's paradigm of intellectual aspiration by pointing out that it leaves no room for feeling: except for a brief glance at the grieving mother before her son's body, there is nothing but the cold sublimity of pure thought. Through her emotional cathexis onto this "kingly" figure, on the other hand, Lynch's seeker invests the realm of "aspiring thought" with the feelings associated with heart and hearth. Lynch imagines an identity happily subsumed into that of a greater force. Yet unlike Osgood (and in spite of Willis) she presents this not as a primarily erotic union but an intellectual one.

Likewise, Lynch's "Thoughts in a Library" advises that "when thy brothers pass thee by / With stern, unloving eyes," the ambitious soul should find refuge in a library, among "the monarchs of the mind," the "Poets" and "Prophets." In the hortatory mode of Longfellow's Psalmist, she urges, "Be thou companion here / And in the mighty realm of mind, / Thou shalt go forth a peer!"[54] Again, the individual's attainment of intellectual or spiritual goals depends upon her ability to create companionable relationships with those "mighty," "kingly" monarchs of thought—an ability that the unloving "brothers" of the poem do not possess. It remains unclear whether this companionate relationship is one that raises the seeker to the status of an equal, or of a privileged lesser partner, a wifely collaborator: Lynch's "To a Poet's Wife" compares the fame of a poetess to the glory of such companionship and insists, "A higher happiness is thine."[55] Yet when published in a different context—in Coates's *Fireside Anthology,* for instance— "Thoughts in a Library" sheds its attachment to gender and takes on the tone of Longfellow's aspiration poems, such as "A Psalm of Life."

In 1855, at the age of thirty-nine, Lynch surprised her friends and followers by marrying Vincenzo Botta, a Dante scholar somewhat younger than herself who came to be widely known as an advocate for Italian independence. She also moved with increasing confidence from the parlor to the library. Her writing became more cosmopolitan and academic, more metaliterary: in 1860, she published the compendious, exhaustively researched *Hand-Book of Universal Literature,* which went through multiple editions and sold widely even into the next century.[56] Like Longfellow in *The Poets and Poetry of Europe,* Lynch's aim is prescriptive as well as descriptive, with distinctly cosmopolitan aims: "The literatures of different nations are so related, and have so influenced each other, that it is only by a survey of all, that any single literature, or even any great literary work, can be fully comprehended, as the various groups and figures of a historical picture must be viewed as a whole, before they can assume their true place and proportions." Along with this scholarly judgment, she sounds a personal note: "This work was begun many years ago, as a literary exercise, to meet the personal requirements of the writer," who felt lost in the immensity of the literary tradition and "in a position not unlike that of the traveler suddenly set down in an unknown country, without guide-book or map."[57] In six hundred pages of small type, Lynch fulfills the fantasy of the lonely seeker in the library, becoming if not a peer then at least an authorized "companion" of those intellectual "masters of mind." Even as she moved to occupy the library, however, Lynch kept up her activities in the front parlor. One visitor described the Bottas' "House Beautiful" as "extending its serene welcome to poet and painter, to critic and story-teller, to sculptor and actor, to scholar and traveler, to cultivated men and women whose lives were not the lives of toys and trinkets. . . . For years it seemed as if this were the one truly cosmopolitan drawing-room in the city, because it drew the best from all sources: Italy and England, France and Germany." The salon itself, then became a living anthology of culture, redacting "the best from all sources." Wielding this authority was a "gracious mistress" who "was versatile in languages, but the language of depreciation she knew not."[58]

Ironically, or perhaps fittingly, the *Hand-Book* project forced Lynch, as the keeper of the library, to revisit her role as mistress of the salon: the text closes with a chapter on American literature, putting her in the position of ranking and assessing the work of her own visitors. About Longfellow, she repeats the frequent criticism that his poems "give little evidence of the power of overmastering passion, but they are pervaded with an earnestness and beauty of sentiment." Of Willis, whom she ranks just after Longfellow, Lynch says, "The poems . . . are characterized by a vivid imagination and a brilliant wit" (perhaps thinking of his overwrought "volcano" letter). In an extensive separate paragraph on "the literary women of the United States," she ranks Frances Osgood highly, noting "a facility of expression which rendered her almost an improvisatrice," and thereby stressing the importance of their original performative context in the salon setting. She praises Julia Ward Howe's "ardor and earnestness" and Greenwood's "fine burst of womanly pride and indignation." In each section of the chapter, she pointedly marks the important contributions of "literary women."[59] About her own poems, however, she has nothing to say.

Lynch turns toward the library as a realm that mediates between other domestic spaces of varying degrees of intimacy and publicity. If the work of the parlor and that of the library drew her away from the work of composing, they also granted her a kind of authority that Willis, with his exclusive focus on the intimate revelation of female passions, was unable to imagine for her. This sense of literary topography might help us account for the particular prestige of "fireside" writing throughout the century, and for Longfellow's status as one of its chief arbiters. Longfellow never edited a periodical, pulling up an imaginary "Editor's Chair" before the family hearth; nor did he use his parlor as a salon at which the Cambridge literati met and performed regularly, as they did at Lynch's home in New York. But he did endow the home library with a mystique that seems both domestic and masculine: hagiographical nineteenth-century accounts of the poet's home life inevitably contain an illustration of Longfellow's private study, down to descriptions of inkwells, luxury bindings, and other fetishes of authorship; the Longfellow House in Cambridge still sells postcards of those images.[60] The story of the death of Frances Appleton Longfellow, which was well-known throughout the century, reinforces this association in a cruelly ironic way: when a stray flame set her dress on fire, she ran into that study, where the poet was working. He covered her first with a rug, then with his own body. At Fanny's memorial service a few days later, he was too ill from his own burns to do more than overhear the words of the mourners gathered in the library.[61] About this deeply traumatic scene—Fanny was a "companion of the mind," who collaborated on projects like *The Poets and Poetry of Europe*—his later writings have nothing, directly, to say. Like the lyre of Lynch's poem, they suppress the word that is meant for one alone. The final stillness in Longfellow's library echoes the dedicatory poem of *The Seaside and the Fireside*, as it gestures toward "the pleasant books, that *silently* among / our household treasures take familiar places"(emphasis added).

NOTES

A preliminary version of this essay was delivered at the 1994 MLA convention in San Diego. Thanks to Carol Sheriff and the editors of this volume for their comments and encouragement.

1. Ron Rosenbaum, "Staring into the Heart of the Heart of Darkness," *New York Times Magazine*, 4 June 1995, 36–44, 50, 58, 61, 72, quotations from 40.

2. Wendy Simonds and Barbara Katz Rothman, *Centuries of Solace: Expressions of Maternal Grief in Popular Literature* (Philadelphia: Temple University Press, 1992), 37. On the crisis of motherhood, see 51–3 and 72–3.

3. Cheryl Walker, *The Nightingale's Burden: Women Poets and American Culture before 1900* (Bloomington: Indiana University Press, 1982), 38. In her later anthology, *American Women Poets of the Nineteenth Century* (New Brunswick, N.J.: Rutgers University Press, 1992), Walker elaborates on her earlier identification of the principal female themes: the free-bird poem, the sanctuary poem, the "power fantasy," and the "poem of secret sorrow" (xxv–xxvi). See also Emily Stipes Watts, *The Poetry of American Women from 1632 to 1945* (Austin: University of Texas Press, 1977).

4. Annie Finch, "The Sentimental Poetess in the World: Metaphor and Subjectivity in Lydia Sigourney's Nature Poetry," *Legacy* 5, no. 2 (1988): 3–15, quotation from 5. Finch acknowledges the similarity of tone between "poetesses" and the male Fireside Poets, but claims that Longfellow (for instance) is "sentimentalistic" rather than "sentimental" because, despite his use of sentimental themes, the *structure* of the poems still "reinforces the central self" (5).

5. This is not to claim that the theme is unique to Longfellow: there are no more hackneyed images in Victorian poetry than the Angel of Death and children associated with flowers. I find the specifics of the two poems close enough, however, to warrant my association: both imagine the "Reaper" as a gardening angel, and both direct attention to heaven's aesthetic and emotional needs, as God arranges his own domestic sphere. The extraordinarily wide circulation of the Longfellow poem makes it a likely progenitor of the other, perhaps at several anonymous levels of remove.

6. Samuel Longfellow, ed., *Works of Henry Wadsworth Longfellow*, 14 vols. (Boston: Houghton Mifflin, Riverside Press, 1886), 1:23 (hereafter cited as *Works*).

7. Samuel Longfellow, ed., *Life of Henry Wadsworth Longfellow*, 3 vols. (Boston: Houghton Mifflin, Riverside Press, 1886) 1:306 (hereafter cited as *Life*).

8. *Life*, 1:317.

9. The Sigourney quotation, from her essay on Felicia Hemans, is cited in Walker, *Nightingale*, 24. The anecdote of the young fan is in William Charvat, *The Profession of Authorship in America, 1800–1870*, ed. Matthew J. Bruccoli (Columbus: Ohio State University Press, 1968), 124.

10. Walker, *American Women Writers*, xv, xvi, quoting Rufus Griswold, *The Female Poets of America*. For competing anthologists who emphasize the gender divide far less than Griswold, see Thomas Buchanan Read, *The Female Poets of America* (Philadelphia: E. H. Butler, 1848) and Caroline May, *The American Female Poets* (Philadelphia: Lindsay & Blakiston, 1849).

11. Rufus Griswold, ed., *The Cypress Wreath: A Book of Consolation for Those Who Mourn* (Boston, n.p., 1844); *Echoes of Infant Voices* (Boston: Crosby & Nichols, 1849).

12. Dana Gioia's "Longfellow in the Aftermath of Modernism" (in *The Columbia History of American Poetry*, ed. Jay Parini [New York: Columbia University Press, 1993]) summarizes this critical split helpfully, yet Gioia, like others, seems concerned with salvaging Longfellow's masculinity by rescuing him from ridicule. Lawrence Buell's strategy in editing Longfellow's *Selected Poems* (New York: Penguin, 1988) is to eschew the more famous "light" domestic lyrics in favor of lesser-known examples of the "dark" Longfellow; John Hollander's *Nineteenth-Century American Poetry*, vol. 1 (New York: Library of America, 1993) does the same. Norman Holmes Pearson's early essay "Both Longfellows" (*University of Kansas City Review* 16 [1950]: 245–53) suggestively describes a poetic personality split between "the court and the camp," arguing that the duality in the work is one of class and cultural aspiration, not one of "tone" or, as we tend to think now, of gendered subjectivity.

13. Eric Haralson, "Mars in Petticoats: Longfellow and Sentimental Masculinity," *Nineteenth-Century Literature* 51, no. 6 (1996): 327–55, quotations from 328–9.

14. Horace E. Scudder, ed., *Poetical Works of James Russell Lowell* (Boston: Houghton Mifflin, 1890), 147.

15. Ibid., 153. See Kenneth Alan Hovey, "Critical Provincialism: Poe's Poetic Principle in Antebellum Context" (*American Quarterly* 39, no. 3 [1987]: 341–54) for a summary of the Poe / Longfellow "war," which he casts in terms of antithetical poetic poles (the Wordsworthian Northerner vs. the Byronic Southerner) that seem open to reading in terms of anxieties of masculinity.

16. Longfellow, "Defence of Poetry," *North American Review* 34 (1832): 56–78. Quotations in this paragraph from 69, 59, 62, 63, 76, 77.

17. In addition to Bertolini's treatment of antebellum fears of "spermatorrhea" in this volume, see G. M. Goshgarian, *To Kiss the Chastening Rod: Domestic Fiction and Sexual Identity in the American Renaissance* (Ithaca: Cornell University Press, 1992), 36–75. David Reynolds, in *Beneath the American Renaissance* (New York: Knopf, 1988), 88–91, gives some typical examples of the rhetoric of sexual continence in antebellum pamphlets.

18. In 1854, in response to an English acquaintance who felt that both "A Psalm of Life" and "Reaper" were simply translations, Longfellow denied the charge, but acknowledged parallels with Goethe's collections of German folk songs. Both poems, he says, were composed "at the beginning of my life poetical, when a thousand songs were ringing in my ears; and doubtless many echoes and suggestions will be found in them. Let the fact go for what it is worth" (*Letters*, 3:443).

19. Charvat, *Profession of Authorship*, 109–11.

20. Kenneth Walter Cameron, *Longfellow Among his Contemporaries* (Hartford, Conn.: Transcendental Books, 1978), 8, 44. For extensive anecdotes about the sense of novelty readers felt in response to *Voices of the Night*, see Loring Hart, "The Beginnings of Longfellow's Fame," *New England Quarterly* 36, no. 1 (1963): 63–76.

21. Edward Wagenknecht, *Henry Wadsworth Longfellow: His Poetry and Prose* (New York: Ungar, 1986), 21.

22. See Kenneth Alan Hovey, " 'A Psalm of Life' Reconsidered: The Dialogue of Western Literature and the Monologue of Young America," *American Transcendental Quarterly* 1, no. 1 (1987): 3–19, for an argument that this poem describes a new, post-Jacksonian masculinity tempering the aggressions of Manifest Destiny.

23. These lines were so universally known through the early twentieth century that it would be impossible to chart their influence fully. One biographer describes a scene in which a working-class man approached Longfellow and said that "A Psalm of Life," handcopied on a worn scrap of newspaper, had saved him from suicide (William Sloane Kennedy, *Henry Wadsworth Longfellow: Biography, Anecdotes, Letters, Criticism* [Akron, Ohio: Saalfield, 1903], 64–5). (See also Hovey, " 'Psalm' Reconsidered.")

24. See Haralson, "Mars in Petticoats," 337 for a discussion of sublimation as the "sublime" of this poem.

25. Charvat, *Profession of Authorship*, 157–60. Though Longfellow continued to publish in the highly visible periodicals as well as in book form, he and other writers complained of their powerlessness over that context. Longfellow wrote to Ward, "I am quite mortified at the fate of *Excelsior*. I would rather have paid the price of it, than have it go into that milk-pan, the *Ladies' Companion*" (Andrew Hillen, ed., *Letters of Henry Wadsworth Longfellow*, 6 vols. [Cambridge: Harvard University Press, 1966–82], 2:336). Periodical publication as a whole seems feminized by association.

26. *Life*, 1:371–2.

27. *Letters*, 2:230.

28. *Life*, 1:343.

29. Kennedy, *Longfellow Biography*, 222.

30. *Life*, 1:384.

31. "The Village Blacksmith," an equally well known text from *Ballads* (and subtitled "Another Psalm of Life"), also illustrates a man's necessary loosening of the bonds of home. David Leverenz, in *Manhood and the American Renaissance* (Ithaca: Cornell University Press, 1989), characterizes the blacksmith as an exemplar of the "autonomous self-sufficiency" of the Jeffersonian artisan, and suggests that Longfellow imagines him nostalgically as a critique of the Jacksonian entrepreneur (78). However, although the blacksmith has muscles "as strong as iron bands," he is also a man of feeling: he stops in the middle of his labor to shed a tear for his dead mother. The blacksmith's alternation between *working* and *weeping* suggests a new version of Shaftesbury's sentimental man: one whose experiences at the maternal hearth carry over into the building of more public fires.

32. *Works*, 1:244.

33. *Works*, 1:270.

34. *Works*, 1:269.

35. Clifford Edward Clark, Jr., *The American Family Home, 1800–1960* (Chapel Hill: University of North Carolina Press, 1986), 114. See also Jane Nylander, *Our Own Snug Fireside:*

Images of the New England Home, 1760–1860 (New York: Knopf, 1993), for images of contrasting fireside family ideals: one, from the 1830s (76), shows a quiet scene of a husband reading to his wife and child; another (101) depicts a nostalgic 1855 rendition of an "old-fashioned New England homestead," in which a large extended family works at separate tasks. For anecdotes of family reading around the fire, see 102, 225, 239; on women's tasks in tending an open fire, see 87 and, in general, chapter 5.

36. Clark, *American Family Home*, 40.

37. For a broad sampling of antebellum reformists' house plans, see Clark, *American Family Home*, chapters 1–2, and Maureen Ogle, "Domestic Reform and American Household Plumbing, 1840–1870," *Winterthur Portfolio* 28, no. 1 (1993): 33–58, especially 38, 53. On these plans, there is some variation in terminology about how to distinguish the public visiting room from the family gathering room (assuming one could afford both); I use "family parlor" here for the latter to avoid such confusion. Beecher's *Treatise on Domestic Economy* (1841; reprint, New York: Source Book Press, 1970) and Beecher and Stowe's *The American Woman's Home* (New York: J. B. Ford & Co., 1869) advise families who cannot afford separate public and private parlors to make strategic use of screens and shades to create limited privacy.

On the influence of the romantic reform movement upon the public parlor space, see Karen Halttunen, "From Parlor to Living Room: Domestic Space, Interior Decoration, and the Culture of Personality," in *Consuming Visions: Accumulation and Display of Goods in America 1880–1920*, ed. Simon J. Bronner (New York: W. W. Norton, The Winterthur Museum, 1989), 157–89. She argues that the "public face" of the parlor was decorated according to a "moral aesthetic" that emphasized beauty, instruction, and signals of the family's propriety; later in the century, this ideal gradually gave way to one of conspicuous consumption (159). For other views on the history of the parlor, see Katherine C. Grier, *Culture & Comfort: Parlor Making and Middle-Class Identity, 1850–1930* (Washington: Smithsonian Press, 1997), and Colleen McDannell, "Parlor Piety: The Home as Sacred Space in Protestant America," in *American Home Life, 1880–1930*, ed. Jessica H. Foy and Thomas J. Schlereth (Knoxville: University of Tennessee Press, 1992), 162–89.

38. Andrew Jackson Downing, cited in Kate Roberts, "Fireside Tales to Fireside Chats: The Domestic Hearth" (*The Arts and the American Home, 1890–1930*, ed. Jessica H. Foy and Karal Ann Marling [Knoxville: University of Tennessee Press, 1994] 44–61), 44. On nostalgia for the open fire of bygone days, see Nylander, *Snug Fireside*, 99–102. James Rocks reads another Fireside Poet's effort to reclaim national unity after the Civil War through a similar nostalgia for fire; see "Whittier's *Snow-Bound*: 'The Circle of Our Hearth' and the Discourse on Domesticity," *Studies in the American Renaissance* (1993): 339–53.

39. The Beechers were particularly opposed to the "poisonous" air of Franklin stoves: "Better, far better, the old houses of the olden time, with their great roaring fires" (Beecher and Stowe, *Woman's Home*, 51).

40. Beecher and Stowe, *Woman's Home*, 300, 293.

41. Mary P. Ryan, in *The Empire of the Mother: American Writing about Domesticity, 1830–1860* (New York: Haworth, 1982), argued influentially that increasingly affordable domestic literature in the early nineteenth century replaced conversation as a way to show mothers how to instruct their children, on the theory that "female literature has a special office . . . to be responsible for moralizing the world" (33). The bibliography of critical works that follow Ryan's links between women, periodical culture, and the moral "office" of female readers is ample and is rehearsed in the introduction to this volume.

42. Clark, *American Family Home*, 40. For house plans that show a library (usually placed across from, or next to, the family parlor), see Clark, 20–1 (from Downing) and 39, and Ogle, "Household Plumbing," 38 (from Woodward and Thompson).

43. Newton Arvin, *Longfellow: His Life and Work* (Boston: Little, Brown, 1962), 59.

44. Henry T. Coates, ed., *The Fireside Encyclopedia of Poetry* (Philadelphia: Porter & Coates, 1878), v. See also the proliferation of "Fireside" miscellanies, such as *Uncle Frank's Pleasant Pages for the Fireside*, ed. Francis Woodworth (New York: H. Dayton, 1859).

45. *Letters*, 2:510. See Susan Coultrap-McQuin, *Doing Literary Business: American Women Writers in the Nineteenth Century* (Chapel Hill: University of North Carolina Press, 1990) for an extended treatment of male-female patronage relationships.

46. It seems clear that Lynch admired Longfellow: her reading table—as described by a friend—featured a typical American Victorian pantheon of "Emerson, Herbert Spencer, George Eliot, Longfellow, Whittier, 'Light of Asia', Tennyson, Wordsworth" (Vincenzo Botta, ed., *Memoirs of Anne C. L. Botta, Written by Her Friends* [New York: J. S. Tait & Sons, 1894], 110). Although the New York literary world was geographically and ideologically distant from Longfellow and he rarely ventured there, Longfellow seems to have become at least acquainted with Lynch: a letter to Vincenzo Botta in 1870, begging off from attending a meeting in celebration of Italian independence, sends "best regards to Mrs. Botta" (*Letters*, 5:388).

I have here followed the practice of Walker, Nina Baym, and others in using Lynch's maiden name to discuss works she published under that name before her marriage.

47. The little biographical information that exists on Lynch can be found in Edward T. James, ed., *Notable American Women*, 3 vols. (Cambridge: Harvard University Press, 1971), 1:212–4 and Lisa Mainiero, ed., *American Women Writers: A Critical Reference Guide*, 4 vols. (New York: Ungar, 1979–82), 1:239–40. Walker mentions Lynch as an important patron encouraging Helen Hunt Jackson's early work (*Nightingale*, 94–5). I have relied also upon Vincenzo Botta's memorial compilation, acknowledging the possibility of loving exaggeration in the reports of mourners. Grace Greenwood's comments are typical: "She formed the most brilliant and successful salon I have ever known in America. Those who had the *entree* to those weekly reunions—almost uninterrupted for a score of years, and never wholly discontinued—must remember them with grateful pleasure mingled with keen regret. . . . Those evenings were *conversazioni* of an informal but most refined character. . . . My friend's admirable feminine traits and social and intellectual equipments most impressed me. . . . Authorship was not so fashionable among Southern ladies as it now is; but the ability was by no means lacking. The wit, the taste, the poetic feeling now put to practical and profitable use in literature, were then prodigially expended in conversation" (43–4). Even Hawthorne apparently felt obliged to visit Lynch on one of his rare visits to New York: see Tamara Jones, "Hawthorne's Appearance after being Lynched," *Nathaniel Hawthorne Review* 18, no. 1 (1992): 21.

48. Page references are to the first edition: Anne Charlotte Lynch, *Poems* (New York: Putnam's, 1849). Lynch also edited *The Rhode-Island Book* (Providence: H. Fuller, 1841) and *Tales of Flemish Life of H. Conscience* (New York: E. Dunizan & Brother, 1849), and translated *The Death of President Lincoln: A Poem by Edouard Grénier* (New York: C. F. Heartman, 1918).

49. Nina Baym, *American Women Writers and the Work of History* (New Brunswick: Rutgers University Press, 1995), 69.

50. Botta, *Memoirs*, 320–1.

51. Lynch, *Poems*, 29.

52. Joanne Dobson, "Sex, Wit, and Sentiment: Frances Osgood and the Poetry of Love," *American Literature* 65 (1993): 631–50.

53. Lynch, *Poems*, 31–3.

54. Lynch, *Poems*, 27–8.

55. Lynch, *Poems*, 182.

56. The *Hand-Book*, first published in 1860, went through twenty-one editions before Lynch's death in 1891, and was revised even after that. It was apparently used widely in college courses; I have found printings as late as 1923. Citations here are from Anne C. Lynch Botta, *Hand-Book of Universal Literature, From the Best and Latest Authorities* (Boston: Houghton, Osgood & Co., Riverside Press, 1879).

57. Botta, *Hand-Book*, iv, iii.

58. Botta, *Memoirs*, 71, 88–9. On the salon in its Lynch and Botta phases, see James, 213.

59. Botta, *Hand-Book*, 539–41.

60. There is a room adjoining this study, closer to the front of the house, referred to as the "library" (there is a separate parlor), but pictures of "Longfellow's Library" are of the study. Harriet Beecher Stowe's upstairs library, in her Hartford home, presents another example of a fetishized author's writing space.

61. For accounts of Fanny's death in July 1861 and Longfellow's response to it, see Edward Wagenknecht, *Henry Wadsworth Longfellow: Portrait of an American Humanist* (New York: Oxford University Press, 1966), 172–3, and Arvin, *Life and Work*, 140–1. Wagenknecht's *Mrs. Longfellow* (New York: Longmans, Green, 1956) portrays a dynamic, intelligent woman whose contribution to her husband's work was considerable.

CHAPTER THREE

▐▲▲▌

Then When We Clutch Hardest

On the Death of a Child and the Replication of an Image

Karen Sánchez-Eppler

Dying is what children do most and do best in the literary and cultural imagination of nineteenth-century America. That the figure of the dead or dying child proves so common, so clichéd even, makes us uncomfortable, precisely because we find the possibility of a child dying so overwhelmingly painful. The loss of a child must be one of the most intimate of griefs, a fundamentally familial loss that makes little apparent rent in the social fabric. And yet the constant reiteration of this figure from Mary Morgan, Eva St. Clare, and Beth March to the myriad of nineteenth-century child elegies suggests that the death of a child serves a public function as well, enacting a loss that the culture needs to evoke and repeat. The repetitive portrayals of a dead or dying child work to articulate anxieties over the commodification of affect in an increasingly urbanized, industrialized, and impersonal America.

Yet the deaths of children are not only or centrally allegorical in this way; they are also and most immediately sites of personal trauma, grief, and mourning. My aim in this essay is to explore the connections between what Esther Schor calls "the exquisite pain of bereavement" and "the calm commerce of condolence."[1] In the nineteenth century's proliferation of mourning paraphernalia (clothes, jewelry, tombstones, portraits, and verse), condolence is quite literally commercial. Yet it is equally clear that grief plays an important part in producing and valuing the private, both the home and the feeling individual cherished there. The replication of the figure of the dead child, its mass production as it were, may thus point to new ways of thinking about the relation between personal emotion and the commerce of the public sphere. I will discuss one such commercial medium of replication and circulation, postmortem photographs of children, and two well-known instances of bereavement that produced generically quite disparate literary effects: the death of Harriet Beecher Stowe's son Charley in 1849 and that of Ralph Waldo Emerson's son Waldo in 1842. Stowe's and Emerson's accounts—

64

Figure 1. Postmortem *carte de visite*, 1864. Squyer Studio, Auburn, N Y. Courtesy of the Carpenter Center for the Visual Arts, Harvard University.

one the favorite exemplum of sentimentalism, the other equally famous for failing to find in grief any capacity to confirm the reality of the feeling self—are in many ways antithetical, yet read together they reveal much about what happens to grief in the whir of mass production and commercial circulation.

In a *carte de visite* photograph made by the Squyer Studio in Auburn, New York, in 1864 (fig. 1), a boy and his smaller sister lie cuddled together, his arm around her shoulder, her whole small body in a fancy checkered dress resting against him; their eyes are closed. It is a picture of tender love between brother and sister, and it is a picture of tragic loss, for both are dead. The Squyer Studio—most likely at the family's request—mounted this image in an oval frame, as if the children were held in cupped hands, treasured in an egg, or reflected, as indeed they are, in the oval of the viewer's eye. We know that brother and sister were placed in this loving posture, that the tenderness with which they hold one another registers the care of other hands that dressed them, brushed their hair, and laid one small corpse in the arms of the other. In depicting the love between these children, the photograph thus alludes back to the love of the family that had this picture taken.

This tableau has been arranged, staged. The articles on making postmortem portraits, written for the trade press by daguerreotypists and later photographers, reveal that, in practice, arranging the bodies of the dead is a necessary but quite "unpleasant duty."[2] The aim of these manipulations is to produce out of these dead bodies a meaning that exceeds the fact of death. This tableau measures the worth of the family, whose love and intimacy are here poignantly confirmed, even in a sense produced, in the image of the children it has lost.

This sense of the dead child as the most powerful sign of right sentiment—for the family and for the individual—is itself one of the founding tropes of sentimentalism. Karen Halttunen argues that "death had come to preoccupy sentimentalists, who cherished it as the occasion for two of the deepest 'right feelings' in human experience: bereavement, or direct mourning for the dead, and sympathy, or mournful condolence for the bereaved."[3] Harriet Beecher Stowe would offer the experience of bereavement as the deepest truth of her individual heart and as the means of forging a sympathetic connection with both the lives of slaves and the lives of her readers. *Uncle Tom's Cabin,* she averred, began in the death from cholera of her eighteen-month-old son Charley: "It was at *his* dying bed, and at *his* grave that I learnt what a poor slave mother may feel when her child is torn away from her. . . . I felt that I could never be consoled for it, unless this crushing of my own heart might enable me to work out some great good to others. . . . [M]uch that is in that book ('Uncle Tom') had its root in the awful scenes and bitter sorrows of that summer."[4] In the novel, this "root" becomes the central mechanism and emblem for Stowe's abolitionist project, and so grounds public political change in personal domestic affect.

In a scene that explicitly enacts Stowe's own novelistic procedures, the escaping slave Eliza Harris elicits sympathy and succor by responding to Senator and Mrs. Bird's questions as to why she ran away with a question of her own: "have you ever lost a child?" Mrs. Bird feels the question as "unexpected, and . . . thrust on a new wound." But Stowe is clear that Eliza's question is also calculated, for Eliza had "looked up at Mrs. Bird, with a keen, scrutinizing glance, and it did not escape her that she was dressed in deep mourning."[5] Like Eliza, scrutinizing Mrs. Bird's black dress, Stowe's knowledge of her readers is cultural knowledge; she knows (as we historicist readers of nineteenth-century sentimental fiction are always reminding ourselves) that one out of six children died in the 1850s before reaching the age of five. Her task is to make those broad cultural statistics novelistically and politically efficacious, to replace the undifferentiated mass of death with the more precise connections of condolence—to make of the corpse a love-affirming tableau.

In making such a connection, Senator Bird, too, thinks about clothes:

"Mary, I don't know how you'd feel about it, but there's that drawer full of things— of—of—poor little Henry's." So saying, he turned quickly on his heel, and shut the door after him.

His wife opened the little bed-room door adjoining her room and, taking the candle, set it down on the top of a bureau there; then from a small recess she took a

key, and put it thoughtfully in the lock of a drawer, and made a sudden pause, while
two boys, who, boy like, had followed close on her heels, stood looking, with silent,
significant glances, at their mother. And oh! mother that reads this, has there never
been in your house a drawer, or a closet, the opening of which has been to you like
the opening again of a little grave? Ah! happy mother that you are, if it has not been
so. (153–4)

Stowe's image of a bureau drawer, "the opening of which has been to you like the
opening again of a little grave," imagines that all homes are built, like Stowe's
novel, around a child's grave. This image does not denote a rupture in the domestic, or imply that the abysses of loss accessed through bureau drawers are antithetical to the protective goals of home, but rather that this capacity of drawers to
become like graves, of homes and hearts to harbor loss, is precisely what constitutes the ideal sentimental reader and the ideal nineteenth-century American
family. Indeed, it is only when Mrs. Bird approaches her grave-drawer and puts
the key in the lock that her living sons are suddenly conjured into the text. The
grave locked within the home serves to produce and focus the family tableau.
Stowe ends by imagining some other home, a home without graves. But when she
offers as an alternative to her searing question the exclamation "Ah! happy
mother that you are, if it has not been so," this affirmation feels full of doubt and
threat. Can such happy ignorance ever last? Indeed, can this "happy mother"
truly be a mother if she has known no loss?

Explicitly adding the readers' presumed losses to the novel's chain of mourning, Stowe casts the reader as a participant both in Eliza's pain and in Mary Bird's
capacity for sympathetic action. That Eliza's and Mary's two little boys have the
same name and can fill the same clothes tries to erase the racial divide, and insists
on the overdetermined, almost tautological nature of these links; all children
mean the same once they are gone. What they mean is, egocentrically perhaps,
your own child, your own loss, your own pain. David Marshall defines sentimentality as "not just the capacity for feeling, but more specifically the capacity to feel
the sentiments of someone else," and goes on to conclude—following Adam
Smith—that this poses "an epistemological and aesthetic problem: since we cannot know the experience or sentiments of another person."[6] The figure of Mrs.
Bird standing before the bureau drawer is an instance of just such a projection of
the self. In a letter to Sarah Allen, who had also lost a child, Stowe described her
own scene of mourning—"I cannot open his little drawer of clothes now without
feeling it through my very heart"—and then asked: "How is it with you in your
heart of hearts when you think of the past—I often wonder how your feelings correspond with mine."[7] Like Marshall, Stowe realizes that she cannot know
another's heart of hearts, that one person's grief may not correspond to another's,
and yet in assigning the scene that cuts through her very heart to the character of
Mrs. Bird, in asking her readers the same wounding question that Eliza asks Mrs.
Bird, indeed in imagining that the "crushing of [her] own heart" at Charley's

death "may" feel like the separations of slavery and "might enable [her] to work out some great good to others," Stowe risks offering her readers just such a mesh of correspondence. At once calculated and unexpected, the "new wounds" of grave and drawer suggest that the site of mourning is not only secret and deep (unknowable), but also and importantly open.

Marianne Noble astutely links Stowe's treatment of sentimental identification as a "wound" with Roland Barthes's assertion that he was "interested in Photography only for 'sentimental' reasons; I wanted to explore it not as a question (a theme) but as a wound."[8] The open wound provides a site where internal pain remains internal and yet becomes externally visible. What I find most lacerating about the Squyer photograph is the tension between what is held close and what is laid open: the two children appear so protectively enclosed in this image (curled around each other, encircled by the frame, wrapped by death), and yet the oval aperture permits us to see into this intimate space. Such photographs are memorial treasures, carried in purse or pocket, kept secret in a bureau drawer; what they keep is not only the particular lost loved one, but more importantly the loss itself. They work to keep the wound open as it were.

Stowe had a daguerreotype of her son Charley taken after his death (fig. 2), and her letters tell how tormenting his cholera was: "I have just seen him in his death agony, looked on his imploring face when I could not help nor soothe nor do one thing, not one, to mitigate his cruel suffering, do nothing but pray in my anguish that he might die soon."[9] The daguerreotype confirms her anguished hope that death might be, for Charley, an end to pain; it represents him lying peacefully on a bed or sofa, his head resting, smooth browed, on a soft white pillow, a small bouquet clasped in his hands. In the daguerreotype image there is no agony, no imploring face, no cruel suffering. Death and the daguerreotypist have made him instead into a memorial object, a small material thing with which to keep and cherish loss.

Roland Barthes writes of "that rather terrible thing which is there in every photograph: the return of the dead." What Barthes recognizes here is the uncanny nature of photography. "What the Photograph reproduces to infinity has occurred only once: the Photograph mechanically repeats what could never be repeated existentially."[10] The Daguerreotype, of course, reproduces a moment only once, upon a single unique plate; but when Daguerre unveiled his and Niepce's invention in 1839, even that single act of replication astounded its viewers. Period accounts of the daguerreotype stress its occult character: one of the first American descriptions of the invention published in *The New Yorker* proclaimed that with these pictures "the real black art of true magic arises and cries avaunt"; practitioners later noted that "this art has been termed magic," "the spells and incantations of the device" surpassing the "enchantress'[s] wand." Even over a decade later, when daguerreotypes had been displaced by the infinitely replicable process of negative-positive photography, Oliver Wendell Holmes would describe for his *Atlantic* readers the process of making a photographic portrait in the occult imagery of "the ghost we hold imprisoned in the shield we have just brought from the camera."[11] As

Figure 2. Postmortem daguerreotype of Samuel Charles Stowe, July 1849. Porter and Fontayne's Gallery, Cincinnati, Ohio. Courtesy of the Schlesinger Library, Radcliffe College.

Barthes's notion of the returning dead suggests, there may indeed be no more accurate name for a photograph than that of ghost.

The relation between death and photography becomes even more literal when it comes to the problems of photographing children. The first daguerreotypes required a fifteen-minute exposure, this was quickly reduced to thirty seconds, and by the mid-1850s the switch to a collodion or wet-plate process had reduced exposure times to as little as half a second, yet even this is still a long time to expect stillness from a living child.[12] Photography not only imitates death, but requires a deathlike stillness to make that replication possible. If it lacks other definite markers or inscriptions, contemporary historians of photography routinely conclude that a sharply focused early daguerreotype of a baby is likely to be postmortem.[13] Nineteenth-century photography journals frequently published articles sharing tactics for photographing restless infants ("arrangements for the babies should be made so as not to interfere with their daily sleep, as they look and feel so much better and sweeter after a nap"), while advertisements claimed skill in photographing children ("We are always glad to take a reasonable amount of pains with children. They are subjects that make lovely pictures, but they are often difficult to secure. We can always get *something* of them"), and many child photographs reveal restraining sashes or even hands.[14]

Such responses to the frustrations of photographing young children extend well beyond the long exposure days of the 1840s and 1850s, which only emphasizes how, in more than a straightforward, technical way, a dead baby was a far more satisfactory photographic subject than a live one, even when the goal of such mortuary photography was to produce a lifelike image. In his 1855 article, "Taking Portraits After Death," N. G. Burgess acknowledges that "all likenesses taken after death will of course only resemble the inanimate body, nor will there appear in the portrait anything like life itself, *except* indeed the sleeping infant, on whose face the playful smile of innocence sometimes steals even after death. This maybe and is oft-times transferred to the silver plate."[15] The lovely Southworth and Hawes photograph of a dead child, nestled on a pillow with seemingly relaxed, gently crossed limbs and a peaceful, innocently "sleeping" face, testifies to the truth of these claims (fig. 3). Especially for children, mortuary photography promises to preserve the ideal of childhood—to present a child more pliant and open to adoration than any live subject could be. The coercion of death preempts the need for photographic coercions of sash, hand, or rod. That Burgess knows such an appearance of life rarely characterizes postmortem photographs of adults, suggests in part that the desired image of adulthood—certainly for adult men, but even for adult women—is never so passive. If the dead child serves better than the live one, it may be because of the ways that a child is imagined like a bureau drawer, a receptacle for parental aspirations and feelings.

From the first, the miracle of photography has been understood as a miracle of memorialization: the capacity to let us see again, as it was, a moment that is in all other ways irretrievably past. For a parent to commission a photograph like the Southworth and Hawes image must involve contradictory emotions: the image invites its viewers at once to deny death—to retain the living child, at least as an image—and to record the fact of death, to acknowledge that the child has died. The girl in the Southworth and Hawes print clasps the ribbon of a small crucifix, half obscured by the folds of her white dress, ensuring that however skillfully the photographers have arranged her corpse to imitate sleep, no viewer could long mistake the image for that of a living child. I want to suggest that mortuary photographs are in this way not a special case, but rather almost the paradigmatic instance of how the daguerreotype portrait was thought to focus familial affect. The family, as locus of love and feeling, constitutes itself sentimentally as an act of memorialization.

Memorialization and mourning are accomplished here not simply in the heart, but quite clearly through commercialization. Daguerreotypes offer a perfect instance of how desire and the market create each other: in 1838 there was no

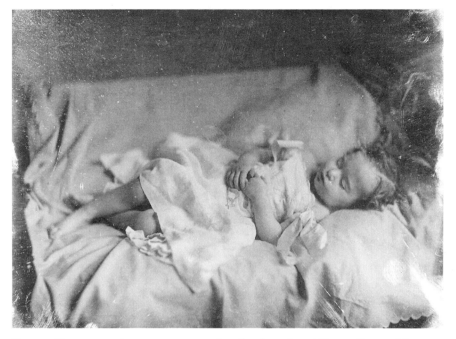

Figure 3. Postmortem daguerreotype, ca. 1850. Southworth and Hawes, Boston, Mass. Courtesy of the George Eastman House.

such thing as a daguerreotype, and though itinerant artists could produce fairly inexpensive portraits, such portraits were still far too costly to let most Americans afford a likeness of themselves or those they loved; a decade later "there were already two thousand daguerreotypists in the country . . . by 1853, three million daguerreotypes were being made annually and there were eighty-six portrait galleries in New York City alone," and nearly everyone could afford to have a portrait made.[16] This tremendous popularization and growth make clear that to have one's portrait taken was both to participate in the creation of a new market and to act on a new desire: one rarely practicable before this new technology. Daguerreotypes made the relation between desire and the market more obvious because of this newness, and more glaring because the thing to be purchased was a replication of a beloved face. Perhaps more perfectly than any other object for sale, daguerreotype portraits meld commercial replication and unique, emotional individuality, for what is replicated and commodified by these portraits is not the unique plate or the individual's image, so much as a form, the standard poses, accouterments, and presentation of the daguerreotype portrait. The daguerreotype of the mother holding both her dead child and an elaborate hat displays the ambivalence of making the commercial act of visiting a portrait studio into a ritual of bereavement (fig. 4). This is not a funereal hat; indeed the family paid extra

Figure 4. Postmortem daguerreotype, ca. 1850. Courtesy of Stanley B. Burns, M.D., and the Burns Archive.

to have its ribbon hand-colored a festive blue. Thus, as the mother literally balances on her lap the dual rites of grieving for her child and dressing for the photographer, she epitomizes the relation between memorialization and this new commodity—the daguerreotype portrait. After all it is the hat, that incongruous effort to assert status and make a good picture, that most distinguishes and individualizes this image, letting us glimpse something of what it meant for this woman to use photography as a means of posing and preserving her grief. The image of young Max Anderson lying in his perambulator provides a similar instance (fig. 5). It reminds us, moreover, that the same argument holds for the way

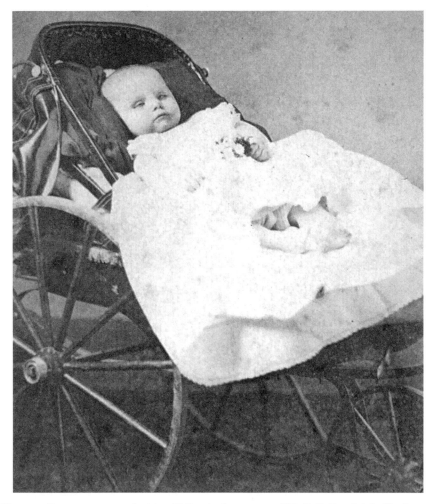

Figure 5. Postmortem *carte de visite* of Max Anderson, ca. 1868. D. S. Randolph, Xenia, Ohio. Courtesy of Stanley B. Burns, M.D., and the Burns Archive.

that the manufacture of goods specifically for children—also a new mid-nineteenth-century development—allies the creation of marketable desires with familial affection and status. In 1868, when this card was made, the fine carriage would have been almost as recognizably new a commodity in Xenia, Ohio, where the photograph was taken, as the *carte de visite* itself.[17]

The commodification of childhood and photography reveal how deeply the processes of commercialization depend upon emotions traditionally understood as inherently individual, intimate, and hence noncommodifiable. Of course, this understanding of mourning is itself a new product of that era, the legacy of nineteenth-century discourses of sentiment and domesticity that would claim in heart and hearth a lone haven from commercial taint. The scorn with which most scholarship has viewed the nineteenth-century commercialization of death and mourning rests on the assumption that mortality and grief are incompatible with commerce, and therefore that the creation of these new commodities and their professionals (funeral directors, embalmers, cemetery designers, as well as daguerreotypists) ultimately functions to strip bereavement of its emotional authenticity.[18] As the examples of photography and childhood make clear, however, the commercial, the public, and the emotional need not be viewed solely in oppositional terms. If commodification exploits feelings to yield profit, it is equally possible for emotions to use the commercial as a means of expression and a form of circulation. Sentimentalism is, among other things, the genre that accompanied American expansion and industrialization. The literary preference for producing tears, for voicing what we often describe as "excessive," repetitive emotion, coincided with the advent of mass production and its way of making surplus. Emerson's grim search for emotional authenticity oddly serves to reveal the social utility of repetition, and so to suggest what mass production and wide circulation might accomplish as a response to death.

In a journal entry of 24 October 1841, Ralph Waldo Emerson writes of having his own daguerreotype portrait made:

> Were you ever daguerreotyped, O immortal man? And did you look with all vigor at the lens of the camera, or rather, by direction of the operator, at the brass peg a little below it, to give the picture the full benefit of your expanded and flashing eye? and in your zeal not to blur the image, did you keep every finger in its place with such energy that your hands became clenched as for fight or despair, and in your resolution to keep your face still, did you feel every muscle becoming every moment more rigid; the brows contracted into a Tartarean frown, and the eyes fixed as they are fixed in a fit, in madness, or in death? And when at last you are relieved of your dismal duties, did you find the curtain drawn perfectly, and the hands true, clenched for combat, and the shape of the face or head?—but, unhappily, the total expression escaped from the face and the portrait of a mask instead of a man? Could you not by grasping it very tight hold the stream of a river, or of a small brook, and prevent it from flowing?[19]

Here, all the daguerreotype can image is death. Expression, the immortal soul of "O immortal man," proves to be precisely what this technology seems unable to grasp. The ironic barb of Emerson's questions points, of course, to how little faith men have in their immortality, and hence their desire to be daguerreotyped, to preserve at least a death-mask face against an uncertain future. Emerson may ridicule this desire for photographic immortality, but he also shares it; he too has gone before the operator. Most significantly, his final image for the futility of photography—the absurd goal of stopping the flow of a river with one's grasping hands—returned to haunt him just three months later when, on 27 January 1842, his only son and beloved first child, Waldo, died of scarlet fever.

Emerson speaks explicitly of Waldo's death in only one paragraph of his essay "Experience," yet, as Sharon Cameron and others after her have argued, Waldo's death is not simply "set forth and set aside, in fact the essay is a testament to the pervasiveness of a loss so inclusive that it is suddenly inseparable from experience itself."[20] Emerson follows his specific words on his son's death with this same, no longer foolish, image of hands vainly clutching at an ungraspable flow: "I take this evanescence and lubricity of all objects, which lets them slip through our fingers then when we clutch hardest, to be the most unhandsome part of our condition."[21] What is "unhandsome" is indeed our "hands": both that they would clutch at life—where clutching is useless—and that for all their clutching they will never grasp.[22] The daguerreotyped hands clenched in combat or despair gain a new poignancy. The fight to possess and the despair of possessing, how hands are unhanded, characterizes our condition by locating it in the body, and more specifically locating it in that portion of the body which differentiates the human capacity to manufacture the objects of our world. All our making cannot grant us possession. The death-mask daguerreotype of immortal man is one instance of this vain clutching, an instance clearly grounded in a market economy where daguerreotype portraiture sells. The impossibility of preventing Waldo's death, or of keeping him truly present once he has died, is another. The unhandsomeness of our hands characterizes both the consumerist quest for ever more having and the grief of bereavement.

The pain of no longer being able to have his son is the theme of many of Emerson's letters and journal entries in the days after Waldo's death:

> For this boy in whose remembrance I have both slept and waked so oft decorated for me the morning star, & the evening cloud, how much more all the particulars of daily economy; for he had touched with his lively curiosity every trivial fact & circumstance in the household, the hard coal and soft coal which I put in my stove; the wood of which he brought his little quota for grandmother's fire, the hammer, the pincers, & file, he was so eager to use, the microscope, the magnet, the little globe, & every trinket & instrument in the study; the loads of gravel of the meadow, the nests in the henhouse and many & many a little visit to the doghouse and to the barn— For everything he had his own name & way of thinking, his own pronunciation & manner. And every word came mended from that tongue.[23]

These pages are imbued with a sense of how Waldo's presence permeated his father's life, inhabiting the hearth—that conventional image for the heart and center of the home—but also Emerson's study, and language itself. The belief that Waldo's touch endowed the world with value characterized his role in the family all along; it was not simply a response to his death. So, for example, in a journal entry written when Waldo was not yet two, Emerson quoted Lidian's maternal prizing of two apples the boy had carried home "one in each hand. . . . 'See where the dear little Angel has gnawed them. They are worth a barrel of apples that he has not touched.' "[24] But if Waldo had "touched" and "mended" all this—both with his hands and tongue, and with the "lively curiosity" of his mind—he himself is no longer lively and can no longer be touched, so that the question of what it would mean to mend such a loss straddles the gap between all the specific, graspable things Emerson can list and the ungraspable thing he has lost.

A few days after Waldo's death, Emerson would write to Caroline Sturgis:

> I chiefly grieve that I cannot grieve; that this fact takes no more deep hold than other facts, is as dreamlike as they; a lambent flame that will not burn playing on the surface of my river. Must every experience—those that promised to be dearest & most penetrative—only kiss my cheek like the wind & pass away?[25]

Following Cameron, it is important to see this grief over the loss of affect as a displacement of grief over the death of the son that incorporates and reiterates that loss: it is not only an abstract "experience" that has "passed away," but also the boy who used to kiss his father's cheek. Still, this pattern of displacement as reiteration differs from the idea of mourning which characterizes the sentimental ideology I detailed above: mourning as a keeping of loss, a clutching at loss. Not only does Emerson fail, in this account, to grasp evanescent experience, but the "fact" of his son's death also fails to "hold" him. The vainness of clutching and the impossibility of being held prove one and the same. In "Experience," Emerson elaborates it this way:

> So it is with this calamity: it does not touch me: some thing which I fancied was part of me, which could not be torn away without tearing me, or enlarged without enriching me, falls off from me, and leaves no scar. It was caducous. I grieve that grief can teach me nothing, nor carry me one step into real nature. The Indian who was laid under a curse, that the wind should not blow on him, nor water flow to him, nor fire burn him, is a type of us all. The dearest events are summer-rain and we the Para coats that shed every drop. (473)

This image of a ripping of flesh that "leaves no scar" is the perfect antithesis of the sentimental cultivation of the new and open wound. Mrs. Bird has no scar not because her loss has seamlessly healed, but rather because the wound will not close. Stowe offers Mrs. Bird (in a scene that recapitulates her own personal experiences of loss) as "a type of us all," assured that readers, reading this passage, will claim and feel Mrs. Bird's wound as their own. In claiming no scar, Emerson asserts his loss as an utter loss. "It was caducous," like, as my dictionary says (offering notably sentimental examples), the sepals of a flower or a baby's milk teeth, a palpable part of the self that is shed without trauma, leaving no mark of the initial connection. Similarly, the connection to his readers that Emerson proffers, what he finds "of us all," is not shared feeling but rather the shared curse of an inability to feel.

In passages like these, Emerson clearly and strongly rejects the sentimental conception that the cherishing of the dead can in any way relieve loss, or produce emotional ties. "Intellect always puts an interval between the subject & the object," he would muse in his journal some months later, "Affection would blend the two. For weal or for woe I clear myself from the thing I contemplate: I grieve, but I am not a grief: I love but I am not a love."[26] Death and grief, especially for what is loved, are simply loss: they do not remake the self in their own image, they build no connections, they teach nothing. Yet as Emerson's imagery reveals, this very claim of impermeability and disconnection—"the Para coats that shed every drop"—simultaneously expresses how grief and loss permeate the world: the mourner may believe that loss will not bring him "one step into real nature," nor forge the precise connections of sentiment, but the skies themselves cry in summer-rain the father's tears.[27] This double sense of loss as both caducous and diffusely all-permeating clearly differs from the sentimental conception of loss as grounding both individual affective identity and precise emotional bonds to others. It is, however, this Emersonian conception of loss—ungraspable and all-permeating—that best reveals the way grief, even in the sentimental guise of "Affection" that Emerson disavows, bears on issues of production, commerce, and possession.

From his earliest writings, Emerson had positioned himself, and his call for a national rebirth, in opposition to mourning. Mourning entails homage to the dead: "Our age is retrospective. It builds the sepulchers of the fathers" he asserts in the first lines of *Nature,* and famously goes on to ask "Why should not we also enjoy an original relation to the universe?" (7). Emerson's scorn for retrospect and sepulchers sees in mourning's attachment to the past, its effort to keep the dead present in the feelings and thoughts of the living, a profound threat to the original relation he imagines. He wants not a remembrance but a making new, even if it must be, as his "also" admits, always only the repetition of making new again. But what happens when the sepulchers prove not for the fathers but for the son; when what is mourned is not the past, but the future? "It is true that the Boy is gone," Emerson writes to his wife Lidian when he is away lecturing in Providence, a scant two weeks after Waldo's death, "the far shining stone that made home glitter to me when I was farthest absent—for you & I are passing, and he was to remain."[28] The lost boy is figured as the "far shining" future, but he is also the source, the buried past, and no doubt the "little man" of the poem which begins "Experience," to whom nature whispers "The founder thou! these are thy race!" (469).

Part of what Waldo has founded for his father is precisely this refusal to hold on to grief. "We are finding again our hands & feet after our dull & dreadful dream which does *not* leave us where it found us," Emerson wrote to Margaret Fuller in the week after Waldo's death. He goes on to admonish himself for being thus altered by bereavement, so that what follows this passage already points to the claim in "Experience" that even the most grievous loss "would leave me as it found me" (473).

Lidian, Elizabeth, & I recite chronicles words & tones of our fair boy & magnify our lost treasure to extort if we can the secretest wormwood of grief, & see how bad is the worst. Meantime the sun rises & the winds blow Nature seems to have forgotten that she has crushed her sweetest creation and perhaps would admonish us that as this Child's attention could never be fastened on any death, but proceeded still to enliven the new toy, so we children must have no retrospect, but illuminate the new hour if possible with an undiminished stream of rays.[29]

It is the child, particularly the child who has died, who together with nature teaches the parent not to fasten onto death. And so the mourning parents—to whom what is lost is a treasure—become instead "we children," relinquishing retrospect by returning to youthful origins, and claiming each "new hour" as a "new toy" so as to find not loss but abundance in the passage of time that makes us mortal. Thus one way that Emerson fastens on to his son, even as he resists fastening on to death "if possible" (this lesson is in no way easy), is by recording this capacity to let go as one of the things his child taught him.

There is much that is disturbing about Emerson's notion of "Compensation," as he titled his essay on loss as a source of abundance. The confidence in redress Emerson offers here can feel like a callous discounting of loss. "Compensation" was published in *Essays: First Series,* and so was written long before Waldo's death, but in the wake of the deaths of Emerson's first wife, Ellen, and his brother Charles.[30] Comparing the soul to a shellfish that must periodically quit its "beautiful stony case, because it no longer admits of its growth and slowly forms a new house" (301), Emerson writes:

> A fever, a mutilation, a cruel disappointment, a loss of wealth, a loss of friends, seems at the moment unpaid loss, and unpayable. But the sure years reveal the deep remedial force that underlies all facts. The death of a dear friend, wife, brother, lover, which seems nothing but privation, somewhat later assumes the aspect of a guide or genius; for it commonly operates revolutions in our way of life, terminates an epoch of infancy or of youth which was waiting to be closed, breaks up a wonted occupation, or a household, or style of living, and allows the formation of new ones more friendly to the growth of character. (302)

Emerson undoubtedly found this deep remedial force harder to believe in by the time he wrote "Experience," but this is at most a shift of emphasis.[31] The recompense claimed here is, after all, nothing more sanguine than the recognition that our lives are not fractured by deprivations but made whole through them, because ultimately all ways of life are "waiting to be closed." The sense that even the gravest calamities can be assigned meaning and thus transmuted into value, that loss may prove the source of abundance, remains Emerson's most insistent response to death. There is a chilling solipsism here—the mirror image of the sentimental egoism that would absorb all losses in one's own bereavement. In both of these texts, loss and grief become sources of value, more "payable" than one had ever imagined. Letting go of the dead, the very opposite of the sentimental preservation enacted by photographs and bureau drawers, ultimately shares with sentimentalism the recognition that loss confers worth, that it enriches and empowers the self because it prompts new beginnings and the work of self-making.[32] Yet, ungraspable and all-permeating, bereavement in Emerson's account confers value not by the hoarding of the heart's treasure but rather, as the very multiplicity and variety of Emerson's illustrations suggest, through acts of fabrication. All lives, he insists, must be remade—replicated—again and again. The empty place which loss creates requires filling, so that bereavement proves ultimately useful as the occasion for invention and production.

Critics have found the way Emerson writes of Waldo's death in "Experience" as scandalous as they find sentimental responses trite, because Emerson insists on the insufficiency of grief and, worse yet, depicts the loss of a child with peculiarly economic analogies.[33]

> In the death of my son, now more than two years ago, I seem to have lost a beautiful estate,—no more. I cannot get it nearer to me. If tomorrow I should be informed of the bankruptcy of my principal debtors, the loss of my property would be a great inconvenience to me, perhaps, for many years; but it would leave me as it found me,—neither better nor worse. So it is with this calamity: it does not touch me. (473)

I realize that I may risk sounding like Emerson's original audience: young men of the new commercial classes who, Mary Kupiec Cayton argues, misconstrued Emerson's message and applauded his examples ("Steam was as abundant 100 years ago as now but it was not put to so good a use as now. [Applause]") while remaining oblivious to the "higher theory" Emerson intended such examples to illustrate.[34] Still, it seems to me that Emerson's comparison of the death of his son to the loss of an estate and the bankruptcy of debtors is significant, not only because it jars sentimental expectations (such losses are not comparable and to compare them seems an affront to feeling, or a mark of disassociation), but also because it insists upon a relation between grief and economic possession. What the boom and bust cycles of the 1830s amply illustrate is the insecurity of possession: how easily beautiful estates may be lost; how—in the figure of the debtor whose bankruptcy incurs losses for others—possession is not singular but rather forges flexible and multiple links. This is not, of course, the vision of commercial progress that mechanics, clerks, and aspiring merchants would want to applaud, but it is an understanding of the economic world which stresses the exchange and fluidity of America's new commercial structures, and which suggests that these could be reimagined as a source of renewal.[35]

The impossibility of securing possession is not only a general economic fact, but moreover one which Emerson recognized as specifically relevant to his own work as a lecturer and writer. As he writes in "Experience":

> So many things are unsettled which it is of the first importance to settle,—and, pending their settlement, we will do as we do. . . . Law of copyright and international copyright is to be discussed, and, in the interim, we will sell our books for the most we can. Expediency of literature, reason of literature, lawfulness of writing down a thought, is questioned; much is to say on both sides, and while the fight

waxes hot, thou, dearest scholar, stick to thy foolish task, add a line every hour, and between whiles add a line. Right to hold land, right of property, is disputed, and the conventions convene, and before the vote is taken, dig away at your garden, and spend your earnings as a waife or godsend to all serene and beautiful purposes. (481)

Here the joy of what "we do" is identified not with possession but with expenditure. Emerson's own early collections of essays circulated far more widely and successfully through pirated British editions and the often inaccurate and certainly fragmenting reprint mechanisms of periodical notices and reviews than in authorized editions.[36] If Emerson takes pleasure in how "things are unsettled" and how the "right of property" is unrealizable, it is clear that this pleasure derives from how the inability to grasp leaves unhindered the ability to sell and write and spend. Susan Stewart has argued that the memento or souvenir—of which the postmortem photograph is a particularly affect-laden example—is like a book in "the way in which an exterior of little material value envelopes a great 'interior significance.'" "Yet at the same time," she adds, "these souvenirs absolutely deny the book's mode of mechanical reproduction. . . . Because of its connection to biography and its place in constituting the notion of the individual life, the memento becomes emblematic of the worth of that life and of the self's capacity to generate worthiness."[37] I want to argue against this that most souvenirs, including mementos of the dead, are in fact collaborations between the modes of commercial and mechanical production and the emotions and desires of an individual life.[38] Books and mementos are both instances of how thought and memory may be endowed with a commodifiable form. What Emerson concludes of his books—that commercialization and replication are valuable not as a means of (re-)possession but as ways to facilitate both circulation and production ("and between whiles add a line")—proves equally true of his grief.

I am finally suggesting reading "Experience," and its sense of bereavement's failure to confirm the reality of the feeling self, as a critique of the notions of memorialization and preservation characteristic of nineteenth-century sentimental mourning practices, including mortuary photography. But I am also suggesting that his critique is strongly marked by the wish that sentimental claims might be true, and hence that one could, as photography advertisements urged, "secure the shadow ere the substance fades," and find in replication and commodification a form of keeping.

> This morning I had the remains of my mother & my son Waldo removed from the tomb of Mrs. Ripley to my lot in "Sleepy Hollow." The sun shone brightly on the coffins, of which Waldo's was well preserved—now fifteen years. I ventured to look into the coffin. I gave a few white oak leaves to each coffin, after they were put in the new vault, & the vault was then covered with two slabs of granite.[39]

Enacting his own most shocking comparison, Emerson would make the re-interred body of his child a physical part of the "beautiful estate" of Concord's Sleepy Hollow Cemetery. But if this effort at preservation seems more absolute than any keepsake memento—insisting as it does on the actual body rather than accepting the mediations offered by graphic reproduction—it is also and necessarily undermined by this very materiality. Emerson does not say what he finds in that coffin, but surely it is not preservation. Peering into the grave, Emerson embodies sentimental efforts to keep the dead present, and thereby proves the disintegration of the dead, ungraspable but also therefore uncontainable even by slabs of granite.

There is nothing to possess but dust. Yet if having must always be an occasion for loss, it is equally true for Emerson that loss will always be an opportunity for production and renewal. What Emerson accomplishes is a reimagining of possession as a limitless circulation. He explains in "Experience" that "when I receive a new gift I do not macerate my body to make the account square, for, if I should die, I could not make the account square. The benefit overran the merit the first day, and has overran the merit ever since" (491).[40] The image of his son as something "I fancied was part of me, which could not be torn away without tearing me," haunts this passage, for the father had wished in those lines for a body that could be macerated, for experience that could be clutched and could therefore wound. The inability to square the account suggests not debt or loss but rather excess, a world overrun with "new gifts."

Years later, Emerson would write about gifts in his journal, offering as one "capital example" a birdhouse that has housed bluebirds each of the years since its giving. He then "think[s] of another" example,

> quite inestimable. John Thoreau, Junior, knew how much I should value a head of little Waldo, then five years old. He came to me, & offered to carry him to a daguerreotypist who was then in town, & he, Thoreau, would see it well done. He did it, & brought me the daguerre which I thankfully paid for. In a few months after, my boy died, and I have ever since had deeply to thank John Thoreau for that wise & gentle piece of friendship.[41]

In Emerson's economy, what is valued in the daguerreotype of the now dead child is its capacity to overrun, to renew and multiply like the generations of bluebirds. What is valued is the excess that replication permits and loss initiates. Thus, even as we may read "Experience" as a critique of sentimentalism and its vain clutching at what is gone, Emerson's theory of bereavement expresses more explicitly than sentimentalism itself how sentimentalism's structures of excess, replication, and circulation reflect not only the repetitive characteristics of mourning, but also the commercial and replicating mechanisms that place those feelings in circulation. Photography and bureau drawers can never really preserve the dead, but they can make of loss a "new toy." As the figure of the dead child becomes itself a commodity of sorts, and as the market tools of replication and circulation are harnessed to the act of mourning—that is, as a figure innocent, intimate, static, and unique becomes an object of mass production—the dead child carries intimacy and affect into the commercial, industrial world where such feelings appear most threatened. To say this is not to abstract and disavow the pain of a child's death; the intensely and almost exclusively emotional loss that is the death of a child, and the more diffuse and public trauma of national and commercial progress, can elaborate each other because, in nineteenth-century America, both are urgent sites of bereavement and circulation.

NOTES

1. Esther Schor, *Bearing the Dead: The British Culture of Mourning from the Enlightenment to Victoria* (Princeton: Princeton University Press, 1994), 3.

2. Charles E. Orr, for example, wrote an article for *The Philadelphia Photographer* of 1877 to give "assistance to some photographers of less experience, to whom it might befall the unpleasant duty to take the picture of a corpse." He explains that photographers should "secure sufficient help to do the lifting and handling, for it is no easy matter to bend a corpse," and advises that mourners should be "politely request[ed] . . . to leave the room to you and your aides, that you may not feel the embarrassment incumbent should they witness some little mishap liable to befall the occasion" (quoted in Jay Ruby, *Secure the Shadow: Death and Photography in America* [Cambridge: MIT Press, 1995], 58). In "An Address to the National Photographic Association" in 1872, published in the *Philadelphia Photographer* (June 1872), Albert S. Southworth recalled his first postmortem daguerreotypes, reporting how by bending the joints they can be made pliable so that "you may do just as you please so far as handling and bending the corpses is concerned," and going on to detail his procedures for removing fluid from the mouth of the corpse so that none will be "ejected" during the sitting (in *Secrets of the Dark Chamber: The Art of the American Daguerreotype*, ed. Merry A. Foresta and John Wood [Washington: Smithsonian Institution Press, 1995], quotation from 308).

3. Karen Halttunen, *Confidence Men and Painted Women: A Study of Middle-Class Culture in America, 1830–1870* (New Haven: Yale University Press, 1982), 124. Halttunen's argument focuses on the ironies of seeking to perform sincerity in both of these right feelings, and how such performances become a means of claiming genteel status. My concern with the relation between commercialism and mourning would see nineteenth-century expressions of grief less as a tool of status than as interdependently bound to it.

4. Harriet Beecher Stowe to Eliza Lee Cabot Follen, 16 December 1852, in Charles Edward Stowe, *The Life of Harriet Beecher Stowe Compiled from her Letters and Journals* (Boston: Houghton and Mifflin, 1889), 198–9.

5. Harriet Beecher Stowe, *Uncle Tom's Cabin or, Life Among the Lowly* (New York: Penguin, 1981), 149. Subsequent citations will be given in parentheses in the text.

6. David Marshall, *The Surprising Effects of Sympathy: Marivaux, Diderot, Rousseau, and Mary Shelley* (Chicago: University of Chicago Press, 1988), 3, 5.

7. Stowe to Sarah Allen, 2 December 1850. The Allens had been the Stowes' next-door neighbors in Cincinnati, with Diarca Howe Allen teaching with Calvin Stowe at the Lane Seminary. In 1844, Sarah and Harriet, without a doctor or midwife present, delivered the baby of one of the Stowes' boarders. Letter quoted and discussed in Joan D. Hedrick, *Harriet Beecher Stowe: A Life* (New York: Oxford University Press, 1994), 158–62, 199.

8. Roland Barthes, *Camera Lucida: Reflections on Photography,* trans. Richard Howard (New York: Hill and Wang, 1981), 21. I want to thank Marianne Noble for sharing with me the manuscript of her paper "Ecstasies of Sentimental Wounding in *Uncle Tom's Cabin.*" The

version of this paper published in the *Yale Journal of Criticism* 10, no. 2 (1997): 295–320 does not mention Barthes, but her point is the same: to recognize the psychological and erotic content of wounding as central to the pleasures of sentimentality and the construction of sentimental identifications.

9. Stowe to her husband Calvin Stowe, 26 July 1849, in Charles Edward Stowe, *Life Compiled*, 124.

10. Barthes, *Camera Lucida*, 9, 4.

11. "New Discovery in the Fine Arts," *New Yorker*, 13 April 1839, in Foresta and Wood, *Secrets of the Dark Chamber*, 223–5, quotation from 224; N. G. Burgess, *Photographic and Fine Art Journal* 8 (January 1855): 80; Oliver Wendell Holmes, "Doings of the Sunbeam," *Atlantic Monthly*, 12 July 1863, in *Photography: Essays and Images, Illustrated Readings in the History of Photography*, ed. Beaumont Newhall (New York: Museum of Modern Art, 1980), 63–77, quotation from 66.

12. For a table of exposure times from the 1840s, see Beaumont Newhall, *The Daguerreotype in America* (New York: Duell, Sloan and Pearce, 1961), 124.

13. Bill Jay, "Infantry Tactics," in Sue Packer, *The Babies* (Manchester, Mich.: Cornerhouse, 1989).

14. Edward L. Wilson, "To My Patrons" (Philadelphia, 1871), in Newhall, *Photography: Essays and Images*, 129–33, quotations from 130, 133.

15. Quoted in Ruby, *Secure the Shadow*, 44 (emphasis added).

16. John Tagg, "A Democracy of the Image: Photographic Portraiture and Commodity Production," in *The Burden of Representation: Essays on Photographies and Histories* (Minneapolis: University of Minnesota Press, 1988), 43.

17. See Karin Calvert, "Cradle to Crib: The Revolution in Nineteenth-Century Children's Furniture," in *A Century of Childhood: 1820–1920*, ed. Mary Lynn Stevens Heininger et al. (Rochester, N. Y.: Margaret Woodbury Strong Museum, 1984), 33–64.

18. Both *Passing: The Vision of Death in America*, ed. Charles O. Jackson (Westport, Conn.: Greenwood Press, 1977) and *Death in America*, ed. David E. Stannard (Philadelphia: University of Pennsylvania Press, 1975) organize their essays so as to tell an overarching story about the fall from the colonial period's authentic and communal if rather grim relation to mortality, through the nineteenth century's sentimental and lamentable commercialization and beautification of death, to the twentieth-century attempt to deny death, or at least make it invisible. This, of course, is an American elaboration of the trajectory traced by Philippe Ariès's *Western Attitudes Toward Death: From the Middle Ages to the Present*, trans. Helen Weaver (New York: Alfred A. Knopf, 1981). See also Ann Douglas, who has interpreted the cult of death and its sentimental commodifications as a symptom of the feminization of American culture: "the dying infant was made supremely to flatter [women and clergymen] . . . : he shared their weakness while he dignified and extended their authority" (*The Feminization of American Culture* [New York: Avon Books, 1977], 246).

19. Ralph Waldo Emerson, *The Journals and Miscellaneous Notebooks of Ralph Waldo Emerson*, 16 vols., ed. William H. Gilman and J. E. Parsons (Cambridge: Harvard University Press, 1970), entry of 24 October 1841.

20. Sharon Cameron, "Representing Grief: Emerson's 'Experience,' " in *The New American Studies: Essays from Representations*, ed. Philip Fisher (Berkeley: University of California Press, 1991), 201–27, quotation from 202.

21. Emerson, "Experience," in *Essays and Lectures* (New York: Library of America, 1983), 473. Subsequent citations from this and other essays will be given in parentheses in the text.

22. Stanley Cavell brilliantly calls attention to the connection between "the hand in unhandsome and the impotently clutching fingers" of this passage, although he sees unhandsomeness only in the desire "to deny the standoffishness of objects by clutching at them," a desire he associates with language but which I would also associate with the urge to possess which characterizes consumerism (*This New Yet Unapproachable America: Lectures after Emerson after Wittgenstein* [Albuquerque, N. M.: Living Batch Press, 1989], 86–8).

23. Emerson, *Journals*, 6:150–1.

24. Emerson, *Journals*, entry of 16 July 1838. See also Lidian's adoration of a tower Waldo has built (4:432–3). In both of these cases the "fit of affection" is depicted as Lidian's—a maternal valuation—but the writing father presents his words as an endorsement of her effusions.

25. Emerson to Caroline Sturgis, 4 February 1842, in *The Letters of Ralph Waldo Emerson*, 8 vols., ed. Ralph Rusk (New York: Columbia University Press, 1939), 3:9.

26. Emerson, *Journals*, entry of September 1842.

27. See Cameron, "Representing Grief," 210 and 215–6 for more extended readings of these passages, including her recognition that the kiss of the wind and the tears of summer rain, in passages that might seem to mourn the loss of affect and not the loss of a son, actually evoke Waldo and the act of grieving for him. My work has been deeply influenced by these readings.

28. Emerson to Lidian Emerson, 15 February 1842, in *Letters*, 3:12.

29. Emerson to Margaret Fuller, 2 February 1842, in *Letters*, 3:9.

30. See James Cox, "Ralph Waldo Emerson: The Circle of the Eye," in *Emerson: Prophecy, Metamorphosis and Influence*, ed. David Levin (New York: Columbia University Press, 1975), 57–81, especially 71–3, on how the deaths of Ellen and Charles inspired and empowered Emerson's writing.

31. Stephen Whicher's seminal study of Emerson, *Freedom and Fate: An Inner Life of Ralph Waldo Emerson*, 2d ed. (Philadelphia: University of Pennsylvania Press, 1971) posits Waldo's death as the pivot which turns Emerson from optimism to skepticism. This basic structure still organizes most critical work on Emerson, although increasingly critics—and I would count myself here—have focused on the continuity of Emerson's thought and the way fate haunts even such early work as "Nature" and "Self-Reliance." See Cavell, *New Yet Unapproachable America*, and Richard Poirier, *The Renewal of Literature: Emersonian Reflections* (New York: Random House, 1987), on the pervasiveness of Emerson's skepticism. Christopher Newfield's *The Emerson Effect: Individualism and Submission in America* (Chicago: University of Chicago Press, 1996) takes this revision farther than I find convincing, in depicting Emerson's fatalism as his most significant (and damning) contribution to the nature of American liberalism.

32. Michael Lopez, *Emerson and Power: Creative Antagonism in the Nineteenth Century* (DeKalb, Ill.: Northeastern University Press, 1996), in chapters on "The Doctrine of Use" and "The Uses of Failure," richly explores Emerson's conviction that loss should be apprehended as a source of power.

33. Mark Edmundson gets well beyond the "scandal" in noting how these economic figurations of loss "anticipate Freud's own economic tropes for the psyche" ("Emerson and the Work of Melancholia," *Raritan* 6 [Spring 1987]: 120–36, quotation from 128; see also his specific economic comparisons with "Mourning and Melancholia" on 131).

34. Mary Kupiec Cayton, "The Making of an American Prophet: Emerson, His Audiences, and the Rise of the Culture Industry in Nineteenth-Century America," *American*

Historical Review 92 (June 1987): 597–620, especially 612–3, quoting a report on Emerson's lecture "Wealth" by the *Daily Cincinnati Gazette*, 13 December 1852.

35. I share Richard F. Teichgraeber's sense that Emerson, in his use of economic imagery, is not merely illustrating philosophical and ethical issues outside the market economy, but also offering ways of reimagining that economy. See *Sublime Thoughts / Penny Wisdom: Situating Emerson and Thoreau in the American Market* (Baltimore: Johns Hopkins University Press, 1995).

36. See Teichgraeber, *Sublime Thoughts / Penny Wisdom,* especially 173–99. Lawrence Buell's account of antebellum balancing acts between the increasing commercialization of authorship and "the persistence of the ideal of art as a form of cultural service" finds in Emerson a perfect instance of the capacity to have it both ways, since Emerson simultaneously "resisted depicting art as a commodity" and yet made Transcendentalism into "an eminently marketable commodity that (as legions of late-century imitators found) lent itself to mass production" (*New England Literary Culture: From Revolution through Renaissance* [New York: Cambridge University Press, 1986], 62–5).

37. Susan Stewart, *On Longing: Narratives of the Miniature, the Gigantic, the Souvenir, the Collection* (Durham, N. C.: Duke University Press, 1993), 139.

38. Helen Sheumaker's study of hair fancy work provides a particularly rich example of how even so personal and "authentic" a memento as a lock of hair could be made into a sentimental consumer object (paper presented at the American Studies Association conference, Kansas City, October 1996). A prime use of hair wreaths, of course, was to frame memorial photographs of the dead.

39. Emerson, *Journals,* entry of 8 July 1857.

40. Wai-chee Dimock uses nineteenth-century economic debates to elaborate on how the self's felt lack, what she calls its "constitutional scarcity," distinguishes it from the abundant world and permits it to receive endlessly. Her essay makes a strong case for the centrality of economic concerns to "Experience," and my notion of an economy of grief is largely indebted to her. See "Scarcity, Subjectivity and Emerson," *Boundary 2* 17 (Spring 1990): 83–99.

41. Emerson, *Journals,* entry of 17 January 1862.

PART TWO

Public Sentiment

CHAPTER FOUR

The Black Body Erotic and the Republican Body Politic, 1790–1820

John Saillant

Two entirely new elements in American writing appeared in antislavery writings published and republished in America between 1790 and 1820: an erotic representation of the black male body—its visage, hands, muscle, skin, height, sex—unparalleled by the representation of any other body, black or white, male or female, and a *communitas*, blending sentimentalism and homoeroticism, shared by black men and white men who were united in opposition to slavery. Earlier than the polemics of the antebellum abolitionists, these writings expressed an alternative to the republican racialism of postrevolutionary America, in a time when ideas about race and slavery were in flux. The eroticized black male body figures in antislavery variations on eighteenth-century sentimentalism and revolutionary republicanism, two strains of thought linked by the sentimentalist reconstruction of the classical ideal of martial virtue into an ideal of affection, benevolence, sentiment, and sympathy shared among men, the virtuous citizens of the American republic.[1] The black man who appeared between 1790 and 1820 in antislavery narratives, essays, and poems is the "poor negro," deserving benevolence but denied it by his white masters.[2] This sentimentalized "poor negro," on American soil, became an eroticized "friend," echoing the homoeroticism of classical martial virtue as well as gesturing toward nineteenth-century blackface and its interracial homoerotics.[3] Rooted in the eighteenth century, the sentimentalized and eroticized black friend of the turn of the nineteenth century predates the eroticized figures of antebellum sentimental women's writing concerned with race and slavery.[4]

White men eroticized black men in antislavery writings because the American sentimental and republican ideologies grounded their vision of the body politic in a fundamental likeness among men that produces benevolence.[5] Republicans believed some fundamental likeness to be required in a free society like postrevolutionary America. This notion of likeness echoed some prominent elements of the American past—Puritan covenant theology, the Calvinist doctrine of a benevolent providential design inhering in all people and things, the idealized communalism of farming communities, and the idealized unity of the patriots in the War of Independence. It also echoed some prominent elements in eighteenth-century European thought—for example Montesquieu's notion of a "spirit" uniting a society, and British sentimentalism and common sense philosophy.[6] Republicans lacked a proslavery argument, accepting merely the Montesquieuian view that any group that could not join in the spirit of a society should be enslaved or banished. The American Colonization Society, an expatriationist effort to remove black Americans to Africa or the Caribbean, flowed from this view of the black man as alien to the unifying likeness required in a republic whether Democratic-Republican or Federalist, deist or orthodox, Americans like Thomas Jefferson, James Monroe, James Madison, Samuel Hopkins, and Jonathan Edwards, Jr., believed that blacks and whites could never share the likeness and the unity of common sense and experience required for benevolent relations, and thus benevolence could never exist between black and white in America.[7] So dogmatic was this notion that when James Monroe suggested that a settlement far in the west might suit both America and its blacks, Jefferson scolded him that even there blacks would be a "blot" and reminded him that the time to commence the expatriation was short. Still, Montesquieu, one of the greatest European influences on revolutionary and postrevolutionary American thought, had made it clear in 1750 that one "likeness" white men share with black men is precisely a sexual likeness.[8] Attacking "Negro slavery," Montesquieu savaged the making of "eunuchs" as a way of depriving "blacks of their likeness to us in a more distinctive way."[9] Interracial likeness and interracial benevolence were understood by antislavery writers to be rooted in physical similarities between the black male body and the white male body, and the eroticization of black men in antislavery writing confirmed this likeness by uniting black men and white men in an affectionate and physical bond. Indeed, antislavery writing introduced the body as such into American writing, for no figure other than the black male is represented in such bodily detail and in such a sexualized fashion before 1790.

The sentimentalization and eroticization of black men by white men was a counterdiscourse to republican ideology, rubbing against one of its sorest points: the persistence of an enslaved, oppressed class in a republic founded by a liberty-loving people. The racial dimension of republican thought placed leading republicans in an uncomfortable position, one impossible to sustain. Colonization, which men like Thomas Jefferson and James Madison viewed as essential to republicanism, was impractical, while republican discourse could not quell the notion that oppressed black men were like white men and thus were worthy of liberty and dignity. Republicans freed themselves from this uncomfortable position only by freeing themselves from the eighteenth-century underpinnings of republican thought. The impulses to enslave blacks and to deny them an equal place in the social order, in the North as well as in the South, proved to be stronger than the commitment to revolutionary ideology. As liberal thought transformed the republican commitment to likeness, benevolence, and unity into a commitment to Protestant pluralism, economic freedom, and individualism, the dialectic between the view of the black man as an alien and the view of the black man as a sentimental friend came to an end. The writings examined in this essay were printed and reprinted in the decades before that end, when it seemed that revolutionary republicanism would determine the character of American culture and its race relations. These writings were part of a debate, sometimes lively and sometimes desperate, about race, but insofar as their nexus was a black man and a white man in a sentimental friendship, they lost their potency after 1820 in a new, liberal America.

In the postrevolutionary decades, republican leaders promoted various strategies for fortifying likeness among white men: universal common education, the division of society into small "ward-republics," and an empiricism that would unite people in common sense, not divide them by a fissiparous idealism. The black male, in the republican mind, threatened such unity not only because he was in some sense outside it—whites had alienated blacks by slavery, while by nature the races were already divided—but also because he had a claim to benevolence that white Americans at large were unwilling to recognize.[10] This claim to benevolence was made explicit by black spokesmen of postrevolutionary America, who modulated their claims through religious doctrine, republican principles, and reminders of the virtuous service of blacks in difficulties like the revolutionary battles and the yellow fever epidemic.[11] Certain that the black man threatened the republic because he was both socially and naturally "heterogeneous," republican leaders planned to maintain slavery until blacks could be expatriated, a plan that simply paralleled other republican strategies for creating white unity.

Essential to white thought on race and slavery in the early republic is the opposition between, on the one hand, the schemes of the republican literati to remove blacks physically from America and, on the other hand, the newspaper essays and pamphlets in which white men eagerly embraced black men and their claims to benevolence. Antislavery writings centering upon benevolent relations between a black man and a white man were not antirepublican, but rather the result of a different understanding of the connections among race, sentiment, and republicanism. Unlike the republican literati, none of whom conceded that the benevolence required in a republic could cross the race line, the white men who *could* imagine interracial benevolence had no place in the central republican discourse of postrevolutionary America; they published their thoughts anonymously in pamphlets and newspapers, creating an almost subterranean republican commentary on race. As the Jeffersonians and other expatriationists monopolized political philosophy and religious discourse, other men with a vision of interracial benevolence modulated their ideas and values through the erotics of masculine relationships. In other words, when it became all but impossible to address interracial benevolence, which was the heart of the matter, in republican political philosophy and religion, a handful of white men turned to a union of bodies. Eros, one urge behind sentiment, became an eroticism of black men and white men when American ideology condemned interracial benevolence.

A French Montesquieuian provided Americans with a model for eroticization in antislavery writing. Joseph LaVallée's *Le nègre comme il y a peu de blancs,* published in Paris in 1789, appeared almost immediately in English.[12] Two different English translations appeared in London in 1790, *The Negro As There Are Few White Men* and *The Negro Equalled by Few Europeans.* A Philadelphia periodical, the *American Museum, or Universal Magazine,* carried *The Negro Equalled by Few Europeans* in installments in 1791. Finally, in 1801, an American book edition appeared in Philadelphia.[13] The status of LaVallée's *Negro* as an important antislavery text is suggested by the long list of subscribers for the American edition, including two eloquent spokesmen for black rights and dignity, Richard Allen and Absalom Jones (2:239–44). The novel, presented as an autobiography of the African Itanoko, seems to have directly influenced American writing about slavery, as well as capturing the spirit of the republican age in which slavery became a problem in political philosophy. The language and the incidents of the novel are echoed in American writings about slavery, while two of LaVallée's themes—the beauty of the black male body and the value of intimate, benevolent relations between a black man and a white man—became central in newspaper and pamphlet writings about race and slavery. Although its male protagonists love women, LaVallée's *Negro* both valorizes an erotic relationship between Itanoko and a white man intent on securing his enslaved friend's liberty, and condemns sexual connections between enslaved black men and white men who exploit them sexually but are uninterested in their freedom.

In its homoeroticism, LaVallée's *Negro* presented Americans a new object of representation—the black male body. The most remarkable element in postrevolutionary American periodical essays and religious tracts concerning slavery is the emergence of the black male body as an object of representation—a new object framed by the sentimentalism, republicanism, and Christianity that defined American ideas and values. Eighteenth-century republican thought, like all systems of ideas and values, led its adherents into beliefs about their own sexuality as well as the sexuality of those defined as Other. The sexuality attributed to black men, the republican Other, was sometimes a wild rapaciousness and sometimes a sentimental adhesiveness. But in any case, as white Americans wrestled with the problem of slavery in a new democratic and Christian republic, they were thrust by their ideas and values into this new zone—the black male body.

An announcement that whites must accept blacks either as "slaves" or as "friends" sounds the opening note of LaVallée's *Negro,* which chronicles the African's adventures with men who seek to enslave or to befriend him (1:5). Whatever their intention, the men who encounter Itanoko are immediately enthralled by his pulchritude. In its antislavery sentiments and its tales of black-white relationships, the novel casts the black male body as the supremely important object of representation. Itanoko is first heard in the narrative as he addresses the "beauty" he shares with the black "nation": "I have not to complain of Nature. She endowed me with a robust form, a distinguished height. To that she added the beauty of my nation: a jet black, a full forehead, piercing eyes, a large mouth, and fine teeth" (1:8). Constant elements in the narrative, Itanoko's "height and muscle" are admired by all the men he meets, both black and white (1:87). Not content with height and muscle, the translator of the first London edition emphasized the nudity of Itanoko, who lacks "pudicity"—modesty concerning his genitalia.[14] When Itanoko is seized by a neighboring African prince who seems to desire him as a caged companion—Itanoko is given free run of the palace but is forbidden to leave the premises—these circumstances are explained thus: "My height, my air, my figure struck him" (1:40). When Itanoko escapes from the palace by means of a prodigious swim to a ship anchored offshore, a ship's officer, upon pulling him out of the water and first glimpsing the African's physique, exclaims, "This is the finest negro I have ever seen" (1:48). As the ship's captain admires him, Itanoko notes, "My fine figure struck him" (1:61). Again the first translator emphasizes Itanoko's sexuality, by indulging in a double entendre on "bodily parts" and "bed": Itanoko swims to the French slaver at night and when he climbs nude into the light he reports, "If the reader observed what I said above respecting my bodily parts, he will not wonder at the air of astonishment with which they received me. Zounds! cries the officer on watch, with an energetic oath, that's the finest black I ever clapt my eyes on; how lucky is the captain, why, fortune hunts him even in bed."[15]

Itanoko's beauty distinguishes him not only from the white characters of his narrative, whose bodies are almost never represented, but also from the white figures who appear in American writing of the late eighteenth century in general. In American writing, informed by sentimentalism, republicanism, and Christianity, a white man appears ideally as a neighbor, brave citizen, loyal family man, or pious believer, but never as a body endowed with remarkable beauty. "The good husband, the good father, the good friend, the good neighbour," announced the *American Museum, or Universal Magazine,* "we honor as a good man worthy of our love and affection."[16] LaVallée's identification with Itanoko's beauty—the narrator's projection into a beautiful black male body as well as the whites' frank appreciation of the African—engendered a subgenre of American writing in which Itanoko's black sons displayed their beauty.

Itanoko's brave swim makes him a slave, since he has unknowingly swum to a French slaver, but it sets him in the benevolent relationship that dominates the rest of his narrative. Itanoko's capacity for male-to-male benevolence is well established by the time he swims to the slaver, since he has two such connections in his past. One was with his boyhood friend Otourou, his "friend" and "brother," with whom Itanoko shared "one soul" and, as boys, "one cradle" (1:21–2).[17] Mutual devotion and disinterestedness characterize their friendship. The other was with Dumont, a Frenchman who survived a shipwreck on the Senegalese coast to become Itanoko's tutor in French and Christianity. "Sympathy," "analogy," "sentiment," "love," and "the ties of the heart" unite Itanoko and Dumont, while Christianity shapes their intimacy. Finding Dumont in prayer, for instance, Itanoko reports, "I threw myself into his arms. 'Inform me,' said I, 'why do you do this.' He embraced me. Tears of joy sprang from his eyes" (1:12–4). Yet Otourou and Dumont merely prefigure the man whose friendship Itanoko comes to value most: the slave ship captain's son, Ferdinand. Hungry after his great swim to the ship, Itanoko is fed European food for the first time, but he finds even the "pleasing" new tastes overwhelmed by the young man who feeds him. "Nothing," Itanoko declares, "gave me such pleasure as the sight of Ferdinand. Tall and finely formed, he possessed also an ingenuous countenance, which ever attaches to the heart in the first instance. I could not resist it" (1:51).[18]

The intimacy that immediately burgeons between the young black man and the young white man seems to be blighted when Ferdinand's father has Itanoko chained in the hold with the other captives. Having remarked several times on the African's beauty, the slave ship's captain plots to sell Itanoko into a servitude particularly suited to his appearance, presumably a position of sexual service (1:61–75). Associating Ferdinand with the slave traffic, Itanoko locks his heart against the young white man who nevertheless visits him in the hold. "Many times during the day did Ferdinand approach me," Itanoko recalls, but "my heart was entirely shut up" (1:58). Only when Ferdinand declares himself against slavery can Itanoko reopen his heart. For, undaunted by the African's coolness, Ferdinand undoes the leg irons of the friend he desires and promises Itanoko that things will be better, despite his current pain. "I answered not a word," Itanoko states.

> I could not speak. If I had possessed that power, resentment alone would have furnished my expressions. But, as no one was then near us, he seized my irons, and threw them into the sea with such indignation, that this action, which did not escape me, instantly disarmed me. I took his hand and pressed it to my heart. He understood my language, and answered with sobs (1:59).

As Ferdinand's "tears" serve to resurrect their mutual benevolence, Itanoko reports that these entreaties "penetrated me" (1:63). Ferdinand keeps his promise to Itanoko by giving him money with which to buy his freedom; they will be separated soon, but Itanoko, Ferdinand explains, can pass the money to a confidant in St. Domingue, who will buy the African from his new master and orchestrate a reunion between the two friends. The gold coins exchanged between Ferdinand and Itanoko are themselves homoerotically charged, since they are given while the African is chained and are to be hidden while he is in the hold, in the slave market in St. Domingue, and on a plantation, until he can meet Ferdinand's confidant. Only by hiding the gold coins in his rectum can Itanoko secure the liberty Ferdinand provides him (1:76–7).

If Ferdinand loves Itanoko, then Ferdinand's father, Urban, seemingly rapes Itanoko. Urban's plan to sell Itanoko into a position of sexual service seems to require that the white slaver rape the black man. Calling Urban a "ravisher" and then a "perfidious ravisher," Itanoko reports that the slaver "was struck by my comeliness" and pushed into a state of "covetousness." Urban was led to "violate, what is most sacred among men," forcing Itanoko into this position: "I bore resemblance to a man, who, weary with struggling against a tiger, that threatened his life, would fall into a voluptuous sleep, between the clutches of the monster." As several white men examine Itanoko, Urban leers, in what is probably an eighteenth-century version of a phallic joke, "He will be taller yet."[19]

Commitment to the black man's liberty fosters intimacy between Itanoko and Ferdinand. However, in St. Domingue, in his quest for liberty and reunion with Ferdinand, Itanoko encounters a different sort of young white man. As the slavers zero in on Itanoko, Ferdinand's friends spirit him off to a sugar cane plantation where he will be cached, surrounded by slaves. On the plantation, Itanoko encounters Theodore, whose "criminal complaisance with the overseer" allows him to give "free scope to his irregular passions" with the plantation slaves, who around 1790 were mostly male.[20] These "irregular passions" apparently include sexual activity with black men, which LaVallée calls "crime," "vice," and "rapine," all "enormities" resulting from "unbridled disorders" and "passion" (1:86, 109–11). Moreover, Itanoko discovers, Theodore seems intent on the new African on the plantation:

> Theodore at first regarded me only as a young man who would serve as a companion for his irregularities. He had not the usual prejudice of the Europeans who think they dishonor themselves by admitting us to their society; but it was debauchery alone which gave him this apparent philosophy. . . . His amusements were too far removed from my taste to permit me to accept an equality to which my principles must have been sacrificed. (1:111)

As the first British translation has it, Theodore indulged "shameful pleasures, only fit for darkness" on the plantation, far from those who might hear "the moans of the victims of his violence"; he "at first, saw in me but a young man, whose inexperience gave him hope of complaisance."[21] When Itanoko proves not to be complaisant, Theodore plots the African's death.

LaVallée condemns Theodore not for desiring black men, but for the refusal to join this desire with an opposition to slavery. Itanoko and Ferdinand embrace precisely because the white man opposes slavery: their intimacy reflects their commitment to freedom. When they embrace upon parting, Ferdinand reminds Itanoko of that commitment. Itanoko recalls that "melting into tears, I precipitated myself into his arms. 'Cherish,' cried he, 'the principles which we have cultivated together.' . . . We held each other long embracing without speaking" (1:93). Sentimentalist opposition to slavery, presupposing that the black man is either "slave" or "friend" of the white, assures us that Itanoko must resist the advances of a white man who desires the slave's body but not his liberty. Indeed, LaVallée uses the very man who spirits Itanoko away from the slavers to emphasize that a man's desire for black males is immoral only if joined to a toleration of slavery. Itanoko immediately notes that his new companion, the middle-aged Frenchman Dumenil, is unmarried—LaVallée's cliffhanger leads the reader to believe that Dumenil has purchased the African for sexual service—and so queries the white man's servants about his marital status. Dumenil "has never taken a companion to his bosom," reply the servants laconically (1:101–2). After such suggestions of homosexuality, Dumenil is revealed to be a Christian helpmate of Itanoko and Ferdinand, not a sexual predator like Theodore. LaVallée could hardly have emphasized more strongly that white men's interest in black men and love of them leads to black liberty, while white men's exploitation of black men and passion for them leads to black slavery.

As an originating text, LaVallée's *Negro* reads like a textbook of the themes appearing in American writing about slavery in the 1790s and early 1800s. Its forthright republicanism is evident in the notion that slavery is unlawful because "the liberty of man is an inalienable right" (1:67). Avarice, passion, and a desire for luxury lead to the enslavement of some human beings by others, according to LaVallée's republicanism (1:63, 66, 69). Extending both antislavery and proslavery thinking into a zone centered on the black male body, LaVallée's antislavery characters develop intimacy across the race line, while his proslavery characters reveal their obsession with the black male body even within their desire to enslave and break it. The homoerotic feeling that apparently receives LaVallée's blessing is one elevated by republican brotherhood and Christian love, not one vitiated by passion. LaVallée's naturally benevolent black men, moreover, help one another escape slavery and its cruelties. This notion is well represented in the natural benevolence shared by Itanoko and Otourou, who disinterestedly places his friend's interest before his own and seeks his friend's liberty out of a spirit of "friendship alone" (1:153). Finally, LaVallée introduces a scene that would be replicated again and again in American antislavery writing: a black man and a white man go off alone into a sublime setting, at which point the writer turns to a rhapsody about the beauty that the two men together encounter. For instance, Itanoko and Dumont retreat, as the "sun [descends] toward the horizon," to a beautiful spot in Senegal, where they breathe in the "sweet perfumes" of flowers under a "serene" sky. This scene "ravishes my senses," cries Itanoko. With nightfall they return, the African finding that his "heart was full" (1:15–8). In general, this scene of two people going off alone into a sublime setting is highly eroticized in writings about race and slavery; whether the two are a black man and a white man or a black man and a black woman—and even the latter case is homoerotic, since it is written by a white man who identifies with both the black male and the female with whom he shares his "happiness"[22]—the same turn to a rhapsody about beauty appears.

A new Itanoko appeared in American newspapers as "Quashi; or, the Desperate Negro," in the 1790s.[23] His narrative itself is simple. Quashi and his master share benevolent affection, happily based in boyhood intimacy but fractured by the master when he wrongly credits an accusation made against his devoted slave. The meaning of Quashi's narrative is that benevolence can characterize black-white relations, while slavery is essentially a violation of benevolence. Quashi's narrative ends improbably in his suicide after he reproaches his master for the white man's abandonment of their mutual "attachment" (8). Within this series of events, Quashi's beauty is joined to benevolence, while the violation of his beauty by the whipping his master plans is joined to slavery and its abnegation of benevolence. Quashi's body, specifically his skin and even his thighs, is central to the narrative, while his master, a typical white character, hardly appears as a body.

Reared as "playfellow to his young master," Quashi, "a lad of parts," became as a man the "driver" or "black overseer, under his master." (One newspaper here substitutes "companion" for "master."[24]) Within this benevolent master-slave relationship, Quashi retains "the tenderness" and "the affection" for his master that had been nourished in "their boyish intimacy," while possessing "no separate interest" for himself. "The most delicate, yet most strong, and seemingly indissoluble tie that could bind master and slave together" seemed to be the fruit of their lifelong intimacy (5). However, when the master wrongly believes Quashi guilty of a minor infraction of plantation discipline, slavery is revealed as a violation of benevolence and Quashi's beauty enters the narrative. The master resolves to whip Quashi, who, never having been whipped, has maintained "the smoothness of his skin" (6)—in the original, "the glossy honours of his skin"[25]—precisely because of his benevolent connection with his master. This scourging of black skin rivets attention on the black man's body and his beauty:

> A Negro, who has grown up to manhood, without undergoing a solemn cart whipping (as some by good chance will), especially if distinguished by any accomplishment among his fellows, takes pride in what he calls the smoothness of his skin, and its being unrased by the whip; and would be at more pains, and use more diligence to escape such a cart-whipping, than many of our lower sort would to shun the gallows. (6)[26]

Quashi's response to his master's resolution is to avoid the white man and to seek a white "mediator" or "advocate" to intercede, since Quashi himself feels unable to speak.

After Quashi is unable to secure a mediator and unable to speak directly to the friend who is betraying him, the black man and the white man struggle on the ground in a morbid travesty of sexual intercourse:

> Quashi ran off, and his master who was a robust man, pursued him. A stone, or a clod, tripped Quashi up, just as the other reached out to seize him. They fell together, and struggled for the mastery; for Quashi was a stout man, and the elevation of his mind added vigor to his arm. At last, after a severe struggle Quashi got firmly seated on his master's breast, now panting and out of breath, and with his weight, his thighs, and one hand, secured him motionless. He then drew out a sharp knife, and while the other lay in dreadful expectation, helpless and shrinking into

himself, he thus addressed him:—"Master, I was bred up with you from a child; I was your playfellow when a boy; I have loved you as myself; your interest has been my own. I am innocent of what you suspect; but had I been guilty, my attachment to you might have pleaded for me; yet you condemn me to a punishment of which I must ever have borne the disgraceful marks,—thus only can I avoid it." With these words, he drew the knife with all his strength across his own throat, and fell down dead, without a groan, on his master, bathing him in his blood. (8–9)

While benevolence is possible between black and white, Quashi's narrative instructs, slavery violates black beauty as well as benevolence. Indeed, a newspaper that reprinted Quashi's narrative made explicit, one week before the appearance of the black man's tale, the value of the benevolence his master violated:

> The social principle in man is of such an expansive nature, that it cannot be confined within the circuit of a family, of friends, or a neighborhood; it spreads into wider systems, and draw [sic] men into larger confederacies, communities and commonwealths. It is in these only that the higher powers of our nature attain the highest improvement and perfection of which they are possible.[27]

Other young black men replicated Itanoko's and Quashi's beauty in American writing of the late eighteenth and early nineteenth centuries. One was Selico, whose narrative began appearing in 1798, in the *American Universal Magazine* and the *Philadelphia Minerva*. "Of all the negroes of Juida," the narrator assured his readers, "Selico was the blackest, the best made, and the most amiable."[28] Zami, who also appeared in the *American Universal Magazine* in 1798, was "aged eighteen, beautiful in shape as the Apollo of Belvedere, and full of spirit and courage." Zami's associate, Makandal, who is quite self-conscious about his allure and sexual prowess, states to his fellow slave, "Zami, you know the formidable power of my image."[29] Zembo appeared in the *Monthly Anthology and Boston Review* in 1807, "Tall and shapely as the palm, / A storm in war, in peace a calm; / Black as midnight without moon, / Bold and undisguised as noon."[30] This string of valorizing adjectives culminating in "undisguised" (that is, nude) is an early example of what Eric Lott identifies as "white men's investment in the black penis."[31] The vibrant sexuality of such young black men arises in their narratives, and the white men who penned these tales clearly identified with the sexual prowess they attributed to black men; even a prim condemnation of sexual excess does nothing to mask the enthusiastic language used to describe black men's sexual exploits.

In his adventures, Selico "penetrates" a sultan's seraglio and launches himself into a rollicking series of events in which he is rescued from torture and immolation only when he explains to the sultan that he is not a rapist, but a votary of love.[32] Zami is linked to the Apollo of Belvedere, a male nude of the young god known as the lover of Daphne, Coronis, and Cassandra. Significantly, perhaps, Apollo was the god of divine distance, who warned from afar of humankind's guilt and who spoke through oracles of the future and the will of his father, Zeus. Also, Apollo was a victim of his brother Hermes's thievery, but became reconciled to Hermes through Zeus's judgment. The significance of a black American Apollo—an erotic brother, betrayed and prophetic—is easy to see, whether or not this anonymous writer was fully aware of the resonance of his analogy. The remarkable sexual prowess of Zami's friend Makandal began early, according to the narrator of his tale:

> At the age of fifteen or sixteen, love began to inflame his breast, and to rule with the most astonishing impetuosity. He did not, however, entertain an exclusive passion for one object, but any woman who possessed any charms, received part of his homage, and inflamed his senses. His passion acquired energy and activity in proportion as the objects which inspired it were multiplied. In every quarter he had a mistress. It is well known, that among the negroes, enjoyment soon follows desire; and that satiety and indifference are the usual consequence; but Makandal, on the contrary, appeared always to be more enamored of those who had contributed to his felicity.

But Zami shares his fellow slave's avid sexuality, for Zami and his lover, Samba, meet "at a private place, where, amidst a grove of odiferous orange trees, on the turf, ever crowned with verdure, under a serene sky, never obscured by clouds, in the presence of the sparkling orbs of heaven, and favored by the silence of night, they renewed the ardent testimonies of their affection and comforted each other by the tenderest caresses." Unsurprisingly, "this happiness" leads Samba to discover that "she was about to become a mother."[33] Recalling LaVallée's men paired before nature's ravishing beauty, this scene involves two characters paired in a beautiful natural setting and a turn of the writer away from explicit description of the characters to an evocation of the sublimity of nature. The manly young Zembo, after slaying a tiger, similarly envelops a woman with "his eager arms" in "the broad palmetto shade."[34]

Itanoko, Otourou, Quashi, Selico, Zami, Makandal, and Zembo are revived in William, another young black man who becomes a white man's object of representation. An Anglican minister's account of his conversion of a black servant, William, appeared in 1815; it equally describes the minister's conversion to an erotic Christian love for the young black man. First a pamphlet, the story of William's conversion was reprinted as a newspaper account soon afterward.[35] William's story opens with an association of benevolence, liberty, and Christianity. The minister encounters William because, in the words attributed to the black man, his "master" is "good" and has made him "free" by awarding him his "liberty." William resides with his former master, who notices a spark of Christian faith in his black protégé and thus asks the minister for guidance. The minister visits William, discovering that he can read the Bible and that he is "a very young looking man with a sensible, lively, and pleasing turn of countenance." William, the minister discovers, is seeking "Christian friends" and is prone to "cry" upon contemplating Jesus. The manumitted slave's desire for friendship and his Christian sentimentalism not only recall LaVallée's distinction between "slave" and "friend," but also augur a benevolent consanguinity between the minister and the black man. Yet not everyone, the minister also discovers, regards William benevolently, for when he speaks of his love for Jesus, some white people call him "negro dog, and black hypocrite." The minister's interest in William intensifies when the black man describes his idea of Christian love, a straightforward version of universal benevolence: "Me love all men, black men and white men, too" (59–61).

After this first interview, the minister reports, he found himself drawn to visit William again soon. Mounting his horse, the minister soon finds himself in a scene echoing Itanoko and Dumont before the ravishing beauty of nature in Senegal, Zami and Samba "on the turf," and Zembo with his lover in his eager arms under the tropical trees. Choosing a scenic route along the coast in order to admire the beauties of nature, the minister discovers William alone there, an object in nature's beauty yet also an apparent soul mate who has likewise come out along the coast on a Christian mission—reading his Bible. In the minister's words:

> The road which I took lay over a lofty down or hill, which commands a prospect of scenery seldom equalled for beauty and magnificence. It gave birth to silent but instructive meditation. I cast my eye downwards a little to the left, towards a small cove, the shore of which consists of fine hard sand. It is surrounded by fragments of rock, chalk cliffs, and steep banks of broken earth. Shut out from human intercourse and dwellings, it seems formed for retirement and contemplation. On one of these rocks, I unexpectedly observed a man sitting with a book.

Peering down, the minister recognizes William. "The black color of his features, contrasted with the white rocks beside him," reports the minister, revealed the man as "my Negro disciple. . . . I rejoiced at this unlooked-for opportunity of meeting him in so solitary and interesting a situation." Roping his horse to a tree, the minister scrambles downhill to meet William. Even the description of the path suggests that the minister finds William in a masculine paradise, for the way to the black man was "formed by fishermen and shepherds' boys in the side of the cliff."

The minister's inference that he has found a soul mate who shares his appreciation of nature and his Christian commitment is soon amply confirmed, as their talk immediately turns to religion, leading William and the minister to address their likeness. "Me wish me was like you," declares William. "Like me, William? Why, you are like me, a poor helpless sinner," responds the minister. Both agree that the black man should fly to the minister who represents God. "Come to Jesus," says the minister. " 'Yes, Massa,' said the poor fellow weeping, 'me will come: but me come very slow; very slow, Massa; me want to run, me want to fly.— Jesus is very good to poor Negro, to send you to tell him this.' " After this positive evidence of William's faith, the minister uses a religious trope to broach the subject of William's semen and helps William fill his heart with God in a conversion experience. God's promise, asserts the minister, is that "he will not only 'pour water upon him that is thirsty,' but 'I will pour my Spirit upon thy seed, and my blessings upon thine offspring.' "[36] The understanding of blessing that the minister attributes to William is rooted in the body and its orifices, for the black man desires, he says, that God "purge me with hyssop, and I shall be clean." William's purgation is that of the body as well as that of the spirit (Ps 51:7). The biblical hyssop was probably a type of caper, but the hyssop long known to European and American folk medicine, a variety of mint, indeed purges the body. After purgation, William is filled with God:

> This was a new and solemn "house of prayer." The sea-sand was our floor, the heavens were our roof, the cliffs, the rocks, the hills, and the waves, formed the walls of our chamber. It was not indeed a "place where prayer was wont to be made;" but for this once, it became a hallowed spot: it will by me ever be remembered as such. The presence of God was there.—I prayed—The Negro wept. His heart was full. I felt with him, and wept likewise.

The praying finished, William and the minister must leave. The minister finds that he must trust in William's body as he ascends to his horse. "It was time for my return, I leaned upon his arm, as we ascended the steep cliff in my way back to my horse, which I had left at the top of the hill," reports the minister. "Humility and thankfulness were marked in his countenance. I leaned upon his arm with the feeling of a brother. It was a relationship I was happy to own—I took him by the hand at parting." As he rides out of the woods, the minister muses that his experience with William "produced a sensation not easy to be expressed." Still, the minister advances hopefully, "The last day will shew, whether our tears were not the tears of sincerity and Christian love."

The minister is again unable to be apart from William. Riding to the home of William's master, he finds the black man awaiting him in a grove. "Ah! Massa," cries William, "me very glad to see you, me think you long time coming." The minister then begins to call William "brother from Africa." Both William and the minister rivet their attention on the black man's body, William humbly claiming that his "soul" is "more black" than his "body" and the minister borrowing from the Bible to add new verses to a hymn featuring William: "Though he's black, he's comely too." Even the saintly William seems inevitably physicalized in the imagination of the minister, who declares of the black man, "He was a monument to the Lord's praise" (65–6). The point of William's tale is that the affectionate, eroticized consanguinity shared by the black man and the white man overturns the violent seizure that brought the African to America: "Me left father and mother one day at home, to go to get sea shells by the sea shore; and, as I was stooping down to gather them up, some white men came out of a boat, and took me away" (60).

White men opposed to slavery seem to have been captive to the black man's body and to the physical likeness between black and white. In 1803, Rhode Island slaveholder turned abolitionist Moses Brown interpreted a black man with white marks on his skin as "evidence of the sameness of human nature and corresponding with the declaration of the Apostle, that, 'God hath made of one blood all nations of men.' " Brown found likeness to the "easy and agreeable" Henry Moss through the black man's body: "His back below his shoulders is mostly as white as white people of his age, as are parts of his breast and even his nipples. The white parts of his skin and especially his anus are so transparent as to show the vains [*sic*] as distinct, as a white mans [*sic*]." Julie Ellison has accurately noted that "sensibility" encouraged attention to "the body [of] color," along with hope for an encounter defined by "interpersonal transparency." Here, in the writings of white antislavery men on black men, a transparency of the body as well as of the consciousness is invoked. The white man's benevolence to the black man seems inevitably to involve the latter's body.[37]

Revolutionary republicanism taught Americans that benevolence is the unifying force of society and that benevolence helps gird the virtuous man to fight against oppression. Republican ideology, liberal religion, and Calvinist orthodoxy all led Americans to believe that while monarchy had traditionally united society through authority, cruelty, and force, a new society in the United States could cohere by means of the natural benevolence inherent in humankind. The same newspapers that printed white-penned narratives of young black men in the 1790s told readers that "society being formed, it becomes essentially necessary that universal benevolence founded on the true principle of friendship should be its base and support."[38] "Friendship," Americans were encouraged to believe, "is the grand tie of society."[39] The analogy between black loyalty and republican loyalty is especially clear in the tale of "Scipio," a teenaged slave "greatly attached" to his master's son, with whom he had been reared. Scipio presciently refuses to trust a nurse hired to care for the sick white boy and, concealed under the boy's bed, comes to the rescue when the nurse fails in her duty.[40] Scipio's loyalty is likened to that of the "Patriots" during the War of Independence—the heart of the matter in white thinking about blacks and benevolence.

Between 1790 and 1820, antislavery writings represented intimacy between a black man and a white man with the sentimentalist vocabulary of benevolence: affection, attachment, brotherhood, disinterestedness, friendship, heart, intimacy, love, sentiment, sympathy, and tenderness. This antislavery writing usually noted that while slavery violates a natural right to liberty, it is also an abnegation of benevolence. According to this critique, which shared little with the individualistic abolitionism of the antebellum decades, the black must be either the "slave" or the "friend" of the white. Lamenting the cruelty of slavery, a 1791 newspaper article stated the essence of this critique: "The Negro has no friends."[41] Antislavery writers of the 1790s, moreover, sought to emphasize an irony they perceived in slavery. Blacks, they were often convinced, are especially benevolent and sympathetic, but are not accepted within the circuit of society. Thus white Americans in the postrevolutionary decades were in the remarkably complex situation of hearing that republican society could cohere only through benevolence, while they were living with blacks, whose enslavement and oppression surely violated benevolence and likeness and yet who were like whites in language, religion, and sex, and were even commonly believed to be especially benevolent.

Defenses of slavery in the revolutionary era and the early republic shared with antislavery writing the sentimentalist presuppositions about the unifying force of benevolence, but presupposed that affection and the other ties that unite individuals could not cross the race line. This defense of slavery was not an abandonment of sentimentalism—indeed its major spokesman, Jefferson, was both slave holder and sentimentalist—but rather was a revelation of the grim face of sentimentalism. Society must enslave or banish those who cannot join it benevolently, reasoned Jefferson, as he affirmed Montesquieu's arguments of the middle of the eighteenth century. The accumulated cruelties of slavery and the seemingly natural differences between black and white suggested to proslavery Americans that blacks were better slaves than free. Almost never did eighteenth-century Americans defending slavery claim that slavery is ultimately just. Rather, they claimed that blacks and whites, separated by past cruelties and by nature and, thus, unable to coexist benevolently in a free society, would turn on each other. Slavery's justice, therefore, was provisional, for only colonization—the expatriation of black Americans to Africa or the Caribbean—would allow manumission. Such American defenders of slavery could reveal their concern with black sexuality, whether in the notion that black men are more "amorous" or in the fear that miscegenation would become even more widespread in a free society in the Southern states than it was in a slave society. It was a commonplace of the day that liberating the slaves would lead to "a general commixture" and "Ethiopians [in] sexual intercourse with the whites," were the freed slaves to remain in the United States.[42] Indeed, this fear of future miscegenation, especially in the South, was a tacit affirmation of the desirability of the black male, since a slave society already offered white men considerable access to black women and any great increase in miscegenation would likely then be intercourse between black men and white women.

Erotic representations of black men by white men are not records of sexual activity, but rather records of beliefs and feelings.[43] The beliefs and feelings inscribed in these representations resulted from an encounter of white men, who were heirs and affiliates of sentimentalism, republicanism, and Christianity, with black men, who represented to white men a peculiar Other—like yet unlike, compatriot yet slave, masculine by nature yet restricted as lovers, husbands, fathers, and citizens by society. Erotic representations of black men by white men resulted from a rupture in the national (or hegemonic) discussion of race and slavery in postrevolutionary America. As discussed above, separation of the races, not benevolent association, was the standard of white leaders in postrevolutionary America. The means of this separation was to be the expatriation of black Americans to Africa or the Caribbean, and its fruit was the American Colonization Society. Despite this standard, there is considerable evidence that white Americans saw a likeness within black Americans, a likeness whose recognition they usually suppressed, perhaps because of guilt about slavery, or a reluctance to share with an underclass the benefits of their new society, or ambivalent feeling about blacks as at once near and far, an Other to white Americans. Even Jefferson, for instance, considered blacks to be natural republicans and Benjamin Banneker to be a true scientist—an ideal to which Jefferson himself aspired.[44]

As a new object of discourse, the black male body entered through this rupture in republican discourse about slavery. The white experience of likeness in blacks—feeling benevolence for them, recognizing their republican desire for liberty and their worship of the same God—could not be entirely suppressed, even if it could be barred from standard forms of social thought and religion. The account of one participant at a revival provides an excellent example of how the presence of blacks could be marginalized but not suppressed: he "cried out . . . 'God is among the people' " as he saw "prostrate on the ground . . . the learned pastor, the steady patriot, and the obedient son, crying 'Holy, holy, holy, Lord God Almighty,' " and then he listed those he saw in succession as he cast his "eyes a few paces" onwards. After the men were the women praising God, after the women were the worst sinners now converted, and after the worst sinners, at the limit of the sanctified, was "the poor oppressed African with his soul liberated, longing to be with his God."[45]

Neither in black writing nor in the white imagination would the figure of the black male remain at the margin; instead that figure came to the center to address the issue of masculine likeness. When William's minister brings the black man bodily as well as spiritually into the circle of benevolence, he emphasizes their sameness: "The religion of Jesus is everywhere the same. Its real possessors, whether black or white, all use the same language—all are actuated by the same love and animated by the same hopes through faith in the same Savior"(59). Like William's minister, some white American men, even an ardent expatriationist like Jefferson, found black men "like" themselves, an experience of likeness "not easy to be expressed" (as William's minister says) precisely because it was effectively barred from white discourse. Blurring the line between benevolent and erotic feelings, representations of the black male body became the means of saying what otherwise could barely be said, for the body of one man possesses an undeniable likeness to that of another. Representations of the black male body allowed physical equality to hint of political equality, while homoeroticism hinted of the likeness and benevolence that might join black and white.[46]

This black male, eroticized and republicanized, therefore reveals something essential in postrevolutionary American ideology. Black and masculine, the first body to be so fully represented in American publications extended and revealed the masculine likeness on which revolutionary republicanism was grounded, a likeness that became either threatening or inviting when it crossed between black and white. The republican literati recognized this likeness by acknowledging black men's natural republicanism and their alleged desires for white women, but explained the threat such likeness posed to the republic by arguing that the historic cruelties of slavery would always undermine a black-and-white republic. Republicans sought to expatriate blacks precisely to preserve the likeness required by American republicanism, but the figure of black man himself—oppressed, similar to white men, impossible to banish—helped to upset the precarious balance of late-eighteenth-century American thought.

Long noted by historians, this precariousness has been attributed to the republican effort to balance civic virtue with commercial development, as well as natural aristocracy with participatory democracy.[47] But this precariousness derived also from the republican insistence on setting black against white in a sentimentalist system of ideas and values. As antislavery pamphlets and newspaper writings of the era demonstrate, this balance could not be maintained in a slave society—nor, as leading republicans apprehensively recognized, in a postslavery republic. The black man disrupted republican ideology because he was too close to white men—too close to the affections, too much a republican—in a system of ideas and values demanding that he be separate. The response of leading republicans to the existence of the black man—expatriate him and other blacks to Africa—was so impractical that some other adjustment, ideological if not geographical, was required.

Liberal individualism, well known as a response to new economic, political, and geographical circumstances in the new republic, was also a readjustment of thought about slavery, race, and the future of a multiracial America. Liberal individualism recast the abolitionist understanding of slavery as no longer a violation of benevolence, but an infringement upon an individual's natural liberty. It allowed Americans to jettison the notion, on which eighteenth-century thought about race rested, that the black man is inevitably either "slave" or "friend" to the white, by replacing it with the notion that an ex-slave would rather be another atomistic individual in a free society.[48] As Americans came to realize that blacks and whites would inhabit the same continent, but could share little of the benevolence esteemed in eighteenth-century theology and social thought, revolutionary republicanism died and liberal individualism quickened.

The black man, in short, stirred questions about the possibilities of sentiment and liberty. Leslie A. Fiedler has argued that the "relationship between a white man and a colored one" in American literature was homoeroticized because the colored man represented white men's desire for uncivilized freedom, "a life of impulse and instinct," a life that could not be conceived heterosexually. This, in relation to black men, is wrong, and it has led to Fiedler's error in writing that "the Negro is a late comer to our literature, who has had to be adapted to the already existing image of the original Noble Savage. Our greatest Negro characters, including Nigger Jim, are, at their most moving moments, red men in blackface."[49] In his own right and in the white imagination, the black man is his own figure in American writing and thought, not a derivative of the Indian. At the transition from the eighteenth century to the nineteenth century, the black man represented in one part of the white imagination not uncivilized freedom but the eros and union of sentiment. William and his minister in the cove yearn for union, not a wild freedom. Paradoxically, the black man stirred questions about sentiment and liberty in a time when white Americans were not only developing a new notion of

freedom, free from the sentimentalist conditions of republicanism, but also grop-
ing towards a new, liberal ethos of race relations, one made inevitable by the
impracticality of expatriation.

NOTES

1. Sentimentalism, republicanism, and Christianity in late eighteenth-century and
early nineteenth-century America are well treated in the following works: A. Owen
Aldridge, *Thomas Paine's American Ideology* (Newark: University of Delaware Press, 1984);
Bernard Bailyn, *The Ideological Origins of the American Revolution* (Cambridge: Harvard Uni-
versity Press, 1967); James T. Kloppenberg, "The Virtues of Liberalism: Christianity,
Republicanism, and Ethics in Early American Political Discourse," *Journal of American His-
tory* 74 (1987): 9–33; Adrienne Koch, *The Philosophy of Thomas Jefferson* (New York: Columbia
University Press, 1943); Mark Valeri, "The New Divinity and the American Revolution,"
William and Mary Quarterly 46 (1989): 741–69; Garry Wills, *Inventing America: Jefferson's Declaration of Independence* (Garden City, N.J.: Doubleday, 1978); Gordon S. Wood, *The Creation of the
American Republic, 1776–1787* (New York: W. W. Norton, 1969). Gordon S. Wood, *The Radicalism of the American Revolution* (New York: Knopf, 1992); Conrad Edick Wright, *The Transformation of Charity in Postrevolutionary New England* (Boston: Northeastern University Press,
1992). Republicanism is a contentious issue in American historiography. A recent overview
with contributions by Drew R. McCoy, Isaac Kramnick, Robert E. Shalhope, Lance Ban-
ning, Peter S. Onuf, Cathy Matson, Gordon S. Wood, and George Athan Billias appears as
"The Republican Synthesis Revisited: Essays in Honor of George Athan Billias," *Proceedings of the American Antiquarian Society* 102 (1992): 69–224. My goal here is less to take a side in
the republican / liberal debate than to suggest that the evolution from republicanism to
liberalism was driven not only by economic factors (as is commonly accepted) but also by
racial and sexual factors in which the black man is a commanding presence. For recent
examples of the emphasis on economic factors, see the following: Robert E. Shalhope,
"Republicanism, Liberalism, and Democracy: Political Culture in the Early Republic,"
Proceedings of the American Antiquarian Society 102 (1992): 99–152, especially 117. Carroll Smith-
Rosenberg, "Dis–covering the Subject of the 'Great Constitutional Discussion,'
1786–1789," *Journal of American History* 79 (1992): 841–73, especially 847–49; Steven Watts,
The Republic Reborn: War and the Making of Liberal America, 1790–1820 (Baltimore: Johns
Hopkins University Press, 1987).

2. These writings share in the eighteenth-century "centrality of sentiment and pathos"
(see Janet Todd, *Sensibility: An Introduction* [New York: Meuthen, 1986] 1–9). Part of an
Americanization of British sentimentalism, the "poor negro" is a black, American variation of "virtue in distress," prey to racism and economic exploitation. Remodelling conventional representations of distressed women, the sentimentalist depictions of black men
were meant to elicit "humanity" from the reader. See G. J. Barker-Benfield, *The Culture of
Sensibility: Sex and Society in Eighteenth-Century Britain* (Chicago: University of Chicago Press,
1992), 219–34. The British background of sentimentalism is discussed in John Mullan, *Sentiment and Sociability: The Language of Feeling in the Eighteenth Century* (Oxford: Oxford University Press, 1988). I agree with a recent argument that the use of the term "Age of Sensibility" has been too narrow because it has not included the way in which "race relations and
sexual relations [were] represented in terms of sympathetic transactions" (Julie Ellison,

"Race and Sensibility in the Early Republic: Ann Eliza Bleeker and Sarah Wentworth Morton," *American Literature* 65 [1993]: 445–74, quotation from 446).

3. Paul Rahe, *Republics Ancient and Modern: Classical Republicanism and the American Revolution* (Chapel Hill: University of North Carolina Press, 1992), 128–33, 154–5. Eric Lott, *Love and Theft: Blackface Minstrelsy and the American Working Class* (New York: Oxford University Press, 1993). The songs of blackface minstrels of the middle of the nineteenth century were not as overtly political as those examined in this essay, specializing instead in verbal legerdemain such as the story of "Unkle Ned [who] had no wool on de top of his head." "De gals lub him so," apparently because "he had fingers like de cane brake, / Dough he had no eyes for her to see, / He hadn't any teeth to eat de corn cake, / So he had to leave de corn cake be" (*The Ethiopian Glee Book; Containing the Songs Sung by the Christy Minstrels, with Many Other Popular Negro Melodies, . . . by Gumbo Chaff, A.M.A., First Bango Player to the King of Congo* [Boston: Elias Howe, 1849], no. 3, 116).

4. Karen Sánchez-Eppler has noted the way in which a sentimentalism attributed to women led in the 1840s and 1850s to alluring depictions of black bodies, since "sentimental fiction constitutes an intensely bodily genre." "Miscegenation," she thus argues, "provides an essential motif of virtually all antislavery fiction" ("Bodily Bonds: The Intersecting Rhetoric of Feminism and Abolition," in *The New American Studies: Essays from Representations*, ed. Philip Fisher [Berkeley: University of California Press, 1991], 228–59, especially 235–40.

5. For some of Jefferson's statements on "benevolence," "emulation," "imitation," and "virtue," see the following: *The Writings of Thomas Jefferson*, ed. Andrew A. Lipscomb and Albert Ellery Bergh, 20 vols. (Washington: Thomas Jefferson Memorial Association, 1903), 1:116–9; 2:121, 177; 3:318; 12:393–4; 16:73; *The Papers of Thomas Jefferson*, ed. Julian P. Boyd et al. 25 vols. (Princeton: Princeton University Press, 1950–1992), 1:76–7; 8:637.

6. "How to attach people to one another and to the state? That was one of the central obsessions of the era," Gordon S. Wood has written of the revolutionary and postrevolutionary years. "The Enlightenment came to believe that there was 'a natural principle of attraction in man towards man,' and that these natural affinities were by themselves capable of holding the society together" (*Radicalism of the American Revolution*, 214). See also Wood, "Illusions and Disillusions in the American Revolution," in *The American Revolution: Its Character and Limits*, ed. Jack P. Greene (New York: New York University Press, 1987), 355–61, especially 358. For Montesquieu on sentiment and social unity, see Ann M. Cohler, *Montesquieu's Comparative Politics and the Spirit of American Constitutionalism* (Lawrence: University Press of Kansas, 1988), 45–55. For Montesquieu's influence on Jefferson, see Garrett Ward Sheldon, *The Political Philosophy of Thomas Jefferson* (Baltimore: Johns Hopkins University Press, 1991), 67. For the "ward-republics," see Richard K. Matthews, *The Radical Politics of Thomas Jefferson: A Revisionist Approach* (Lawrence: University Press of Kansas, 1984), 81–9.

7. *Writings of Thomas Jefferson*, 2:192, 201, 10:294–7; Drew R. McCoy, *The Last of the Fathers: James Madison and the Republican Legacy* (New York: Cambridge University Press, 1989), 277–303. Colonizationist efforts are discussed in the following works: Robert McColley, *Slavery and Jeffersonian Virginia*, 2d ed. (Urbana: University of Illinois Press, 1973), especially 129–30; Duncan J. MacLeod, *Slavery, Race, and the American Revolution* (New York: Cambridge University Press, 1974), 78–85; John Chester Miller, *The Wolf by the Ears: Thomas Jefferson and Slavery* (New York: Free Press, 1977), 164–70; P. J. Staudenraus, *The African Colonization Movement, 1816–1865* (New York: Columbia University Press, 1961); Larry E. Tise, *Proslavery: A History of the Defense of Slavery in America, 1770–1840* (Athens: University of Georgia Press, 1987), especially 190–1, 356–61.

8. For Montesquieu's influence in America, see the following: Thomas L. Pangle, *The Spirit of Modern Republicanism: The Moral Vision of the American Founders and the Philosophy of Locke* (Chicago: University of Chicago Press, 1988), 89–94; Paul Merrill Spurlin, *Montesquieu in America, 1760–1801* (Baton Rouge: Louisiana State University Press, 1940).

9. Charles-Louis de Secondat, baron de La Brede et de Montesquieu, *The Spirit of the Laws,* trans. and ed. Anne M. Cohler, Basia Carolyn Miller, and Harold Samuel Stone (New York: Cambridge University Press, 1989), 250.

10. *Writings of Thomas Jefferson,* 1:72–3; Rahe, *Republics,* 619, 636–7, 648; Dumas Malone, *Jefferson and His Times: The Sage of Monticello* (Boston: Little, Brown, 1981), 341–2.

11. Indeed, articulate black Americans of the postrevolutionary years, whether sophisticated ministers like Richard Allen and Lemuel Haynes or societies that left their beliefs inscribed in constitutions and proclamations, set their claims for black dignity exactly in the circle of benevolence. Richard Allen, *The Life Experience and Gospel Labors of the Rt. Rev. Richard Allen, To Which Is Annexed the Rise and Progress of the African Methodist Episcopal Church in the United States of America, Containing a Narrative of the Yellow Fever in the Year of Our Lord 1793, With an Address to the People of Color in the United States* (New York: Abingdon Press, 1960) (see 19–26, 50, 72, 75–89 for comments on benevolence); Ruth Bogin, "Liberty Further Extended: A 1776 Antislavery Manuscript by Lemuel Haynes," *William and Mary Quarterly* 40 (1983): 85–105 (see 98–104 for Haynes's use of "natural Effections" and "Disinterested Benevolence"); Lemuel Haynes, *The Nature and Importance of True Republicanism, with a Few Suggestions Favorable to Independence: A Discourse Delivered at Rutland (Vermont) the Fourth of July 1801, It Being the 25th Anniversary of American Independence* (Rutland, Vt.: Fay, 1801), 7–13; *Laws of the African Society, Instituted at Boston, Anno Domini, 1796* (Boston: The African Society, 1802); *The Proceedings of the Free African Union Society and the African Benevolent Society, Newport, Rhode Island 1780–1824,* ed. William H. Robinson (Providence: The Urban League of Rhode Island, 1976), 145–6.

12. Joseph LaVallée, *Le nègre comme il y a peu de blancs* (Paris: Buisson, 1789). The work was reprinted in France in 1795 and 1800. "Antislavery" deserves a comment here that applies to all the texts examined in this essay. The antislavery thought expressed in these texts is at least as much sentimental and paternalistic as fraternal and egalitarian. The African American antislavery thought of its day, such as that of Lemuel Haynes and John Marrant, rejected its paternalism. Lacking interest in the self-determination of African Americans, the authors of the texts examined here partook of a white paternalism that would come to be important in antebellum proslavery thought. A belief in sentiment as the force that would alleviate slavery led the authors examined here into a paternalism in which the white man frees the black as the two come to recognize their sentimental ties. Thus even the claims of black superiority in beauty and sentiment could serve to subordinate the black man waiting for the recognition of his sentiments and for his liberation.

13. Joseph LaVallée, *The Negro As There Are Few White Men,* 3 vols., trans. J. Trapp (London: n.p., 1790); *The Negro Equalled by Few Europeans* (London: Robinson, 1790); *The Negro Equalled by Few Europeans* (Dublin: Byrne, 1791); "The Negro Equalled by Few Europeans," *The American Museum, or Universal Magazine* 9 (Jan.–June 1791): 53–60, 99–107, 145–53, 205–13, 257–65, 313–24; 10 (July–Dec. 1791): 29–40, 77–88, 129–44, 185–200, 241–56, 285–303; *The Negro Equalled by Few Europeans,* 2 vols. (Philadelphia: William W. Woodward, 1801). All citations, except as noted, are from the 1801 printing, and will be made in parentheses in the text.

14. *The Negro As There Are Few White Men,* 1:14.

15. *The Negro As There Are Few White Men*, 1:61. By the end of the eighteenth century, the word "parts" had a well established sexual connotation as meaning "privy parts" (see *Oxford English Dictionary*, 2d ed., s.v. "parts").

16. *The American Museum, or Universal Magazine* 9 (1791): 275. Jefferson's republican "good man" is "he whose every thought and deed by rules of virtue moves," who assumes a "neighbor's" role, "not stranger-like" but integrated into his community and uninterested in profiting from his peers (*Writings of Thomas Jefferson*, 16:110-1). For Timothy Dwight's Federalist ideal of masculine neighborliness, see *Greenfield Hill*, in *The Major Poems of Timothy Dwight*, ed. William J. McTaggart and William K. Bottorff (Gainesville, Fla.: Scholars Facsimiles & Reprints, 1969), 481-95. Neither Jefferson nor Dwight includes any notion of masculine beauty in these representations of white men.

17. This notion of black benevolence was probably related to a belief that blacks were likely to participate in what modern social scientists describe as "same-sex dyadic ties," which, some scholars speculate, were extensions of "shipmate relationships" formed in transport from Africa. See Sidney W. Mintz and Richard Price, *An Anthropological Approach to the Afro-American Past: A Caribbean Perspective* (Philadelphia: Institute for the Study of Human Issues, 1976), 22-3.

18. The first translation takes a slightly different approach to this meeting: "Well shaped, straight, endowed with the happiest and sweetest countenance, he was possessed of those secret charms which conquer the heart at first sight. I did not hold out. . . . Sit by me, said I, so beautiful a face, cannot be without a noble soul" (*The Negro As There Are Few White Men*, 1:65).

19. *The Negro As There Are Few White Men*, 1:80-98. By the end of the eighteenth century, according to the *OED*, the word "embrace" had a long history of association with sexual intercourse, the word "violate" had a long history of meaning rape, and the word "voluptuous" had a long history of meaning sensual; "ravish" had a long history of meaning rape, while "ravisher" meant in particular rapist.

20. Caribbean plantation owners preferred buying new stocks of young Africans to encouraging indigenous slave families, since the cost of buying an African was considered less than the cost of rearing a child to be a slave.

21. *The Negro As There Are Few White Men*, 1:152, 155. Itanoko also reports that when Theodore chose a manservant, "[o]ne may sufficiently guess that luxuriance of shape had been more consulted, than personal qualifications" (156).

22. In *White over Black: American Attitudes toward the Negro, 1550-1812* (Chapel Hill: University of North Carolina Press, 1968), 136-78, Winthrop D. Jordan explores the sexual implications of the fact that white "desire and aversion rested on the bedrock fact that white men perceived Negroes as being both alike and different from themselves" (137). Winthrop's interest is in explaining both miscegenation and the "fundamentally sexual" character of "white men's insecurity vis-à-vis the Negro" (156). My interest, however, is in white men's eroticization of black men as an extension of sentiment, part of a counterdiscourse to republicanism that still shared the sentimentalist presuppositions of leading republicans.

23. Two periodical versions are "Quashi, or the Desperate Negro," *Massachusetts Magazine, or Monthly Museum of Knowledge and Rational Entertainment* 5 (1793): 583-4, and "Quashi the Negro, a True Story," *Vergennes Gazette* 1 (18 October 1798): 4. A pamphlet version which nearly duplicates the 1793 version, is *The Story of Quashi; or, the Desperate Negro* (Newburyport: W. & J. Gilman, 1820); all citations, except as noted, are from this version, and will be made

in parentheses in the text. The source is apparently Reverend James Ramsay, *An Essay on the Treatment and Conversion of African Slaves in the British Sugar Colonies* (London: James Phillips, 1784), 248–53.

24. "Quashi the Negro," 4.

25. Ramsay, *Essay*, 251.

26. The 1820 version's "unrased" replaces "unraised" in the 1793 version: either an error or else a self-conscious effort to use "unrased" (a variant of "unrazed") to suggest even more of the violence of whipping than does "unraised." Since there are no other misspellings in the pamphlet, and since it is a well-produced, illustrated booklet, I suspect that the change was made self-consciously.

27. "Duties of Society," *Vergennes Gazette* 1 (11 October 1798): 4.

28. "Selico, an African Tale," *American Universal Magazine* 4 (1798): 183–92, quotation from 185. Selico's tale was also printed in the *Philadelphia Minerva* 4 (1798): 13–21, but citations are taken from the former.

29. "Account of a Remarkable Conspiracy Formed by a Negro on the Island of St. Domingue," *American Universal Magazine* 4 (1798): 193–7, quotations from 196, 197. This was reprinted in the *New York Minerva* 2 (1823): 74–5, but the 1798 version is the source of all references here.

30. James Montgomery, "Zembo and Nila: An African Tale," *Monthly Anthology and Boston Review* 4 (1807): 603–4, quotation from 604.

31. Lott, *Love and Theft*, 121.

32. "Selico," 188–9. By the end of the eighteenth century, according to the *OED*, the word "penetration" had a well established sexual meaning of penile penetration.

33. "Account of a Remarkable Conspiracy," 193–4, 197.

34. Montgomery, "Zembo and Nila," 604.

35. I have used "Narrative of a Negro Servant," *Christian Messenger* 1, no. 8 (13 November 1816): 59–61; no. 9 (20 November 1816): 65–6. Further citations will be made in parentheses in the text. At least seven other printings appeared before 1820: *The Negro Servant, and the Young Cottager* (New York: Whiting and Watson, 1815); *The Negro Servant, an Authentic and Interesting Narrative* (Andover, Mass.: Flagg and Gould, 1815); *The Negro Servant, an Authentic and Interesting Narrative* (Boston, 1815); *The Negro Servant, an Authentic and Interesting Narrative* (New York: Fanshaw and Clayton, 1815); *The African Servant* (Andover, Mass., 1816); *The Negro Servant: An Authentic Narrative* (Boston: American Tract Society, 1816[?]); *The Negro Servant* (Philadelphia: Wm. Bradford, 1817).

36. Again according to the *OED*, the word "seed" had a long history of meaning semen by the end of the eighteenth century.

37. Moses Brown Anti-Slavery Papers, 1803 folder, Rhode Island Historical Society; Ellison, "Race and Sensibility," 447–9. For Moses Brown and other Quaker opponents of slavery, see David Brion Davis, *The Problem of Slavery in the Age of Revolution, 1770–1828* (Ithaca: Cornell University Press, 1975), 213–54.

38. "On Friendship," *Herald of Vermont* 1 (23 July 1792): 4.

39. "Friendship," *Vergennes Gazette* 2 (27 February 1800): 4.

40. "Fidelity; or, Scipio, the Negro Boy," *Christian Messenger* 1 (12 March 1817): 196.

41. "A Fragment," *Morning Ray* 1 (29 November 1791): 3.

42. "On the Moral and Political Effects of Negro Slavery," *Middlebury Mercury* 2 (6 July 1803): 1–2. See also Jonathan Edwards, Jr., *The Injustice and Impolicy of the Slave-Trade,*

and of the Slavery of the Africans (Providence: John Carter, 1792), 35–7, for the necessary choice between miscegenation and separation after the end of slavery.

43. Thomas W. Lacqueur is obviously right in noting that discourse about sexual activity is quite different from the activity itself ("Sexual Desire and the Market Economy during the Industrial Revolution," in *Discourses of Sexuality: From Aristotle to AIDS*, ed. Domna C. Stanton [Ann Arbor: University of Michigan, 1992], 185–215, especially 200).

44. For Jefferson on blacks' natural republicanism, see *Writings of Thomas Jefferson*, 1:72–3. An excellent analysis of Jefferson's ambivalent feelings about blacks, touching on his thoughts about Banneker, is Frank Shuffelton, "Thomas Jefferson: Race, Culture, and the Failure of the Anthropological Method," in *A Mixed Race: Ethnicity in Early America*, ed. Frank Shuffelton (New York: Oxford University Press, 1993), 257–77.

45. "Religious Intelligencer," *Vermont Mercury* 1 (10 May 1802): 2. Albert J. Raboteau notes that worship of the same God implied an egalitarianism across the race line; see "Slave Autonomy and Religion," *Journal of Religious Thought* 38 (1981–2): 51–64, and "The Slave Church in the Era of the American Revolution," in *Slavery and Freedom in the Age of the American Revolution*, ed. Ira Berlin and Ronald Hoffman (Charlottesville: University Press of Virginia, 1983), 196–211.

46. Carroll Smith-Rosenberg has argued that the idea of the black slave was used by white Americans to define and stabilize, by way of contrast, the idea of a middle-class individual, free and productive ("Dis-covering the Subject," 861–2). The likeness recorded in the texts I discuss here threatened to subvert that contrast, so discussion of black-white likeness was pushed out of postrevolutionary white discourse.

47. The most distinguished commentary on commercial development and participatory democracy in postrevolutionary America is that of Joyce Appleby: "The Social Origins of American Revolutionary Ideology," *Journal of American History* 54 (1978): 935–58; "What Is Still American in the Political Philosophy of Thomas Jefferson?" *William and Mary Quarterly* 39 (1982): 287–309; "Commercial Farming and the 'Agrarian Myth' in the Early Republic," *Journal of American History* 58 (1982): 833–49; *Capitalism and a New Social Order: The Republican Vision of the 1790s* (New York: Oxford University Press, 1984); "Republicanism and Ideology," *American Quarterly* 37 (1985): 461–73; "Republicanism in New and Old Contexts," *William and Mary Quarterly* 43 (1986): 20–34.

48. See Louis S. Gerteis, *Morality and Utility in American Antislavery Reform* (Chapel Hill: University of North Carolina Press, 1987), 20–2; Daniel J. McInerney, " 'A Faith for Freedom': The Political Gospel of Abolitionism," *Journal of the Early Republic* 11 (1991): 371–93, especially 374–5.

49. Leslie A. Fiedler, *Love and Death in the American Novel*, rev. ed. (New York: Stein and Day, 1966), 159, 339, 366, 375–7.

CHAPTER FIVE

Remembering Metacom

*Historical Writing and the Cultures of Masculinity
in Early Republican America*

Philip Gould

No figure was more vilified in colonial New England than Metacom, or "King Philip" as he was called, the Wampanoag sachem (or leader) who in June 1675 precipitated the conflict that would forever bear his name. King Philip's War destroyed half of New England's towns, decimated its population, and left the region's economy all but ruined.[1] Although historians today have come to acknowledge the colonial aggression that brought on the war, their Puritan forebears were not so objective. Puritan histories, such as Increase Mather's *A Brief History of the War with the Indians in New-England* (1676) and William Hubbard's *A Narrative of the Trouble with the Indians in New-England* (1677), typically figured the conflict as part of the archetypal struggle between God's saints and Satan's minions in the American wilderness. Like Milton's Satan in *Paradise Lost*, the Puritan version of Metacom was an evil demagogue who unleashed violent passions to disorder the world.

In the early republic, however, the historical representation of Metacom significantly changed. Now demonized *and* eulogized, Metacom stood as a cultural trope for the complex and tenuous relations between republicanism and sentimentalism from the 1780s into the 1830s. The contrast between colonial and republican historians attests to the cultural influence of gendered ideologies about the nature of "manhood," which not so much displaced as refigured the representation of race in the early republic. This essay relocates the meaning of "racial" history in the context of issues of masculine identity, political authority, and republican citizenship, as opposed to the entire critical tradition which views nineteenth-century representations of Native Americans in light of the period's westward expansion. Despite the methodological differences among works by Richard Slotkin, Ronald Takaki, Brian Dippie, and Lucy Maddox, their original and unique discussions of literary complicity in the claims of Manifest Destiny are premised on a historically simplified dichotomy between "savagery" and "civilization."[2]

I would like to complicate this racial dichotomy by invoking the gendered ideology of sentiment as a context for race. In this way, I want to propose an androgynous model of republican manhood in postrevolutionary culture. My conception of androgyny is less concerned with psychosocial pathologies[3] than with issues of citizenship and political authority in the early republic. Susan Juster, for example, has explored both the psychological and the political dimensions of androgyny, employing Victor Turner's concept of "liminality" to show how, for eighteenth-century New Englanders, the evangelical state of grace was an ephemerally androgynous zone "in which the masculine and the feminine [were] dissolved into an undifferentiated whole."[4] According to Juster, this religious dynamic had political significance as well during the postrevolutionary era, since communally minded women asserted their individual "moral agency," and individualistic men resituated their identities, in the androgynous *communitas* of believers: "The metaphor of androgyny for the state of grace connoted far more than a sexual middle ground: it signaled the ultimate compromise between two competing principles of social organization ["individual" and "community"] which had frayed the evangelical community from its inception."[5] I want to pursue the political significance of such a model of androgyny by considering historical rather than evangelical discourses.[6] In both, the virtue of the "affections" characterized the converted saint and the republican citizen equally. Yet in the realm of civic politics with which historical writing was concerned, the androgynous realm of sentimental affections mediated not between individual and community but between competing—and gendered—conceptions of community itself. The historical figure of Metacom registers this cultural mediation and reveals the political slippage in the modern ideal of sentimental manhood itself.

ı⁴ı

Between 1776 and 1787, revolutionary America negotiated both the institutional and the ethical meanings of a "republic." The foundational text for this reformulation of modern republicanism is, of course, James Madison's *Federalist* #10, which departed from a tradition that had stretched from Aristotle to Montesquieu by incorporating "interests" and "factions" into republican theory. Yet it is important to realize that the Constitutional settlement of 1787–8 did not so much abandon as recontextualize the importance of republican "virtue." The reformulation, in other words, of "mixed" government based upon institutional checks and balances was accompanied by a republican culture that still openly acknowledged the importance of civic behavior. The norms of "republican" virtue, however, changed significantly during the eighteenth and early nineteenth centuries. Virtue, after all, traditionally derived from the Roman concept of *virtu* (the etymological source of "virility"), and in this classical context signified the patriotic vigilance and martial valor requisite to the republic's survival. As J. G. A. Pocock has argued, the classical understanding of citizenship, which later influenced

American Revolutionaries, allowed for the full expression of male personality within the context of the *res publica*. The *vivere civile*—the ideal of active citizenship—described an exclusively masculine politics whereby elites served in government and the masses in military defense.[7] The ability to fully express one's identity, in other words, was restricted to republican men.

The emergence of sentimental culture in eighteenth-century Anglo-America gradually eroded this exclusively masculine political ideology. Commensurate with eighteenth-century ideals of "enlightenment," which privileged the modern virtues of benevolence, refinement, and sociability, virtue underwent a process of feminization. As Gordon S. Wood has argued,

> Virtue became less the harsh self-sacrifice of antiquity and more the willingness to get along with others for the sake of peace and prosperity. Virtue became identified with decency. Whereas the ancient classical virtue was martial and masculine . . . the new virtue was soft and feminized and capable of being expressed by women as well as men.[8]

Indeed one might argue, along with Ruth Bloch, that virtue became associated fundamentally (though not exclusively) with women: "Virtue, if still regarded as essential to the public good and republican state, became ever more difficult to distinguish from private benevolence, personal manners and female sexual propriety."[9]

The androgynous nature of early national manhood lay in the simultaneity of these gendered forms of virtue describing the elusive concept of "republicanism." These gendered forms of identity also describe competing modes of relation in which the distinctions between the "citizen" and the "member of the human family" became morally problematic. This is apparent, for example, in the preface to Charles Goodrich's *The History of the United States* (1829), one of the many popular, didactic histories of the antebellum period, and one which was reprinted numerous times for both adults and schoolchildren: "In general, it may be said, that the proper end of all reading is to make '*good men and good citizens.*' But by what particular steps is History [*sic*] to subserve this end."[10] Such a distinction between manhood and citizenship, however, suggests significant slippage in republican masculinity itself. Why even distinguish between the two?

The revolutionary era's most renowned medical and educational theorist, Benjamin Rush, confronted this problem at a crucial moment in "A Plan for the Establishment of Public Schools and the Diffusion of Knowledge in Pennsylvania" (1786). Claiming that sentimental humanitarianism was completely compatible with American republicanism, Rush notably recoils when he considers the American schoolboy's civic instruction:

> He must be taught to love his fellow creatures in every part of the world, but he must cherish with a more intense and peculiar affection, the citizens of Pennsylvania and of the United States. . . . [W]e impose a task upon human nature, repugnant alike to reason, revelation and the ordinary dimensions of the human heart, when we require him to embrace, with equal affection, the whole family of mankind.[11]

The stability that Rush would bring to this ontological and political problem of citizens and the human family did not, however, provide a satisfactory solution for the postrevolutionary generation. As American political culture was gradually democratized over the next thirty years, it nevertheless continued to restrict political rights according to gender and race, and thereby allowed the problematic distinction between citizenry and humanity to fester. As late as 1834, an article in one of the more influential literary journals of the early nineteenth century, the *North American Review*, considered historical writing's ability to inculcate virtue and claimed that "[t]he great object of history is to teach us how we may become good citizens, not only as the ancients understood the word, but as its present and broad comprehensive meaning denotes,—considering every individual as a member of the human family."[12]

Joan Scott has argued persuasively that "gender identification, although it always appears coherent and fixed, is, in fact, highly unstable. . . . The principle of masculinity rests on the necessary repression of feminine aspects—of the subject's potential bisexuality—and introduces conflict into the opposition of masculine and feminine."[13] In postrevolutionary America, this process was highly contingent upon shifting rhetorical and political contexts. Whereas Andrew Jackson's cultivation of the political persona of "Old Hickory"—the war hero who had saved the republic during the Battle of New Orleans—appropriated the languages and cultural forms of classical, masculine republicanism, the androgynous representation of the republican man whose vigorous industry and vigilant selflessness were refined by the sentimental capacities of the affections was far more characteristic of the era. In *American Biography* (1794–8), for example, the didactic minister and historian Jeremy Belknap praises the Pilgrim founder William Brewster as a model of republican manhood in just these terms: "In his private conversation, he was social, pleasant and inoffensive, yet when occasion required, he exercised that fortitude which *true virtue* inspires, but mixed with such tenderness, that his reproofs gave no offense."[14] Such gendered rhetoric, moreover, could actually confuse sexual identity. Consider the following two passages from Samuel Knapp's *Female Biography* (1834):

> A sweetness of temper, obliging courtesy, and mildness of manners, joined to an engaging candor of sentiment, spread a glory over his reputation, and endeared his person to all his acquaintances.

> [She] was a woman of singular endowments. She was beautiful, accomplished, pious and learned. She was eloquent and fascinating, and wrote with genius and facility. . . . Her temper was sweet and her conversation fascinating.[15]

Without any pronominal clues, the sexual identities of Aaron Burr, Sr., the eighteenth-century minister and President of the College of New Jersey, and his wife, the famous colonial diarist Esther Edwards Burr, would be hopelessly confused. The Burrs' shared virtue of "sweetness" suggests the androgynous potential of the norm of a refined, enlightened sensibility. Yet, as Belknap's description of Brewster indicates, the cultural legacy of Whig republicanism simultaneously demanded an exclusively "masculine" vigilance that was crucially premised upon clear distinctions between the citizen and the noncitizen.

This gendered tension suggests two cultural problems endemic to historical narratives. The first concerns the inequities of the revolutionary settlement itself. Who *were* "American" citizens? Why would benevolence be relegated to the national family instead of the human family? Hence the rhetorical instability of "civic humanism" as the phrase that signified the paradox of humanity and citizenship. The second issue concerns the problem of "effeminacy." How could republican men negotiate traditionally "masculine" virtues amidst an emergent sentimental culture privileging their affective identities?[16]

᛭

Historical accounts of Metacom during the early republic inscribe this political form of androgyny and the problematic cultural issues attending it. Critics have begun to articulate the importance of gender to literary treatments of race in the early antebellum era's historical writing. Nina Baym has argued, for example, that both male and female writers of "Indian stories" during the 1820s "revised each other from gendered perspectives." According to Baym, the epic poem *Yamoyden* (1820) by James W. Eastburn and Robert C. Sands prompted Lydia Child's novel, *Hobomok* (1824), which in turn elicited James Fenimore Cooper's *The Last of the Mohicans* (1826).[17] Yet such a summation delimits critical attention to "literary" texts. Early nationals, however, read historical romances alongside nationalist histories written for young and old alike. Both genres self-consciously aimed to cultivate the proper, albeit elusive, codes of republican virtue.[18]

Metacom's historical representation during this era registers the political tensions inhering in the trope of sentimental republican manhood. National-minded and generally conservative historians rewrote the history of King Philip's War in the image of the American Revolution: they used the event metaphorically to recover an anachronistically masculine form of republicanism. This involved extolling not just Puritan combatants but often Metacom himself. After vilifying the Wampanoag sachem as an evil demagogue who nearly ruined colonial New England, these historians uncannily transformed him (often in the very next breath) into an exemplar of republican *virtu*. No less than Old Hickory himself, Metacom "was one worthy of the most sagacious statesmen of any age."[19] As a classical republican icon, of sorts, Metacom was likened to Caesar or Alexander the Great, and the Wampanoags lauded as "a free and independent people."[20] In their *Compendious History of New England* (1808), the staunch Calvinists Jedidiah Morse and Elijah Parish finally admitted that Philip "was a deep politician, with a heart glowing with love of his country, and burning with indignation against the prosperous strangers, who were extending themselves over the inheritance of his fathers."[21] As both hero and villain, then, Metacom's bifocal reputation marked an important ambiguity over the very status of masculine "passions," which could be configured alternatively as selfless patriotism or unrestrained ambition. A demagogue during the war, a heroic patriot afterwards: the uncertain political status of the passions made the Other into the paradoxical bane and savior of republicanism.

Yet the affective language surrounding Metacom, even in these staid historical accounts, registers the emergence of a culture of sentimental republican manhood during this era. As a historical symbol, Metacom helped to mediate cultural changes in the meanings of republican manhood. One sees this particularly in early nineteenth-century belletristic writings, where genteel romantics capitalized on the nostalgic potential of Native American heroism to produce sentiment for purposes of melodrama. In Washington Irving's portrait of Metacom in *The Sketch Book of Geoffrey Crayon, Gent.* (1820), for example, Metacom's benevolent heart becomes the site of both cultural and literary transformations. "Philip of Pokanoket" recycles the cant of Whig republicanism to codify an exclusively male conception of civic virtue: "Proud of heart, and with an untameable love of natural liberty," Crayon exults, "[Philip] preferred to enjoy it among the beasts of the forests . . . rather than bow his haughty spirit to submission and live dependent and despised in the ease and luxury of the settlements."[22] Note here how Crayon reinforces the noble savage stereotype by invoking a masculine, Whiggish rhetoric of "luxury" to declaim the very "march of civilization" that the sentimentality itself validates. Philip's demise is both sentimental and tragic, as Crayon affectively humanizes him in ways that *necessitate* his ultimate removal. Such a formula is made possible by the infusion of benevolent humanitarianism into Whig patriotism. Philip, Crayon emphasizes, was "alive to the softer feelings of connubial love and paternal tenderness, and to the generous sentiment of friendship."[23] So, by ascribing the modern virtues of republicanism to the Native American sachem, Crayon runs dangerously close to suggesting a place for Native Americans in colonial—and, by extension, nineteenth-century—America. Through the logic of sentimental manhood, however, this place is ultimately erased. Only in Metacom's death are the historical drama and sentimentalization of manhood equally achieved.

Women writers of this period pursued even further the cultural changes in the meaning of republican manhood. Although she did not take up Metacom per se, Lydia Maria Child used one of his Wampanoag forebears to explore the androgynous possibilities of sentimental masculinity in her first novel, *Hobomok* (1824). Set in first-generation New England, *Hobomok* recounts the story of a Puritan woman, Mary Conant, who marries and conceives a child with a Native American, Hobomok, only to return to a "normal" life in the Puritan community. The presence of the Native American complicates the typical marriage plot of historical romance, for Hobomok's virtues make him—at least until the end of the novel— the appropriately "republican" mate for Mary. In order to sanction miscegenation, Child feminizes Hobomok in a way that still draws upon the language of Whig republicanism, thereby reconstituting the contexts for republicanism and manhood through the novel's thematics of marriage. All of Hobomok's virtues—his "manly beauty," "vigor and elasticity," and "vigorous elegance of proportion"—essentialize him according to a recognizable model of gender rooted in Revolutionary republicanism.[24]

In this androgynous synthesis lies revision as well. As in *The Sketch Book*, the Native American hero is cast in the image of enlightened virtues. In this regard, Hobomok's refinement is crucial: "His long residence with the white inhabitants of Plymouth had changed his natural fierceness of manner into haughty, dignified reserve; and even that seemed softened as his dark, expressive eye rested on Conant's daughter" (36). Hence his final transformation—the moment when he realizes Mary's enduring love for the newly reappeared Charles Brown, her Episcopalian suitor, and therefore relinquishes her—conveniently forecloses the novel's miscegenation plot according to the enlightened norms of reciprocal, affectional marriage relations. The cultural refinement of Hobomok, moreover, politicizes sentimental benevolence as a mode of relation inconsistent with the classical norms of the *vivere civile*. For Hobomok's heart consistently undermines his political sense of "duty": his rival, Corbitant, taunts him for sensitivities that derive from female "influence"—" 'Hobomok saves his tears for the white-faced daughter of Conant' " (33)—and when Hobomok recites to Mary the legend of Tatobem, a Pequot sachem torn between political duty and conjugal affections, he actually is acting more as autobiographer than folklorist. In confessing his own dilemma, and in ultimately giving himself over to Mary, Hobomok undergoes a process that in effect describes the domestication of a "manly" ideal.

What Child accomplishes in *Hobomok* is to sentimentally politicize the historical romance's marriage plot in a way that suggests the possibility of miscegenation in Puritan—and republican—society. Even though she ultimately recoils from such a radical vision of racial relations, she reinterprets the stereotype of the "noble savage" into a model of feminized republican manhood that Charles Brown eventually must emulate. Not only does Hobomok sacrifice political authority for conjugal love, but he also abdicates authority within conjugal relations in the name of disinterested benevolence. As Mary acknowledges, it is a " 'kind noble-hearted creature' " (137) who relinquishes her in the end. Hobomok's displacement from the text is made possible only by Charles Brown's simultaneous feminization at the Conant hearth. As Carolyn Karcher has argued, Brown and Hobomok are doubles throughout the novel,[25] yet this doubling is consummated only by Brown's eventual capacity for "chastened tenderness" (63). Only when Brown can emulate the Native American hero's holy act of self-denial can the marriage plot be resolved.

Native American heroism thus provided the emotive materials for creating historical melodrama, and the political materials for renegotiating republican virtue. Male writers who followed Child, however, used the life of Metacom to revise this script for American manhood. They continued to exploit the sentimental effects necessary to historical melodrama, but Metacom's death now began to encode different political messages. The most obvious instance of this is John Stone's play, *Metamora; or the Last of the Wampanoags*, which opened at the Park Theater in New York in 1829. The renowned actor, Edwin Forrest, had announced a five-hundred-dollar prize for the best new play whose hero was a Native American, and he of course played the role of Philip in the first production. Modern critics of *Metamora* (yet another name for Metacom) have emphasized the importance of masculine sentiment to both the play's representation of Native Americans and its effects on contemporary audiences.[26] Yet *Metamora*'s contemplation of androgyny and its politicization of gender reveal larger problems in the relations between gender and authority in early republican America.

What is crucial in *Metamora* is the gendered source of republican tragedy: the Native American hero's sentimental virtues doom him politically. Indeed, what Juster has called "the feminine realm of flux and dissolution"[27] within androgynous identity undermines Metamora's political authority. In this way, the play registers the fragility of the trope of republican manhood. Throughout the drama, Metamora wavers between republican vigilance ("Death! Death, or my nation's freedom!" he cries, paraphrasing Patrick Henry[28]) and New Testament love and altruism. In these oscillations, the text actually capitalizes upon the very affective epistemologies that its thematic design shows to be destructive: its melodramatic power derives from the same masculine form of sentiment that eventually sinks the Native American sachem. In Metamora himself, Stone dramatizes irreconcilable tensions within the cultural trope of masculinity, pointing up inconsistencies where other writers had glossed over them. The sachem hates the English yet discourses on religious toleration, and is a consummate warrior yet tenderly refuses to execute an adversary who will surely betray him.

Metamora's chastened heart, moreover, results from the very female "influence" that transforms figures like Hobomok and Charles Brown. In parallel scenes, both Puritan and Native American women successfully appeal to his sentimental capacities and refine his better nature. When his wife, Nahmeokee, convinces him to spare the life of a political enemy, Metamora's words resound with verbal irony foreshadowing his political demise: "Come not near me," he admonishes her, "Or thou wilt make my heart soft, when I would have it hard like the iron" (37). But it is much too late—his avowal of classical *virtu* is full of sound and fury but signifies absolutely nothing. Thus Stone's play dramatizes Metamora's destruction as a way of thematizing the politically untenable nature of sentimental republicanism. Moreover, Metamora's death belies a political paradox at the heart of the "Indian" melodrama: the Native American hero exhibits republican virtues that implicitly legitimate claims both for Native American citizenship and public identity, but these claims are ultimately erased by either his death or (in Hobomok's case) his disappearance.

The gendered stakes of historical romance allow for reconsideration of the genre's treatment of captivity. Most discussions of the process by which the Indian captivity narrative was adapted by the early American novel focus on race rather than gender; this is certainly the case with scholarship on the work of James Fenimore Cooper.[29] Less well known to most readers than the popular Leatherstocking Tales is Cooper's *The Wept of Wish-ton-Wish* (1829), which takes place on the Connecticut frontier during King Philip's war. Like *The Last of the Mohicans,* however, this novel is structured as a series of captivities, and, I would argue, Cooper actually makes racial captivity the means by which the novel meditates on the nature of gender, power, authority, and republican citizenship.

The captivity of Conanchet, the sachem of the Narragansetts and Metacom's most important ally in the war against the English, as I will show, testifies to Cooper's hostility toward the feminized revisions of masculine sentiment by women writers like Child. Early on in *The Wept,* Conanchet is taken captive by the Heathcote family and held there for quite some time until a Native American attack finally releases him. If Conanchet is a "wavering" hero in the tradition of Sir Walter Scott, his divided nature arises as much from sentimental as racial loyalties. While in captivity, Conanchet is much less susceptible to the zealous Puritan Mark Heathcote's proselytizing than he is to Ruth Heathcote's unqualified benevolence. The changes Conanchet undergoes at the Heathcote hearth later destroy him. His embodiment of these gendered modes of republican virtue is apparent, for example, during the novel's first battle scene, when his "gentle expression" contends with his "dark visage." During this scene, Ruth trusts Conanchet with the lives of her children:

> The flashing of his eye as it lighted on this sad object [a human bone] was wild and exulting, like that of the savage when he first feels the fierce joy of glutted vengeance; but gentler recollections came with the gaze and kinder feelings usurped the place of the hatred that he had been taught to bear a race who were so fast sweeping his people from the earth. The relic fell from his hand, and had the gentle Ruth been there to witness the melancholy and relenting shade that clouded his swarthy features, she might have found pleasure in the certainty that all her kindness had not been wasted.[30]

Conanchet's apparent transformation belies Cooper's awkward negotiation of Native American nature, since the behavior of the "savage" is ambiguously "taught." In this crucial transformation, however, Conanchet is ultimately divested of political authority as a warrior. The influence of Ruth Heathcote, moreover, would seem to be reinforced by her daughter, whom Conanchet takes back to the Narragansett settlements and marries. Just as in *Hobomok* and *Metamora,* conjugal affection produces not merely children but the qualities of sentimental manhood expressed through the capacity for benevolence:

> The firmness [of Conanchet's look] had passed away, and in its place was left the winning softness of affection, which, as it belongs to nature, is seen at times in the expression of the Indian's eye, as strongly as it is ever known to sweeten the intercourse of a more polished condition of life. (315)

Cooper's convoluted syntax typically confuses the relations among nature, cultivation, and empire. Is the Native American—under the proper, feminized conditions—capable of civilized republican behavior? Or is this just the momentary and unpredictable pulse of nature? In either case, the sentimentalization of manhood simultaneously humanizes the Native American and erases his political efficacy.

The novel's politics of androgyny actually inscribes itself on the very body of Conanchet. Indeed, readers who look for ideological significance in Cooper's landscapes might also consider the Native American body as a text meant to signify historical and political processes. At the moment *The Wept* brings Conanchet into focus, one sees Cooper's atavistically masculine revisions of cultural changes in gender during the early nineteenth century:

> In form and features, this young warrior might be deemed a model of the excellence of Indian manhood. The limbs were full, round, faultlessly straight, and distinguished by an appearance of extreme activity, without however being equally remarkable for muscle. In the latter particular, in the upright attitude, and in the distant and noble gaze, which so often elevated his front, there was a close affinity to the statue of the pythian Apollo; while in the full, though slightly effeminate chest, there was an equal resemblance to the look of animal indulgence, which is to be traced in the severe representations of Bacchus. (293–4)

Through the contrast between Apollonian masculinity and Dionysian femininity, the figure of the Native American sachem is decidedly androgynous. In representing Conanchet in this manner, moreover, Cooper invokes the cant of Whig republicanism—Conanchet's "effeminate chest"—to suggest political connotations of luxury, weakness, corruption and decay. As the social conservative Noah Webster put it in his original *American Dictionary* of 1828, the word "effeminate" meant "destitute of manly qualities." Conanchet's symbolic form, then, suggests less an androgynous synthesis and more the contamination of a "masculine" ideal.

In this way, *The Wept* recasts an ideal of sentimental manhood as a political problem. As in *Metamora*, Native American virtue becomes the site of the fragile relations between social and political forms of virtue. Keep in mind who Conanchet actually is: the Narragansett sachem has seen his father betrayed by the English and his tribe all but massacred during the war, and while Conanchet knows the politics of retribution, he cannot execute it. Cooper goes to great lengths to show the political impracticality of sentiment in Conanchet's three successive acts of selfless love. First, Conanchet spares the Heathcotes' lives, which prompts the scorn of both his Narragansett warriors and Metacom himself. Like Hobomok, Conanchet also relinquishes his wife in the name of selfless love: "The Manitou of your race is strong," he tells his wife, cradled now in her mother's arms, "He telleth a mother to know her child" (319). Finally, Cooper stages a reciprocal exchange of male sentiment between Conanchet and Submission (the regicide figure who saves the Puritan settlement from destruction), which culminates in Conanchet's willingness to sacrifice himself for his symbolic white father. At Conanchet's execution, Cooper draws verbatim from the Puritan minister William Hubbard's *Narrative of the Trouble with the Indians* (1677), which claimed that Conanchet died bravely, in order to expose the problem—in strictly political terms—of sentimental manhood. Like Metamora lamenting to his wife, the wasted Conanchet whispers to his adversary Uncas, "Mohican I die before my heart is soft" (389). Conanchet, however, dies *because* his heart is soft.

ıⁱı

The cultural legacy of the American Revolution left complex rhetorical and ideological frameworks for reading the gendered forms of virtue in the early American historical novel. Native American heroism became one site of larger cultural negotiations over the gendered meanings of "republicanism," and Metacom's representation reveals the complexity of new, gendered possibilities, and new political implications, for the meaning of "manhood." Historians, ministers, aspiring playwrights, male and female novelists: all of these social-literary groups appropriated colonial history to envision and re-envision the social and political nature of American manhood. If, as historians today argue, the categories of "public" and "private" spheres distort the historical experiences of nineteenth-century women,[31] so too does the time-honored distinction between the "masculine" valor and "feminine" sentiment that allegedly correspond to these spheres.

NOTES

1. For historical accounts of the conflict, see Douglas Edward Leach, *Flintlock and Tomahawk: New England in King Philip's War* (New York: Macmillan, 1958); Francis Jennings, *The Invasion of America: Indians, Colonialism, and the Cant of Conquest* (New York: Norton, 1976), 254–326; Russell Bourne, *The Red King's Rebellion: Racial Politics in New England, 1675–1678* (New York: Oxford University Press, 1990); and Richard Slotkin and James K. Folsom, eds., *So Dreadfull a Judgment: Puritan Responses to King Philip's War, 1676–1677* (Middletown, Conn.: Wesleyan University Press, 1978).

2. See Richard Slotkin, *Regeneration Through Violence: The Mythology of the American Frontier, 1600–1860* (Middletown, Conn.: Wesleyan University Press, 1973); Brian Dippie, *The Vanishing American: White Attitudes and U.S. Indian Policy* (Middletown, Conn.: Wesleyan University Press, 1982); Lucy Maddox, *Removals: Nineteenth-Century American Literature and the Politics of Indian Affairs* (New York: Oxford University Press, 1991); and Ronald Takaki, *Iron Cages: Race and Culture in Nineteenth-Century America* (New York: Knopf, 1979). While Slotkin is most representative of myth criticism, all of these studies in some way articulate a political mythology of American expansionism.

3. See, for example, T. Walter Herbert, *Dearest Beloved: The Hawthornes and the Making of the Middle Class Family* (Berkeley: University of California Press, 1993), for analysis of

Nathaniel Hawthorne's tortured struggle to negotiate within himself "the essence of the masculine and the feminine" (6). The problematic correlation of masculine / feminine with public / private also informs E. Anthony Rotundo's discussion of early-nineteenth-century gender: "After all, if the doctrine of separate spheres was a critique of 'the world' and the world was man's realm, then the doctrine was also a critique of manhood" (*American Manhood: Transformations in Masculinity from the Revolution to the Modern Era* [New York: Basic Books, 1993], 25).

4. Susan Juster, *Disorderly Women: Sexual Politics and Evangelicalism in Revolutionary New England* (Ithaca: Cornell University Press, 1994), 21.

5. Ibid., 207.

6. For the importance of history writing in cultivating virtuous citizens in the republic, see, for example, George H. Callcott, *History in the United States, 1800–1860* (Baltimore: Johns Hopkins University Press, 1970) and Nina Baym, *American Women Writers and the Work of History, 1790–1860* (New Brunswick, N.J.: Rutgers University Press, 1995).

7. J. G. A. Pocock, *The Machiavellian Moment: Florentine Political Thought and the Atlantic Republican Tradition* (Princeton: Princeton University Press, 1975), 49–80.

8. Gordon S. Wood, *The Radicalism of the American Revolution* (New York: Knopf, 1992), 216.

9. Ruth Bloch, "The Gendered Meanings of Virtue in Revolutionary America," *Signs* 13 (1987): 37–58, quotation from 56.

10. Charles A. Goodrich, *A History of the United States of America* (New York: G. C. Smith, 1829), 5–6 (emphasis added).

11. Benjamin Rush, *Essays, Literary, Moral, and Philosophical* (Philadelphia: Thomas and Samuel Bradford, 1798), 11.

12. Anon., "The Philosophy of History," *North American Review* (July 1834): 30–54, quotation from 46.

13. Joan Scott, *Gender and the Politics of History* (New York: Columbia University Press, 1988), 38–9.

14. Jeremy Belknap, *American Biography; or an Historical Account of Those Persons Who Have Been Distinguished in America* . . . (Boston: Thomas and Andrews, 1798), 2: 265, (emphasis added).

15. Samuel Knapp, *Female Biography; Containing Notices of Distinguished Women, in Different Nations and Ages* (Philadelphia: Thomas Wardle, 1834), 103–4.

16. Cf. G. J. Barker-Benfield's summation of this problem in eighteenth-century England: "It was in the interest of commerce that men cultivated politeness and sensibility. This tendency coincides with the goals of the 'reformation of manners.' Men wanted this reformation, and they associated it with greater heterosociality abroad and at home. At the same time, they marked their apprehensions over relinquishing the older male ideals associated with classical warriors and farmers at a boundary they named 'effeminacy' " (*The Culture of Sensibility: Sex and Society in Eighteenth-Century Britain* [Chicago: University of Chicago Press, 1992], xxv).

17. Nina Baym, "How Men and Women Wrote Indian Stories," in *New Essays on Last of the Mohicans,* ed. H. Daniel Peck (New York: Cambridge University Press, 1992), 67–86, quotation from 68.

18. For the relations between these genres, see my *Covenant and Republic: Historical Romance and the Politics of Puritanism* (New York: Cambridge University Press, 1996).

19. Samuel Knapp, *Lectures on American Literature* (New York: Elam Bliss, 1829), 229.

20. See, for example, David Ramsay, *History of the United States of America* (Philadelphia: Mathew Carey, 1818), 1: 286; Abiel Holmes, *The Annals of America from the Discovery of Columbus in the Year 1492 to the Year 1826* (Cambridge, Mass.: Hilliard and Brown, 1829), 383; and

Epaphras Hoyt, *Antiquarian Researches: Comprising a History of the Indian Wars* (Greenfield, Mass.: Ansel Phelps, 1824), 140–1.

21. Jedidiah Morse and Elijah Parish, *A Compendious History of New England* (London: William Burton, 1808), 39–40.

22. Washington Irving, *The Sketch Book of Geoffrey Crayon, Gent.*, ed. William Hedges (New York: Penguin, 1988), 246–7.

23. Ibid., 246.

24. Lydia Maria Child, *Hobomok*, in *Hobomok and Other Writings on Indians*, ed. Carolyn Karcher (New Brunswick, N.J.: Rutgers University Press, 1987), 36, 84. Further quotations will be cited parenthetically in the text.

25. See her introduction to the volume cited above, especially xxix–xxxi.

26. See, for example, Roy Harvey Pearce, *Savagism and Civilization: A Study of the Indian and the American Mind* (Berkeley: University of California Press, 1988), 176, and Bruce A. McConachie, *Melodramatic Formations: American Theater and Society, 1820–1870* (Iowa City: University of Iowa Press, 1992), 121–7.

27. Juster, *Disorderly Women*, 21.

28. Eugene Page, ed., *Metamora and Other Plays* (Princeton: Princeton University Press, 1941), 37. Further quotations will be cited parenthetically in the text.

29. For discussion of race in the novel that I treat below, see, for example, Leslie A. Fiedler's *Love and Death in the American Novel*, rev. ed. (New York: Stein and Day, 1966), 184–5, 203–4; George Dekker, *James Fenimore Cooper: The Novelist* (London: Routledge and Kegan Paul, 1967), 75–85; and, more recently, James D. Wallace, "Race and Captivity in Cooper's *The Wept of Wish-ton-Wish*," *American Literary History* 7 (Summer 1995): 189–209. For a notable exception to this critical trend, which analyzes the role of gender in captivity in *The Last of the Mohicans*, see Lora Romero, "Vanishing Americans: Gender, Empire, and New Historicism," *American Literature* 63 (1991): 385–404.

30. James Fenimore Cooper, *The Borderers; or The Wept of Wish-ton-Wish* (London: Richard Bentley, 1833), 187. Further quotations will be cited parenthetically in the text.

31. See, for example, Mary P. Ryan, *Women in Public: Between Banners and Ballots, 1825–1880* (Baltimore: Johns Hopkins University Press, 1990), and her essay "Gender and Public Access: Women's Politics in Nineteenth-Century America," in *Habermas and the Public Sphere*, ed. Craig Calhoun (Cambridge: MIT Press, 1992): 259–88. See also Lori D. Ginzberg, *Women and the Work of Benevolence: Morality, Politics and Class in the Nineteenth-Century United States* (New Haven: Yale University Press, 1990).

[◫]

CHAPTER SIX

Bloated Bodies and Sober Sentiments

Masculinity in 1840s Temperance Narratives

Glenn Hendler

In 1842, unprecedented numbers of American men were weeping in public. Throughout the country hardened drunkards—mostly artisans and mechanics—sobbed convulsively in front of large crowds at meetings of the Washington Temperance Society.[1] By the end of each evening, many went through a physical and emotional conversion experience that led them to sign, before dozens or even hundreds of their peers, a standardized pledge of total abstinence from alcohol. The Washingtonians' greatest innovation was the form of these gatherings, which they called "experience meetings."[2] Earlier incarnations of the temperance movement had mostly been controlled by mainstream Protestant ministers, were often linked to specific denominations, and consisted mainly of didactic sermons preached to parishioners and reprinted in pamphlets by the American Temperance Union and the American Tract Society.[3] The experience meeting, in contrast, was an exceptionally nonhierarchical, nonsectarian, and populist cultural form. It opened not with prayer and sermonizing, but with one or two featured lecturers telling the stories of their own drunken past and conversion to teetotalism: their "experiences." Their listeners were drawn not to condemn these men for their indulgence or their horrible treatment of families, but to empathize with their plight, and to display that compassion through tears. The *Boston Mercantile Journal* wrote of an experience meeting run by the celebrated Washingtonian John H. W. Hawkins: "We believe more tears were never shed by an audience in one evening than flowed last night. . . . Old gray haired men sobbed like children, and the noble and honorable bowed their heads and wept."[4]

Tears were not only the medium through which these men's conversions took place; they were also the means by which the Washingtonian movement reproduced itself. After the initial storytelling, the experience meeting was given over to men in the audience who spontaneously stood up to describe their own alcohol-induced depravities. Like the professional speakers, they dwelt at length upon their abuse of mothers, wives, and children, as well as on the horrible deeds they had committed to keep themselves supplied with alcohol. Some followed the lead of John Bartholomew Gough, another popular Washingtonian, by graphically describing the physical sensations and hallucinations of delirium tremens. Many concluded with an account of the act of sympathetic kindness from another man which had brought them to the meeting, and attested to the power of such sympathy by walking to the front of the hall and signing the temperance pledge in full view of all present. Each performance of sentimental manhood thus recommenced and re-enacted an emotional and narrative formula.

In 1842 these spectacles attracted enthusiastic attention from three prominent public figures representing different versions of nineteenth-century masculinity. Early in that year, Timothy Shay Arthur, soon to be a regular contributor of sentimental tales to *Godey's Lady's Book* and a decade later the best selling author of *Ten Nights in a Bar-Room*, published *Temperance Tales; or, Six Nights with the Washingtonians*, a linked series of short stories based on experience narratives he had heard at some of the earliest Washingtonian meetings held in Baltimore.[5] In February, Illinois lawyer and legislator Abraham Lincoln delivered an address to the Washington Temperance Society of Springfield, Illinois, and afterward helped lead reformers and converts in a grand parade.[6] And in November, Walter Whitman followed up a series of pro-Washingtonian editorials in the New York *Aurora* with the publication of a novel: *Franklin Evans; or, The Inebriate,* which appeared as a special edition of the *New World*.[7] Whitman continued to evince his interest in temperance two months later with the publication in the New York *Washingtonian and Organ* of an installment of *The Madman*, which was apparently to be a second temperance novel.[8] Though they use different forms and genres, each man repeats the same story—that of the seemingly irredeemable drunkard restored to respectable manhood through the medium of a voluntary association—and promulgates the same affective politics, in which the sentimental experience of sympathy is both personally and socially transformative so long as it is mediated by such a voluntary association.

In other words, these texts advocated, participated in, and further developed the political logic of temperance, which Michael Warner has aptly characterized as "a civil society phenomenon, arguably the largest and most sustained social movement in modernity."[9] Beginning as a group of six Baltimore drinking buddies who wrote and signed the pledge in May of 1840, the Washingtonians claimed that over 200,000 had signed up by the end of 1841, and that their membership passed the one million mark during 1842. Even though this figure was probably exaggerated, the fact that in March of 1842 thirty-eight separate Washingtonian organizations existed in New York City alone, several with over a thousand names on their membership lists, indicates that the movement's new tactics were remarkably successful, especially since mainstream temperance groups had for years been losing members and momentum.[10]

More is at stake in analyzing the cultural products of the Washingtonian phenomenon than providing an historical context for a minor, though widely read, genre of writings. The Washingtonian narrative, in both its oral and printed manifestations, is an unlikely but significant progenitor of many popular cultural forms that rely on the affectively transformative effects of sympathetic identification, including much of the sentimental and sensational fiction that dominated the literary marketplace in succeeding decades. In that sense, the reformed and transformed drunkard stands near the beginning of a history of American mass culture. He also represents a paradigm shift within another history, a larger political and social history of gendered sentimentality. His widespread popularity and emotional power are evidence that nineteenth-century sentimentality has been too quickly categorized as a form of feminization and a force of privatization. Feminine sentimentality, by this argument, is defined in opposition to masculine rationality, and the two correspond to interdependent but distinct domestic and public spheres.[11] The Washingtonians, however, were able to deploy an expressively emotional form of sentiment as a way of making heterosocial alliances—bringing more women into the temperance movement than ever before—while at the same time tearful male sentiment served to refigure and buttress the homosocial bonds that underlay the masculine character of the public sphere. Moreover, their representations of the bloated, red-faced, lustful, uncontrolled male inebriate, both in literature and in experience meetings, made him the most vividly embodied figure in antebellum fiction and public life, except perhaps for the black slave with whom he was often compared. The drunkard's conversion, through tearful narration, into a sentimental, sympathetic, responsible man demonstrates that the boundaries between sentimentality as a characteristically feminine form of embodiment and publicity as a legitimating form of disinterested masculine abstraction were more porous than we usually assume.

One implication of this observation is that antebellum sentimentality needs to be analyzed as more than a feminine literary genre or mode, and as more than a rhetoric that women deployed in political and proto-political efforts to redraw the boundaries between public and domestic, to rewrite domestic ideology in their own interests.[12] In this essay, I analyze the formal structures of both the experience meeting and the Washingtonian temperance novel as exemplary of an antebellum sentimental masculinity that complicates such definitions. The sentimental experience of "sympathy" is the narrative and affective core of this structure of feeling, and the forms and conventions developed by the Washingtonians are articulations of new social formations only then being preliminarily experienced by the white working-class men and artisans who largely made up the movement. Experience meetings, oral Washingtonian narratives, and the temperance novels by Arthur and Whitman were all attempts to shape what might later be seen as private experience into something social—or, to use a more historically and theoretically specific term, into something *public*. At the same time, I argue that these social practices were not just expressions of preexisting identities; they constructed whiteness and masculinity as definitional of both the public sphere in which they took place and the embodied subjects who populated that sphere.[13]

SOBER SENTIMENTS

Washingtonianism was the first massively popular movement organized around the experience of sympathy. Its proselytizers differentiated their organization from earlier temperance movements on precisely this basis. Most notably, the Washington Temperance Societies were the first such groups to believe that habitual drunkards could be redeemed. Previous activists had largely agreed with the blunt assessment put forward by a founder of the American Temperance Society, Justin Edwards: "Keep the temperate people temperate; the drunkards will soon die, and the land be free."[14] In contrast, Abraham Lincoln argued in his address to the Springfield Washingtonians that such a callous stance was "so repugnant to humanity, so uncharitable, so cold-blooded and feelingless, that it never did, nor never can enlist the enthusiasm of a popular cause. We could not love the man who taught it—we could not hear him with patience."[15] By Lincoln's account, not only is the earlier temperance position not "charitable" enough to be effective in the conversion of a drunkard; it also prevents the temperance advocate from receiving "love" in return, and therefore limits the potential scope of temperance as a "popular cause." The rejection of all limitations on compassion, as well as the insistence that such compassion be reciprocal, is typical of the newer movement's rhetoric, and recurrent in its fiction. Whitman's novel, for instance, contains several subplots which emphasize not the dangers of drinking, but the risks of failing to extend compassion and humanity to a drunkard.

As such, the Washingtonian temperance crusade exemplifies the tendency of sentimental politics to, in Philip Fisher's words, "experiment with the extension of full and complete humanity to classes of figures from whom it has been socially withheld." Sympathy is here not extended to its "typical objects . . . the prisoner, the madman, the child, the very old, the animal, and the slave."[16] Instead, the Washingtonians brought crowds of ethnic and working-class drinkers into the movement, thereby alienating many of the ministers and middle-class men who made up the core of earlier temperance drives.[17] Older temperance regulars also resisted the new activists' insistence that sentiment, rather than reason or religion, was to be their primary weapon against intemperance.[18] A drunkard could be redeemed, the Washingtonians argued, if he could be induced to exercise his sympathy while listening to the story of a reformed drunkard. This sympathy was designed to produce an emotional equivalence between speaker and audience; as Lincoln said, "out of the abundance of their hearts their tongues give utterance. . . . And when such is the temper of the advocate, and such of the audience, no good cause can be unsuccessful."[19] Interpellated by such emotionally egalitarian rhetoric, the debased alcoholic subject becomes the protagonist of a new narrative whose telos is the restoration of his masculinity: "The drunkard found himself unexpectedly an object of interest" one observer wrote, "[h]e was no longer an outcast. There were some who still looked upon him as a man."[20]

The affective exchanges that are both the plot and the purpose of the story are designed to replicate themselves, diegetically and extradiegetically, in the resolution of the protagonist's narrative problems and in the concomitant moral and physical transformation of the listener or reader, whose responses set the narrative circuit in motion once again. Thus Washingtonian speeches elicited spontaneous public confessions from their auditors, stories in which the drunkard was not just "an object of interest," but narrator and protagonist as well. This activity was modelled in the opening speeches; both Gough and Hawkins concluded their standard conversion narratives with a scene in which they found themselves in front of a crowd, almost involuntarily describing their harrowing experiences with alcohol. Listeners were quick to follow their lead, narrating their life stories up to the present moment of redemption. Narratives and emotions are figured as objects that should be freely exchanged: "Let us have your experience," calls out the organizer of a meeting in *Six Nights with the Washingtonians* at the end of one story, and a new narrator begins a new story (SN 1:93).

Whitman's *Franklin Evans* reproduces the affective logic of the experience meeting without actually representing such a gathering in the story. First of all, Whitman exhorts his reader to move into an intimate and sympathetic proximity with his first person narrator: "Reader! perhaps you despise me," he writes, "Perhaps, if I were by you at this moment, I should behold the curled lip of scorn, and the look of deep contempt. Oh, pause stern reverencer of duty, and have pity for a fellow-creature's weakness" (*FE* 179). The narrator also displays a marked willingness to allow other characters to tell their own stories, stories that are made to serve a role like that of the spontaneous narration of the experience meeting. Whitman underscores the homologous functions of these different levels of narration when, late in the novel, Franklin Evans's benefactor tells him a story about a young man who is saved from a life of intemperance by the sentimental sight of his young sister's death. After he has finished his tale he confesses that "he had indeed been relating a story, the hero of which was himself" (*FE* 200). A paragraph later, Franklin has signed a temperance pledge. The novel itself begins with a similar narratorial shift, with two lengthy paragraphs referring to a "stranger" in the third person, only to reveal in the third paragraph: "Reader, I was that youth" (*FE* 129). The Washingtonian strategy of narration is parallelled in Franklin's own experience as an auditor, an experience his readers are meant to share.

The power of the experience narrative derived from the egalitarian equivalence it established between its participants as well as its spontaneity and direct emotional appeal, the sense that "those unlettered men . . . spoke from the heart to the heart," as one contemporary writer put it.[21] As such, their nearest relative as a narrative form was the nascent genre of sentimental women's fiction, which was similarly centered on the enactment or performance of sympathetic identification, an exchange of affective experience among author, character, and reader. Writers like Catharine Maria Sedgwick and Sarah Josepha Hale had already established many of the conventions that later best-sellers by Maria Susanna Cummins and Susan Warner would follow, depicting the trials and tribulations of young women of the same gender, age, race, and class as the readers they intended to address. Sentimental writers did not simply presume that their mostly female readers would sympathize with their protagonists; the heroines themselves are characterized primarily by their capacity to sympathize. Readers, along with the heroine, are witness not only to suffering itself but to numerous examples of the power of sympathy to relieve that suffering. They are then asked, often explicitly, to extend the chain of sympathetic identifications into the real world. That extension of sympathy is typical not only of those sentimental novels like *Uncle Tom's Cabin* whose concerns reach beyond the domestic sphere; even novels overtly intended to reinforce women's domestic role deploy the same logic in trying to make their readers into more loving and sympathetic wives and mothers.[22]

Both defenders and critics of women's fiction characterized the sympathy it performed and evoked as a kind of affective contagion, communicated by the immediacy with which suffering was depicted. Women readers had long been associated with a sometimes excessive propensity to sympathize and an insufficiently mediated relation to the narratives that absorbed them. Whether these ostensibly feminine characteristics were viewed as the source of woman's moral superiority or as the sign of her inadequate rationality, sympathetic absorption in narrative was by the 1840s seen as a—perhaps *the*—quintessentially feminine characteristic. It is all the more surprising, then, that the Washingtonians built a mass movement around a compulsively repeated primal scene of tearful, sympathetic identification with another *man's* suffering.[23] Descriptions of experience meetings make them sound like collective scenes of sentimental reading, with the pale, solitary, emotionally responsive woman reader replaced by a mass of tipsy but tearful red-nosed auditors. "The simple tale of the ruined inebriate," one observer stated, "interrupted by a silence that told of emotions too big for utterance, would awaken general sympathy, and dissolve a large portion of the audience in tears."[24] Like the female reader "forgetting herself" in her novel, listeners lose their individuality in the flow of sympathetic identification with the reformed inebriate; another writer reported that after an experience speech the audience's "hearts were melted, tears glistened, and that human mass became knit together by a common spell."[25] Despite its male focus, then, the Washingtonian experience narrative possessed a prototypically sentimental structure.

BLOATED BODIES

In both women's fiction and male temperance narratives, sentimentality is more than an exchange of ideas and emotions; it is a form of embodiment, a "bodily bond" in Karen Sánchez-Eppler's phrase, that links character and reader to each other and to the social body. Analyses of feminine sentimentalism have recently reconceived it as "a project about imagining the nation's bodies and the national body," arguing that "[i]n sentimental fiction bodily signs are adamantly and repeatedly presented as the preferred and most potent mechanisms both for communicating meaning and for marking the fact of its transmission."[26] The "bodily signs" most often used as the means of this communication are, of course, tears, and these signs function similarly in the Washingtonian narrative apparatus. Tears are consistently cited as evidence of each step of the restorative process: the drunkard cries when he is first approached by the kindly Washingtonian; he cries again as he narrates his tale to the larger audience; the audience cries in response; and the fictionalized retelling of the experience inevitably concludes with tears that practically flow off the page onto the reader.

According to Sánchez-Eppler, the "feminist-abolitionist discourse" she analyzes deployed sentimentality in order "to transform the body from a site of oppression into the grounds of resisting that oppression." The logic of abstract personhood characteristic of republican and constitutional discourse was so capable of disconnecting the citizen from his body that "it did not seem absurd for the founding fathers to reckon slaves as 'three-fifths of a person' " without imagining that such a division would entail "amputations." In contrast, she argues, feminist-abolitionist discourse insisted on "acknowledging the corporeality of personhood," in part by making bodily signs like tears the goal of the narrative and the sign of moral humanity.[27] Washingtonian discourse was equally insistent upon representing corporeality, but it formulated the sentimental relation between the (male) person and his body differently. However fundamentally it relies on bodily signs, the experience narrative has as its goal the diminution and metaphorical dissolution of the body that serves as its "object of interest." Ultimately the embodied subject of the narrative is replaced by a person who aspires to the disembodied abstraction that is the prerequisite and privilege of white male citizenship.[28]

Of course the white male body does not disappear in this transaction. In fact, the physical manliness of Washingtonians was constantly reiterated in narratives and newspaper accounts of their meetings. Such descriptions may have focused on the virility of the men's bodies in part to counteract the conception, still prevalent amongst working-class men, that strong spirits strengthened the body and abstinence led to effeminacy.[29] But contemporaneous accounts of the best experience speakers also linked their visible masculinity to their ability to reduce a sympathetic crowd to tears; manliness is depicted as an effective form of sentimental rhetoric. In 1841 the *Boston Daily Mail* described Hawkins as "a man of forty-four years of age—of fine manly form—[who] said he had been more than twenty years a confirmed inebriate. He spoke . . . [in a] free and easy, off-hand, direct, bang-up style; at times in a simple conversational manner, then earnest and vehement, then pathetic, then humorous—but always manly and reasonable." Hawkins's "fine manly form" and "direct, bang-up style" had their desired effect on his listeners: the article goes on to describe the "fountains of generous feeling" that "gushed forth in tears" in the lecture hall.[30] Gough's performances were even more melodramatically masculine: carried away in his own performance, he would stride across the stage acting out the violent acts to which Demon Rum had driven him or his intemperate acquaintances, pantomiming "a man laying his child on an open fire or clutching his wife's throat with a death grip."[31] Gough's audiences, according to a writer in the *New York Observer*, "were under the spell of this young charmer . . . alternately elevated by the grand, thrilled with the horrible, dissolved with the tender, enchanted with the beautiful."[32]

The seductive physical immediacy projected in these speakers' styles was underscored in the stories they told, which focus obsessively on the bodies and faces of their protagonists. The drunkard is described as red, blotched, bleary-eyed, and, most consistently, "bloated." Gough, for instance, repeated in virtually every one of his autobiographical narratives the tale of his return home after a long binge; his mother's greeting at the door is "Son, you are bloated." Michael Moon notes that vivid descriptions of the body often appeared in anti-onanism writings of the period; in temperance discourse such words similarly designate a person's excessive devotion to bodily desires that are often simultaneously alcoholic and erotic.[33] Whitman's use of the trope of bloating is quite typical; before his first wife wastes away due to his neglect, Franklin Evans speaks of her "hot tears that fell upon my bloated face," describes one drunkard's "red and swollen eyes," and says of another that "his face was bloated, his eyes inflamed, and he leaned back in that state of drowsy drunkenness which it is so disgusting to behold" (*FE* 175, 153). Overall, Evans is depicted as a murderous personification of libido; in the course of the novel he manages to acquire two wives and one mistress, all of whom die as a result of his drinking.

The alcoholic body in Washingtonian discourse is clearly sexualized; its manliness is marked racially as well. Typically, at one stage in the narration of a drunkard's descent into absolute abjection he is described as a man so far from normative masculine identity that he has also lost his whiteness, at least insofar as whiteness is a visible condition of the skin. The narratives repeatedly decry the physical discolorations that alcoholism produces, remarking on the "unnatural redness" of one drinker's face, while another's is "flushed with a deep red" that contrasts vividly with the "pale" and "colorless" face of his worried daughter (*FE* 129; *SN* 1:12, 33). At one of the lowest points in Franklin Evans's life, when he describes himself as "a miserable object," the clearest sign of his fall is his skin color: "My face, I felt, was all dirty and brown, and my eyes bleared and swollen. What use had I for life?" (*FE* 186). After his rescue from "the forces of the Red Fiend," a former drunkard is invariably whitened, not only by the cleansing baths that usually accompany his being taken in by the Washingtonians, but also by the restoration of his face's "natural" color (*FE* 237).

Such color coding, the passage from red and brown to white, might be legible in other than racial terms if not for the consistency with which temperance tales make reference to both Native Americans and black slaves. An otherwise gratuitous narrative inserted early in Whitman's novel is introduced by a man who "can conceive of no more awful and horrible, and at the same time more effective lesson, than that which may be learned from the consequences of the burning firewater upon the habits and happiness of the poor Indians" (*FE* 133).[34] Stories of Native American alcoholism typically serve to illustrate the social and especially *national* repercussions of alcoholism: in Whitman's novel, the man goes on to say that a "whole people—the inhabitants of a mighty continent—are crushed by it, and debased into a condition lower than the beasts of the field. Is it not a pitiful thought? . . . They found themselves deprived not only of their lands and what property they hitherto owned, but of everything that made them noble and grand as a nation!" (*FE* 45). Curiously, the ensuing narrative makes no mention of alcohol after this moralizing preface. The story instead serves the purpose of attributing to Native American men a pure masculinity against which white men can measure themselves: at a climactic moment, a young man exclaims "Wind-Foot is not a girl. The son of a chief can die without wetting his cheek by tears" (*FE* 53). Conjoined with the elegy for Indian nationhood, the story produces, as in James Fenimore Cooper, a transracial emotional identification while simultaneously placing the equivalence between white men and native men implied by that sympathy into an irretrievable past.

Temperance fiction's pervasive deployment of the figure of the black slave is more ambivalent and complex, but it also entails a powerful and temporary bodily identification with a racial Other. Arthur, for instance, describes his first attendance at an experience meeting as a crowd of "mostly mechanics and working men":

> We pushed our way close up to the speaker's stand, and then turned to survey the countenances of the assembly. It was a sight to move the heart. . . . Men who had been slaves, some for a long series of years, to the most degrading vice. But now they stood up as freemen, and there was scarcely a face, marred sadly as some were, that had not an expression of serious, manly determination and confidence. (*SN* 1:3)

The drunkard's liberation from his excessive embodiment is not only a passage to manhood, but also a passage from slavery to freedom.[35] Alcoholism in temperance discourse is regularly figured as bondage either to "King Alcohol" or to the body itself, and the other people, aside from sentimental women, who were regularly portrayed as excessively and oppressively embodied were black slaves.[36] Indeed, that embodiment was, according to Sánchez-Eppler, one basis for the always conflicted alliance between feminists and abolitionists. The same connection extends to the figure of the drunkard, making available a metaphorical equivalence between alcoholism and slavery.

As a rhetorical figure, the comparison between alcoholism and slavery could be articulated in various ways. In his history of the antebellum black temperance movement, Donald Yacovone describes a shift from the 1820s and 1830s, when black temperance was seen by its advocates as part of a movement for universal moral reform, to the 1840s, when "temperance and abolitionism had become virtually synonymous." Yacovone cites two exemplary phrases from Frederick Douglass's speech to the World Temperance Convention: one where he declares that "I am a temperance man because I am an anti-slavery man" and another in which he represents slaveholding itself as a form of intoxication and addiction, proclaiming that "Mankind has been drunk" and that if man were sober "we could get a public opinion sufficiently strong to break the relation of master and slave."[37] A sober public, it seems, would be rational, democratic, and free.

While Washingtonian discourse posits a similar equivalence, it narrates the connection in reverse. Again the Washingtonian body follows a trajectory opposite to that of the bodies in feminist-abolitionist discourse, whose embodiment is an assertion of their gendered personhood. The body moves not only toward the abstracted masculinity described earlier; at the same time it also takes on a newly valorized whiteness, visible in its contrast with both the "unnatural" bloated redness of the drunkard's body and the slave's inability to own his body and exercise his will over it. This contrast between these two deployments of sympathy and embodiment is evident even at moments when white Washingtonians explicitly connect the two. Somewhat later in his career Gough invoked a scene from *Uncle Tom's Cabin* as a parallel example of the transformative power of sympathy, but with a significant difference in emphasis. Gough compares the treatment the drunkard receives from the world with the moment in the novel "when Ophelia shrank back from little Topsy [and] 'the girl felt it.' You shrink back from the drunkard, and he feels it. The finger of scorn pointed at him, stings the seared heart as if a burning brand were pressed upon the quivering flesh."[38] Rather than figuring sympathy itself as a form of embodiment, Gough represents its *withdrawal* as a painful physical sensation that makes the drunkard, like Topsy, all too aware of his body. Though the project of Washingtonianism is typically articulated in gendered terms—an attempt, as Whitman says, to abolish "those pestilent places, where the mind and the body are both rendered effeminate together" (*FE* 239)—and although it defined itself as a working-class movement in contradistinction to other branches of temperance, it was equally a "racial project" that constituted working-class masculinity as a form of whiteness.[39]

Washingtonian sentimentality is thus more than an effective rhetoric; it discursively constructs its male subjects in a way that articulates together racialized, classed, and gendered forms of identity into an affective whole, a sentimental structure of feeling. White working-class masculinity can be viewed as sentimental in this discourse because its defining opposite, alcoholism's involuntary servitude, is depicted as an inability to sympathize. As one of Arthur's speaker / narrators describes his intemperate state, "All natural affection seemed gone from my bosom. I loved only myself, and sought only the lowest sensual gratifications" (*SN* 1:58). It is this lack of "natural affection" which allows the drunkard to abuse and abandon his wife and children, and it is the restoration of such affections that Washingtonian sentiment enables. Two pages later, the same speaker describes a

Washingtonian speaking to him "in a kind sympathizing tone. . . . This melted me right down. For years a kind word had never been spoken to me" (*SN* 1:60). Sentimental personhood is thus restored by both the reciprocal sympathy of the experience meeting and its concomitant dissolution of the hardened, sinful body of the drunkard. The male bodies in these stories are transformed first into grotesque, bloated, red and brown monsters, then, through the power of Washingtonian sympathy, they are "melted down" into their properly white "manly forms"—pale, respectable, docile.

For the Washingtonians, then, the male body is the site of the audience's transformative identification. The narrative trajectory of the body in the experience narrative is from an excessive physicality toward a more contained and controllable sentimental personhood. Even as readers or listeners cry over the death of a child or wife, they identify with the tearful feeling of regret expressed by the vividly embodied, lively, and perversely interesting perpetrator of the crime, not the pale, sickly victims whose narrative function is to waste away, and not even the virtuous reformed drunkard, whose interest only lasts as long as he narrates his depravities. Of course, the reader's sympathy with the alcoholic's violent desire is meant to be prelude to an identification with his more respectable later self, but the Washingtonian narrative was notoriously ambivalent about how to maintain an affective connection with a figure whose main characteristic is his lack of exciting affect. Critics of the movement often argued that the real appeal of these stories was in the sensational depravities they depicted, noting quite accurately that they rarely focus at all on the less eventful later life of the sober convert.[40]

Whitman acknowledges this tension in *Franklin Evans* in the midst of the weirdest and most gothic episode of the novel. When Evans tries to escape his depraved past by moving to Virginia, his hypermasculinity displays itself in its most destructive manner, leading to the abject "disgust with myself" that is prerequisite to a Washingtonian transformation (*FE* 216). He has won the affections of a beautiful light-skinned slave woman, whom he has freed, married, then promptly begun to neglect in favor of a visiting white widow. He then describes how his inattention drives his wife to murder the white woman by deliberately exposing her to a wasting illness. Immediately after narrating these events, but before his conversion to teetotalism, he opens a chapter by rhapsodizing:

> How refreshing it is to pause in the whirl and tempest of life, and cast back our minds over past years! I think there is even a kind of satisfaction in deliberately and calmly reviewing actions that we feel were foolish or evil. It pleases us to know that we have the learning of experience. The very contrast, perhaps, between what we are, and what we were, is gratifying. . . . The formal narration of them, to be sure, is far from agreeable to me—but in my own self-communion upon the subject, I find a species of entertainment. (*FE* 219)

As his use of the word "experience" signals, Whitman is here describing—and perhaps struggling to legitimate—the reformative strategy of Washingtonian narrative form. As a reader of his own life history, Franklin finds "entertainment" in accounts of his own virile sexuality, even as he sheds tears over the victims of his voracious, "bloated" body and asks his readers to applaud that body's transformation into a more respectable masculine form. He also claims that the conversion to teetotalism represents a complete bodily metamorphosis, asking rhetorically: "What if the whole system must undergo a change, violent as that which we conceive of the mutation of form in some insects? What if a process comparable to flaying alive, have to be endured?" (*FE* 179). The function of the experience narrative, as well as Whitman's novel, is to enact such a physical and affective transformation, first constructing a mammoth and monstrous figure of "discolored" masculinity, only to dissolve that body in tears, leaving a sober, respectable white man in its place.

COUNTERPUBLIC SENTIMENTS

Discussing a different moment in the history of sentimentality, Eve Kosofsky Sedgwick asks: "[I]f the sentimental, as we have been taught, coincides topically with the feminine, with the place of women, then why should the foregrounded *male* physique be in an indicative relation to it?" Her claim is that gradually after 1880 "the exemplary instance of the sentimental ceases to be a woman per se, but instead becomes the body of a man who . . . physically dramatizes, *embodies* for an audience that both desires and cathartically identifies with him, a struggle of masculine identity with emotions or physical stigmata stereotyped as feminine."[41] So far I have demonstrated that the dynamic Sedgwick analyzes here was in operation in American popular culture earlier than she claims. Sentimentality was never as feminine nor as private an affective structure as we assume it was in the nineteenth century.[42] As early as the 1840s, when the ideology of gendered separate spheres was being forcefully inscribed in American culture, sentiment and male embodiment were already being deployed together as part of a public discourse of political reform and masculine self-fashioning.

The final section of this essay argues that Washingtonian sentimentality strove for more than the reformation of individual moral character or the restoration of broken families. The movement's critique was aimed less at private behavior than at the social formations that produced such behavior. At the same time, it was not a political movement in any simple sense; indeed, one distinguishing feature of Washingtonianism was its opposition to legal prohibition, its commitment to "moral suasion," or noncoercive social reform through voluntary association. In much of the fiction, "talking about politics" is seen as just as degrading as drinking itself, in part of course because party political activism usually involved a great deal of drinking; political campaigns at least since George Washington had budgeted money to "treat" prospective voters to alcohol. As Arthur says, "Elections . . . were carried by drinking. An electioneering campaign resembled, in some respect, the Bacchanalian orgies of old, rather than a general rational movement of the people, preparatory to an expression of their honest sentiments at the polls" (*SN* 2:82).[43] The group so emphatically avoided electoral politics that many of its members opposed prohibition legislation; indeed, one reason for the group's factionalization later in the 1840s was the ongoing debate between prohibitionists and those devoted to moral suasion.[44]

Although it used individual bodies as its instruments and eschewed electoral and legislative politics, the Washingtonian movement's remedy for social ills was a transformation of the public sphere. Indeed, one thing that distinguished these scenarios of men crying from a potentially feminizing sentimentality was their public nature, which both implicitly and explicitly marginalized women. The publicity of the experience narrative and the abstinence pledge, the Washingtonians argued, provided the regenerate man with a collective source of emotional support; it also drove home the threat of collective public censure were he to backslide. No less important, though, was the way an act of public speech reinforced gender distinctions that the sentimental responses of the crowd might otherwise have thrown into question. Women provided at least half the audience at most experience meetings, were encouraged to sign the pledge, and Washingtonianism was noted even at the time for involving an unprecedented number of women in temperance activity through auxiliary Martha Washington societies.[45] Women figured in the narratives as well, of course, though most often as passive victims of alcoholic male brutality. But women were not allowed to speak in the experience meetings themselves; they could neither lecture from the podium nor narrate their experiences from the floor.[46] The narrative and affective exchange of the experience meeting was meant to be a transaction between men.

Even as the Washingtonians emphasized their homosocial exclusivity, they fit Sedgwick's description of sentimental male embodiment as "a struggle of masculine identity with emotions . . . stereotyped as feminine." Writers and speakers constantly described Washingtonian sympathy as maternal: "We don't slight the drunkard; we love him, we nurse him, as a mother does her infant learning to walk."[47] Making this maternal sympathy into a form of public masculinity was not as easy as writing rules to exclude women speakers. In "The Widow's Son," one of the embedded tales in *Six Nights*, Arthur expostulates at length about the proper relation between these two sets of values, embodied in the relationship between a widowed woman and her son, an aspiring lawyer. "A mother who truly loves her son, has perceptions of right and wrong, far above his rational discriminations," Arthur writes, and at first these perceptions, combined with the young man's rationality, are sufficient to keep him from drink (*SN* 2:54). "He did not, of course, as a man, lay aside his rationality, and allow himself to be blindly influenced. He only sought the aid of a woman's perceptions to enable him to see a doubtful point in a truly rational light. . . . She was cautious not to make him feel restraint—nor to destroy his rational freedom; but, rather, to guard him by counsels that did not seem, and were not felt as such" (*SN* 2:56). But eventually the young man loses touch with his mother's sense of right and wrong, and she is horrified by "the discovery that her pure-minded, noble-spirited boy had fallen from the calm, rational dignity of manhood by a weak self-indulgence" that has cost him his reputation as a lawyer (*SN* 2:60–1). The story depicts at length the various ways in which Alfred is tempted to drink, including an argument presented by a rival attorney that "seems rational" to Alfred (*SN* 2:73), and conversations in which the young man's friends claim that it is "manly" to drink (*SN* 2:75). Each time the thought of his suffering mother descending further into poverty is almost enough to recall him to sobriety, but then a new challenge to his "manhood" makes him fall back off the wagon.

Revealingly, one of these challenges comes in the form of a political campaign; Alfred "sink[s] lower and lower" to the point of running for office. For Arthur, the problem goes beyond the fact that this activity gives Alfred more opportunity to drink. Even though his campaign is described relatively positively as a form of "active service" that allows him to "rise above" the memory of what he has lost due to alcoholism, the loss of the election, combined with his reaching the limits of his finances, brings him to the point of vowing abstinence from alcohol (*SN* 2:82–3). Politics is not the public realm that will lead him to redemption, however, for this vow depends on a faith in self that does not fit in with the Washingtonian formula for public redemption. So Alfred relapses again until he encounters a more authentic public sphere in the form of a Washingtonian meeting. As in most Washingtonian stories, it is only this that permanently cures Alfred of his drinking, leading him to financial success, a happy marriage, and a reconciliation with his mother.

The Washingtonian theory of moral suasion, then, is based neither on individual will nor on political force, and it depends on more than a balance between the power of maternal sympathy and the force of manly rationality.[48] To be effective, both of these individual faculties have to be made collective and, most importantly, public. Indeed, the Washingtonian project was ultimately the construction of what critical theorists Oscar Negt and Alexander Kluge have called a "counterpublic," defined by Nancy Fraser as a "parallel discursive arena . . . where members of subordinated social groups invent and circulate counterdiscourses to formulate oppositional interpretations of their identities, interests, and needs."[49] In a number of ways, notably in its intimate imbrication with the restricted family and domestic ideology, the Washingtonian counterpublic was comparable to the middle-class liberal public analyzed by most theorists and historians.[50] The trajectory of Washingtonian narratives leads almost invariably toward the reconstitution of such a family, even if that family unit has been ravaged by alcohol; this emphasis is paralleled in feminine and middle-class sentimental fiction, as is the constitution of the public by a circuit of publicly mediated sympathetic identifications. The Washingtonian public, however, was primarily working class or artisanal rather than middle-class and entrepreneurial, with its leisure activities and spaces far less rigorously divided from the workplace and less closely tied to the domestic sphere than the increasingly gender-and class-segregated leisure spaces of the bourgeoisie.[51] Thus the Washingtonians organized "fairs, picnics, concerts, balls, and processions" in the 1840s, as well as coffeeshops, temperance restaurants, reading rooms, and meeting places furnished with cold water. According to Ian Tyrrell, one issue of the Washingtonian weekly *New York Crystal Fount* "listed a half-dozen temperance concerts; one such meeting in December 1842 attracted over 4,000 persons, although attendances of around six hundred were more common at such functions."[52]

The ubiquity of stories about Washingtonians in the newspapers of the early 1840s, as well as the fact that Whitman's novel was published as a special issue of a New York weekly, underscore the centrality of print as the medium that brought even this oral narrative form and voluntary association to the attention of a wider public. As if they were not getting enough coverage from mainstream newspapers, they also founded innumerable new publications. Not all were based in major cities like the *Crystal Fount;* Jackson, Michigan, was the site of publication of *The Michigan Washingtonian* as late as 1846.[53] The Washingtonians were especially fond of positing an alternative nation by sponsoring Fourth of July picnics, "complete with games, feasts, toasts (in cold water), and bombastic orations on the 'second declaration of independence,' " from "King Alcohol."[54]

The experience meeting and other social forms produced in the Washingtonian movement were, then, all moves toward the construction of a counterpublic sphere, but to argue the same thing about the temperance novels of Whitman and Arthur is to contradict claims that pervade the theory of the novel from Ian Watt to Nancy Armstrong: claims that the modern novel, especially in the early stages of its development, is quintessentially middle-class precisely because of its individuating and privatizing narrative form, construction of character, and relation to its readers.[55] And it is true that the fictional narratives are far less likely than newspaper stories to represent the movement's alternative institutions. Indeed, they tend to deal with the conversion itself and anything afterwards in an almost perfunctory manner, concluding that there is nothing more to tell once the drunkard has been cured, no narrative of sober life as engaging, as provocative of sentiment, as the iniquities of the inebriate.

The narrative's failure to thematize Washingtonian publicity is, I would argue, a result of the fact that the novels themselves are meant to instantiate that publicity. The novels do not need to represent such alternative institutions because they *are* such institutions themselves. Of course all fiction aimed at social reform depends to some degree on the idea that publication is a public act in this sense. But it is important to remember that such a use of the novel was a relatively new phenomenon, especially within the temperance movement; it was not until 1836 that the American Temperance Union voted to approve the use of fiction to further the cause. Accordingly, the prefaces of both Arthur's and Whitman's texts, amidst standard claims not to be "a work of fiction" and to be built on "a basis of real incidents" announce themselves as "powerful auxiliaries in the promotion of [a] noble cause," and proclaim that the "New and Popular Reform now in the course of progress over the land, will find no trifling help from a TALE OF THE TIMES" (*FE* 126–8; *SN* I: iii–iv). In other words, for them the novel is in Michael Warner's phrase, "an exemplary public instrument."[56] And even when it is focussing on ostensibly domestic and private events like family reconciliation, Washingtonian fiction is far more explicitly and directly oriented towards the public than either the novels Habermas cites or subsequent sentimental fiction. As one small example: Arthur's "The Widow's Son" ends happily when a newspaper prints a paragraph entitled "A Pleasing Scene," which recounts the lawyer Alfred's recovery from alcoholism and his return to the "vigor, depth, and brilliancy of mind that distinguished his best efforts at the Bar, more than ten years ago" (*SN* 2: 105). His lover Florence, who had rejected him years before due to his drinking, reads this paragraph and the couple is thereby reconciled. Even romance and marriage, in the Washingtonians' world, are mediated through the publicity of print.

Both Whitman and Arthur emphasize the affective core of the reform movement to which their texts contribute; public opinion takes the form of public *sentiment*. As Arthur says, the guarantee of the "truth" of his tale is that "[at] every step of his progress in these tales, the writer has felt with the actors—sympathising with them in their heart-aching sorrows, and rejoicing with them when the morning has broken after a long night of affliction" (*SN* 1:iii). Such sentiments are designed to transcend the individual subject; they become public and specifically national in scope. Arthur concludes his introduction with the hope that "the whole country can now attest their power to move the heart," and Whitman even remarks on the medium of distribution of his text in "the cheap and popular form you see . . . wafted by every mail to all parts of this vast republic" in such a way as to affect "the mighty and deep public opinion" of Americans (*SN* 1:iv; *FE* 126–7).

Seeming to target individual moral transformation, Washingtonian sentiment in fact aims at a total reformation of American society and nationality. The group's often grandiose rhetoric of social transformation is in part a reflection of the millenialist character of most antebellum reform movements.[57] Those who lived through the period saw the relatively secular Washingtonian tide as a part of this phenomenon; one observer recalled that "[t]he 'Washingtonian' movement had swept over our land like a moral tornado, giving sight to the blind, healing to the broken-hearted, deliverance to the captives, a year of Jubilee. Miracles of healing had been wrought, and many hoped that the millennium had dawned!"[58] Whitman's representation of this "Jubilee" demonstrates that the Washingtonian millennium integrated sentimental and national rhetorics into its transformation of the public sphere. Near its conclusion, *Franklin Evans* contains a chapter in which its eponymous protagonist dreams that he is wandering through a "mighty and prosperous empire." In typical Whitmanian fashion, this nation—identified as America by the ubiquitous display of "the Star-Flag—emblem of Liberty"—is uncontained by national borders: "And how countless were the inhabitants of that country! On I went, and still on, and they swarmed thicker than before. It was almost without boundary, it seemed to me—with its far-stretching territories, and its States away up in the regions of the frozen north, and reaching down to the hottest sands of the torrid south—and with the two distant oceans for its side limits" (*FE* 220).

Evans has arrived in this phantasmatic nation on "some general holyday," which turns out to be the celebration of the last drunkard's signing of the temperance pledge. He looks on in pleasure at the spectacle, which includes a parade:

> First came a host of men in the prime of life, with healthy faces and stalwart forms, and every appearance of vigor [who] had once been under the dominion of the Tempter, but were now redeemed. . . . Then I saw a myriad of youths, with blooming cheeks and bright eyes. . . . Not the least beautiful part of the procession, was composed of bands of women and young girls. (*FE* 221)

This pleasurable display of gendered bodies is succeeded by a banner depicting the victory of feminine sentiment over masculine embodiment, picturing "the figure of a fair female, robed in pure white. Under her feet were the senseless remains of a hideous monster, in whose grapple thousands and millions had fallen, but who was now powerless and dead" (*FE* 222). Finally this display of "public joy" reorganizes itself around "the Last Vassal," who signs the pledge. In the process, however, the crowd has been refigured: "Far around, on every side, countless multitudes of nothing but human heads were to be seen, in one compact body" (*FE* 222). The man signs the pledge, and "the people are regenerated!" (*FE* 223). Introduced by Evans's rhapsody to the pleasures of looking back on his "experience," this dream sequence stands in for the experience meeting which is never actually depicted in the novel. In its imaging of an imperialist nation apparently engaged in perpetual public display, it also clearly represents the utopian outcome of Washingtonian publicity, as the display of virile, desiring bodies is supplanted by the affective unity of a single public body whose "rational sentiments" are signalled by the fact that its only visible feature is its multiplicity of heads.

Describing the body around which this celebration is organized with the peculiar archaism and Old World associations of the word "Vassal," however, again points up the unstable valence of the rhetorical equivalence between alcoholism and slavery, for this time it is articulated to an explicitly proslavery discourse.[59] Imagined by a man who has escaped the seductive temptations of the Northern city only to be more fatally tempted by the conflicted pleasures of miscegenated Southern desire, who has just narrated the story of his black wife's murder of his white mistress, and who has a few pages earlier almost gratuitously apostrophized the virtues of Southern slavery—a "merely nominal oppression" when compared to "the stern reality of starvation and despotism" in Europe (*FE* 202)—this version of the Washingtonian counterpublic is subtly but significantly racialized. Its central figure, like the novel's protagonist, has publicly performed an odd version of the blackface minstrelsy that was a popular form of temperance entertainment amongst the Washingtonians, playing "The Last Slave of Appetite" before an audience only recently and tentatively able to identify with the position of white masculinity to which he aspires: "I joy that I occupy my position before you now, as I do!"[60] And now he has emerged "regenerated" from his downward spiral, free from the bodily bonds that are figured as unambiguously parallel to those binding black slaves: " 'This day,' continued he, "I throw off the chains, and take upon myself the pleasant bondage of good' " (FE 222).

Even in its most phantasmatic and utopian incarnation, access to the Washingtonian counterpublic depended upon acquisition of the status attributes that were prerequisite to full participation in the bourgeois public sphere of antebellum America: whiteness, maleness, self-possession. In themselves, none of these attributes are made unambiguously appealing in temperance narratives, whether they are depicted as a "pleasant bondage" or especially when they are characterized as pure negations, as the absence of color, of sentiment, of bodiliness, of affect. What this public fantasy offered the ethnic drinkers who were the Washingtonians' newest recruits was the capacity for abstracting and unmarking the bodily particularities that constituted their racial and gender attributes. Washingtonian whiteness and masculinity are constructed through a dialectic of identification and disavowal; the drunkard, and those who sympathize with him, become white men by dissolving their bodies in tears. The temperance story provides a narrative form for that process, restructuring the ambiguous affective responses embodied in the figure of the alcoholic and transforming them into a more legible sentimental experience.

NOTES

1. While the new organizations that arose in the early 1840s took on a variety of names, the general phenomenon was known then as the Washingtonian movement and historians still refer to it as such.

2. The term "experience meeting" and the form of public confessional narrative used by the Washingtonians were products "of English working-class teetotalism of the 1830[s]," which in turn derived from Methodism, with its enthusiastic emotionality (Wesley himself refers to it as a "religion of the heart"), egalitarian sense of community, and rigorous internalization of moral and labor discipline (Raymond Williams, *Keywords: A Vocabulary of Culture and Society* rev. ed. [New York: Oxford University Press, 1983], 128). The movement drew support from a range of evangelical churches, especially those whose parishioners were mostly poor, such as the Primitive Methodists and the Universalists.

3. In 1837, the American Temperance Society reorganized as the American Temperance Union. This and other historical points about the Washingtonians and the mainstream temperance movement are drawn from the many temperance histories that deal with the period, including Jack S. Blocker, Jr., *American Temperance Movements: Cycles of Reform* (Boston: Twayne, 1989); Jed Dannenbaum, *Drink and Disorder: Temperance Reform in Cincinnati from the Washingtonian Revival to the WCTU* (Urbana: University of Illinois Press, 1984); Bar-

bara Leslie Epstein, *The Politics of Domesticity: Women, Evangelism, and Temperance in Nineteenth-Century America* (Middletown, Conn.: Wesleyan University Press, 1981); Joseph R. Gusfield, *Symbolic Crusade: Status Politics and the American Temperance Movement* (Urbana: University of Illinois Press, 1970); Robert L. Hampel, *Temperance and Prohibition in Massachusetts, 1813–1852* (Ann Arbor: University Microfilms International Research Press, 1982); John Allen Krout, *The Origins of Prohibition* (New York: Alfred A. Knopf, 1925); and especially Ian Tyrrell, *Sobering Up: From Temperance to Prohibition in Antebellum America, 1800–1860* (Westport, Conn.: Greenwood Press, 1979). A useful compendium of earlier histories of the Washingtonian phenomenon is Milton A. Maxwell, "The Washingtonian Movement," *Quarterly Journal of Studies on Alcohol* 11 (1950): 410–51.

4. Quoted in Maxwell, "The Washingtonian Movement," 419.

5. T[imothy] S[hay] Arthur, *Temperance Tales; or, Six Nights with the Washingtonians*, 2 vols. (1842; reprint, 2 vols. in 1, St. Clair Shores, Mich.: Scholarly Press, 1971). Further citations will be made parenthetically within the text, and abbreviated *SN.*

6. Abraham Lincoln, *An Address Delivered by Abraham Lincoln, Before the Springfield, Washingtonian Temperance Society, at the Second Presbyterian Church, Springfield, Illinois, On the 22d Day of February, 1842* (Springfield, Ill.: O. H. Oldroyd, 1889).

7. Walt Whitman, *Franklin Evans, or The Inebriate*, in *The Early Poems and the Fiction*, ed. Thomas L. Brasher (New York: New York University Press, 1963), 124–239. Further citations will be made parenthetically within the text, and abbreviated *FE.* For a complete account of *Franklin Evans's* publication history, see Brasher's footnote 1 on 124–6. Two of Whitman's pro-Washingtonian editorials are reprinted in *Walt Whitman of the "New York Aurora": Editor at Twenty-Two*, ed. Joseph Jay Rubin and Charles H. Brown (State College, Penn.: Bald Eagle Press, 1950), 35–6.

8. Walt Whitman, *The Madman*, in Brasher, *Early Poems and Fiction*, 240–3. No subsequent installments of *The Madman* have been located.

9. Michael Warner, "Whitman Drunk," in *Breaking Bounds: Whitman and American Cultural Studies*, ed. Betsy Erkkila and Jay Grossman (New York: Oxford University Press, 1996), 30–43, quotation from 34.

10. See Tyrrell, *Sobering Up*, 135–51.

11. For a discussion of the key critical and historical texts that developed and institutionalized the domestic / public opposition as central to an understanding of nineteenth-century American culture, especially the "women's sphere" and sentimental fiction, see the introduction to this volume. Much recent work on American masculinity is based on this feminist work and to a large extent shares its conceptualization of the public / private split; a list of such scholarship is also in the introduction. While acknowledging the usefulness and productivity of this formulation, feminist critics and historians have in recent years discovered its limitations: see for instance Mary P. Ryan, *Women in Public: Between Banners and Ballots, 1825–1880* (Baltimore: Johns Hopkins University Press, 1990) and Linda K. Kerber, "Separate Spheres, Female Worlds, Woman's Place: The Rhetoric of Women's History," *Journal of American History* 75, no. 1 (June 1988) 9–39.

12. Whether they value the sentimental novel positively or negatively, most participants in the debate over its politics characterize it in these terms: see especially Nina Baym, *Woman's Fiction: A Guide to Novels by and about Women in America, 1820–1870* (Ithaca: Cornell University Press, 1978); Ann Douglas, *The Feminization of American Culture* (New York: Avon, 1977); and Jane Tompkins, *Sensational Designs: The Cultural Work of American Fiction, 1790–1860* (New York: Oxford University Press, 1985).

13. I argue for the use of Raymond Williams's term "structure of feeling" in the analysis of sentimental culture in "The Structure of Sentimental Experience: A Response to Marianne Noble," *Yale Journal of Criticism* (forthcoming). Joel Pfister has recently suggested that the entire concept of the psychological—the development of which includes the history of sentimentality—can be viewed through the lens of Williams's concept. See "On Conceptualizing the Cultural History of Emotional and Psychological Life in America," in *Inventing the Psychological: Toward a Cultural History of Emotional Life in America*, ed. Joel Pfister and Nancy Schnog (New Haven: Yale University Press, 1997), 43 n. 2. For a definition of a "structure of feeling," see Raymond Williams, *Marxism and Literature* (Oxford: Oxford University Press, 1977), 128–35.

14. Quoted in Maxwell, "The Washingtonian Movement," 412.

15. Lincoln, *Address*, 7.

16. Philip Fisher, *Hard Facts: Setting and Form in the American Novel* (New York: Oxford University Press, 1985), 99.

17. For details on the class composition of Washingtonian chapters see Tyrrell, *Sobering Up*, 162–71. He argues that the group was not exclusively working-class; it included members from various class positions, most notably artisans displaced by upheavals of rapid industrialization whose livelihood had been damaged by the depression of 1837. "What distinguished the Washingtonians of the early 1840s," he concludes, was not a homogeneously working-class constituency, but "the relative absence of the older evangelicals and wealthy and upwardly mobile captains of industry from controlling positions in the new societies" (167). As Bruce Laurie argues, it is this relative autonomy from direct bourgeois supervision that makes the Washingtonian movement less easy to fit into the argument that temperance movements were a form of middle-class social control (*Working People of Philadelphia, 1800–1850* [Philadelphia: Temple University Press 1980], 40–2).

18. The Washingtonians also differed from many of their predecessors in their insistence on total abstinence; most regular temperance organizations had not completely rejected wine and beer. However, the teetotalist position had been gaining strength for some time; the new movement was responsible for popularizing it, but it was not their innovation. For instance, the mainstream American Temperance Society adopted a total abstinence pledge in 1836 (Tyrrell, *Sobering Up*, 137, 144).

19. Lincoln, *Address*, 5.

20. Quoted in Krout, *Origins of Prohibition*, 189. "Interpellation" is Louis Althusser's term describing the way that ideology addresses and constitutes the subject, constituting identity through the very act of "hailing" the individual. See Louis Althusser, *Lenin and Philosophy*, trans. Ben Brewster (New York: Monthly Review Press, 1971), 127–86.

21. Quoted in Krout, *Origins of Prohibition*, 189.

22. For more on the logic of sympathetic identification, see my essay "The Limits of Sympathy: Louisa May Alcott and the Sentimental Novel," *American Literary History* 3 (1991): 685–706.

23. The exclusive homosociality of Washingtonian stories differentiates this from other moments in the history of the temperance narrative. Though the stories include other stock tropes, including the long-suffering wife and the neglected but still loving child, what has redemptive power is most often the sympathy of other men. On the power of the child in temperance fiction, see Karen Sánchez-Eppler, "Temperance in the Bed of a Child: Incest and Social Order in Nineteenth-Century America," in *American Quarterly* 47, no. 1 (1995): 1–33, and on the figure of the wife see Jerome Nadelhaft, "Alcohol and Wife Abuse

in Antebellum Male Temperance Literature," *Canadian Review of American Studies* 25, no. 1 (1995): 15–41.

24. Quoted in Krout, *Origins of Prohibition*, 189.

25. W. H. Daniels, ed., *The Temperance Reform and Its Great Reformers. An Illustrated History* (New York: Nelson & Phillips 1878), 127.

26. Shirley Samuels, introduction to *The Culture of Sentiment: Race, Gender, and Sentimentality in Nineteenth-Century America.* (New York: Oxford University Press, 1992), 3–8, quotation from 3; Karen Sánchez-Eppler, *Touching Liberty: Abolition, Feminism, and the Politics of the Body* (Berkeley: University of California Press, 1993), 27.

27. Sánchez-Eppler, *Touching Liberty*, 1, 49.

28. For an account of how disembodied abstraction, or "the principle of negativity," constitutes American citizenship, see Michael Warner, "The Mass Public and the Mass Subject," in *Habermas and the Public Sphere*, ed. Craig Calhoun (Cambridge: MIT Press, 1992). Warner's account of this mechanism is concise: "Access to the public came in the whiteness and maleness that were then denied as forms of positivity, since the white male qua public person was only abstract rather than white and male. . . . Self-abstraction from male bodies confirms masculinity" (382–3).

29. Dannenbaum, *Drink and Disorder,* 44.

30. Quoted in Krout, *Origins of Prohibition*, 187.

31. David S. Reynolds, *Beneath the American Renaissance: The Subversive Imagination in the Age of Emerson and Melville* (Cambridge: Harvard University Press, 1989), 359. In *Walt Whitman's America: A Cultural Biography* (New York: Knopf, 1995), Reynolds confirms that Whitman attended Gough's Washingtonian lectures in New York, and in general provides more information on Whitman's connection to the temperance movement (92–7).

32. Quoted in Krout, *Origins of Prohibition*, 197. Gough himself was charmingly self-deprecating about his physical strength and appearance in his *Autobiography*. Thanks to John Crowley for pointing me to the earlier, 1845 version of Gough's *Autobiography*, in which he is much more interestingly and systematically Washingtonian in his self-presentation than in his more widely available 1870 version. See *An Autobiography of John B. Gough* (Boston, 1845) and *Autobiography and Personal Recollections of John B. Gough, With Twenty-Six Years' Experience as a Public Speaker* (Springfield, Mass.: Bill, Nichols & Co., 1870).

33. Moon argues persuasively that Whitman's poetic practice in the 1855 *Leaves of Grass* refashions for his own literary-political purposes contemporary discourses on the body, most notably anti-onanist and temperance discourses. His emphasis on the metaphorics of fluidity common to literary and political discourses is especially illuminating. The only disagreement I have with Moon's argument is that I think the "fluidity" between politics and sexuality, and between the text and the body, is present in at least potential form in Washingtonian discourse itself; I give Whitman somewhat less credit for bringing that potential out. Put another way: while Moon argues that Whitman queers temperance discourse, I argue that it was pretty queer already. See Michael Moon, *Disseminating Whitman: Revision and Corporeality in "Leaves of Grass"* (Cambridge: Harvard University Press, 1991), 1–87.

34. The story's ambiguous link to the temperance cause was further evinced when Whitman revised and republished it in the *American Review* in 1845 as "The Death of Wind-Foot," but then republished it without further changes later the same year in the *Crystal Fount and Rechabite Recorder.* Though there are some minor differences between the story in the novel and the later versions, in none of its incarnations is alcohol mentioned. See Brasher's note to *Franklin Evans*, 126 n. 1.

35. The dual nature of the drunkard's transformation parallels the connection Frederick Douglass makes between freedom and manhood in his *Autobiography* and *The Heroic Slave*. See Richard Yarborough's analysis "Race, Violence, and Manhood: The Masculine Ideal in Frederick Douglass's *The Heroic Slave*," in *Frederick Douglass: New Literary and Historical Essays,* ed. Eric J. Sundquist (Cambridge: Cambridge University Press, 1990), 166–88.

36. The temperance movement was at this point just beginning to invent the idea of addiction, a concept that internalizes the causes of the compulsion to drink and thus makes its comparison with slavery less plausible. See Eve Kosofsky Sedgwick, *Tendencies* (Durham, N. C.: Duke University Press, 1993), 130–42, and Warner's use of her argument in "Whitman Drunk," 33–4.

37. Donald Yacovone, "The Transformation of the Black Temperance Movement, 1827–1854: An Interpretation." *Journal of the Early Republic,* 8 (1988): 281–97, quotations from 290–1.

38. *Orations of John B. Gough, with Sketch of his Life* (Toronto, William Briggs, 1886), 28.

39. For historical accounts of the social construction of working-class whiteness, see David Roediger, *The Wages of Whiteness: Race and the Making of the American Working Class* (London: Verso, 1991) and *Towards the Abolition of Whiteness: Essays on Race, Politics, and Working Class History* (London: Verso, 1994), and Noel Ignatiev, *How the Irish Became White* (New York: Routledge, 1995). Michael Omi and Howard Winant define a "racial project" as "simultaneously an interpretation, representation, or explanation of racial dynamics, and an effort to reorganize and redistribute resources along particular racial lines. Racial projects connect what race means in a particular discursive practice and the ways in which both social structures are racially *organized*, based upon that meaning" (*Racial Formation in the United States: From the 1960s to the 1990s,* 2d ed. [New York: Routledge, 1994], 56).

40. See Sean Wilentz, *Chants Democratic: New York City and the Rise of the American Working Class, 1788–1850* (New York: Oxford University Press, 1984), 312.

41. Eve Kosofsky Sedgwick, *Epistemology of the Closet* (Berkeley: University of California Press, 1990), 142, 146.

42. Here too, however, I am in a sense agreeing with Sedgwick, who argues that "[t]he immense productiveness of the public / private crux in feminist thought has come, not from the confirmation of an original hypothesized homology that male:female::public:private, but from the wealth of its deconstructive deformations" (*Epistemology,* 109).

43. Tyrrell cites several sources claiming that the elections of 1842 and 1844 were major causes of backsliding amongst Washingtonians (*Sobering Up,* 206–7).

44. The two major debates that factionalized the Washingtonians and led to the end of their phase of the temperance movement were over the value of "Maine Laws" prohibiting the sale of alcohol, which were antithetical to the Washingtonian commitment to "moral suasion," and over the appropriateness of newly formed secret societies like the Sons of Temperance and the Good Templars, which contradicted the Washingtonians' commitment to publicity. The former debate had its counterpart in the abolitionist movement, but with quite different implications; see P. Gabrielle Foreman's essay in this volume. Arthur, despite his early commitment to moral suasion, was an enthusiastic prohibitionist by the time he wrote *Ten Nights in a Bar-Room* in 1854. For differing accounts of the tensions between the Washingtonians and prohibitionism, see Tyrrell, *Sobering Up,* 191–224, and Leonard U. Blumberg, "The Significance of the Alcohol Prohibitionists for the Washington Temperance Societies," *Journal of Studies on Alcohol* 41, no. 1 (1980): 37–77.

45. Tyrrell cites several groups whose membership lists were predominantly female, and claims that in New York City "Washingtonian women usually outnumbered men at temperance functions" (*Sobering Up*, 179).

46. See Dannenbaum, *Drink and Disorder*, 34.

47. Quoted in Maxwell, "The Washingtonian Movement," 415.

48. Nor did the Washingtonians put much stock in the power of prayer. After his first vow, Alfred prays for the strength to remain temperate, and his mother does little in the story but pray for him. Such prayers are rarely answered in Washingtonian fiction, more evidence that although the organization appropriated the forms of religious revivalism, especially Methodism, they significantly secularized those forms.

49. Nancy Fraser, "Rethinking the Public Sphere: A Contribution to the Critique of Actually Existing Democracy," in Calhoun, *Habermas and the Public Sphere*, 109–42, quotation from 123. The term "counterpublic" derives from the work of Oscar Negt and Alexander Kluge in *Public Sphere and Experience: Toward an Analysis of the Bourgeois and Proletarian Public Sphere*, trans. Peter Labanyi, Jamie Owen Daniel, and Assenka Oksiloff (Minneapolis: University of Minnesota Press, 1993). The concept has been especially fruitful for feminists; see Rita Felski's positing of a feminist public sphere in *Beyond Feminist Aesthetics: Feminist Literature and Social Change* (Cambridge: Harvard University Press, 1989) 164–74.

50. The major theorization of the bourgeois public sphere is Jürgen Habermas, *The Structural Transformation of the Public Sphere: An Inquiry into a Category of Bourgeois Society*, trans. Thomas Burger and Frederick Lawrence (Cambridge: MIT Press, 1989), 31–43. The history of the rise of the public sphere in the United States is told in Michael Warner, *The Letters of the Republic: Publication and the Public Sphere in Eighteenth-Century America* (Cambridge: Harvard University Press, 1990). I discuss the usefulness of Habermas's formulation for nineteenth-century American literature and culture in "Pandering in the Public Sphere: Masculinity and the Market in Horatio Alger," *American Quarterly* 48 (1996): 415–38, as well as in my forthcoming *Public Sentiments: Fictions of the Public Sphere in Nineteenth-Century America*.

51. On the development of class differences in leisure, see Lawrence W. Levine, *Highbrow / Lowbrow: The Emergence of Cultural Hierarchy in America* (Cambridge: Harvard University Press, 1988), and Kathy Peiss, *Cheap Amusements: Working Women and Leisure in Turn-of-the-Century New York* (Philadelphia: Temple University Press, 1986).

52. Tyrrell, *Sobering Up*, 177–8.

53. Brother Roger Jamison, *Temperance Movement in South Bend and St. Joseph County, 1830 to 1855* (master's thesis, Notre Dame, Ind., 1938), 34.

54. See Tyrrell, *Sobering Up*, 178.

55. Thanks to Gloria-Jean Masciarotte for pointing out this continuity running from Watt to Armstrong, whose arguments are otherwise quite different. See Ian Watt, *The Rise of the Novel: Studies in Defoe, Richardson, and Fielding* (Berkeley: University of California Press, 1957), and Nancy Armstrong, *Desire and Domestic Fiction: A Political History of the Novel* (New York: Oxford University Press, 1987).

56. Warner, *Letters*, 154; he applies this description to Charles Brockden Brown's novel *Arthur Mervyn*.

57. On evangelism and reform, see Mary P. Ryan, *Cradle of the Middle Class: The Family in Oneida County, New York, 1790–1865* (Cambridge: Cambridge University Press, 1981); Paul Johnson, *A Shopkeeper's Millennium: Society and Revivals in Rochester, New York, 1815–1837* (New York: Hill and Wang, 1978); and Steven Mintz, *Moralists and Modernizers: America's Pre–Civil War Reformers* (Baltimore: Johns Hopkins University Press, 1995).

58. Quoted in Dannenbaum, *Drink and Disorder*, 36.

59. Warner characterizes the dream sequence as condensing the Washingtonians' "fantasy of stateless public association," but also remarks that "[i]f it weren't so queer, this passage would be a true nightmare of democratic totalitarianism," identifying as mitigating queerness the man's spectacular self-relation, Evans's presence as spectator, and the "campy feudalism involved in calling John Doe the Last Vassal" ("Whitman Drunk," 34). What is left out of this dialectic of stateless association and democratic totalitarianism is the racialized basis of this fantasy that I identify below: if the Last Vassal's performance is a form of camp, his claim to be a slave breaking his chains is a form of blackface.

60. The Washingtonians' appreciation for blackface minstrelsy was one of the aspects of the movement that temperance regulars saw as less than respectable. Horace Greeley campaigned in the *New York Daily Tribune* against Charley White's Kentucky Negro Minstrels, who first came to public attention performing at the Washingtonian Teetotaler's Hall (see Tyrrell, *Sobering Up*, 195). For more on how the popularity of blackface minstrelsy contributed to the social construction of whiteness in the 1840s, see Eric Lott, *Love and Theft: Blackface Minstrelsy and the American Working Class* (New York: Oxford University Press, 1993).

CHAPTER SEVEN

Sentimental Abolition in Douglass's Decade

Revision, Erotic Conversion, and the Politics of Witnessing
in The Heroic Slave *and* My Bondage and My Freedom

P. Gabrielle Foreman

> If the volume now presented to the public were a mere work of ART, the history
> of its misfortune might be written in two very simple words—TOO LATE. The
> nature and character of slavery have been subjects of an almost endless variety
> of artistic representation; and after the brilliant achievements in that field, and
> while those achievements are yet fresh in the memory of the million, he who
> would add another to the legion, must possess the charm of transcendent
> excellence, or apologize for something worse than rashness.
>
> EDITOR'S PREFACE TO FREDERICK DOUGLASS, *MY BONDAGE AND MY FREEDOM* (1855)

Frederick Douglass stands as the only African American of the nineteenth century to receive sustained and serious critical attention. Amidst the celebration
and republications of previously underaddressed works by African Americans,
Douglass's work continues to be central; in the 1990s, two volumes of critical
essays and an additional award-winning biography have taken their places
amongst Douglass scholarship. Criticism that addresses Douglass's artful narrative representations is now plentiful enough that another essay might easily be
dismissed with the two words from my epigraph—"TOO LATE."[1] Yet, in the opening sentences of his preface, the editor of Douglass's *My Bondage and My Freedom*
refers to the very dynamics that also justify another article that takes Douglass as
its subject. The subtle, though not oblique, reference to Harriet Beecher Stowe's
Uncle Tom's Cabin[2]—the brilliant achievement "fresh in the memory of the million"—alerts contemporary readers of Douglass's post-Stowe writings not only
to the politics of authority and revision at work in his novella *The Heroic Slave*
(1853) and his second autobiography (1855), but also to his complicated negotiation of sentiment.

Douglass distances himself from Garrisonian moral suasion, at the same time that he adopts a heightened sentimentality as a rhetorical strategy in his own fictional and autobiographical writings. While the Douglass of the *Narrative* (1845), his first autobiography, does not engage in consistent sentimental renderings of domesticity, the 1855 narrator does. Recent critics acknowledge Douglass's use of sentiment and Stowe, while some emphasize his simultaneous search for, relation to, and reconstruction of (white) paternal power and the rhetoric of the U.S. revolution.[3] While I touch upon Douglass's articulation of reconstituted manhood, my focus is on Douglass's rhetorical use of sentimentality.

Deborah McDowell notes that "*My Bondage and My Freedom* reveals more clearly than the first narrative that Douglass's rewriting of his own origins does more than satisfy the dictates of abolitionism. It also makes intelligible Douglass's and the movement's problematical relation to the feminine."[4] To McDowell's analysis I would add that Douglass's genealogical revisions also illuminate his, and abolitionism's, complicated relation both to the feminized, and to the erotically fraternal. In paradoxical ways, Douglass's post-Stowe writings bring to the fore questions of how domestic ideology informs abolitionist strategies. Douglass's autobiographical projects call for the consideration of racial aspects of sentimentality that take into account domesticity's influence beyond a woman's sphere.

What I call "sentimental abolition"[5] renames, and, I hope, allows us to retheorize, the heightened connection between abolition and what is too often considered the separate sphere of sentimentality.[6] Sentimental abolition coincides with, and borrows from the power of, the extended domestic spheres popularized in reformist communities and culture in the 1830s and 1840s; it stresses the affectional over the authoritative, emphasizing that the heart is the only true site of change and redemption. Sentimental abolition's emphasis on the affectional also distances it from political reform,[7] but these terms are not dichotomous: Douglass's sentimental abolition allows him to explore emotive arenas in order to energize political protest. In claiming sentimental abolition as a category, I would further assert that its emphasis on transforming the public through the affectional realm facilitates a particularly eroticized means of conversion to the antislavery cause. Not only do the heroines Georgianna in William Wells Brown's *Clotel* and Mrs. Bird in *Uncle Tom's Cabin*, for example, bring their partners to espouse abolition, but fictional slave *heroes* also convert white male characters by first touching their hearts.

In *The Heroic Slave* and *My Bondage and My Freedom*, Douglass revises Stowe both by de-emphasizing women's centrality and by striving to convert his characters and readers by linking emotive sympathy to judicial standing. As Douglass moves away from Garrisonian abolition and embraces political action and the promise of the constitution, he is aware that although his gendered strategies and his political positioning have changed, his political position as a legally disenfranchised African American man has not. In the years leading to the Dred Scott decision (1857), Douglass is increasingly concerned with questions of Black social and political agency: although he is exasperated with being a moral witness, an objectified icon on the Garrisonian abolitionist platform, he is acutely aware that white men are the only reader-citizens imbued with legal standing as witnesses; they are his only politically embodied readers; the only ones, that is, with a "vote."

White men become, then, the primary object of Douglass's political desire, and he turns them into the objects of desiring in *The Heroic Slave*. Douglass makes a representational choice to recognize that only the white male gaze and ear have the actual power to confirm his slave protagonist Madison Washington's subjectivity.[8] Douglass pairs the patriarchal and political power of the gaze with what both contemporary critical discourse and slave narrative discourse cast as the feminized vulnerability and penetrability of the ear. Through the white male response to Madison's invasive sensorial presence, Douglass attempts to seduce white male readers to antislavery activism as a means of achieving future Black rights and subjectivity.

In this paper I will address Douglass's quest for status as an independent agent in the sphere of political rights, where witnessing, converting witnesses, and gaining standing as witness in one's own right are increasingly problematic. Examining Douglass's rewriting in *The Heroic Slave* of Stowe's famous *Uncle Tom's Cabin* chapter "In Which It Appears That The Senator Is But a Man," Douglass's revision of his own autobiographical account of his Aunt Hester's beating,[9] and *The Heroic Slave*'s conversion to abolitionism of the white man Listwell, will reveal how Douglass weds sympathy to standing. Ultimately, in his revision of himself and of Stowe, I contend that as he (again) writes women's voices out of his texts, he locates his political intervention within the language of domestic affection and sentimental abolition. Furthermore, instead of simply mimicking the cultural norms of heroic manhood,[10] his recognition of available representational strategies and Black racial and sexualized positioning combines to produce an eroticized bond between men.

ı⁴ı

A glance at the historical record can contextualize Douglass's move away from Garrisonian moral suasion and his continuous use of the rhetoric of sentimental abolition. After two years of forced, if pleasant, post-*Narrative* exile, Douglass came back from London in 1847 with his freedom papers and enough money to begin his own newspaper—both gifts, so to speak, from English abolitionists. He was disappointed with the Garrisonians' response to his initiative, for they were "opposed to the idea of [his] starting a paper, and for several reasons. First, the paper was not needed; secondly, it would interfere with [his] usefulness as a lecturer; thirdly, [he] was better fitted to speak than to write; fourthly, the paper could not succeed."[11] As a result of Garrison's opposition, Douglass moved to Rochester, N.Y., and founded *The North Star*, which he soon merged with political abolitionist Gerrit Smith's paper and renamed *Frederick Douglass's Paper* to reflect his continued editorial control. Douglass began to reconsider his position on voting; he endorsed political candidates and, in 1852, became actively involved in Gerrit Smith's successful bid for Congress. Douglass also rethought his previously Garrisonian ideas about the antislavery nature of the constitution, and crystallized his former uneasiness about nonviolence as an abolitionist strategy.

Although Douglass's descriptions in *Bondage* gloss over the explosiveness of his split with the Garrisonians, and the bitter melee that ensued, Douglass was in fact maligned as an apostate in one of the most public personal divisions of the abolitionist movement. In the 9 December 1853 edition of *Frederick Douglass's Paper,* he described the break as an attack charged "with a bitterness ever increasing and a steadiness and violence only characteristic of malice, deep, broad, lasting in its worst form."[12] Douglass devoted almost a whole issue of his paper to reprinting the attacks on his personal life and political stances, and responding to them.

By 1853, Garrison was not the only major antislavery figure with whom Douglass had to reckon. The historical record also elucidates the overlappings and convergences between Douglass's *The Heroic Slave* (1853) and Stowe's *Uncle Tom's Cabin* (1852). Douglass himself had written a glowing review of *Uncle Tom's Cabin* in 1852. The next year Stowe's *The Key to Uncle Tom's Cabin* was greeted with panegyric praise in *Douglass's Paper,* and when Douglass accepted Stowe's invitation to visit at her home, the two authors had much to discuss. While other Black leaders had condemned the colonizationist stance in *Uncle Tom's Cabin* and, in strong language, had raised questions about Stowe's free use of slaves' stories as her own, Douglass had been relatively gentle and had tried to forge alliances. With James McCune, a doctor who held advanced degrees from the University of Glasgow and was the most prominent Black reformer in New York City, and James Pennington, another renowned fugitive narrator, Douglass petitioned Stowe to help them raise funds for a Black industrial college. In 1853, it looked as if their alliance would be successful.[13] In that year, the National Negro Convention also reconvened and acknowledged the two writers' prominence: The organizers listed as reasons for reconvention the Fugitive Slave Act; segregated schools; colonization; social, economic, and political barriers; and "withal the propitious awakening to the fact of our condition at home and abroad, which has followed the publication of *Uncle Tom's Cabin*." They went on to cite Stowe's influence in their opening address, and to elect *Frederick Douglass's Paper,* where *The Heroic Slave* was first published, as their official organ.[14]

A final important piece of historical background is that the actual life of *The Heroic Slave*'s protagonist, a successful slave mutineer named Madison Washington, converged with Douglass's life in ways that might have made Madison appealing to Douglass. Both made their initial escapes in 1835, and both came to the fore as public figures in 1841. But Douglass also uses Stowe's hero as a point of departure for Madison Washington. When, in Madison's opening soliloquy, he refers to a disembodied character, Tom, as if his readers would know who Tom is, of course they would: "if Tom can do it [survive and escape]," Madison muses, "so can I."

As he breaks away from Garrisonian abolitionism, Douglass consciously circulates the image of Madison Washington to rewrite Stowe's pacifist vision and to counter the figure of ex-slave autobiographer Josiah Henson, whose popularity surged after he became known as the "authentic" model for Stowe's religious martyr, Uncle Tom.

This historical aside helps clarify the cultural context in which Douglass was maneuvering. Despite his shift to political abolition, in 1853 both he and Stowe were more rhetorically invested in conversion than in coercion. As a literary strategy, this situates them within a model of internal change rather than external regulation, a model aligned with what Richard H. Brodhead calls "disciplinary intimacy." Brodhead explains that:

> A first feature of this *collectively* composed disciplinary model is that it requires authority to put on a human face. A second feature is a purposeful sentimentalization of the disciplinary relation: a strategic relocation of authority relations in the realm of emotion and a conscious intensification of the emotional bond between the authority figure and its charge.[15]

Disciplinary intimacy leads to a move from an authoritative to an affectional regime and regimen. Garrison's pronouncement, "Let us aim to abolitionize the *consciences* and *hearts* of the people, and we may trust them at the ballot-box, or anywhere else,"[16] is a direct example of this type of affectional rule. Douglass never rejects this model, but he does invert who the authority is and who is the charge. He insists that Garrison's "us" and "them" must be freed of the white paternalism and prejudice of both the movement and the broader culture.

What I would like to suggest is that affectional desire and regulation is slippery terrain. Abolitionist Lyman Cobb suggests that "the parent or teacher should, first of all, secure the LOVE and AFFECTION of his children or pupils. He will then have an unlimited control over their minds and conducts."[17] Madison Washington and Douglass are of course nothing if not teachers in an affectional realm that leaves the field of eroticized pedagogy wide open. *The Heroic Slave* also serves as a postscript to Douglass's 1852 letter to Charles Sumner in which he had written that in relation to Garrison he stood "something like a child to a parent."[18] Douglass publicly realigns his relation to Garrison by becoming Listwell's abolitionist teacher and "father," thereby reclaiming slave authority and upsetting abolitionist paternalism. As a result, the categories of fraternal and erotic love blend into each other in *The Heroic Slave* as they do in *Uncle Tom's Cabin*.[19]

In 1853, Douglass consciously replicates and revises Stowe's strategies, carefully shifting the meanings Stowe assigns to Tom's body, its circulation, and Tom's "escape," in an effort to attract, rather than alienate, both Stowe and her readers. His "Section II" of *The Heroic Slave*, a scene at the home of the Listwells, is a case in point; it is an explicit refiguration of the oft-quoted Senator and Mrs. Bird chapter in *Uncle Tom's Cabin*. One might characterize Listwell as the co-protagonist of *The Heroic Slave*. He is a Northerner who is so overwhelmed by Madison's speech and presence that, when he happens upon the slave on a trip South, he becomes an abolitionist. In both Douglass and Stowe, a fugitive interrupts a white Ohio familial scene replete with the familiar signs of domesticity. Douglass echoes Stowe's opening, which reads: "The light of the cheerful fire shone on the rug and carpet of a cosey parlor, and glittered on the sides of the teacups and well-brightened teapot, as Senator Bird was drawing off his boots."[20] In his own first lines, Douglass writes, "Five years after [Listwell's trip South], Mr. and Mrs. List-well sat together by the fireside of their own happy home. . . . The children were all gone to bed. A single lamp burnt brightly within."[21] Yet Douglass's virtual replication of the fugitive Eliza's appearance at the Birds' door will soon overturn the maternal ethic Stowe advances. Mrs. Bird is the moral force that both Eliza and Stowe's readers recognize; it is Eliza's appeal to her that convinces the sena-tor to follow his heart and, faced with a fugitive slave, to act differently than he votes. In contrast, Madison relates his story at the sympathetic request of *Mr.* List-well, who, of course, listens well. Even when he interrupts Madison, he facilitates and affirms Madison's story; as Robert Stepto puts it, Listwell authenticates rather than questions.[22]

Mrs. Listwell's interruptions, unlike her husband's, distract from rather than advance Madison's story and cause. When she breaks in on Madison's description of a hairsbreadth escape and exclaims "Oh! The old wretch! He had betrayed you," Madison calmly responds, "I think not" (42). Mrs. Listwell, pointedly, does not listen well, and Douglass brings this home when he has her interrupt Madison a second time, the only other instance in which she speaks during the text. As Madison again recalls stealing chickens in order to feed himself, an activity that Mr. Listwell earlier defended, she instead exclaims "But you didn't eat food raw? How did you cook it?" (44). "It seemed quite a relief to Mrs. Listwell to know that Madison had, at least, lived upon cooked food," the narrator quips; "women have a perfect horror of eating raw food" (44). While in Stowe good women under-stand slavery's evil better than their male counterparts, in Douglass's novella, as in his narratives, actual women (as opposed to woman-as-mother-as-trope) are ridiculed or erased.

In *The Heroic Slave*, both home and family—familiar tropes of domestic rheto-ric in antislavery writing—are displaced onto the primary ties between Madison and Listwell. When Madison ventures back to the South to rescue his wife Susan, she, like Douglass's own wife Anna Murray, and like the image of his mother in his autobiography, is mute.[23] Susan's one direct vocalization, a shriek, leads to their discovery, her death, and Madison's recapture. Moreover, neither Listwell's nor Madison's children are any more than props, whereas the loss of children is precisely what provides the bond between the Birds and Eliza. Madison mentions this as an afterthought; he never tries to see or rescue them; and after Susan's death Douglass does not even bother to account for what happens to them.

Douglass's revision of Stowe's Bird passage could be interpreted as an example of male revolutionary politics displacing a domestic ethic. Even though Douglass does incorporate domestic rhetoric and insist that slavery contradicts the morality of a Christian nation, one could argue, as Eric Sundquist does, that for Douglass "the primary tropes of family and home became archetypes of the nation-state not by virtue of a visionary feminism, a new rule of domesticity, but by their identification with the 'manly' principles of revolutionary politics."[24] Sundquist hints at the difference between, on the one hand, the affectional models of visionary feminism and moral suasion as I would configure them, and on the other hand bourgeois individual rights. Yet his opposition between a "visionary feminism" and the " 'manly' principles of revolutionary politics" resists taking fully into account the feminized rhetorical grounding of Douglass's move to a political and paternal arena. Douglass incorporates "womanly" models more fully than Sundquist's argument admits. In attempts at conversion—religious in Stowe, or secular in Douglass—sentiment and sympathy are affectionately bound, that is, they fall within the realm of visionary feminism and sentimental abolition. They will in turn slide into a masculinized discursive economy which escapes the sanitized boundaries for "proper" viewing and hearing relations.

ıᴵı

Douglass revises himself rather than Stowe as he translates into writing what he overhears and oversees in the beating of his Aunt Hester; it is, for him, "the blood stained gate," his "entrance to the hell of slavery." The two versions work quite differently; in the *Narrative*, his framing emphasizes sentiment, while in *Bondage* he moves from language's inability to convey sentiment to language's inadequacy without attendant rights. In the *Narrative* he writes: "I have often been awakened at the dawn of day by the most heart-rending shrieks of an own aunt of mine. . . . No words, no tears, no prayers, from [the master's] gory victim seemed to move his iron heart from its bloody purpose." Douglass affirms his emphasis on the heart, on the connection of language, of words, to tears and prayers, when he goes on, "I wish I could commit to paper the *feelings* with which I beheld it." Deborah McDowell points to the voyeuristic reproductions Douglass both is complicit in and creates in this rendition. That he testifies to witnessing such an "exhibition," and it being a most terrible "spectacle," actualizes his lamentation of being doomed to be "a witness and *participant*" in such "outrages."[25]

Without mitigating the force of McDowell's fine argument, I would add that Douglass's language in the *Narrative* positions the author's character, young Frederick, as a witness *against* slavery, through the medium of sentiment and feeling, inexpressible but shared with the reader whom he hopes to convert into being a similar witness. Douglass may move the reader to excitement, to borrow his description of Listwell's feelings upon overhearing Madison's laments, but then the question is what to do with the aligned feelings of fear and paralysis that he experiences, "so terrified and horror-stricken at the sight [of Hester's beating that he] hid [him]self in a closet, and dared not venture out till long after the bloody transaction."[26] Douglass cannot risk his readers' becoming overwhelmed into continued passivity. By creating a sympathetic link between the young Frederick and the reader—both experience the inexpressiveness of language—he provides an interpretative path of sentiment: even if readers cannot process the feelings that Douglass's description evokes, Douglass counsels that they should use those feelings to prompt a protest against slavery.

Douglass's rendition in the second narrative shifts his focus from sympathetic bonds, through the inexpressible feelings that Hester's beating elicits, to the language of judicial redress. After describing the beating in detail, he writes: "language has no power to convey a *just* sense of its awful criminality."[27] Douglass implies in the first passage, and makes explicit in the second, that language is not adequately expressive; it has "no power to convey." Yet language in both instances is simply a medium. What does not remain constant is Douglass's focus on its purpose: he moves the reader from language's inadequacy in relation to the feelings of the heart as he writes in 1845, to an emphasis on criminality and justice ten years later. One reason language has "no power" in 1855 is that the African American witness still has no standing in the judicial sense. Douglass's position as outsider, looking through the slats of Master Anthony's kitchen closet in which he sleeps, simulates his position as outsider in the court—as a witness he, like his language, has no power. By making white readers witnesses, and by implicitly offering judicial means as a more effective medium for their language, he attempts to grant antislavery witnessing standing, and to imbue language with political power.

Douglass attempts to affect wider white antislavery endorsements in part because he recognizes the increasing encroachment upon and instability of Black rights. He thus anticipates Justice Taney's pronouncement, in *Dred Scott,* that slaves and free Blacks are so inferior, that they have no rights which the white man is bound to respect.[28] Douglass's changing description of Hester's beating reflects his translation of the "subjective" language of sentiment into the "objective" codification of official discourse. When, for example, in *Bondage,* Douglass reports how many lashes Hester receives, the numbers, unlike her cries, seem to leave little room for any proslavery meaning. By 1853 Douglass already simultaneously accepts and resists what contemporary legal critic Patricia Williams forwards: that "white statements of Black needs suddenly acquire the sort of stark statistical authority that lawmakers can listen to and politicians hear. But from Blacks, stark statistical statements of need are heard as strident, discordant, and unharmonious."[29] Douglass does not appeal to the court itself, but provides the data to those who can; he encourages white witnessing as a temporary measure in the fight for collective Black standing, standing that would promote more than individual Black self-expression.

In both descriptions of Hester's beating Douglass works to form a sympathetic link with his readers; how he directs the energy that connection creates differs in each account. Robert Levine argues that for Douglass "the ability to sympathize was a key indication of one's humanity, and those whom he believed possessed capacities for sympathy—such as Stowe—were viewed as *nearly* transcending the limits of race. . . . Between Douglass and Stowe, as Douglass in 'The Heroic Slave' presents it between Washington and Listwell, power is shared and mutually constitutive."[30] Douglass, I would counter, is considerably less idealistic, for he realizes that the reader / listener / Listwell does not transcend race, and that power is not shared. That is precisely why Douglass needs white readers as witnesses, why, again, he weds sympathy, tears, or language's emotive power, to standing in his rewriting of Hester and in his description of Listwell's and Madison's relationship.

Because the racial and gendered identities of Douglass's characters are compound, we never find ourselves, simply, in the company of equally endowed men, who have, through sympathy, transcended race. Nor does Douglass use "the male couple as a figure of an inherently democratic union of equals which could serve as the basis for a new social organization" as Robert K. Martin argues Melville does in the same decade.[31] One might expect that the definitively male discourse of rights, as Douglass employs it in his move toward adopting the founding fathers and individual liberalism, might provide fertile ground for the kind of homoerotic play that Martin outlines. Yet liberalism's emphasis on private rights, self-sufficiency, and individualism excludes the collective, inwardly binding, affectional ways of knowing and exchanging that issues of witnessing bring to the fore. Douglass does make fraternity at once erotic and social, but the politics of his narrative conversions in *The Heroic Slave* presuppose the fact that his transracial couplings are not democratic unions of equals.

Douglass also elicits sympathy by connecting it to the horror and titillation of the sexualized (and tortured) bodies of Hester and Madison, and by positioning their bodies as objects of the reader's voyeuristic gaze. This sexualization of representation is a crucial marker in the shift from affectional relations to erotic ones in antislavery literature. In countless narratives, sexual exploitation—not, for example, issues of desire, self, and liberty, framed by relations of capital and property—is presented (at least ostensibly) as the ultimate reason to speak against slavery. Slavery often "begins" for its narrators at the moment they understand the sexual threat it presents; narrators often inscribe the difficult politics of witnessing in these sexualized passages. Witnessing is almost always bound up with sex in slavery. Finally, representations of abolitionist conversion are often sexually encoded as well. Within the affectional model of disciplinary intimacy, where Douglass and Stowe make their protagonists teachers, Black men instigate white male transformation as often as white women do. In the textual economies of these two authors at least, one result of "successful" male interracial interaction is the shift from elicited abolitionist love to (illicit) homoeroticized prose.

Heterosexualized attraction, so often a part of the hero's stature, is not an option in Douglass's portrait of Madison Washington. For Douglass to give voice to what Karen Sánchez-Eppler characterizes as the "always suppressed possibility of the white woman's desire for the black man"[32] would almost certainly alienate his readers of either race. Black female affirmation, on the other hand, would be ineffective as a medium of conversion, because the Black female's desire was continually ignored, denied, or denigrated. Only white male desire, then, can affirm Madison's status as hero. Happening upon the unaware Madison in the woods, Listwell observes that he was

> of manly form. Tall, symmetrical, round, and strong. In his movements he seemed to combine, with the strength of the lion, a lion's elasticity. His torn sleeves disclosed arms like polished iron. His face was "black, but comely." . . . His whole appearance betokened Herculean strength.

After taking note and stock of Madison's overwhelming physicality, Listwell turns from appraising Madison's body to appraising his interiority:

> As our traveller gazed upon him, he almost trembled at the thought of his dangerous intrusion. Still he could not quit the place. He had long desired to sound the mysterious depths of the thoughts and feelings of a slave. . . . He listened again for those mellow and mournful accents, which, he says, made such an impression upon him as can never be erased. He did not have to wait long. There came another gush from the same full fountain; now bitter, and now sweet.

The erotic nature of Douglass's language here is fairly self-evident, especially since Listwell has little reason to "tremble" for his personal safety—he himself notes that despite Madison's Herculean strength, "there was nothing savage or forbidding in his aspect. A child might play in his arms, or dance on his shoulders."[33] Douglass's language both explicitly refers to the "behemoth" Uncle Tom on whose shoulders Little Eva plays,[34] and simultaneously imbues Madison with a manly, rather than maternal, aspect. Listwell's voyeuristic (and appreciative) gaze catches Madison in a state of mental and physical undress, and the switch from the visual to the aural to the gustatory confirms the suggestive scopophilic frame. Listwell has long desired to "sound" "depths" and is rewarded with an ejaculatory "gush," "now bitter, now sweet." It is the heightened invasiveness of his senses that assures Listwell's conversion / seduction. Far away from the rights rhetoric of the founding fathers, Douglass's language transfers the affectional model of sentimental sympathy into a highly eroticized exchange.

In the erotically fraternal version of sentimental abolition that Douglass presents here, his discourse of conversion insists upon the sexual charge of listening, and so anticipates Harriet Jacobs's use of the ear as a metaphor for sexual violation. Douglass creates "a narrative situation that he must have desired in his journalistic career . . . an interdependent relationship [with] the white abolitionist . . . guided by an authoritative black leader," as Shelly Fisher Fishkin and Carla Peterson aptly point out.[35] Yet in the passage describing Listwell's first encounter with Madison, testifying and witnessing become not only interdependent acts but interpenetrative ones. In case the reader has missed this point, Douglass writes that, after Madison has left, Listwell "stood half hoping, half fearing the return of the sable preacher to his solitary temple. The speech of Madison rung through the chambers of his soul, and vibrated through his entire frame." Listwell's titillated state is followed by a *petite morte* of sorts. The Northerner has been taken; he has been possessed, and through this, reborn. Later in this passage, Listwell declares: "from this hour I am an abolitionist."[36] Douglass merges the penetrative power of speech and the dangerous description of sexual titillation and release into a conversion to the antislavery cause.

Ultimately, the bonding that takes place between Madison and Listwell leads back to a rhetoric of conversion that readers can recognize as both fraternal and feminized, where the two terms are not oppositional but mutually constitutive. When Listwell later happens upon the recaptured Madison, to whom he imagines he is linked by a "supernatural power, a wakeful providence or an inexorable fate," it is sentiment, rather than revolutionary rights rhetoric, that is the site of their link. Douglass describes Listwell's thoughts in affectional language: "His feelings were . . . bitter and excited and his heart was full with the fate of poor Madison (whom he loved as well as admired)."[37] Despite this masculinized arena, Douglass's homoeroticism, like Stowe's, finds itself expressed in the affectional language of sentiment and suasion rather than through rights discourse.

ı᛫ı

Douglass extends his use of sentimental tropes and language regularly deployed to express an expansive and empowering sentimental ideology as he simultaneously embraces individual and formal rights. While Douglass replaces Stowe's maternal ethic with a fraternal one, he does not dispense with affectional rhetoric, a central ideological linchpin of domesticity and sentimental abolition. Although by the early 1850s Douglass has actually supported Free-Soil candidates and embraced the constitution—that is, he has moved away from moral suasion's central tenets—Madison Washington's narrative role parallels Douglass's authorial one: both depend on persuasive speech's emancipating power. Madison's liberatory strategy reflects Douglass's rendition of the slave who counters his master's arguments about the peculiar institution and persuades his master to grant him his freedom in Douglass's first formal primer, "The Colombian Orator." Each of the narratives and the novella he writes during what I call "Douglass's decade" seek to convert whites through language that touches their core and compels them to work for abolition. Douglass offers affectional means of relation, voice, and sentiment, as the medium for change.

Sentimental abolition is significant as a critical category because it names the models and mechanisms of domesticity that inform, but are not limited to, moral suasion. Domestic ideology's influence—which is not simply contained in the bodies and presences of women—provides the weft between sentiment and standing, between the fraternal and the feminized. Moreover, in antislavery writings that deal with the erotically charged representations of Black bodies engaged in transracial relations, affectional discourse acts as a catalyst for further sexualization, whether the object of desire be a man or a woman, whether the subject of desiring be a woman or a man.

NOTES

I would like to thank the Center for African American and African Studies (CAAS) at the University of Michigan, Ann Arbor, for the fellowship that allowed me to research and write this essay. The University of Chicago's CAAS invited me to present an earlier draft, and I appreciate the helpful feedback I received there. I would also like to thank Arthur Aubin Saint-Flannigan, Tyler Steben, and especially Jacqueline Goldsby and Eric C. Williams for their useful suggestions during the final stages of writing this piece.

1. See William Andrews, ed., *Critical Essays on Frederick Douglass* (Boston: G. K. Hall & Co., 1991); Eric J. Sundquist, ed., *Frederick Douglass: New Literary and Historical Essays* (New York: Cambridge University Press, 1990); William S. McFeely, *Frederick Douglass* (New York: W. W. Norton and Co., 1991). My epigraph is from Frederick Douglass, *My Bondage and My Freedom* (New York: Dover, 1969), v. All subsequent Douglass quotations are cited from this and the following texts: *The Narrative of the Life of Frederick Douglass*, ed. Houston Baker (New York: Penguin Books, 1982); *The Heroic Slave*, in *Three Classic African-American Novels*, ed. William L. Andrews (New York: Mentor, 1990).

2. Harriet Beecher Stowe, *Uncle Tom's Cabin* (New York: Macmillan, 1962). Slave narrators in the 1850s often make explicit reference to Uncle Tom or to Stowe.

3. I refer here most recently to Richard Yarborough, Eric J. Sundquist, and William Andrews. The latter two lament that Douglass's second narrative has been largely overlooked, and argue for its centrality by addressing the paternal issues the text raises (see William Andrews, *To Tell a Free Story* [Illinois: University of Chicago Press, 1988] and "*My Bondage and My Freedom* and the American Literary Renaissance of the 1850s," in Andrews, *Critical Essays*, 133–47; Eric J. Sundquist, *To Wake The Nations: Race in the Making of American Culture* [Cambridge: Harvard University Press, 1993] and "Frederick Douglass: Literacy and Paternalism," in Andrews, *Critical Essays*, 120–32). For the most thorough treatment of *The Heroic Slave*, see Yarborough, "Race, Violence, and Manhood: The Masculine Ideal in Frederick Douglass's *The Heroic Slave*," in Sundquist, *New Essays*, 166–88. For work on Douglass's objectification of the Black female, see especially Deborah E. McDowell, "In the First Place: Making Frederick Douglass and the Afro-American Narrative Tradition," in Andrews, *Critical Essays*, 192–214, and Valerie Smith, "Three Slave Narratives," in *Self-Discovery and Authority in Afro-American Narrative* (Cambridge: Harvard University Press, 1987), 9–43.

4. McDowell, "In the First Place," 199.

5. The term "sentimental abolition" was used in the early 1860s to connote an extremely diluted abolitionism, but I mean to situate the term here within the very different register defined by recent work on the interconnections between abolition, domesticity, and feminism.

6. For important work that illustrates "the degree to which domestic and sentimental antislavery writings are implicated in the very oppressions they seek to reform," see Karen Sánchez-Eppler, "Bodily Bonds: The Intersecting Rhetorics of Feminism and Abolition," 92–114 (quotation from 93), and Laura Wexler, "Literary Eavesdropping, Domestic Fiction,

and Educational Reform," 9–38, both in *The Culture of Sentiment: Race, Gender, and Sentimentality in Nineteenth-Century American Culture,* ed. Shirley Samuels (New York: Oxford University Press, 1992).

7. Current "needs" vs. "rights" debates in contemporary Critical Legal Studies (CLS) both echo and help to illuminate the practice and politics of abolitionist fractures. Moral suasion loosely corresponds to what CLS calls "needs discourse." CLS's skepticism about the law as a place of resort for the disenfranchised corresponds to moral suasionists' distrust of the law and constitution. In the other direction, CLS's utopian strain, its emphasis on contractual alienation, and its wish for a more communal world echo the secular extensions of Garrisonian, radical, non-sectarian, and antisabbatarian activism and belief in morality as the highest authority.

8. The various ramifications of Douglass's choice are precisely what mar his novella in Yarborough's estimation (see "Race, Violence, and Manhood," 179–83). See also Robert Stepto, "Storytelling in Early Afro-American Fiction: Frederick Douglass's *The Heroic Slave,*" in *Black Literature and Literary Theory,* ed. Henry Louis Gates, Jr. (New York: Methuen, 1984), 175–86.

9. In the first narrative she is called Hester, in the second Esther; he explains the shift by saying he is writing from sound. For simplicity, I will refer to her throughout as Hester.

10. Smith and McDowell, in the essays cited above, argue that Douglass revises but ultimately reinscribes male patriarchal norms, and Yarborough argues that Douglass "was unable or unwilling to call into question the white bourgeois paradigm of manhood itself" in *The Heroic Slave* ("Race, Violence, and Manhood," 182).

11. Douglass, *My Bondage and My Freedom,* 393.

12. *Frederick Douglass's Paper,* 9 December 1853.

13. After promising that she would raise monies for the school, Stowe changed her mind; she never fully explained why. See Waldo Martin, *The Mind of Frederick Douglass* (Chapel Hill: University of North Carolina Press, 1984), 125–6, and also Robert Levine, "*Uncle Tom's Cabin* in *Frederick Douglass's Paper:* An Analysis of Reception," *American Literature* 64 (1992): 71–93, especially 81.

14. See Eric Foner, ed., *The Life and Writings of Frederick Douglass,* vol. 11 (New York: International Publishers, 1950), 29.

15. Richard H. Brodhead, "Sparing the Rod: Discipline and Fiction in Antebellum America," in *The New American Studies,* ed. Philip Fisher (Berkeley: University of California Press, 1991), 141–70, quotation from 145.

16. *The Liberator* 10, no. 11 (13 March 1840): 42.

17. Quoted in Brodhead, "Sparing the Rod," 161.

18. Quoted in Andrews, "*My Bondage and My Freedom,*" 143.

19. See P. Gabrielle Foreman, " 'This Promiscuous Housekeeping': Death, Transgression, and Homoeroticism in *Uncle Tom's Cabin,*" *Representations* 43 (Summer 1993): 51–72, for a reading of homosocial desire between St. Clare, Tom, and St. Clare's manservant Adolph. For work on earlier models of emergent homosexual relations and representation, see Michael Lynch, " 'Here is Adhesiveness': From Friendship to Homosexuality," *Victorian Studies* 29, no. 1 (1985): 67–96, especially 68, and Robert K. Martin, "A Note on the Use of the Term 'Homosexual,' " in *Hero, Captain, and Stranger: Male Friendship, Social Critique, and Literary Form in the Sea Novels of Herman Melville* (Chapel Hill: University of North Carolina Press, 1986), 12–16. In contrast see Donald Yacovone, "Abolitionists and 'The Language of Fraternal Love' " In *Meanings for Manhood: Constructions of Masculinity in Victorian America,* ed. Mark C.

Carnes and Clyde Griffen (Chicago: University of Chicago Press, 1990), 85–95, especially 89–93, and Nancy Cott, "Passionless: An Interpretation of Victorian Sexual Ideology, 1790–1850," *Signs* 4, no. 2, (219–36, 1978): especially 233.

20. Stowe, *Uncle Tom's Cabin*, 132.

21. Douglass, *Heroic Slave*, 31.

22. Stepto, "Storytelling," 183.

23. In *My Bondage and My Freedom*, Douglass writes: "It has been a life-long standing grief to me, that I knew so little of my mother; and that I was so early separated from her. The counsels of her love must have been very beneficial to me. . . . I take few steps in life, without feeling her presence; but the image is mute, and I have no striking words of hers treasured up" (57).

24. Sundquist, *To Wake the Nations*, 108.

25. All quotations in this paragraph are from Douglass, *Narrative*, 51 (emphases added). McDowell's essay is perhaps the best work on Douglass's narrative objectifications of women: see "In the First Place," especially 201–4.

26. Douglass, *Narrative*, 52.

27. Douglass, *My Bondage and My Freedom*, 88 (emphasis added).

28. *Dred Scott v. Sanford, Reports of Cases Argued and Adjudged in The Supreme Court of The United States*, December term, 1856 (Washington: William Morrison and Co., 1857), 19:407.

29. Patricia Williams, *The Alchemy of Race and Rights* (Cambridge: Harvard University Press, 1991), 152.

30. Levine, "Analysis of Reception," 85.

31. Robert K. Martin, "Note on 'Homosexual,' " 11.

32. Sánchez-Eppler, "Bodily Bonds," 103.

33. Douglass, *Heroic Slave*, 28.

34. Stowe, *Uncle Tom's Cabin*, 222.

35. See Shelley Fisher Fishkin and Carla Peterson, " 'We Hold These Truths to be Self-Evident': The Rhetoric of Frederick Douglass's Journalism," in Sundquist, *New Essays*, 189–204, quotation from 199–200.

36. Douglass, *Heroic Slave*, 29.

37. Douglass, *Heroic Slave*, 58, 57.

CHAPTER EIGHT

Chivalric Sentimentalism

The Case of Dr. Howe and Laura Bridgman

Cassandra Cleghorn

Shirley Samuels suggests that sentimentalism's interest in the social and material facts of bodies and of bodily responses should come as no surprise. Such facts are, after all, bound up in its most basic project: that of sympathy, or its intensified form, empathy:

> As a set of cultural practices designed to evoke a certain form of emotional response, usually empathy, in the reader or viewer, sentimentality produces or reproduces spectacles that cross race, class, and gender boundaries. . . . [W]hile frequently operating as social commentary or critique, sentimentality acts in conjunction with the problem of the body and what it embodies, how social, political, racial, and gendered meanings are determined through their differential embodiments.[1]

Phrases such as "differential embodiments" reveal the pressure experienced by interpreters of history working within a Foucauldian schema which posits both that the body is the final, irreducible site and that it matters not who's speaking. The double push toward a materialist study of bodies as localized effects and toward a highly abstracted appreciation of discourses operating in what Foucault called "a pervasive anonymity" is, at the very least, awkward.[2] To their credit, the essayists in Samuels's collection balance their discursive overview with a narrower attention to the particular bodies of viewer and viewed that comprise the freighted spectacles of sentimentalism. But what emerges from this volume is still a view of sentimentalism's ideologies, practices, and spectacles as largely the business of women.[3] When it comes to gender, these essays suggest, the differential embodiments of nineteenth-century sentimentality were less different from each other than Samuels's introductory remarks imply.

The basic term of Ann Douglas's classic attack thus endures: in most accounts, sentimentalism still amounts to feminization.[4] And yet sentimentalism permeated antebellum American language, literature, and culture to such an extent that the accumulating accounts of its expression invite reconsideration of the very notion of separate spheres. We might well ask which antebellum men played the field of sentimentalism, and how, and in which spectacles of sentimentalism they participated as producers, as audience, and as knowing or unwitting actors.

In what follows, I investigate Samuel Gridley Howe, an antebellum philanthropist whose lifework required constant negotiation with sentimental forms. In his celebrated treatment of the deaf and blind girl Laura Dewey Bridgman, Howe staged for his audience gendered narrative patterns powerfully associated with sentimentalism: the passive, silent girl brought to civilization by her benevolent, all-powerful surrogate father. So described, the structure of their relationship is susceptible to a feminist reading. We might imagine a critique of the case that would rescue Bridgman from the claustrophobic hold of her benefactor, putting Howe in his place and restoring Bridgman to herself. Howe's reputation was as a zealous Hollingsworth whose style gave frequent offense (his disciplinary methods, for example, were often quite harsh), and as a preoccupied husband who offered only slight support of his wife's literary endeavors; Hawthorne may well have been thinking of Howe, in fact, as he composed his harsh portrait of the Blithedale reformer. And before Henry James refashioned Hawthorne's novel to produce *The Bostonians*, he wrote to Howe's daughters in praise of their book, *Laura Bridgman: Dr. Howe's Famous Pupil and What He Taught Her.* "It is a most American document," James told Florence and Maud Howe, referring in all probability to its account of the voracious appetite and mesmeric power of a reformer who absorbs his objects into himself.[5]

But this was only one side of Howe's public persona, and to confront it alone would be to miss the complex, chiastic structure at work. For if Howe played father and disciplinarian to Bridgman, he was also her mother and sentimental tutor: "He stroked my hand when he perceived how dirty or shabby I looked," wrote Bridgman, "he patted my cheeks expressing to me his love and affection."[6] Insofar as Howe approached Bridgman as a sentimental project and offered her back to her antebellum supporters in sentimental terms, the case can become for historians something more than the expression of a voracious, if well-meaning, philanthropy. Howe's representative status as a male practitioner of a mode commonly associated with women suggests that sentimentalism as a "structure of feeling" blurred the boundary between masculine and feminine practices.

The domestic and sexual dynamics at work in Bridgman and Howe's case were merely the common vocabulary of a less readily recognized eros: that of antebellum philanthropy itself. Bridgman was for Howe an emblem of philanthropy's powers of rescue. The erotic charge of the case was divided between Howe's hunger for the measurable effects of benevolent sociality and Bridgman's need for a civilizing and humanizing education. These needs may be seen as themselves effects of sentimentalism, that totalizing bundle of tropes and types that turns the world into a testing ground for social experimentation. An investigation of Bridgman's treatment by Howe—and of antebellum responses to that treatment—

reveals chivalric sentimentalism as a literary and social mode nervously poised on the edge of crisis.

ıⁱı

To most of his contemporaries, Samuel Gridley Howe—Byronic hero of the Greek Revolution, tireless do-gooder in every field from abolition to prison reform, dashing husband of poet Julia Ward Howe and close friend of Charles Sumner and Horace Mann—was best known for his association with Laura Dewey Bridgman. Their association began in the early fall of 1837 when Howe travelled to Hanover with a few of his friends from among the Boston literati: Howe "drove to the Bridgman house in quest of his prize. He won it and came back to the hotel triumphant," one of the party recalled (quoted in Howe and Hall, 39). Howe's "prize" was the girl who, under his tutelage, would become the first deaf and blind American to learn to read and write, and to communicate by alphabetic sign language. He "won" Bridgman's from her parents who, frustrated by their inability to communicate with their daughter and unable to control her occasionally violent temper except by force, agreed to send her to Boston as the first blind and deaf resident of Howe's institution. For all intents and purposes, Bridgman became Howe's ward from that moment on: although she continued to correspond with and visit her family over the years, she lived at the institution until her death in 1889.

"I perfectly recollect his exultation at having secured [the girl]," his friend continues, "and the impression he made on me by his chivalric benevolence" (quoted in Howe and Hall, 39). This "chivalric," pseudomedieval language (c.f., "in quest of his prize," returning "triumphant") was not peculiar: chivalry was Howe's preferred mode, as revealed in everything from his nickname—"Chev," coined by his wife and used by his closest friends—to his involvement in revolutions abroad, as well as his pedagogical methods.[7] Chivalry is the term that joins antebellum philanthropy and sentimentalism, bringing into focus some of the social effects of cultural forms. By the time he met Bridgman, Howe was an extremely active benefactor and educator of the blind in America. As director of the New England Institution for the Education of the Blind (renamed the Perkins Institution in 1833), he put his students on display in their home institution and travelled with them through seventeen states, lobbying state legislatures to support the education of the blind. Drawing on accounts by Howe's staff, one historian describes the outpouring of public interest in Bridgman:

> Thousands of Bostonians and foreign visitors came to the Perkins Institution to witness this philanthropic miracle for themselves. The Institution raised funds through regular exhibitions of the students' abilities . . . which could draw more than a thousand visitors a day. . . . One of Perkins's instructors reported in her journal that the crowd "has become so great at the monthly exhibitions, and presses so closely about Laura, that we are obliged to surround her desk by settees, thus making a little enclosure to protect her."[8]

Howe's demonstratively chivalric philanthropy functioned as social theater; through performance, publication, and personal networking, Howe built for himself and Bridgman a national reputation.

Howe's success at what Lori D. Ginzberg calls "the work of benevolence" stemmed from his understanding of publicity and, more profoundly, from the identificatory dynamics involved in public spectacle.[9] Describing Howe's "enchantment" of various state legislatures to the English phrenologist George Combe, Horace Mann captured the involuntary, almost coercive aspects of philanthropic identification:

> The success of an appeal to the sympathies of our people in behalf of the blind may be now calculated upon as one of the natural laws. It has been tried in nearly half of the states of the Union, and has never failed. At the painful sight of the deprivation of their unfortunate children, followed by the gladdening spectacle of the results of the wonderful art by which that deprivation can be supplied, avarice itself relents, and opens its coffers, and suffers the almoner of this bounty to thrust in its arm elbow-deep.[10]

As Mann's passage indicates, the essential role of the philanthropist was not to give money, but to stage the opportunity for others' benevolence through the rhetorical display of philanthropic effects. While Howe's "patient and persevering" methods with Bridgman and his other blind students were part of his attraction, a miraculous element was also essential; indeed, the cultural significance of the case was generated in its movement between the mundane and the miraculous. Time and again, Howe was likened to Christ, to Cadmus, to Columbus. (Such language was not unique: any high-profile philanthropist who performed social work was subject to similar comparisons.) The predictability with which such spectacles could incite giving is revealed in Mann's language of natural law; the principles of sentimental philanthropy had permeated his and Howe's culture as ideology.

Such ideological effects involved complex processes. For Howe and his cohort, philanthropy required, first, acts of reconnaissance, and second, the subsequent translation of that information into reports and recommendations for action. It was not enough, in other words, for social needs to be met; the range of solutions for different social problems each needed to be articulated and rehearsed. Scenes of charity proliferated in magazines, newspapers, and novels, scenes in which states of neediness and processes of giving were condensed and replayed for the middle-class readership.[11] Howe's "Reports of the Perkins Institution," identified as "classics of pedagogy," had a remarkably wide readership, since they were reviewed, reproduced, or responded to in popular magazines (*Godey's Lady's Book*) and literary journals (*North American Review*), as well as in more specialized venues (*American Annals of the Deaf and Dumb*).[12] Like Mann's contemporary "Reports of the Massachusetts Board of Education" and his *Common School Journal,* Howe's

"Reports" gained their readership in part from the author's involvement in a wide variety of social reforms.[13]

The doctor's access to the *terra nova* within Bridgman thus became a key "exploit of philanthropy" (Julia Ward Howe's term), inspiring a lay audience of benefactors. If Howe's style was more flamboyant than that of other philanthropists, his assumptions and methods were not. Along with Mann, Dorothea Dix, Charles Sumner, and others, Howe contributed more generally to the philanthropic education of the consolidating middle class: he encouraged a group of people whose energies were increasingly spent in benevolent societies, home-visiting, and other forms of charitable work to define themselves as society's benefacting class. In short, Howe helped to shape what was quickly becoming a self-consciously middle-class public, and then supplied them with objects for their benevolent energies.[14]

Howe's early case studies of Bridgman include her curriculum, transcriptions of their conversations, descriptions of their daily routine at the institution (daily baths in the river, long walks), and interpretations of his patient's progress.[15] The doctor achieved the triumphant development of Bridgman's moral and mental capacities by bringing her to language, as if language were the place where humanity happens. The trick was in the transportation. In linguistic terms, his project was to bring Bridgman from her rudimentary "natural language" of mimetic signs (whereby "a motion of her two first fingers like cutting with scissors, would signify her thought of that instrument . . . because there was, so to speak, in all these [signs] a tangible likeness" [Howe and Hall, 48]) to alphabetic language, communicated by means of finger spelling ("dactylology") or raised type. Howe's initial methods of teaching Bridgman the names of simple objects—and, more generally, the *idea* of words—literalized the popular notion of linguistic correspondence often attributed to Swedenborg, embraced by Emerson and others, and diffused throughout common-school textbooks in antebellum America. As a corollary to the fundamental identification between spirit and matter, there was said to be an originary identification between signifier and signified, whose traces could be discerned in words' etymologies. Gluing twine to cardboard to form the letters of each word, Howe then fastened each word to its object, and brought Bridgman, by sheer force of repetition, to understand their association. Then, moving toward abstraction, he would remove the cards and have Bridgman place them back on their respective objects. Only once she had perfected this process and understood the underlying concept did he break each word into its constituent letters and teach her the truly abstracted alphabet which she might then manipulate for her own purposes.

While the curriculum is reported in straightforward terms, Howe describes Bridgman's character and genealogy in terms better suited to nineteenth-century fiction:

> The child inherited most of the physical peculiarities of the mother, with a dash of what, from want of a better name, is called the scrofulous temperament. This tem-

perament makes one very liable to certain diseases, but it gives great delicacy of fibre, and consequent sensibility. Laura had a physical organization like that of a delicate plant,—very liable to derangement, because very sensitive; also, very difficult as an organization to bring maturity, but promising great capacity and beauty. (Quoted in Howe and Hall, 31).

In this account, Bridgman's "scrofulous temperament" carries a double valence, signifying at once a blinding disorder and moral degeneration; yet Howe also goes to some lengths to characterize the girl as an exotic plant requiring exquisite care. Combining the stories of her physiological and moral development, Howe presents Bridgman's life as an almost naturalistic struggle, conducted on and through her severely recalcitrant body, and made possible by the environment he creates around her:

> As the brain and other parts of the nervous system were developed, there arose a necessity for the development of the mental and moral capacities. Her mind and spirits were as cruelly cramped by her isolation as the foot of a Chinese girl is cramped by an iron shoe. Growth would go on; and without room to grow naturally deformity must follow. The child began to have a will of her own. . . .
>
> It is often one of the parent's hardest lessons, to learn to yield up timely and gracefully the authority which was once necessarily despotic, but which should soon become responsible, and soon afterwards be abdicated altogether. The inner man will not go long on all fours, any more than will the outer man. It will get up, and insist upon walking about. If it cannot go openly and boldly, it will go slyly, and this of course makes it cowardly. You may as well refuse to let out the growing boy's trousers as refuse larger and larger liberty to his growing individuality. . . .
>
> It is true, hers was a woman's gentler nature; but, to offset this, it must be borne in mind that nothing can compensate for want of development of moral sense. That alone can properly regulate the development of the animal nature. Laura had the capacity, it is true, for becoming a gentle, docile woman; but she had the liability also of becoming a ferocious and unmanageable one.[16]

In such passages, Howe transforms the story of a child wracked by scarlet fever into a complicated moral fable. Bridgman's moral and mental capacity is figured as a thoroughly physicalized will, cramped in its growth as by an iron shoe or ever more constraining trousers. Howe describes Bridgman, already embodying the limits of sensual deprivation (without sight and hearing, and with only the barest sense of smell and taste), as poised on the cusp of humanity, potentially either a feral child or the feminine paragon of a liberating socialization. (One writer readily compared the case to the accounts of Kaspar Hauser, "which were of late such a blessing to the circulating libraries" [*Review*, 469].) The inexpert parents "yield up" the girl to the young bachelor doctor, a moral and intellectual strongman who breaks the iron bonds holding back the natural development of her moral sense. Although she remains necessarily encumbered by her body, she is brought by Howe into mediated contact with the hearts and minds of other people.

Howe's project thus went beyond imparting literacy as a set of skills; he maintained that Bridgman's new language—which, unlike her natural language, was capable of expressing "abstract matters and moral qualities"—would bring her into social communion.[17] In moments like the following, Howe witnesses Bridgman realizing the spiritual benefits of humanity:

> The poor child had sat in mute amazement, and patiently imitated everything her teacher did; but now the truth began to flash upon her, her intellect began to work, she perceived that here was a way by which she could herself make up a sign of anything that was in her own mind, and show it to another mind, and at once her countenance lighted up with a human expression; it was no longer a dog or parrot,—it was an immortal spirit, eagerly seizing upon a new link of union with other spirits! I could almost fix upon the moment when this truth dawned upon her mind, and spread its light to her countenance; I saw that the great obstacle was overcome, and that henceforward nothing but patient and persevering, plain and straightforward efforts were to be used. (Quoted in *Review*, 472)

Here is the encapsulated vision at the heart of Howe's project, the scene always quoted in stories about Bridgman. Bridgman's progress is measured as a series of such miraculous episodes; in this instance, her face offers the physiognomic evidence of spiritual and intellectual growth, from strictly imitative animal to "immortal spirit." In the literature of charity such moments operate as miniature narratives, synecdochically embodying the processes by which the sick are made well. Bridgman was the perfect expression of such narrative condensation: her "disease" (the physiological effect of her scarlet fever) coexists with her "cure" (her coming to language), constantly reminding the observer of her original state of need. Because the cure, in the case of deafness and blindness, is the compensation for the disease, not the eradication of it, Bridgman is thus simultaneously sick and well, needy and satisfied; as such, she represents at once the pitiable object and the attainment of charity's goal to eradicate pain or neediness. Bridgman's status as a collapsed emblem of this narrative movement from point A to point B meant that, under Howe's guidance, her story could move its observers to pity and satisfaction in an instant.

Representations ranging from Howe's anecdotal case studies to Lydia Sigourney's poetry and Francis Lieber's technical account of the girl's "vocal sounds" were alike in their concern with her affectlessness and with the sentiments produced by the sight of her.[18] Their common denominator was an interest in her anomalous, senseless state and its paradoxical generation of human contact and feelings, the generation of which was, of course, the central function of sentimentalism. "Few things that I ever read have interested me more than this of your dear little Laura Bridgman," wrote Thomas Carlyle to Howe after reading the Perkins "Report" of 1842, "probably one of the beautifulest phenomena at present visible under our Sun." For Carlyle, Bridgman stood as an embodiment of the "child of *genius*"—"isolated, as within fivefold iron gates, from all men and all things!"[19] And Charles Dickens, visiting the Perkins on his American tour, was so moved by the spectacle of Bridgman and her peers that he reproduced several extracts from Howe's case studies in his *American Notes*. For Dickens, as for many of his contemporaries, Bridgman performed an essentially spectacular public function, and the observation of this child performing the seemingly impossible task of communicating with her fellow blind pupils had, in turn, the potential to uplift her spiritually impoverished audience. "Nothing can more forcibly show the power of mind in forcing matter to its purpose than a meeting between them," Dickens quoted Howe's report as saying. "For if great talent and skill are necessary for two pantomimes to paint their thoughts and feelings by the movements of the body, and the expression of the countenance, how much greater the difficulty when darkness shrouds them both, and the one can hear no sound!"[20]

Carlyle and Dickens were not alone in their appropriation of Bridgman as a larger spiritual emblem for sentimental sociality. The case satisfied at least two of its culture's narrative needs: on the one hand, it generated a series of stories about Bridgman's sublimely destitute body—senseless, wordless, and seemingly beyond description; on the other hand, Howe's role was seen as the quintessential expression of heroic benevolence, the miraculous accomplishment of social communion where none was thought possible. Because the spectacle of Bridgman was precisely that of the acquisition of language, the culture's literary representatives were privileged, and in the context of a culture that fetishized pedagogy and the literary production of emotion, the medium (literature) was exactly suited to its subject (how language works, what it means to be brought to language). Like sentimental literature more generally, representations of Bridgman's case may be understood as reified forms of human sociality.

Jonathan Elmer's brilliant rendering of the limits of sentimentalism's affective project may be taken as a helpful gloss on Bridgman and Howe and their effect on one another and on antebellum readers:

> Sentimentalism promotes the penetration of reader by affect as the validation of a principle of social cohesion, of the social unity of feeling and sympathy; but then it will seek for ways to close the hole, to control the affect, to modulate grief into mourning. . . . The dead body that doesn't stay dead, the grave that doesn't stay closed, the reader who cannot overcome, cannot manage, the affective ties linking individuals at and across the social limit—all of these are at once failures of the sentimental project and realizations of the sensational underside of that project.[21]

In Elmer's reading of Poe, sensationalism is the answer to sentimentalism's failure to contain the excesses it produces. Howe's fervent expression of chivalrous philanthropy is a similar attempt to channel and shape the challenge that Bridgman poses to the culture. Introducing Bridgman as a body existing at the social limit, Howe means to incorporate her into the sentimental social body. But Bridgman is an especially difficult case. She is neither dead (sentimentalism's favorite body), nor undead (sensationalism's choice); she is a living body, yet one which is still to be brought into the social fold.

Both the promises and the failure of sentimentalism are expressed in an anonymous account of Bridgman published in the *North American Review* of April 1841.
Appearing between a review of Lowell's poetry and an article on Anna Jameson
(the author of *Shakespeare's Heroines* [1832]), the article is consistent with this journal's
ethos of improvement. The stock pieties about Howe's benevolent work suggest the
article's function as a lofty example of social work in action: "This is a wide and
busy world," it concludes, "but it has exceedingly few things for the ambition or
enjoyment of a wise man, to be compared with the consciousness of services like
these in the cause of afflicted humanity" (*Review*, 486). Yet the article is about Howe
only insofar as he is our conduit to the deaf and blind girl, and the heightened tone
surrounding the presentation of Bridgman suggests that this writer is not merely
being didactic. As in Howe's writings, this article's rhetorical framing reveals a desire
to understand Bridgman as a test case for the challenges of human intercourse.

The article's opening remarks orient the reader to the potentially contradictory
reasons for Bridgeman's attraction: first, because her plight unexpectedly emblema-
tizes something about human existence (the common ground is the essential help-
lessness of our minds stranded within our bodies); but second, because Bridgeman
is finally so reassuringly *unlike* her readers. The article generates its emotion in the
movement between identification and alienation. "This imperial mind of ours," it
begins with outrageous fanfare,

> as it sits enclosed from view, within the folds of its fleshly tabernacle, has, by the
> grant of benevolent nature, three principal channels of communication with the
> world outside. Debarred from their use, it is lonely, receiving nothing, bestowing
> nothing, except so far as benevolent art can provide some substitute. By speech
> chiefly, it sends out ideas; by sight and hearing chiefly, it takes them in. (*Review*, 467)

Here is the inclusionary gesture: we are all alike, fundamentally removed from the
world and tethered only by the slender cord of our senses. Communication is an
equilibrated system, the exchange of signs or ideas as effortless or unconscious as
the intake and release of breath; if one channel is disturbed, our other senses ideally compensate for the loss. In abnormal situations, the guidance of "benevolent
art" may simulate the condition originally bestowed by "benevolent nature," thus
saving that unfortunate soul from its potential isolation.

But this evocation of blindness or deafness artfully remedied is mostly a device
for setting up the climax of Bridgman's sublime destitution. Before the facts in the
case of Laura Bridgman may be presented, indeed before we even know that
what follows will be about Bridgman, we are schooled in the affective environment such a case should induce. Having drawn us into the commonality of such a
plight (we are all trapped in our bodies), the article now refuses any easy identification, rendering such a figure abject and utterly inaccessible.

> But what if sight and hearing both fail? Where may the lever then be placed, which
> shall move, with the slightest impulse, the waiting world within? There stands a
> human body, and encased in it, you suppose, are a human mind and heart. But were

> it in its shroud and coffin, could it be more utterly unapproachable, as to any communication or sympathy? You speak, but the anomalous being before you cannot hear; you listen but it cannot speak. . . . How address it with any sign, any appeal, any inquiry, any consolation? Feed it, and it will swallow. Touch it, and it will know—what? How mysterious, how dread, how remote such a presence. What is that awfully independent mind doing in its inaccessible cave? What is more to the purpose,—has art any resources to perforate its prison walls, and mercifully to convey it some tidings of humanity, and some alleviations for the woeful dreariness of its solitude? (*Review*, 468)

This is our introduction to Bridgman. It is the generic *idea* of such destitution, rather than the particulars of her existence, that produces the sublime effect, as we are faced with a body vacant of senses and stripped of even the most basic sexual identity, a "presence" "mysterious," "dread," and "remote."

Through these urgent questions, the reader is ushered into a Poe-like world of buried selves: shrouds, coffins, dungeons, and caves comprise the *mise-en-scène* of the case, and the "anomalous being" with its "awfully independent mind" forcefully poses the problem of utter social breakdown between individuals. "Communication"—via verbal or tactile clues—is aligned here with "sympathy," "signs" with "consolation" and "alleviation." To be face-to-face with this remote creature is to be confronted with our inability to meet its insensate needs, but also, and more pressingly, to be confronted with *its* inability to accommodate *our* need to be heard, to be talked to, to be recognized by a touch. This dramatization of an encounter with a Bridgman-like being ("You speak, but the anomalous being before you cannot hear; you listen but it cannot speak. . . . Touch it, and it will know—what?") thus epitomizes failed contact: the sentence itself breaks off in the telling. Insofar as our minds are separate from our bodies, we all exist in lonely isolation; but here is a figure whose utter solitude seems to defy commiseration, and in so doing calls the very possibility of communication into question.

Or, perhaps, dramatizes what its success means. For if Bridgman is a limit case, her story is one in which those limits are breached. Here is an almost an-aesthetic, almost insensible body whose signs are ultimately conveyed through sentimental tropes realized through bodily touch. Howe's project, after all, was to bring Bridgman into human intercourse and, in important ways, he succeeded. Lines from a poem by Bridgman attest to her sentimental catechism:

> A heart is the candlestick and is lighted by love of Jesus.
> Let not thy love dim. [A]dmit friends without inviting them.
> Yield the beam of sun to those around thee.
> A candle cannot be overblown which is hid in the midst of the pure heart.
> Ye shall not die if ye dwell in the love of the Lord. (Quoted in Howe and Hall, 353)

The lesson Bridgman learns, and in turn teaches, is that the liquid and light-bearing soul lodged within her recalcitrant body can be freed. Bridgman reflects the doctor's teachings.[22] In a letter written to Bridgman from Europe, Howe tried to describe the soul without using complex metaphors drawn from sight, and the result is a primer of sentimental sympathy infused with Christian idealism:

> Nobody knows what the soul is, but we know it is not the body . . . and cannot die. . . . When I say there is a spirit of love in the world, I mean that good people love each other; but you cannot feel the spirit of love with your fingers, it has no shape, nor body; it is not in one place more than in another, yet whenever there are good people there is a spirit of love. . . . God wants every body to be happy all the time, every day, Sundays and all, and to love one another; and if they love one another they will be happy; and when their bodies die, their souls will live on, and be happy, and then they will know more about God.[23]

Between them, the rhetorical postures of Howe's letter, Bridgman's poetry, and the *North American Review* article accurately represent the writing surrounding the case. Bridgman's condition simultaneously gave rise to metaphors of dread inaccessibility and closed architectural spaces (the absolute darkness of caves, prisons, and wells), as well as to prose and poetry of soulful contact. These metaphors reveal a gothic relation between the spiritual and the material self, the former encrypted within the latter. The well and the pit were favorite images of Howe's, used most often for Bridgman but also for other deaf and blind people he examined.[24] In his final Perkins report of 1875, Howe elaborates such an image in summary.

> It sometimes occurred to me that she was like a person alone and helpless in a deep, dark, still pit, and that I was letting down a cord and dangling it about, in hopes she might find it; and that finally she would seize it by chance, and, clinging to it, be drawn up by it into the light of day, and into human society. And it did so happen; and thus she, instinctively and unconsciously, aided in her happy deliverance.[25]

Howe's story concisely explains how such a "happy deliverance" actually came about: a combination of her almost accidental initiative, his repeated effects at rescue, and an element of chance. Recounting the familiar movement from darkness into light, from isolation into human society, Howe collapses his long labors with Bridgman into a virtual fairy tale. One is struck by the frequency with which Howe uses stock narrative structures, not as though by default (as if he could think of no other way to describe his experience), but as though these clichéd images were fresh and original—as though they occurred to *him first* in his unique encounter with Bridgman. Nor is Howe alone in this: in reading contemporary accounts, one repeatedly finds writers discovering the problem of how to put what is beyond words into words. Working with the constraints of sentimental convention, the writers who encounter Bridgman name and rename her anomalous state. In their cumulative force, accounts of Bridgman thus encourage a view of sentimentalism as that which seeks to disprove the very possibility of indescribability, to domesticate the unknown with deeply familiar phrases.

There is a persistent tension in these works between the desire to maintain Bridgman's status as sublime object (her ineffable, wordless state), and the characterization of her as a normal little girl immured within the prison of her body. Bridgman becomes the literal embodiment of gothic stories of enclosure, imprisonment, and enforced silence; and, in the next breath, of blessed release. Like Howe, Lydia Sigourney sees Bridgman in terms of prison bars and a bit of light through the dungeon window. Here are the second and third stanzas of the poem "Laura Bridgman," which appeared in *Godey's Lady's Book* in 1838.[26]

> All fled!—all gone!—not even the rose
> An odor left behind,
> Faintly, with broken reed to trace
> The tablet of the mind.
> That mind!—it struggles with its doom,
> The sleepless conflict, see!—
> As through its Bastille bars, it seeks
> Communion with the free.
>
> Yet still its prison-robe, it wears,
> Without a prisoner's pain,
> For happy childhood's mimic sun
> Glows in each bounding vein,—
> And blest philosophy is near,
> Each labyrinth to scan,
> Through which the subtlest clue may bind,
> To Nature and to man.

This poem encapsulates many of the elements central to the representation of Bridgman's state. Most importantly, the constant struggle of Bridgman's mind against the limitations of her body is something the reader must visualize: "The sleepless conflict, see!—" And what one sees, when one witnesses Bridgman striving for human contact, is a prisoner (thankfully) "[w]ithout a prisoner's pain." This painlessness is key, for although Bridgman is an abject figure, utterly bereft— as Howe elsewhere describes her, a "wreck—she barely suffers": "For happy childhood's mimic sun / Glows in each bounding vein." Sigourney depicts the girl simultaneously as doomed and yet also strangely unconscious of her misfortune, as though the child in Bridgman keeps her optimistic in spite of herself.

In the end, of course, this abjection (whether noticed or not) is only half of Bridgman's story. Having established Bridgman, narratively, as buried or imprisoned, Sigourney's poem, like the *North American Review* article, immediately rescues her.

> So, little daughter, lift thy head,
> For Christian love is nigh,
> To listen at the dungeon-grate,
> And every want supply.
> Say, lurks there not some beam from heaven,
> Amid thy bosom's night?
> Some echo from a better land,
> To make thy smile so bright?

With this stanza the process of chivalric sentimentalization is completed: what had been in the earlier stanzas a neuter subject (Bridgman's mind), and then a child, is now transformed into a "little daughter," the object of (parental) sympathy. Sigourney's rhetorical questions also gesture to Howe offstage: Howe is, after all, the human embodiment of that "beam from heaven" which saves Bridgman. Sigourney's question ("lurks there not?") is perfectly congruent with the *North American Review*'s concern: "has art any resources to perforate [the independent mind's] prison walls?" For both, the answer is an unhesitating yes, via the resources of the chivalric philanthropist. The images of Bridgman as interred or imprisoned necessarily invites the knightly image of Howe disinterring and disimprisoning her.

For Howe, deprivation was always a call to aid. "The sight of any being, in human shape, left to brutish ignorance, is always demoralizing to the beholders. There floats not upon the stream of life any wreck of humanity so utterly shattered and crippled that its signals of distress should not challenge attention and command assistance." So Howe concludes his report of 1844.[27] But why should what is *de*moralizing drive one to chivalric action? The answer lies in the identificatory dynamics upon which sentimentalism depends. Howe identifies with Bridgman to such an extent that he blurs the distinction between what he sees and how he imagines himself. Bridgman's degraded state metonymically degrades him. Action on behalf of others (in this case through pedogogy) is for Howe both altruistic and self-preserving; to pull Bridgman from the brink of incommunicativeness is to shore up his own threatened identity.

If, from one perspective, Howe's identification with dependent or helpless others looks merely self-serving (Howe did, after all, make a living from philanthropy), this view misses the terror underlying his descriptions. The doctor's physical ailments and psychic neuroses were well-known; he regularly suffered from debilitating headaches which caused him to cancel at the last minute his role in performances before state legislatures. As his daughters recalled, the extreme symptoms of Howe's "deathlike" fits were familiar to those who knew him well: "After the first deadly chill, followed a burning fever, and such racking agony of pain that the prostration and insensibility which followed were welcome to those who knew the regular sequence of the symptoms, though to the stranger it was the most alarming phase of the attack" (Howe and Hall, 270). Dickens experienced the consequences of one such fit on the occasion of a charity dinner in London at which the doctor was scheduled to speak; after taking some trouble to accommodate Howe, Dickens repeated that the doctor "was at the last minute unable to attend even on crutches owing to 'fever and ague.' "[28] At odds with the many hagiographic accounts of Howe was a critical counternarrative in which the temperamental doctor came off as a troublemaker. To cite one example from among many, Howe's participation in the infamous Boston common school investigation was widely criticized: parents and teachers accused him of deliberately frightening their children and of bullying them into answering artificially difficult examination questions.[29]

Diagnosing himself, Howe attributed many of his physical afflictions to a bout of malaria he had suffered in Greece. But his complicated acts of discipline and self-staging also seem to have been a latent response to another trauma. In 1832, during his trip abroad to research methods for teaching the blind, Howe took a detour to Prussia to deliver aid to Polish refugees. After a harrowing tour of a refugee camp, Howe asked permission of the authorities to administer relief; his request was granted, but was immediately reversed, and Howe was sent back to Berlin. Upon his arrival, he was arrested by the police, and, after being questioned about his activities with no sense of the charges against him, Howe spent almost four weeks incommunicado in prison. As Howe's biographer tells the story, "Howe lay *au secrete* in a dungeon eight feet wide, seeing no one but his interrogators who from time to time questioned him." After unsuccessful appeals to the King and to the Minister of Police, his American friends worked with diplomatic officials to get Howe released and transported to France.[30]

As his persistent fascination with imprisonment, social isolation, and discipline suggests, Howe never fully recovered from this experience. Under professional auspices, Howe spent the rest of his career returning to prison: from the actual penitentiaries he visited in America and Europe, through his involvement in slavery and corporal punishment reforms, to his figurative disimprisonment of the insane and disabled. In this context, the wells, pits, and tombs which Howe used to describe Bridgman's situation emerge not merely as literary conceits, but as covert autobiographical references. The "insensibility" of Howe's body during his recurrent illnesses (Howe and Hall 270, quoted above) is suggestively mimetic of Bridgman's extrasensory state, as if, by abreactively identifying with Bridgman's insensate body, he might return to the scene of his traumatic imprisonment. In his plan for the isolated confinement of prisoners, Howe attempts to restage institutionally his personal trauma, to make that trauma socially salutary.[31]

But while it is possible to establish some of the biographical sources for Howe's private interest in Bridgman, she could become "one of the beautifulest phenomena" for the culture at large (in Carlyle's words) only insofar as Howe's personal investment in her intersected with that of his readership. Only after being translated into a series of recognizable tropes by Howe, and the host of other writers and philanthropists who participated in textualizing her case, could Bridgman's situation express her culture's abiding interest in the processes of discipline, language acquisition, and socialization more generally. Bridgman's condition reminded Howe and his sympathetic audiences of the body's fragility, and of their dependence upon that body for human interaction, while Howe's ability to overwhelm Bridgman's body's hold on her represented the triumph of independence from one's own body and intercommunication with others. It is possible, the case seemed to say, to overcome nature's potentially crippling isolation and to *will* one another into sociality. The narrative constructed around and through Bridgman's silent but expressive self, in other words, was one of sentimental sociality.

And yet, like so many representations of antebellum philanthrophy, accounts of Bridgman oscillated between the sentimental and the sublime: at any moment the reader might find herself drawn away from Howe's characteristic flourishes, to be recaptivated by Bridgman's opaque, problematic body, only to be delivered again—"instinctively and unconsciously"—back to the liberating agent. Like Bridgman, readers learn their sentimental catechism; like Howe, they fold those lessons back into a chivalric worldview. But underlying both the catechism and the heroic vision is the unsettling reminder that neither discourse bridges all the gaps. Perhaps no image conveys this oscillation better than Julia Ward Howe's description of Bridgman at Howe's deathbed:

> The pathos of Laura's last meeting with her great benefactor was almost beyond description. The man who, at much cost of heroic effort, had delivered to her the keys of life, lay helpless in the grasp of fatal disease, his closing hour drawing nigh. He was surrounded by those nearest to him in ties of affection and kindred, but in all this sorrow, it was felt that a place belonged to this spiritual child, this creature, who, from childhood to mature womanhood, had been guided by his counsel and shielded by his love, owing him in the first instance the revelation of her own humanity. She could not see—she never had seen him, but she knew that she was in his presence for the last time. She was allowed to touch his features very softly, and a little agonized sound, scarcely audible, alone broke the silence of the solemn scene. (Quoted in Howe and Hall, 310)[32]

Acknowledging the affective potency of Bridgman's relationship to Howe, Julia Ward Howe nonetheless reinscribes Bridgman's subordination to her teacher: the forty-seven-year-old woman is a "spiritual child" making diminutive gestures and sounds.

By the time of his death in 1876, Howe's idealistic mixture of science and sentimentalism was already something of a relic. As Lori D. Ginzberg has shown, the war changed the terrain of social work dramatically: once the bureaucratic networks spawned by the enormous effort of the war were in place, individualist heroics like Howe's were almost unimaginable.[33] And yet, on his own terms, the doctor had succeeded. It is useful in this context to recall Ian Watt's formulation of sentimentalism as based in "an un-Hobbesian belief in the innate benevolence of man, a credo which had the literary corollary that the depiction of such benevolence engaged in philanthropic action or tears was a laudable aim."[34] Bridgman at Howe's deathbed pays tears for philanthropy. Enfolded into Howe's family, Bridgman realizes the abstract social good of the Perkins Institution and Howe's many other enterprises, tendering her emotions—emotions first tapped by Howe himself—on behalf of a figure no one now could rescue from the final prison of death. "[H]elpless in the grasp of a fatal disease," Howe can no longer speak for himself, and, ironically, the silence around his deathbed is broken only by the affective cry of Bridgman's ransomed spirit.

NOTES

1. Shirley Samuels, introduction to *The Culture of Sentiment: Race, Gender and Sentimentality in Nineteenth-Century America* (New York: Oxford University Press, 1992), 3–8, quotation from 5.

2. Michel Foucault, "What Is An Author?" in *The Foucault Reader*, ed. Paul Rabinow (New York: Pantheon Books, 1984), 101–20.

3. Ann Fabian's essay is the exception: "Unseemly Sentiments: The Cultural Problem of Gambling," in Samuels, *Culture of Sentiment*, 143–56. See the introduction to the present volume for a further discussion of this point.

4. Ann Douglas, *The Feminization of American Culture* (New York: Avon, 1977).

5. Maud Howe and Florence Howe Hall, *Laura Bridgman: Dr. Howe's Famous Pupil and What He Taught Her* (Boston: Little, Brown, 1903); further references will be made parenthetically in the text. Julia Ward Howe and her daughters were thorough biographers, producing many memoirs and volumes of letters. The James letter is quoted in Laura Richards and Maud Howe Elliott, *Julia Ward Howe, 1819–1910*, 2 vols. (Boston: Houghton Mifflin, 1915), 1:133.

6. Quoted in Harold Schwartz, *Samuel Gridley Howe: Social Reformer, 1801–1876* (Cambridge: Harvard University Press, 1956), 353. Schwartz's book is the only full-scale scholarly treatment of Howe's life.

7. Howe was named Chevalier of the Order of St. Saviour by the king of Greece in gratitude for his years of active support during the revolution (Schwartz, *Howe*, 38).

8. Ernest Freeberg, " 'An Object of Peculiar Interest': The Education of Laura Bridgman," *Church History* 61 (June 1992): 191–205, quotation from 192.

9. Lori D. Ginzberg, *Women and the Work of Benevolence: Morality, Politics and Class in the Nineteenth-Century United States* (New Haven: Yale University Press, 1990).

10. Mary Peabody Mann, *Life of Horace Mann*, 2 vols. (Boston: Walker, Fuller, and Co., 1865), 1:157.

11. See my "Bartleby's Benefactors: Toward a Literary History of Charity in Antebellum America" (Ph.D. diss., Yale University, 1995).

12. The quotation is from *National Cyclopedia of American Biography*, vol. 8 (1898):372–3.

13. The most important published works by Howe on Bridgman are the annual "Reports of the Perkins Institution" (the first of which was published in 1833 under the title *Address of the Trustees of the New England Institution for the Education of the Blind to the Public*); the first account of Bridgman is in the "Sixth Report" (1838). Excerpts were published in pamphlet form, e.g. *Laura Bridgman: Extracts from the Reports of Dr. S. G. Howe* (Boston, 1873), and were quoted at length in reviews, e.g. "Review of Howe's Ninth Report of the Trustees of the Perkins Institution and Massachusetts Asylum for the Blind, to the Corporation," *North American Review* 52, no. 111 (April 1841), 467–86 (hereafter referred to as *Review*, and cited parenthetically in the text), and "Education of Laura Bridgman," *Mind* 3 (1878), 263–7.

14. See David Rothman, *The Discovery of the Asylum: Social Order and Disorder in the New Republic* (Boston: Little, Brown, 1971); Mary P. Ryan, *Cradle of the Middle Class: Family in Oneida County, New York, 1790–1865* (New York: Cambridge University Press, 1981).

15. These case studies constitute only one example of the midcentury genre of philanthropic reporting, a flurry of functional literature which deserves notice. While today we might well balk at such reading, it was regular fare for antebellum middle-class readers: reports on the conditions of prisons and hospitals, accounts of charity fairs and fundrais-

ers, and debates over school operations or the proper methods of almsgiving sat cheek by jowl with poems and stories designed for pleasure. The prevalence of such reports, and their seemingly incongruous place in a wide range of journals and magazines, strongly suggests that they fulfilled some of the same functions that we commonly associate with imaginative literature.

16. "Laura Bridgman," *American Journal of Education* 4 (December 1857): 383.

17. Howe was dead wrong, of course, in his later characterization of the inherent limitations of sign language. Although he had been a proponent of singing, Howe became increasingly supportive of oralism, beginning with his trip to Europe with Mann in 1844. Toward the end of his life he became obsessed with the necessity of communicating by "articulate" speech, going so far as to claim that he should have taught Bridgman to speak. Debates centered around this split were conducted in the pages of the *American Annals of the Deaf and Dumb*, the *American Journal of Education,* and the *North American Review* throughout the century, culminating in the international decision finally rendered at the Milan Conference in 1881 in favor of articulation over sign. See Harlan Lane, *When the Mind Hears: A History of the Deaf* (New York: Random House, 1984).

18. Lydia Sigourney, herself a teacher of the deaf, corresponded with Howe about Bridgman; Whittier and Lowell wrote paeans to Howe's genius as a teacher and "knight-errant" of philanthropy. Just prior to her marriage to Hawthorne, Sophia Peabody was commissioned by her brother-in-law Horace Mann to sculpt a bust of Bridgman. England's Maria Southworth and America's Catharine Maria Sedgwick continued the roster of admirers; the American philosopher-scientists Francis Lieber and G. Stanley Hall wrote case studies based on their testing and observation of the girl. See G. Stanley Hall, "Laura Bridgman," in *Aspects of German Culture* (Boston: Osgood, 1881), 237–76; Francis Lieber, "On the Vocal Sounds of Laura Bridgman," *Smithsonian Contributions to Knowledge* 2 (1851): 1–32; see also H. H. Donaldson, "Anatomical observations of the brain and several sense organs of the blind deaf-mute, Laura Dewey Bridgman," *American Journal of Psychology* 3, no. 2 (1890): 3–90.

19. Thomas Carlyle to Howe, 23 October 1842, Howe Papers, Chapin Library, Williams College.

20. Charles Dickens, *American Notes for General Circulation and Hunted Down* (Boston: Estes, 1890), 63, quoting Howe's "Ninth Report."

21. Jonathan Elmer, *Reading at the Social Limit: Affect, Mass Culture, and Edgar Allan Poe* (Stanford: Stanford University Press, 1995), 95.

22. As Freeberg recounts, Howe's original intention had been to educate Bridgman according to his own Unitarian beliefs; "he hoped to find that the mysterious workings of some innate religious faculty would guide her to a personal and natural understanding of God" ("Object of Peculiar Interest," 200). But Howe's plan was foiled during his long honeymoon in Europe in 1844. In response to ideas introduced to her by a teacher, Laura fired off a letter full of questions to the doctor: "Is God ever ashamed? . . . When will he let us to go to see him in Heaven? . . . Why is He our Father? . . . Why cannot he let wrong people to go to live with him and be happy—Why should he not like to have us ask him to send us good thoughts if we are not very sad for doing wrong—" (Bridgman to Howe, 28 January 1844, quoted in Schwartz, *Howe,* 85). Freeberg describes Howe's reaction to Bridgman's religious education: it was "the greatest disappointment of his life" ("Object of Peculiar Interest," 204).

23. Howe to Bridgman, 1844, quoted in Schwartz, *Howe,* 86.

24. For further examples, and the larger cultural significance of such imagery, see Douglas C. Baynton, "A Silent Exile on This Earth: The Metaphorical Construction of Deafness in the Nineteenth Century," *American Quarterly* 44 (1992): 216–43.

25. Quoted in Schwartz, *Howe,* 71.

26. Lydia Sigourney, "Laura Bridgman," *Lady's Book and Magazine* [later renamed *Godey's Lady's Book*] 16 (June 1838): 252.

27. Quoted in Schwartz, *Howe,* 381.

28. One of the most vocal champions of Howe's work, Dickens nonetheless had little good to say about him personally. "He is a cold-blooded fellow, that Howe—a regular American," Dickens wrote to a friend (*The Letters of Charles Dickens,* ed. Madeline House, Graham Storey, and Kathleen Tillotson [Oxford: Clarendon Press, 1974], 3:495).

29. Schwartz discusses the common school controversy in detail (*Howe,* 120–36; see especially 133).

30. See Howe, "Letter from Berlin Prison," March 1832, Ford Collection, New York Public Library; quotation from Schwartz, *Howe,* 45.

31. For an account of Howe's support of the solitary system, see Schwartz, *Howe,* 47–9.

32. Describing Bridgman's presence at the memorial service, Howe's daughters presented a similar scene: "Not the least eloquent of those who bore witness that day was the pale silent woman, whose expressive face, wan with weeping, was familiar to many of the company. Laura Bridgman brought her ransomed spirit as a tribute to the memory of her best friend" (Howe and Hall, 313).

33. Ginzberg, *Work of Benevolence,* chapter 6.

34. Ian Watt, *The Rise of the Novel: Studies in Defoe, Richardson and Fielding* (Berkeley: University of California Press, 1957), 174.

◭

CHAPTER NINE

The Gaze of Success

Failed Men and the Sentimental Marketplace, 1873–1893

Scott A. Sandage

How foolish a cry, when to implore help, is itself the proof of undesert of it.

HERMAN MELVILLE, *THE CONFIDENCE-MAN*

In 1890, J. W. Bomgardner turned sixty and surveyed a life of unremitting failure. He often lamented a missed chance of the 1860s, when a friend invited him to join an Ohio grain partnership. Hoping to do better, Bomgardner instead bought into an Indiana mill that folded in the panic of 1873. "I was forced to the wall," he recalled, "losing every dollar I had in the world." Thus deflowered, he set off on the odyssey of the transient failed man. Having started in Ohio and failed in Indiana, "I drifted Westward—Decatur—Springfield—Quincy—Ill—2 years in Iowa." Eventually, he landed as a grain dealer in Atchison, Kansas, where he barely made a living in the enterprise he had shunned as a foolish youth. Swallowing the remnants of his pride in 1890, he at last did what he had contemplated so many times during the hard years. He wrote to beg a steady job from the long-lost friend who had once offered that grain partnership and who, in those halcyon days, had just begun some sideline ventures in oil: John D. Rockefeller. "It is so many years since you have probably seen my name, that you may have entirely forgotten me," he began. "But I have watched your career with considerable interest, some times thinking how near I came to being a Millionaire." The letter was a complex testament about failure and success in nineteenth-century America; the broken man measured his obscure defeats against the self-made magnate's renowned triumphs.[1]

Bomgardner's epistle to Rockefeller was at once a sentimental memoir and a business proposition. "What possibilities I threw away," he mused. "Do you know any thing of my career since then?" His tale of disappointment prefaced a nostalgic appeal for employment. Surely some post might be found if Rockefeller remembered his friend, "kindly as I hope, from our business relations when we were young men." The tycoon replied within days; he remembered Bomgardner but could offer only good wishes, not a job. The millionaire's letter made the failed man feel like a charity case, and he wrote again, to explain himself:

> In writing you, as matter of course there was something of *Sentiment* in it. Or probably I should not have Ventured writing you at all. Yet in asking if you could do any thing for me, it was not in the light of charity. But I thought if the *proper* place could be found for me to *drop into,* I could fill it to your satisfaction. . . . What I am seeking is not a good salary for a *soft* and *easy* place- But I would like a little rest from this care and anxiety.[2]

To this failed businessman, sentiment was not out of place in the competitive sphere of market capitalism. "Business relations," after all, depended on strong bonds of mutual obligation—especially during an era when sudden, catastrophic failure posed a daily threat to nearly every entrepreneur. The sentimentalization of men's economic failures had been a staple of popular fiction and advice literature for half a century. To Bomgardner, however, sentiment offered not just a way to describe his fall but also the means of his resurrection. Bomgardner envisioned a transaction whereby "*Sentiment*" might lead to "Venture."[3]

Struggling against failure, Bomgardner was not alone in imagining that sentimental exchange might resuscitate economic exchange. Rockefeller filed his old friend's letters with heaps of others that poured in from strangers and dimly recollected acquaintances—including not only failed businessmen but often long-suffering wives who wrote on their behalf. The practice apparently began in England early in the century; in America, strangers importuned the du Pont family as early as 1822, and both P. T. Barnum and Jenny Lind were besieged with aid letters during the Swedish Nightingale's tour of 1850. The emerging postwar culture of celebrity bulged the mailbags of the rich and famous whose doings filled the newspapers: Rockefeller, Andrew Carnegie, Thomas Edison, and Mark Twain, to name a few. Begging letters were so commonplace that even the supplicants themselves called them by their colloquial name. "Now Mr. Rockefeller," one correspondent admitted, "I suppose you have come to the conclusion long before this that this is a begging letter, and I suppose it would be called so." It was an outrageous, vernacular genre: correspondents made absurd, rambling requests for jobs, money, or advice, and they intruded with little justification on the patience and privacy of a stranger. The letters' intimacy was exceeded only by their relentless lack of originality; beggars wrote the same things, in almost the same order, from Des Moines, Brooklyn, and other scattered points. Sharing the language of sentiment, correspondents poured what they must have felt as unique heartbreaks into remarkably formulaic letters.[4]

Based upon a close reading of more than five hundred letters to John D. Rockefeller between the Panics of 1873 and 1893, this essay considers the begging letter

as an economic and cultural transaction that expended sentiment to restore correspondents' viability in the competitive marketplace. Epistolary beggars aimed to
reconstruct masculine identity in the wake of failure—a foreclosure at once economic and psychological, that stripped men of the means and opportunity to
achieve normative ideals like manly independence and family breadwinning.
More broadly, this essay traces beggars' attempts to reimagine the relationships
among strangers in a perilous economy that seemed to bestow success and inflict
failure almost arbitrarily. Few correspondents asked for outright charity; instead,
many artfully recast charity as a business arrangement with a stranger. To that
end, beggars ardently sought a kind of scrutiny that would reassure their benefactor and likewise vouchsafe their own worthiness to strive and succeed. Failed men
importuned Rockefeller in hopes of recovering their affirmative power to transact, which I will call "transactional manhood." By extending a job or a loan, the
self-made millionaire could certify what they felt as a manly ambition to buy and
sell, borrow and repay. Why would a famous man help a stranger? He would do it,
correspondents believed, if he scrutinized their character instead of their credit.
To paraphrase the oil man's old friend, J. W. Bomgardner, the begging letter envisioned a kind of economic transaction that retained, as a matter of course,
"something of *Sentiment* in it."[5]

Beyond seeking aid, scribbling women and men used begging letters to make
sense of the tragedies of their lives. Conventional language and familiar master
plots reinforced—for them and for us—the intimate connections between home
and market, between the sentimental and the economic. Nina Baym has described
domestic sentiment as "a value scheme for ordering all of life, in competition with
the ethos of money and exploitation that is perceived to prevail in American society." Begging letters support this view up to a point, but correspondents did not
spurn lucre for sentiment. Rather, their lives and letters obliterated alleged distinctions between the spheres of home and market. By insisting that economic life was
always both rational and sentimental, epistolary beggars reimagined the personal
relationships created and severed by economic exchange and revealed how they
grappled with emerging market-based identities like failure and success.[6]

Inevitably, the begging letter was a confessional and a reflexive crucible of
identity. Its conventions required correspondents to consider their own worthiness
and culpability in the face of failure. Jürgen Habermas has written in another
context that "through letter writing the individual unfolded himself in his subjectivity"; the letter is "a conversation with one's self addressed to another person."
By generic form and by specific example, the begging letter conformed precisely
to this definition. Writing about ourselves always entails figuring out who we are
in our own eyes and in those of others, but begging letters in particular were self-
conscious meditations, sometimes as long as twenty pages, providing a complex,
contradictory venue for confessing sins and redeeming identities. They reveal a
great deal about the advent of failure as a category of identity and about how
people conceded and denied that identity.[7]

BEGGING TO BE LOOKED AT:
THE CULTURES OF SENTIMENT AND SURVEILLANCE

Failure was an ideological anomaly in the age of the "Self-Made Man," a term that entered the American idiom when Henry Clay coined it in 1832. Few conceded that it was also the age of the Broken Man, but he became a familiar cultural figure as great financial panics punctuated the century. A mercantile journal lamented in 1845, "What are the fluctuations of romance writers, compared to some of the realities of human life?" Sentimental fiction hardly matched the pathos of the ruin witnessed daily. One congressman described bankrupts killed by shame, "crippled and enervated by the wounds and bruises they suffer, [who] go halting and maimed all their lives long, with nerves shattered by intense anxiety, and hearts sickened and sad from disappointment, bent down with anguish, miserable objects to behold." The many failures of Herman Melville's father were typical. Reduced to a mere clerkship in his last days, Allan Melvill (the *e* was added to the family name after his death) seemed to a relative to be only "the melancholly [*sic*] spectacle of a deranged man." The coming age of realism found few better words to describe failure. Of the protagonist in his 1885 novel, *The Rise of Silas Lapham*, William Dean Howells wrote: "He was more broken than he knew by his failure; it did not kill, as it often does, but it weakened the spring once so strong and elastic. He lapsed more and more into acquiescence with his changed condition." Together, the Self-Made Man and the Broken Man were among the archetypes that defined nineteenth-century American masculinity.[8]

Just as success commanded public adulation, failure earned public emasculation marked by economic impotence and dependency. Failure meant moral stain as well as financial strain, and men who failed often raged against the popular assumption that ruin was the just desserts of lazy or inept men. A Cleveland grocer undone by land speculations absolved himself in an 1887 letter to Rockefeller: "I have been Struggling incessantly trying to re[g]ain a little foothold but without Success," wrote Fitch Raymond, who had known Rockefeller for years. "Not because I am an imbecile, shiftless, lazy, listlessly, loafing about, no, not a bit of it, but the reverse is true." Bad luck, not bad management, had been his downfall. In conclusion he turned to sentiment:

> I feel somehow in my soul that you will not thoughtlessly cast this letter aside unheeded, but that the generous impulses of your heart will prompt you to kindly reach out your hand in any form that seemeth good with thee & assist a fallen comrade to stand upon his feet once more. Not leave him to faint & perish by the way side friendless & alone.[9]

Raymond's language ("to faint & perish") would hardly seem like manly talk, if sentiment were an exclusively feminine domain. But it was not; Raymond appealed to an implicit understanding among entrepreneurs that unexpected and often irretrievable ruin threatened even the best of them daily, and therefore bound them together in male communities of sentimental obligation. Sentiment was as appropriate in the market as it was in the parlor.

Begging letters were embedded not only in a culture of sentiment but also in what can only be called a culture of surveillance. The genre evolved at a time when people who failed found themselves under increasing scrutiny by charity, reform, and even credit-reporting agencies. Credit firms rated entrepreneurs by gathering detailed, narrative reports from nationwide networks of anonymous informers. This was an effective but controversial system of surveillance; one critic noted that credit agencies "*possesse[d] the coercive power of rating every man in the community*" and wielded "exceptional means of affecting the purse or the pride of every man whose name they choose to put into print." The culture of surveillance depended upon keeping watch and keeping records, and under a bureaucratic gaze, prosperity accrued to men whose life stories, moral and financial, could withstand scrutiny and investigation.[10]

Although the begging letter was chiefly a sentimental genre, both senders and recipients admitted its links to this culture of surveillance. Faced with a tide of requests that rose with his fame, Rockefeller asked business and social acquaintances to investigate his uninvited supplicants. Later he commissioned charity and credit agencies to do so, and finally he hired a full-time administrator in 1891 to make "the most careful inquiry as to the worthiness of the cause." Correspondents, for their part, literally begged for inquisition. "I want you to investigate the truth of the statements made in this letter," asked the sender of a typical missive in 1891, "and if after investigation you are willing to help me you will receive my lifelong gratitude." By inviting scrutiny, beggars conceded that surveillance and expert judgment had become the preferred bases on which money was exchanged and obligations created in the modern market. Consider the reach of the begging letter: reporting on their own homes and families, beggars radically extended the jurisdiction of surveillance into realms that even the prying credit agencies could not normally enter. Men exposed their disgraces—or more often, their wives did it for them in letters that betrayed marital confidences out of sheer desperation. "My husband does not know I wrote this," Mrs. Coryell of Colorado admitted in 1889, "as we have no secrets—I shall tell him, though he will censure me for he is so proud, but pride and poverty do not correspond." Epistolary beggars internalized surveillance, peering more deeply into their own lives than any outsider could have done. Opening the private sanctum to an outsider's gaze, beggars signalled their readiness to snitch on themselves.[11]

Yet beggars used their letters to constitute an alternative mode of surveillance that differed markedly from the watching and reporting, ranking and rating by credit and charity agencies. Rather than having a bureaucratic gaze imposed upon them, the authors of begging letters determinedly (if often shamefully) brought themselves under a "gaze of success." Beggars did not use this term, but it aptly describes the economic and social transformation that they expected if their epistles caught the eye of the great man. Desperate women and men sought more than jobs or money; they believed that the Rockefellers, Edisons, and

Carnegies could remake them and turn their failures to success—just by noticing them, scrutinizing them, and seeing who they *truly* were. A Brooklyn woman expressed this poignantly:

> I do not wish to borrow money, but I want to see you if I can. I want to tell you something of myself and ask advise [*sic*] I am so tired and I have no one to go to.
>   You are one of the greatest men of the age, and if I can feel that you are my friend I will have the courage to go on.[12]

In this letter, as in hundreds of others, the gaze of success promised redemption, in both the spiritual and financial senses of the word. Transubstantiation could only occur under the eye of the Self-Made Man, who was both an idea and a real person.

The cultures of sentiment and surveillance converged in the gaze of success, through beggars' insistence that the market was a site for sentimental, not just rational, obligation. In the sentimental market, honest men would not be blamed for their losses, and the always extenuating circumstances of failure would be forgiven. The simplest manifestation of the gaze of success was not the desire to be investigated, but a more pressing one—the yearning to be noticed. Business failure often resulted in the loss of commercial or social identity; failure was at once a conspicuous stigma and an engulfing anonymity. Epistolary beggars tried to write their way out of this abyss. They sought empathy *and* inquiry; the gaze of success denoted their desire to be understood, not underrated.[13]

To this end, beggars were tormented that their letters might remain unread or unanswered; going unnoticed after pouring one's heart out added unbearable insult to injury. "[D]o not throw this Away and not notice it i beseach you," wrote a drunkard's wife from Cleveland. A Pittsburgh railroad yardmaster promised in 1887, "I will not weary you with a long letter. Please do not consign it to the wastebasket until you have read it through." A Toledo wife preferred rejection to being ignored, writing in 1888, "Please answer at once as the most painful reality has come to be more easily borne than this wearing suspense." To be sure, correspondents begged to be noticed because therein lay the first step toward receiving aid. But they also pleaded to avert a further threat to their beleaguered identities. "I tremble for fear you will throw this aside as worthless," admitted a Colorado wife in 1889. The begging letter was identity reinscribed; it was the elusive, failed self rendered tangible. If the letter were deemed worthless and consigned to the wastebasket, what did that say about the writer? Begging for surveillance offered a chance of exorcising the specter of worthlessness.[14]

The gaze may seem an inapt concept for analyzing correspondence between strangers who, in most cases, never actually set eyes upon one another. What kind of gaze does not actually see? What kind of eyes inspect without looking? This riddle unravels in market culture, where identity—which is to say, value—is always a distillation of hearsay, of rumors about the past and promises for the future. Fortunes are built on commodities that are traded but never seen, using money that does not exist. Market cultures thrive on the transaction of representations; people buy and sell not goods but signs and promises. The answer to the riddle, then—what kind of eyes see without looking?—is the eyes of the market, wherein long-distance transactions among unseen strangers are regulated by rationalization and surveillance. Many who fell under the resulting bureaucratic gaze felt that they were watched without being truly seen—by eyes that recorded everything but understood nothing.[15]

The gaze of success, by contrast, attested to beggars' desires to be seen and judged within a sentimental nexus. A few asked for a personal audience with the millionaire. J. W. Bomgardner offered to travel from Kansas to New York so the magnate could "see me, and take my *measure*"—in other words, size him up as a man. Most beggars, however, could not have traveled to see Rockefeller even had he agreed to receive them. To compensate for their remoteness, many beggars sent along tokens to certify their identities, including deeds, bonds, and even lucky coins. Many scribbled their appeals on the letterhead of long-defunct businesses, as if to verify that they had once been solid and stable. A New Jersey plumber wrote, "I enclose my business card by which you may know who I am." Others included letters of recommendation. Beggars did whatever they could to make themselves tangible and scatter the nebula of failure.[16]

The most compelling talisman of identity was the beggar's photograph, which (like the rare personal audience with the millionaire) rendered the gaze of success literally visual. Beggars who sent photographs entreated Rockefeller to see and understand them. A quarter century after the Civil War, an ailing veteran from Indiana sent both his picture and his discharge papers. He sought only advice on how "to better my condition," and he took great care to explain that he was not at fault for his predicament. "I am nothing better than a wreck both physical and mental," the man explained in his 1890 letter. "I have not been addicted to drink or ill usage of person that would bring on these effects." He sent his army papers and his likeness to vouchsafe his claims, and in the last line of his letter, the old soldier asked for the return of these precious validations.[17]

Whether or not correspondents made it visual, the gaze of success could work some of its transformative magic merely through sentimental understanding. "If you could know and feel what a load you would & could take off of my poor heart I know you would do it," wrote a broke and indebted former oil man from Nebraska. A Pennsylvania woman who asked Rockefeller to help some friends asserted, "*if* you could see the persons yourself, you could not but feel both interested and sympathetic." A woman who had already written twice on behalf of her failed husband wrote a third time: "The thought pursues me day and night.— that if you understood it, you would come to my aid." It was this desire to be understood that inspired beggars to pen autobiographies in the form of begging letters. The wife of a failed feed and grain dealer sent their sad tale to Rockefeller in 1892. She concluded, "I am trying to tell you a little so you will see how it is with us." If he saw, truly saw, he would help.[18]

How did these appeals use the gaze of success to sentimentalize market relations? Empathy might garner the great man's charity, but how did that reimagine the market? Most beggars forswore alms; instead, they sought Rockefeller's intervention to reverse or prevent the verdicts of the competitive market. To seek charity was to reject the market, abandon their own place in it, and admit defeat. On the contrary, epistolary beggars sought aid not to escape the market but to stay in it. Correspondents did not conclude from their own misfortunes that American capitalism did not work; instead, they seemed to say that capitalism did not *quite* work but might be mended through intervention based on sentiment. If the tycoon would help this one time, they would again be fit to succeed. "If I could get out of this Debt," predicted a postman and one-time wildcatter, "I am sure I could get along." A failed salesman wrote from New Orleans: "I am in alarm lest my all should be swept away. . . . I will hold my grip however the best I can & feel I will come out all right yet[,] especially if some one would step up & give me a little boost & encouragement." Here was the quintessence of the gaze of success. Even as they despised the popular mythology of success that stigmatized them, beggars upheld that creed by pointing out their own tenacity and unshakable optimism. The philosophy of the "little boost" was not mere fantasy; rather, it was a vernacular stab at political economy. Beggars used their own experience to aver that only a sentimental market could sustain the competitive one. Failure might be thwarted by "a little boost & encouragement," not just from "some one" but from an addressee who embodied Success. Obscure beggars asked the iconic Self-Made Man neither for alms nor abundance; all they asked was that he avert their current fate by restoring them to a position wherein they could strive again.[19]

In this sense, beggars sought not charity but conversion. Sentiment became sacrament as correspondents scrambled into the gaze of success to be resurrected and restored to plausibility. "Man to man," asked a wistful beggar in 1889, "why am I so left to fight—fight without reinforcements?" His faith in his own abilities would bring him success, he believed, if only the millionaire demigod would intervene. "Before God, Mr. Rockefeller, I have been and am most sincere but weak in the presence of my possibilities," he concluded. "[A] kindly notice of my struggle or a word of encouragement, would give a little strength at least." Strongly echoing Protestant conversion narratives (not to mention the religiosity of the sentimental novel), beggars hoped for a secularized transformation—ascension in the market, rather than assistance outside of it. Beggars placed their faith in Rockefeller's aid, advice, and gaze because they regarded him as a seer. Writing from the Dakota territory in 1889, the daughter of an itinerant minister promised "to tell my wish in few words as possible, believing that the 'brainiest and most unassuming man in America', will hear even me." She imparted her "wish" to a lofty oracle, as one might confide in a wizard who possessed the power to transform. Others imputed even greater authority to the tycoon. A disgraced embezzler on the brink of suicide wrote from New York in 1894, "You have the power to save me from this, as surely as Christ saved that thief at Golgotha. I have thrown myself on the mercy of God may he move you to see me." Beggars deified Rockefeller because only an economic god could save them from the double damnation of financial failure and moral stigma. Failure was capitalist hell.[20]

Beggars' prayers to Rockefeller as confessor and redeemer revealed more about them than about him. Indeed, the salient point about the gaze of success was that it existed mainly in the minds and missives of epistolary beggars. Rockefeller delegated the task of responding to this influx, and rarely cast any kind of gaze at all on beggars or their letters. Yet beggars fell under the gaze of success because they created it within their epistles; to a degree, the redemptive powers of the gaze radiated from the act of writing itself. Like all autobiographical narratives, the begging letter was profoundly reflexive. Before they could ask for aid, beggars had first to admit—to themselves—that they had failed. "Believe me," a boyhood friend assured Rockefeller, "this has been one of the hardest tasks I ever undertook—Could you have but the faintest conception of the effort it has cost me, you would[,] I feel convinced[,] read it with a friendly interest." A bankrupt merchant admitted in 1889, "I humiliate myself by appealing for assistance." Here was the abasement of the evangelical witness transported to the marketplace; writing one's life story, especially a tale of ruin addressed to the personification of Success, was indeed a hard task and a costly effort. Addressing John D. Rockefeller entailed remaking their own identities—and his, as well. Although they begged the Self-Made Man to look upon them (and harnessed the contemporary language and mythology of success to do so), in many ways they abided in a gaze of their own imaginative making. Herein lay the poignancy and power of the begging letter. To put it simply, epistolary beggars created the gaze of success and used it to look at themselves.[21]

THE KINDNESS OF STRANGERS:
INSCRIBING OBLIGATION IN THE SENTIMENTAL MARKET

Beggars' efforts to inscribe a gaze of success were hampered by a fundamental problem: why should Rockefeller help a stranger? "I have no claim upon you whatever and am a total stranger to you," wrote the wife of a failed businessman in 1891. Alongside the question of claim lay the related problem of trust. Economic and social transformations in the nineteenth century increased contact and exchange among strangers, both in person and through long-distance transactions. Economic and social interaction among strangers was a crucial precondition of the begging letter. Yet the expected distrust among strangers also presented a significant barrier to the epistolary beggar's success. Correspondents confronted this barrier in two ways: by adopting a voice of utter (if generic) sincerity and, more subtly, by reimagining the relationships among strangers in a sentimental market.[22]

Most beggars began their letters by admitting the gulf between author and addressee. "You may consider this rather a strange letter comming [*sic*] from a stranger as it does, one whom you never met," wrote a self-described "broken down" veteran in 1885. The confession that the writer was not merely a stranger but also "one whom you never met" may have been more than a redundancy. Perhaps it signaled a new awareness of anonymity in an era that fostered exchanges and communications among people who had no discernable connection, no common ground, except for the act of exchange. One recognized a stranger visually, by "recognizing" his unfamiliar face. But a stranger "whom you never met" was a further step removed—this was a person one could encounter only in a realm of interaction that lacked place and lacked opportunities for face-to-face recognition.[23]

This placeless realm of blind exchange was one of the venues of the nineteenth-century market, wherein debtors and creditors incurred obligations by letter and telegraph over long distances without ever meeting. Such was the conceptual arena of the begging letter. Not just the desperation of failure but, curiously, the logic of the market itself produced an epistolary genre that could transform strangers into intimates "whom you never met." Stripped of its pathos, the begging letter was simply a business letter, a facilitator of long-distance exchange among strangers. From this perspective, the core of the genre was not benevolence but rather market relations generally. If the begging letter succeeded, money or other resources changed hands between strangers. Whether this was defined as charity or business, it was undeniably a kind of transaction. To understand the nature of this bargain—and its significance to what I earlier called transactional manhood—it is necessary to delve further into the making of intimate strangers.

As a genre, the begging letter first constructed a new world of unconnected strangers and then proceeded to transgress its cardinal rule by asserting some kind of connection. "You of course are a stranger to me and mine and I have no right to ask such a great favor," wrote a Cleveland wife who went on to seek a job for her failed husband. A New York woman who wrote to Mrs. Laura Spelman Rockefeller, the magnate's wife, explained that she turned to the famous couple because "those on whom I *had* a natural claim for sympathy & timely aid, stood coldly aloof in these hours of awful darkness and distress." The words "natural claim" spoke volumes. Abandoned by everyone to whom she might reasonably have turned—presumably, her family and community—this woman asserted an unnatural claim of some sort. Such letters begged questions as well as handouts. What could justify an unnatural claim on a stranger? How could such claims be made natural and tenable? These were questions about the bonds that linked far-flung people in both the real and the imagined markets—places that often severed (or rendered irrelevant or impotent) the "natural" obligations of family and friendship.[24]

Although begging letters may have derived from the time-honored genres of political constituent and patronage letters, beggars lacked any obvious claim on their patrons and so had to invent one. Writing to a famous stranger was more than an act of faith; it was an act of imagination. To win the desired prize (be it advice, a loan, a job, or just absolution), the writer had to construct two literary characters—a person worthy of being helped and a person capable of helping—and then proceed to imagine and inscribe an obligation between these two characters. Here was a genre that demanded remarkably sophisticated pieces of imaginative writing, yet was invented and perfected by correspondents who, very often, were barely literate.[25]

Some epistolary beggars imagined that a sort of cultural constituency existed between the famous and the obscure. "In reading your Successful career," a Brooklyn insurance agent wrote to Rockefeller in 1889, "I imagined you might aid me in my struggle to prosperity." Another man wrote, "I trust you will not consider my writing you officious, for I feel almost acquainted with you having heard you speak several times." A woman from Indiana carried this feeling even further, confiding "You will no doubt be surprised to receive this note from an entire stranger, yet I have seen your name so often in the Journal and Messinger [sic] that I feel like I might almost have the right of claiming kinship." This correspondent solved the problem raised earlier, about natural versus unnatural claims, by proposing that celebrity itself authorized a natural claim, one that was "almost . . . the right of claiming kinship." Such assertions underscored that market relations did indeed sanction sentimental obligations among strangers. The begging letter was a genre whose most basic grammar was that of the archetype; merely by writing to a famous stranger, correspondents acknowledged on some level that the categories of success and failure ordered the market and the relationships of the people in it.[26]

Yet, even as they asserted sentimental ties, epistolary beggars consciously employed the impersonal modes of human interaction wrought by national markets. They appealed via pathos and autobiography, but they conveyed their appeals by thoroughly modern and market-oriented means: they solicited a geographically distant stranger in writing. The market, after all, not only made Rockefeller rich and famous, and therefore a target of begging letters; it was also the market that made intercourse among strangers common and conceivable. Thus, while beggars in part blamed a cold and impersonalized market for their troubles, they purposefully adopted the conventions of that same market to advertise for relief.[27]

Many actually preferred the conditions of the faceless and placeless market, because they saw market conventions as a less embarrassing and less painful means of seeking relief than a face-to-face appeal. The wife of a failed Colorado rancher wrote in 1889, "oh it is so hard to ask aid, and I *could not* go to any one and ask them it is easier to write." A Pennsylvania woman seeking aid for a friend explained, "She *cannot* apply to men . . . that live here—as *she* is well known, & is *supposed* this day to be well off & you know it is *much* easier to apply to strangers—." In these passages, beggars sentimentalized the market even as they took advantage of its anonymity.[28]

Such passages suggest that beggars, beyond trying to escape embarrassment, were looking to the conventions of the market for solutions to the market's fundamental problem: failure. Charity and commerce were both forms of financial transaction among strangers that in the nineteenth century came to depend on a blend of self-representation and surveillance. These parallels did not, obviously, collapse fundamental distinctions between business and benevolence—distinctions of which beggars were fully aware. Although the market had made contact and exchange between strangers common and legitimate, beggars knew that importuning a stranger on "personal matters" was not quite a routine transaction. "What prompts me to do this very unbusinesslike thing, requesting a favor of a person who has never heard of me and consequently could have no interest in me I cannot say," wrote H. B. Alvord, a failed businessman from Jamaica Plain, Mass., in 1894. He added, "I fully appreciate the ridiculous position in which I may place myself with you."[29]

Yet was the begging letter inherently "unbusinesslike," as this man thought? His own language (and that used by many other epistolary beggars) echoed, by habit or calculation, the language of the standard midcentury business letter. The word "favor," in that idiom of mutual obligation, meant simply a business order or offer; most mercantile correspondence had the conventional opening "We have received your favor of the fifteenth. . . ." To ask a favor was to seek the privilege of doing business with someone. Alvord asked for a loan (and offered some bonds as collateral) to rescue his business, but he was nearly overcome by shame:

> [I]t is very hard indeed to ask a favor and hard to find it necessary to do so. Much better than a loan would be a position which you might give me possibly. I would serve you to the best of my ability and . . . certainly with perfect honesty. Should you grant me the loan the details of the matter would be arranged as you would wish.[30]

In the end, although Alvord humbled himself nearly to the extent of imagining a feudal bond to his patron, he nonetheless returned to the standard idioms of business. His missive invites analysis of how begging letters blurred the line between benevolence and business and how they renegotiated, indeed reimagined, the compatibility of sentiment and rationality in the modern market.

Many of Alvord's contemporary beggars framed their letters as standard, if desperate, business offers. They attempted to transact with Rockefeller—to strike an honest deal between men—even if shame or self-consciousness sometimes compromised the purely commercial nature of such an offer. "I want you to treat this as a business matter," wrote a New York umbrella merchant who hoped to borrow $1,000 in 1894, although he added, "forget that I am a stranger to you." An old friend who wanted a job promised, "Believe me sir I think I can give you value received for any thing you may do for me." Even while confessing financial sins and straits, beggars recast charity as transaction.[31]

Ultimately, this was untenable: liberal market relations rest on the idea of exchange among equals, a fiction incompatible with the subordinate stance of the beggar. "I know that this is not business," confessed a woman seeking aid for her husband, "also that you are not a money-lender and that there is no reason in the world why I should ask you,—a person to whom I am utterly unknown,—to do me this great favor." The modern market depended on transactions among strangers, but there remained a difference between charity and business. A New Jersey tea merchant wrote Rockefeller in 1888 asking for a secured loan, arguably a respectable transaction. "After mailing my letter," he later explained, "I at once saw the absurdity of what I had done and called to say so and get my letter back. Letter was kindly returned to me." The man had recognized that he was begging, not doing business, and the retrieval of his letter was a last clutch at manly self-respect. Six months later, however, he told this tale of retrieval in another letter to Rockefeller, sent when his business crisis at last forced him to drop the pretense of a transaction. "I am no crank," he vowed, "but a reliable business man driven to despair by no faults of his own."[32]

Whether such letters came from ruined businessmen or by proxy from distressed wives, the pose of "business as usual" aimed to reconstruct transactional manhood. The capacity to transact was a central component in the entrepreneurial calculus of masculinity as beggars understood it. Consider an 1888 dispatch from J. W. Cleland, a Kansas City lumber dealer who faced ruin after buying land for a housing development that proved unsalable. He asked Rockefeller to rescue the land and share in the eventual profits it would bring. Cleland began his letter, however, not with current failures but with past successes:

> I am a native of Ohio. served in the army of the rebellion from that state. going [sic] into the army as a private I came home in the command of my company. Came to Missouri at the close of the War and started life for myself first by working for wages and afterwards in the lumber business for myself with only my credit as my capital at beginning.

Martial valor, wage labor, and credit backed his conviction that he was a true man, not a "crank." Having earned $50,000 in business, he reported this "not . . . with any feeling of braggadoia [sic] but only to show that I have not been a 'dependent.' " This resume was meant to reinforce Cleland's masculinity for two people: not merely the letter's recipient but also, significantly, the letter's author. Cleland did all he could to write away his impending failure as preface to the distasteful necessity of admitting it. The words came hard:

> Why I should write you I do not know. It came to me about two weeks ago I wrote a letter but did not have courage to mail it and concluded to make another pull, but I have so much at stake in this—The accumulation of years of hard work—That I cant see any other way to save than by obtaining help from some where at once, And knowing no place to go and knowing that this amt. [amount] would be but small matter with you if you could be convinced that you would not be imposed upon and you could get a remuneration for its use.

Here Cleland neared outright begging. Amid protests that he was not "a 'dependent,' " the last defense of his manhood was the pose of the transaction—to recast begging as a business opportunity. Cleland knew that gambit rang hollow; this decorated war hero confessed that he "did not have the courage" to mail his first letter to Rockefeller. The one he finally sent concluded with shame: "do me the favor to consider this as confidential and in case you cannot grant my request please 'burn this.' "[33]

Courage was a marker of manhood in business as in war, and Cleland's admitted deficit was telling. Saving face depended on deflecting charity by the pose of the transaction. Buying and selling represented the ideal transaction for entrepreneurial manhood, but borrowing and repaying would do in a pinch. "Should you help me out of my present dilemma [it] will be the proudest effort of my life to honorably pay and discharge the debt," Cleland wrote in closing. The pride to which Cleland looked forward stemmed in no small part from the fact that being in a position to borrow and repay a debt was enough to redeem his failures and recapture his transactional manhood. In a sentimental market, he begged for credibility as much as for credit.[34]

THE BEGGAR AS STORYTELLER

The gaze of success, as constituted in begging letters, is transformative, redemptive, and reflexive. At its core is the curious practice of begging for a sentimentalized surveillance, and in a way that practice was the culmination of nineteenth-century ideas about failure. Uneasily, Americans recognized that seeking and submitting to investigation was not only necessary to authorize economic exchange, but also necessary to authorize self-esteem. Only by begging for surveillance—by surrendering his secrets and inviting scrutiny of various kinds—could a failed man hope to reacquire the credentials that would allow him to try again. Feeling watched, but not truly seen, epistolary beggars scrambled into the gaze of success not just in hopes of lucky transformation, but also to demand sentimental reconsideration, a reevaluation of their whole identity. They asked to be judged as characters rather than as commodities.

The writers of begging letters literally wrote and rewrote their lives; perpetrating what Anthony Giddens has called "a corrective intervention into the past," they tried to save far more than their fortunes. Epistolary beggars, both men and women, understood only too well that success and failure were sentimental stories of praise and blame. One man wrote to Rockefeller, "Your success in life, as related to me is wonderful, and recalls some of the stories in the Arabian Nights." But many correspondents called attention to the fact that they, too, had stories to tell. "Let us go back," a quarry owner began, "for such is the story-tellers privilege. . . ." A young real estate speculator assured, "My story I will tell as briefly as possible." In 1889, a Virginia wife wrote, "I . . . come to you with a simple unvarnished story of my troubles." A farmwoman in Ohio insisted upon Rockefeller's "hearing the end of the story . . . to show you that if we had missed success we had still done well and failed only by a cruelly small chance." This woman knew that the difference between success and failure lay in who got to tell the story.[35]

The writers of begging letters contested the judgments made about themselves and their loved ones. Literally inventing their own genre, they created an unsolicited opportunity to narrate their own lives—to speak directly rather than letting their failures be told by credit reporters or bankruptcy lawyers. The wife of a failed merchant wrote in 1891, "to make a long story short we are greatly embarrassed financially. [Y]ou will very naturally ask the cause of this embarrassment. I will tell you." Another woman railed against the gossip about her husband's failure, writing, "so much explanation is always necessary & people always get things wrong." Seizing the storyteller's privilege was a premeditated contestation. These self-conscious narrators did not tell their stories to just anybody who would listen, nor even to just anybody who could help: they made their apologias to an eminent stranger, someone whose opinions about success and failure mattered.[36]

The gaze of success, embodied in Rockefeller's scrutiny and (it was hoped) certification of worthiness, could verify the beggars' own versions of their lives, allay their doubts, and absolve their failures. Their fondest hopes lay not in being helped but in being seen—which in market culture meant being investigated, appraised, and pronounced both valuable and verifiable. This done, they would, in fact, not be beggars or failures; help from Rockefeller would not be charity but rather a fair transaction in a sentimentalized marketplace. The gaze of success could not make them successful; it could, however, rehabilitate them financially and morally to begin again and strive onward.

Thus the market that made the idea of failure likewise offered hope of exorcism. Not a few epistolary beggars found in market discipline a source of poignant self-revelation and even redemption. In 1886, James D. Reid, a writer enduring hard times, sent his old friend Andrew Carnegie a letter that summarized years of failure and struggle. Reid began his witness by bringing himself within Carnegie's gaze of success, writing, "I am very proud of the memory of our first acquaintance and have felt the glow of your success." Immediately, Reid proceeded to contrast this against his own career:

> I clouded some years of my life by a foolish struggle for freedom from subordinating duties which galled me. My methods were unsuited to my nature. Of course I failed and suffered. But the discipline was useful though severe. I learned to suffer without tears, and to find my mind toned to a better and higher key. If I did not become strong, I at least became patient. I now know the possibility of rest even under the severest economics. That is no mean victory.[37]

Reid's letter vividly blended sentiment and economics. He blamed his own indulgence for his downfall. Galling feelings of unfreedom and the sin of pride made him not a productive striver but a foolish struggler. Reid was "foolish" because he denied his essential identity; his abject "nature" best fitted him for "subordinating duties." In itself, he now recognized, subordination was not failure, but having disavowed his nature for years, "of course I failed and suffered"—with the "of course" signaling Reid's belief that he deserved his pain.

Reid's missive to Carnegie internalized surveillance; like so many epistolary beggars, he snitched on himself. But Reid's letter was simultaneously an edict of self-absolution, albeit a rare one that made no claim to commercial redemption. Although he embraced his suffering, the windfall of Reid's failure was that he had learned to suffer well. Unlike other men, who asserted that the discipline of failure had made them more fit to compete in a sentimental market, Reid did not delude himself. Most likely, he had "not become strong"—not economically, at least. Instead, Reid based his claim to redemption on newfound grace. To "know the possibility of rest," even in financial ruin, was a "victory." Rest did not indicate idleness or capitulation but rather a serene acceptance of his elemental nature. Reid added that he was sixty-seven years old, "yet I never felt so much the freshness of life, or felt my step firmer." Only nominally using Carnegie's eyes via the convention of the begging letter, James Reid constructed his own sentimental gaze of success and, perhaps, "felt the glow" of his own kind of rehabilitation. By accepting his failure he absolved himself of it.[38]

NOTES

The Rockefeller Archive Center, the American Historical Association, and the Library of Congress provided generous grants to support the research and writing of this essay. I thank the Rockefeller Archive Center for permission to quote from its archives and for the reference assistance of Kenneth W. Rose and Thomas Rosenbaum. I am grateful to David Jasper for his sentimental gaze, and to generous critics of drafts: Mary Chapman, Linda Frost, Philip Greven, Glenn Hendler, T. K. Hunter, Karl Kroeber, Jackson Lears, Jan Lewis, James Livingston, Barbara Machtinger, Sonya Michel, Carol Zisowitz, Peter Stearns, Michael Zuckerman, and two anonymous referees. For other assistance, I thank Martha Dennis Burns, Ruth Crocker, Daniel Hack, Dawn Greeley, David Hounshell, Katherine V. Snyder, and Susan Yohn.

1. J. W. Bomgardner to John D. Rockefeller, Sr. (hereafter JDR), 19 November 1890, folder 34, John D. Rockefeller Papers, Office Correspondence series, Rockefeller Archive Center, North Tarrytown, N.Y. Unless otherwise noted, all letters cited below are from this collection, which consists of thousands of letters that fill more than 50 archival boxes. All emphases are in the originals.

2. Bomgardner to JDR, 1 December 1890. See also JDR to Bomgardner, 25 November 1890, JDR Papers, Letterbooks series. Some of Rockefeller's responses to begging letters survive, but space and scope preclude analyzing them here.

3. Failure remains an understudied topic, but see Peter J. Coleman, *Debtors and Creditors in America: Insolvency, Imprisonment for Debt, and Bankruptcy, 1607–1900* (Madison: State Historical Society of Wisconsin, 1974); Peter R. Decker, *Fortunes and Failures: White-Collar Mobility in Nineteenth-Century San Francisco* (Cambridge: Harvard University Press, 1978); and Martha Banta, *Failure and Success in America: A Literary Debate* (Princeton: Princeton University Press, 1978). Recent and insightful contributions include Bruce H. Mann, "Tales from the Crypt: Prison, Legal Authority, and the Debtors' Constitution in the Early Republic," *William & Mary Quarterly* 51 (April 1994): 183–202; Toby L. Ditz, "Shipwrecked; or, Masculinity Imperiled: Mercantile Representations of Failure and the Gendered Self in

Eighteenth-Century Philadelphia," *Journal of American History* 81 (June 1994): 51–81; and Edward J. Balleisen, "Vulture Capitalism in Antebellum America: The 1841 Federal Bankruptcy Act and the Exploitation of Financial Distress," *Business History Review* 70 (Winter 1996): 473–516.

4. M. M. Comstock to JDR, 1890, folder 61. See also Mrs. E. R. Longworth [pseud.] to JDR, June 1886, folder 183. "Demands for information and / or financial assistance," Eleuthera Bradford du Pont Collection, box 7, folder 81, Hagley Museum and Library, Wilmington, Del. On Lind, see "Shameful," *New York Journal of Commerce*, 11 November 1850, 2; thanks to Martha Dennis Burns for this citation.

For new work on begging letters, see Dawn Greeley, "Beyond Benevolence: Gender, Class, and the Development of Scientific Charity in New York City, 1882–1935" (Ph.D. diss., State University of New York, Stony Brook, 1995), chap. 4; Ruth Crocker, *Splendid Donation: The Philanthropy of Margaret Olivia Sage* (Bloomington: Indiana University Press, forthcoming); and Daniel Hack, "The Material Interests of the Victorian Writer," a dissertation in progress at the University of California, Berkeley. I thank each of these scholars for ongoing conversations, exchanged drafts, and shared citations. See also Reynold M. Wik, "Dear Mr. Ford . . . ," in *Henry Ford and Grass-Roots America* (Ann Arbor: University of Michigan Press, 1972), 212–28, and Terry Alford, " '. . . Hoping to Hear From You Soon': The Begging Correspondence of Alexander T. Stewart," *Manuscripts* 40 (Spring 1988): 89–100. Earlier British begging letters are analyzed in Lionel Rose, *"Rogues and Vagabonds": Vagrant Underworld in Britain, 1815–1985* (London: Routledge, 1988), chap. 4, and M. J. D. Roberts, "Reshaping the Gift Relationship: The London Mendicity Society and the Suppression of Begging in England, 1818–1869," *International Review of Social History* 36 (1991): 201–31.

5. Although not the core of the present analysis, Judith Butler's resonant term "foreclosure" aptly describes the loss of subjectivity and threat of abjection felt by many men who experienced economic failure. This context underscores the function of the begging letter as a site for performing and (re-)constructing masculinity, through a discourse that "produces the effects it names." See Judith P. Butler, *Bodies that Matter: On the Discursive Limits of "Sex"* (New York: Routledge, 1993), 2–3, 243 n. 2; Butler, in turn, cites Jean Laplanche and J.-B. Pontalis, *Vocabulaire de la psychanalyse* (Paris: Presses Universitaires de France, 1967), 163–7. A provocative new gloss on theories of abjection is Calvin Thomas, *Male Matters: Masculinity, Anxiety, and the Male Body on the Line* (Urbana: University of Illinois Press, 1996), chap. 1.

6. Nina Baym, *Women's Fiction: A Guide to Novels by and about Women in America, 1820–1870* (Ithaca: Cornell University Press, 1978), 27. I use "sentiment" to refer to a language available to epistolary beggars from contemporary popular literature, as well as to the value system that Baym describes. Although failed men were often "feminized" by the disempowering experience of failure, the discourse of sentiment was neither exclusively feminine nor divorced from the rough and tumble world of commerce. Had sentiment been limited in either of these ways, it would not have served the beggars' purpose to bolster and reconstitute masculine identity in times of failure. For a seminal critique of gendered spheres, see Linda K. Kerber, "Separate Spheres, Female Worlds, Woman's Place: The Rhetoric of Women's History," *Journal of American History* 75 (June 1988): 9–39.

7. Jürgen Habermas, *The Structural Transformation of the Public Sphere: An Inquiry into a Category of Bourgeois Society*, trans. Thomas Burger, with the assistance of Frederick Lawrence (Cambridge: MIT Press, 1989), 48–9; see also Michael Warner, *Letters of the Republic: Publi-*

cation and the Public Sphere in Eighteenth-Century America (Cambridge: Harvard University Press, 1990). Habermas asserts that by the eighteenth century, state papers, novels, and even intimate letters had become not only self-observant but "always already oriented to an audience." This "audience-oriented subjectivity" clearly afflicted the writers of nineteenth-century begging letters. See also note 27, below.

8. Robert V. Remini, *Henry Clay: Statesman for the Union* (New York: W. W. Norton, 1991), 3. On panics and the texts they occasioned, see Ann Fabian, "Speculation on Distress: The Popular Discourse of the Panics of 1837 and 1857," *Yale Journal of Criticism* 3 (1989): 127–35. The classic study (among dozens) of self-made manhood remains Irvin Wyllie's 1954 *The Self-Made Man in America: The Myth of Rags to Riches* (New York: Free Press, 1966); a recent and much needed gender analysis is Judy Hilkey, *Character Is Capital: Success Manuals and Manhood in Gilded Age America* (Chapel Hill: University of North Carolina Press, 1997).

"Ups and Downs in Life," *Cist's Advertiser,* clipping pasted into the diary of Henry Van Der Lyn, 30 March 1845, New York Historical Society. John Sergeant, "Mercantile Character," *Hunt's Merchants' Magazine,* July 1840, 2–22. Peter Gansevoort, quoted in Hershel Parker, *Herman Melville: A Biography* (Baltimore: Johns Hopkins University Press, 1996), 58. William Dean Howells, *The Rise of Silas Lapham* (New York: Penguin Books, 1983), 354. On failure and masculinity in nineteenth-century America, see E. Anthony Rotundo, *American Manhood: Transformations in Masculinity from the Revolution to the Modern Era* (New York: Basic Books, 1993), 178–85.

9. Fitch Raymond to JDR, 23 March 1887, folder 246.

10. James D. Norris. *R. G. Dun & Co., 1841–1900: The Development of Credit-Reporting in the Nineteenth Century* (Westport, Conn: Greenwood Press, 1978). Thomas Francis Meagher [Charles F. Maynard], *The Commercial Agency "System" of the United States and Canada Exposed: Is the Secret Inquisition a Curse or a Benefit?* (New York, 1876), 25; emphasis in original.

11. Allan Nevins, *John D. Rockefeller: The Heroic Age of American Enterprise* (New York: Charles Scribner's Sons, 1940), 1:210–7, 266–73, quotation from 266–7. Thomas N. Walker to JDR, Walkerton, Va., 11 March 1891, folder 357. See also T. S. Nettleton to JDR, Alma City, Minn., 7 March 1889, folder 224. Mrs. George E. Coryell to JDR, Monte Vista, Colo., 15 March 1889, folder 62.

Failure emerged as a category of identity in the nineteenth century largely through such intersections of surveillance and confession. My analysis owes much to Michel Foucault's observation that in modern society "[t]he obligation to confess is now relayed through so many points, is so deeply ingrained in us, that we no longer perceive it as the effect of a power that constrains us" (*The History of Sexuality, Volume 1: An Introduction,* trans. Robert Hurley [New York: Vintage Books, 1990], 60). See also Foucault, *Discipline and Punish: The Birth of the Prison,* trans. Alan Sheridan, 2d. ed. (New York: Vintage, 1995), 170–1.

12. Ella M. White to JDR, n.d., folder 365.

13. My intent is to ground the concept of the gaze in the systems of surveillance deployed in nineteenth-century America by credit agencies and bankruptcy laws, as well as in noninstitutional situations wherein people watched, evaluated, and reported on themselves and those closest to them. Current scholarship emphasizes the reflexive, sexual, and psychological essence of the gaze—currents that are clearly present (and sometimes overt) in begging letters but which remain unexplored here. Much existing literature follows Jacques Lacan, whose formulation "I saw myself seeing myself" implies that we are all being watched (and therefore evaluated) all the time, by ourselves as well as by solitary and

communal others. See Kaja Silverman, *Male Subjectivity at the Margins* (New York: Routledge, 1992), introduction and chap. 3; Lacan is quoted at 407 n. 13.

14. Mrs. J. A. Ackley to JDR, 6 December, no year, folder 1. Alonzo Tripp to JDR, 21 November 1887, folder 350. Jane A. Pierce to JDR, 13 March 1888, folder 239. Coryell to JDR, cited in note 11. See also Frank W. Smith to JDR, 10 February 1888, folder 324.

15. Here I am influenced by interdisciplinary work on the cultural and political connections between literature and money (including credit) as modern ways of assessing and representing value. See, for example, Marc Shell, *Money, Language, and Thought: Literary and Philosophic Economies from the Medieval to the Modern Era* (Baltimore: Johns Hopkins University Press, 1982); Viviana A. Zelizer, *The Social Meaning of Money* (New York: Basic Books, 1994); and Michael O'Malley, "Specie and Species: Race and the Money Question in Nineteenth-Century America," *American Historical Review* 99 (April 1994): 369–95.

16. Bomgardner to JDR, 1 December 1890. Deed in Leopold Seltzer to JDR, 14 December 1889, folder 296. Bonds in H. B. Alvord to JDR, 8 March 1894, folder 5. Coin in Eli P. Babcock to JDR, 10 January 1894, folder 14. Business card in Eugene A. Bleything to JDR, 21 November 1890, folder 32. Recommendations in M. M. Welch to JDR, 8 April 1890, folder 363.

17. M. R. Gardner to JDR, 26 January 1890, folder 119. The photograph and discharge papers are not present with Gardner's letter in Rockefeller's papers. See also Mary E. Newton to JDR, 6 April 1891, folder 225.

18. Albert O. Swift to JDR, 2 January 1893, folder 340. Eva K. Bray to JDR, 5 July 1893, folder 38. Emma K. Tourgée to JDR, Mayville, N.Y., 7 October 1890, folder 349; this correspondent was the wife of the radical Republican novelist Albion Winegar Tourgée, who had been left $50,000 in debt by a bad investment. Mary Elizabeth Bevier to JDR, Elmira, N.Y., 31 July 1893, folder 27.

19. Swift to JDR, cited in note 18. J. H. H. Hedges to JDR, 26 April 1891, folder 146. See also Harry L. Robertson to JDR, Wheeling, W.V., 7 December 1885, folder 253, and Mrs. Babcock to JDR, Washington, D.C., 23 May 1889, folder 14.

Although I argue that beggars' stance was more than a fantasy, a useful contemporary analysis is Salman Akhtar, " 'Someday . . .' and 'If Only . . .' Fantasies: Pathological Optimism and Inordinate Nostalgia as Related Forms of Idealization," *Journal of the American Psychoanalytic Association* 44, no. 3 (1996): 723–53.

20. Samuel Abbott to JDR, Wakefield, Mass., 26 September 1889, folder 1. Ida Claire Baldridge to JDR, 15 May 1889, folder 17. Harold G. Butt to JDR, 17 February 1894, folder 47. On the connections between sentiment, religion, and the market, see Jan Lewis, *The Pursuit of Happiness: Family and Values in Jefferson's Virginia* (Cambridge: Cambridge University Press, 1983), 54–9, 214–29; Susan Juster, " 'In a Different Voice': Male and Female Narratives of Religious Conversion in Post-Revolutionary America," *American Quarterly* 41 (March 1989): 34–62; and Jane Tompkins, *Sensational Designs: The Cultural Work of American Fiction, 1790–1860* (New York: Oxford University Press, 1985), 133–5, 139–46.

21. John P. Bell to JDR, Oswego, N.Y., 7 October 1889, folder 24. H. Bruce to JDR, New York, N.Y., 27 April 1889, folder 43.

22. S. P. Darrah to JDR, Mt. Vernon, N.Y., 12 January 1891, folder 77. On sentiment as a shield against deception in "the world of strangers," see Karen Halttunen, *Confidence Men and Painted Women: A Study of Middle-Class Culture in America, 1830–1870* (New Haven: Yale University Press, 1982), 33–55. For insights on strangers and the sentimentalized marketplace in the novels of Horatio Alger, see Carol Nackenoff, *The Fictional Republic: Horatio Alger and American Political Discourse* (New York: Oxford University Press, 1994), chaps. 3–4.

23. John R. Campbell to JDR, Springfield, Ill., 5 March 1885, folder 49. See also Ackley to JDR, cited in note 14.

24. Mrs. S. T. Berry to JDR, 22 June 1885, folder 26. Adelaide Trowbridge to Laura Spelman Rockefeller, 27 May, no year, folder 350.

25. My argument that begging letters constitute a vernacular genre derives, in part, from Jane Tompkins's insistence that sentimental novels were subtle and sophisticated literature, notwithstanding their "continual and obvious appeals to the reader's emotions and use [of] technical devises that are distinguished by their utter conventionality" (*Sensational Designs*, 125). Similar conventionality characterized the intimate yet formulaic begging letter, the customs and grammar of which depended on its genericity. Historians have pondered the cultural work of genre at least since Perry Miller (inspired by W. H. Auden) unravelled "the tyranny of form over thought" in his analysis of the Puritan jeremiad. See Perry Miller, *The New England Mind: From Colony to Province* (Cambridge: Harvard University Press, Belknap Press, 1981), especially 31–2, 51–2; and Michael Denning, *Mechanic Accents: Dime Novels and Working-Class Culture in America* (London: Verso, 1987), 74–9 and 223–4 n. 7. Recent theoretical debates are introduced in W. J. T. Mitchell, ed., *On Narrative* (Chicago: University of Chicago Press, 1981) and Tzvetan Todorov, *Genres in Discourse* (Cambridge: Cambridge University Press, 1990), chaps. 2–3.

26. John Burrill to JDR, 8 April 1889, folder 46. Henry S. Seaman to JDR, Newburgh, Ohio, 28 October 1885, folder 38. Jennie Burroughs to JDR, 12 July 1886, folder 47. My thinking on the concept of celebrity has been shaped by Charles L. Ponce de Leon, "Idols and Icons: Representations of Celebrity in American Culture, 1850–1940" (Ph.D. diss., Rutgers University, 1992).

27. In more theoretical terms, begging letters mimic the simultaneously vertical and horizontal socioeconomic relations that Habermas attributes to modern capitalism. The transformation of the public sphere that Habermas discusses involved an axis shift from the vertical relations that defined feudalism to the "far-reaching network of horizontal economic dependencies" that proliferated in early capitalism. Yet the ensuing liberal vision of "only horizontal exchange relationships among individual commodity owners" was an insidious fiction, because competitive capitalism continued to ordain vertical relationships between those who succeeded and those who did not (Habermas, *Structural Transformation*, 15, 144, 244). This troublesome nexus of relations purportedly horizontal but actually vertical was writ large in the begging letter. Successful men and failed ones always faced off on both horizontal and vertical terms, and any claims obscure strangers made on the famous had to be expressed dually. Epistolary beggars had to acknowledge their *vertical* relationship to the addressee (which authorized the charitable transaction), while at the same time asserting a *horizontal* relationship (which constituted their worthiness and eligibility to continue striving in the market). Even as beggars deferred to an exalted luminary, they claimed their right to approach any stranger as an equal in the liberal marketplace. This double axis underlies the analysis in this essay; my thanks to Glenn Hendler and Jan Lewis for prompting and contributing to this explanation.

28. Coryell to JDR, cited in note 11. Bray to JDR, cited in note 18. See also Mrs. E. P. Buck to JDR, New York, N.Y., 27 November 1884, folder 43.

29. Butt to JDR, cited in note 20. Alvord to JDR, cited in note 16.

30. Ibid.

31. Franz Blumenstein to JDR, 19 February 1894, folder 32. Bell to JDR, cited in note 21. See also Lizzie B. Allen to JDR, New York, N.Y., 29 August 1892, folder 3.

32. Emma K. Tourgée to JDR, 26 September 1890, folder 349. William Dallas to JDR, 2 January 1889 and 13 January 1889, both in folder 77.

33. J. W. Cleland to JDR, 23 February 1888, folder 57.

34. Ibid.

35. Anthony Giddens, *Modernity and Self-Identity: Self and Society in the Late Modern Age* (Stanford: Stanford University Press, 1991), 72. Nathan C. Brooks to JDR, Philadelphia, Pa., 24 August 1893, folder 40. Jewett P. Cain to JDR, Rutland, Vt., 20 March 1890, folder 48. Butt to JDR, cited in note 20. Ella Busick to JDR, 11 November 1886, folder 47. Mary F. Braddock to JDR, 12 February 1894, folder 38.

36. M. J. Watson to JDR, Cleveland, Ohio, December 1891, folder 362. Mrs. M. G. Browne to JDR, Cleveland, Ohio, n.d., folder 42.

37. James D. Reid to Andrew Carnegie, 24 May 1886, Papers of Andrew Carnegie, Library of Congress. Reid was the author of *The Telegraph in America and Morse Memorial* (New York: Printed for the Author by J. Polhemus, [1886]).

38. Ibid. See also subsequent letters from Reid to Carnegie, dated 1895–1898, as noted in the correspondence index to the Carnegie Papers.

PART THREE

Canonical Sentiments

CHAPTER TEN

ꔪ

Masochism and Male Sentimentalism

Charles Brockden Brown's Clara Howard

Bruce Burgett

The moral is that woman, as nature created her and as man up to now has
found her attractive, is man's enemy; she can be his slave or his mistress but
never his companion. This can only be when she has the same rights as he and
is his equal in education and work. For the time being there is only one
alternative; to be the hammer or the anvil. I was fool enough to let a woman
make a slave of me, do you understand? Hence the moral of the tale: whoever
allows himself to be whipped deserves to be whipped. But as you see, I have
taken the blows well; the rosy mist of supersensuality has lifted.

LEOPOLD VON SACHER-MASOCH, *VENUS IN FURS* (1870)

THE CULTURAL PROBLEM OF MASOCHISM

From Nathaniel Hawthorne's infamous lament that "America is now given over to
a d———d mob of scribbling women" to William Dean Howells's reluctant submission to the literary judgements of the "court of women," from Leslie A.
Fiedler's *Love and Death in the American Novel* to Ann Douglas's *The Feminization of
American Culture,* warnings that male sentimentality leads to male masochism echo
through the United States literary and literary critical canons.[1] Most famously,
Fiedler complains that a "robust masculine sentimentality, turned out, oddly
enough, to have no relevance to the American scene." Rather, male sentimentalism takes the form of what Fiedler calls, in another context, "an abyssal male
masochism."[2] As its title suggests, Douglas's study of New England sentimental
culture bemoans a similar reversal of what she refers to as "masculine" and "feminine" values (though Douglas also suggests that sentimentalism fails because it
disavows "matriarchal values" or, in other words, never affirms its own masochistic subtext).[3] "The liberal minister," Douglas argues, "was pushed into a position
increasingly resembling the evolving feminine one. Who else was barred with him

from the larger world of masculine concerns, who else was confined with him to a claustrophobic private world of over-responsive sensibility, who else but the American lady?"[4] For such writers and critics, the pathology of male sentimentalism results from (and in) its tendency to confound the homosocial worlds of (public) "masculinity" and (private) "femininity." Like Richard von Krafft-Ebing's original sentimental masochist Jean-Jacques Rousseau, the "essential element" for the "over-responsive" male is the irrationality and intensity of the "feelings" that dictate his "subjection to the woman."[5]

The writings of Charles Brockden Brown occupy a privileged position within this literary and literary critical equation of male sentimentalism with male masochism. Brown, critics suggest, "capitulated" to the demands of his allegedly female audience in 1800 when he shifted from his early gothic novels (*Wieland, Ormond, Edgar Huntly,* and *Arthur Mervyn*) to his late sentimental novels (*Clara Howard* and *Jane Talbot*). Evidence of this "capitulation" appears in a letter written by Brown to his brother James in April 1800. Hoping to attract a larger audience and market for his novels, Brown pledged to "[drop] the doleful tone and assum[e] a cheerful one."[6] According to his critics, Brown enacts the masochist's surrender to a feminized law by contracting with his public to produce less "experimental" and "radical" fictions. "Like Edgar [Huntly]," Bill Christophersen suggests in a recent book-length study of Brown's career, "Brown may have come to fear his [psychological] discoveries and their possible repercussions."[7] Fiedler is less oblique: Brown "fails in his direct attempt to recapture passion from the 'female scribblers.' "[8] For the same critics, this failure is heroic rather than pathetic, however. Brown becomes the antetype of nineteenth- and twentieth-century male authors whose art resists sentimentality, even as it eventually falls prey to the demands of the mass market and the interests of a female reading public. The story of Brown's career thus becomes a fable that warns the male reader against the perils of sentimental publication—public displays of male affect—in an increasingly gendered literary public sphere. *Clara Howard* and *Jane Talbot* are, Norman S. Grabo concludes, "trivial and silly."[9]

Of course, many of the critics I have alluded to have never given half as much thought to either *Clara Howard* or *Jane Talbot* as they have to Brown's earlier works. Critical convention seems to require a summary dismissal. The only significant exception to this generalization is Sidney Krause's 1981 article, "*Clara Howard* and *Jane Talbot:* Godwin on Trial."[10] Referring to Clara Howard as the "original iron maiden of American literature" (a phrase he takes from Fiedler), Krause reads the novel as a battle between the Godwinian rationalism of Brown's female protagonist (Clara Howard) and the Rousseauist sentimentalism of his male protagonist (Edward Hartley). Brown's irony, Krause concludes, is aimed at the inflexibility and "coldness" of Clara's law. "Just as Brown had shown the limits of Reason in the breakdown of Ormond, . . . so in *Clara Howard* was he revealing what it would be like to write the Enlightenment's courtesy book, with a Godwinite Iron Maiden as instructress in love." Krause's reading is instructive, especially in its insight into

the intellectual intertexts that inform Brown's novel. More interesting, however, is
Krause's unreflective repetition of the masochistic figures that inform other critical accounts of the novel. Edward Hartley is, according to Krause, "put on the
rack" by the "hard-core Godwinism" of the "Prussian" Clara Howard.[11] Like the
other critics, Krause leaves unanswered the central question raised by the novel.
Why does Brown flout Godwinian and, more generally, Enlightenment conventions by gendering reason female and sentiment male? Why, in other words, does
he place his male character's "over-responsive sensibility" under the rational
authority of his female character's abstract law?

An answer to this question requires a rethinking of the relations among sex,
gender, and sentiment that many critics haven taken for granted. By focusing on
the paradoxical figure of the sentimental male in a cultural context that increasingly aligns masculinity with rational authority and femininity with moral sentiment, *Clara Howard* both marks and contributes to a contemporary ideological
shift in the national understanding of the relation between gender and polity, sentiment and reason. Using the shorthand of intellectual history, this shift could be
described as one from a theoretically ungendered eighteenth-century republic of
letters to a theoretically gendered nineteenth-century empire of the mother.[12]
Under the former regime, the existence of a sentimental male—in Henry
MacKenzie's words, a "man of feeling"—like Edward Hartley remains unprob-
lematic since sentiment is, as yet, ungendered.[13] In a 1775 bookplate from Bell's
Circulating Library, for example, potential subscribers are hailed as "sentimentalists, whether ladies or gentlemen."[14] Under the latter regime, Edward Hartley's
sentimentalism marks his gender cross-identification. Like his literary progeny
Natty Bumppo and Huck Finn, Brown's hero is left with only two options: either
submission to Clara's feminized law or escape from the law altogether. Much to
the critics' dismay, Edward submits. No Edgar Huntly, Edward Hartley remains,
in Grabo's words, "a very domesticated pussycat."[15] By substituting Hartley for
Huntly, Brown produces an early, masochistic version of what would become a
persistent reaction to the postrevolutionary alignment of sentimental authority
with femininity, in novels ranging from Hannah Foster's *The Coquette* to Harriet
Beecher Stowe's *Uncle Tom's Cabin*—the melodrama of sentimental manhood.

SENTIMENTAL AUTHORSHIP IN THE REPUBLIC OF LETTERS

An epistolary novel, *Clara Howard* consists of a series of letters concerning the
relations between three main characters: Clara Howard, Edward Hartley, and
Mary Wilmot. As the novel opens, Edward is in love with Clara, but engaged to
Mary whom he "esteems" but does not "love."[16] In the letters that pass between
Edward and Clara, Clara refuses marriage out of respect for Mary. "You know,"
Clara writes to Edward, "what it is that reason prescribes to you with regard to
Miss Wilmot. If you cannot ardently and sincerely seek her presence, and find in
the happiness which she will derive from union with you, sufficient motives to

make you zealously solicit that union, you are unworthy not merely of my love, but of my esteem" (20). In the letters that pass between Edward and Mary, Mary similarly refuses out of respect for Clara: "This Clara will be yours . . . ," Mary writes, "[S]he will offer you happiness, and wealth, and honor, and you will accept them at her hands" (15–6). Toward the middle of the novel, Edward tires of this romantic double bind and vows to escape civilization altogether. Remembering a map of North America that hung in his uncle's parlor, he decides to "embrute all [his] faculties," to "make [himself] akin to savages and tygers, and forget [he] was once a man"—all by pursing his "juvenile reveries" of travelling West by canoe to the Spanish territories of California (134, 115). Interrupted at the outset of this improbable journey by the chastening summons of both Clara and Mary, Edward returns east. The entire predicament is resolved only in the final pages of the novel when a wealthy suitor (Mr. Sedley) appears for Mary, thus dissolving their troubled threesome into respectable, heterosexual dyads.

These already vexed romantic relations are further complicated by the characters' financial commitments. Clara is the daughter of a wealthy Englishman who befriends and educates Edward, while Mary is both poor and orphaned. Mr. Howard wants to marry Clara to Edward in order to cement the latter's position in the family, while Mary and Edward lack the financial means of supporting a middle-class marriage. In a plot that Brown adopts from *Edgar Huntly,* Mary's brother dies midway through the novel, leaving five thousand dollars in a previously unknown bank account, which appears to solve Mary and Edward's problem until a stranger recently held captive in Algeria (Morton) returns to the United States and claims the money as his own. This plot twist leads Mary to abandon Edward to Clara who, in turn, insists that Edward pursue Mary despite her poverty. Again, this predicament is resolved by the appearance of Mr. Sedley. The money, as it turns out, does not belong to Morton; rather, Sedley gave the money to Mary's brother with the intention of enabling her to marry Edward. The supreme disinterestedness of this gesture ensures that Sedley is himself an appropriate suitor for Mary, who obediently decides to "devote her life to Sedley's happiness" (130). Thus restored to her rightful class and marital status (yet another subplot reveals Mary to be a lost relative of Clara), Mary's happiness frees Clara and Edward to become engaged as well. The novel's final letter from Clara to Mary promises that, if Mary add "one more week of probation to the four already decreed, it is, by no means impossible, that the same day may witness the happiness of both" Clara and Mary (148).

This happy ending would seem to bear out the plot summary that Edward provides in his introduction to the packet of letters that makes up *Clara Howard.* Addressed to an anonymous reader, that introduction promises that the letters will explain Edward's social ascent from the position of a "simple lad . . . sprung from obscurity, destitute of property, of parents, of paternal friends" to that of a wealthy man, "crowned with every terrestrial felicity, in possession of that most exquisite of all blessings, a wife, endowed with youth, grace, dignity, discretion" (3). Read in this fashion, *Clara Howard* becomes a male bildungsroman in which what Fritz Fleischmann refers to as the "patronage model" of Brown's earlier novels reaches a positive resolution.[17] What this reading (and Edward's introductory gloss) misses, however, are the gaps that emerge in this otherwise happy ending. Most importantly, *Clara Howard* concludes with the promise of a dual marriage, but not with the marriages themselves. The penultimate letter from Clara to Edward obsessively pictures the physical obstacles that still stand in the way of their marriage (a "boisterous river," "wind and rain," roads "kneedeep in mire," stagecoach wheels that "groan and totter" [146–7]), while the final letter from Clara to Mary encourages Mary not to perform, but to defer her marriage in the service of Clara and Mary's mutual happiness. "May that day," Clara writes, "whenever it shall come, prove the beginning of joy to Mary, and to her who, in every state, will be [her] affectionate Clara" (148). The ceremony that will transform Clara into Edward's "possession" is simply not performed. Clara maintains her primary attachment to Mary, as well as the power that she enjoys throughout the novel as a wealthy, lettered, and unmarried woman.

Unlike the seduced and abandoned heroines of contemporary sentimental novels, Clara thus remains both publicly powerful and, to use an only somewhat anachronistic term, woman-identified. While this combination led nineteenth-century feminist Margaret Fuller to applaud Brown's characterization for proving conclusively that "the term *feminine* is not a synonym for *weak*," it thoroughly disempowers Edward, who responds by criticizing Clara on both counts.[18] From the beginning to the end of the novel, the sentimental Edward accuses the rational Clara of being "inhumane and insensible" (9), of possessing a "narrow" or "cold" heart (74, 136), and, in a letter that many critics cite as evidence of Brown's own attitude toward Clara, of "reap[ing] the fruits of disinterested virtue" by using her power to make Edward, Mary, and herself miserable (112). At other points, Edward accuses Clara of ignoring the desires of the male suitors in the novel (Sedley and himself) by siding unfairly with Mary. "With regard to us," Edward writes immediately before threatening to "embrute" himself by going West, "you have neither consideration nor humanity. They are all absorbed in the cause of one, whose merits, whose claim to your sympathy and aid, if it be not less, is far from being greater than Sedley's or mine" (113). Forced to account for Mary's own compliance with Clara's presumably homosocial reasoning, Edward adopts the explanation Basil Ransom would repeat some eighty years later in *The Bostonians*. Mary, he suggests, found Clara more seductive than himself: "She was too blind an admirer, and assiduous a follower of Clara Howard, to accept my proffers. I abruptly withdrew" (118). Where Basil responds to a similar situation with an act of "muscular force" (hurrying the tearful Verena away from Olive Chancellor), Edward defers to Mary's desires.[19] Here and throughout the novel, Edward's admittedly passionate appeals to his audiences' sentiments fail either to balance or to refute Clara's dispassionate appeals to their reason.

Mapped elsewhere in the novel as a geographic opposition between East and West, or as an ethnographic opposition between civilization and "embrutement," this battle between Clara's reason and Edward's passion appears in the opening letter as a sexual opposition between women and men. In sharp contrast to the self-assurance of Edward's introduction, that letter begins with self-doubt. "Why do I write?" Edward asks:

> For whose use do I pass my time thus? There is no one living who cares a jot for me. There was a time, when a throbbing heart, a trembling hand, and eager eyes were always prepared to read, and ruminate on the scantiest and poorest scribble that dropped from my pen, but she has disappeared. The veil between us is like death. (5)

Addressed to Clara, the anonymous reader, and the general public, this letter both establishes Edward's subjection to Clara's judgment and suggests an affinity between the author and his male protagonist. Both Brown and Edward begin the novel in search of a sympathetic audience for their letters; both despair that those letters will fail to reach their destination; both explain that failure by gendering their audience female. In a subsequent letter, Brown not only repeats this authorial *mise-en-abyme*, but does so in terms that echo his epistolary pledge to his brother James. "What are you doing now?" Edward asks Clara, "Busy, I suppose, turning over the leaves of some book. Some painter of manners or of nature is before you" (88). Having dropped the "doleful tone" of his earlier "gothic" novels, Brown self-consciously aligns the reader of his first "sentimental" novel with Clara Howard—Brown's figure for the virtuous, female audience that he now represents himself as soliciting. The problem with male sentimentalism, both Brown and Edward suggest, is that any publication of those sentiments subjects their male authors to the moral judgments of a literary public sphere that is worse than anonymous—one that is dominated by women like Clara.

In one sense, then, Brown's critics are right. Clara is one of the "original iron maiden[s] of American literature," and the novel clearly encodes both Edward's and Brown's discomfort with their status as male sentimentalists as a discomfort with the masochistic potential inscribed therein. Yet Brown himself provides Clara with an impressive intellectual pedigree. Educated in accordance with her father's enlightened republican principles, Clara judges others not by the "specious but delusive considerations of fortune or birth, but by the intrinsic qualities of heart and head" (51). Having learned to eschew all arbitrary, antidemocratic markers of individual worth, the republican Clara admires and esteems only "just and disinterested conduct" (20). Indeed, all of her criticisms of Edward concern his inability to abstract his interests from his ethical conduct, to act with proper disinterest in relation to his own sentiments and desires. Ironically, then, the very persistence of Edward's confessions of love for Clara evince the inadequacy of that love. "It shews," Clara writes, "you unable to comprehend that the welfare of another may demand self-denial from us, and that in bestowing benefits on others, there is a purer delight than in gratifications merely selfish and exclusive" (24). As an author of sentimental letters, Edward necessarily fails in the self-abstracting ethics that the republican Clara teaches. Yet the precision of Clara's ethical pedagogy generates a paradox within the ideal of republican citizenship that she upholds. As self-abstracting, disinterested, rational judges of others' sentiments and interests, Clara and Edward must bracket their own sentiments and interests. But if they succeed in this process of self-abstraction, then they are left with no subjective motivation for rendering any judgment. It is this self-abstracting rationalism that informs both Clara's ethical practice and her (ungendered) resistance to Edward's (gendered) desires.

EMBODIMENT AND SELF-ABSTRACTION

While Brown's investigations of the paradox generated by Clara's republican ethics are influenced directly by Godwin, they resonate perhaps even more fully with those of their Enlightenment contemporary Immanuel Kant.[20] As in *Clara Howard*, the central antinomies of Kant's moral philosophy oppose reason to sentiment, duty to interest, morality to legality. These antinomies themselves result from Kant's (and Clara's) republican assumption that acts of moral judgment must begin by bracketing all sentiments and interests as subjective. "The moral law," Kant writes in *The Critique of Practical Reason*, "which alone is truly . . . objective, completely excludes the influence of self-love from the highest practical principle and forever checks self-conceit." Again, the very rigor of this theoretical demand for self-abstraction generates a paradox when Kant poses the question of what sentiments and interests motivate moral practice. At times, the answer to this question seems obvious. The "moral interest," Kant argues in a related passage, "must be the pure nonsensuous interest of the practical reason alone." Yet Kant also recognizes that the ideal of the "moral interest" as "nonsensuous" remains a paradox: "Complete fitness of the will to the moral law is holiness, which is a perfection of which no rational being in the world of sense is at any time capable." The result of this limitation is that the paradox of the moral interest can be resolved only negatively. Since a truly moral interest can never be realized, the effect of the moral law on the sentimental or "feeling" subject is not fulfillment, but "humiliation" due to that subject's recognition of its inadequacy. Neither "sympathy" nor "spontaneous goodness of heart" ensures moral practice. What is required are, in the words of the Prussian Immanuel Kant, "spur," "bridle," and "command."[21]

Edward Hartley would reluctantly, but undoubtedly, agree. "If reason be inadequate to my deliverance," he writes to Clara, "pride should hinder me from disclosing my humiliation; from confessing my voluntary servitude" (117). Despite these hints of hesitation, the self-conceit of pride does nothing to hinder Edward from subjecting himself to Clara's lessons in republican citizenship. Dedicated to reassuring Clara that she wrongs him in calling his "passion by the odious name sensual," Edward spends the majority of the novel in acts of confession and disclosure (23). Indeed, Edward's climactic act in the novel is precisely such an act of disclosure. Caught between the demands of Clara and Mary, Edward chooses to provide Mary with all of the letters that have passed between Clara and himself. "She shall judge," Edward writes to Clara, "with all the materials of a right judgment before her. I am prepared to devote myself to her will" (113). With regard to the disciplining of his sentiments, Edward is, to use his own analogy, "like one set loose upon a perilous sea, without rudder or sail" (115). And Edward's motivational crisis results directly from his successful education in the art of self-abstraction. Having bracketed any interest in who commands him, Edward's search for a captain becomes arbitrary: either Clara or Mary will suffice. While this act of disinterested submission to the moral law marks Edward's emergence as a self-abstracting, republican citizen, it also reveals an important difference between the moral practice of Edward and that required by Kant. The "duty" to which Kant advises submission remains perfectly abstract, disembodied, and unrealizable; the "duty" to which Edward submits is not abstract, but embodied. It can be realized through his submission to either (or both) of the novel's two female characters, Clara and Mary.

In part, this difference between Brown's and Kant's analyses of the practice of republican self-abstraction is a difference between two understandings of the relations among sex, gender, and citizenship. While a dimorphic logic of sexual difference operates throughout *Clara Howard*, gender figures in *The Critique of Practical Reason* at only two points.[22] Both occur late in the *Critique;* both appear as part of Kant's counterargument to any potential criticisms that the ideal of the moral law is simply objective or, in Kant's words, an "empty fantasy." "If we attend to the course of conversation in mixed companies consisting not merely of scholars and subtle reasoners but also of business people and women," Kant writes, "we notice that besides storytelling and jesting they have another entertainment, namely, arguing." For Kant, this interest in moral argumentation demonstrates a subjective "receptivity" to the "objectively practical laws of pure reason."[23] The opposition of "scholars and subtle reasoners" to "business people and women" may be less than enlightened, but Kant's point here is not to exclude such "private" individuals from the public forums within which moral argumentation takes place. Rather, Kant suggests that their interest in such argumentation indicates an ability and desire to participate in public processes of moral decision making. Kant's moral philosophy remains, in this sense, both republican and progressive. Due to its very abstraction, its disembodiment, the moral law militates against any exclusive claims to superior moral judgment grounded in forms of embodiment like sex. Though the art of republican self-abstraction could become, in Michael Warner's words, a "differential resource" that "provide[d] a privilege for unmarked identities: the white, the male, the middle class, the normal," the reverse is also true.[24] Kant's resistance to the restriction of moral judgment through any form of embodiment could equally enable counter-hegemonic claims to republican citizenship by those subjects marked as "non-white," "non-male," "non-middle class," "abnormal."

Kant's second reference to gender is more complicated and revealing. Faced again with a widening gap between the objectivity of the moral law and the subjectivity of the moral interest, Kant bridges that gap through the metaphor of the stepmother. *The Critique of Pure Reason*, Kant reminds his reader, "demonstrates the utter insufficiency of speculative reason to solve the most weighty problems which are presented to it in a way satisfactory to its end." "[B]ut," Kant continues,

> that critique did not ignore the natural and unmistakable hints of the same reason or the great steps that it can take in approaching this great goal which is set before it but which it can never of itself reach even with the aid of the greatest knowledge of nature. This nature here seems to have provided us only in a stepmotherly fashion with a faculty needed for our end.[25]

By grounding the potentially heteronomous authority of the moral law in a "stepmotherly" nature, Kant draws in this passage on the canon of natural law theorists to which his own rationalist moral philosophy is generally opposed. From Rousseau to Sacher-Masoch, this canon employs maternity (often in opposition to paternity) as a figure for embodiment. In his essay on Sacher-Masoch's influential contemporary Johann Bachofen, Ernst Bloch confirms this generalization: " 'Mother nature' was always a powerful ingredient in different phases of natural law. . . . [I]t is through maternal law that this element was transmitted and brought back to natural law." "Mother nature" provides a romantic antidote to the coldness of Enlightenment reason; as Bloch writes later in the same essay, it is "a warm harmony, which in the midst of the history of law of the romantic origin, unexpectedly reminds one of Rousseau's return to nature, of natural law without artificiality."[26]

That Kant draws on this natural law tradition reveals the degree to which the association of maternity with embodiment and non-abstraction lies at the heart of not only the nineteenth-century culture of sentiment, but also the most rational of eighteenth-century republicanisms. That Kant refers to a nature that operates in a specifically "stepmotherly fashion," however, indicates his rationalist critique of that tradition. In Sacher-Masoch's novelizations of Bachofen's gynocentric legal philosophy, the male masochist both betrays the gender to which his sex has assigned him (through his alignment with paternity) *and* becomes fulfilled as a subject through that betrayal. As Gilles Deleuze observes in his reading of *Venus in Furs*, the "masochist experiences the symbolic order as an intermaternal order in which the mother represents the law . . . she generates the symbolism through which the masochist expresses himself."[27] In contrast, Kant's rigorous opposition between rationality and embodiment disables both the gendering of reason (as either maternal or paternal) *and* the experience of an undivided subjectivity. Kant's figure of a nature that operates in a "stepmotherly fashion" indicates a nature that is not natural but legally sanctioned, a mother who rules over her children not by natural but by contractual right. A "stepmotherly" nature is, in other words, a nature that supplements Enlightenment rationality and republican self-abstraction, not one that negates them. Both of Kant's references to gender point toward a logic of embodiment which potentially restricts claims to rationality, yet neither reference pursues that logic to the point of sanctioning such restrictions. Despite Freud's assertion that Kant's categorical imperative is "a direct inheritance of the Oedipus-complex," *The Critique of Practical Reason* pursues an ideal of rationality that remains both ungendered and, in psychoanalytic terms, anti-Oedipal.[28] Its authority is grounded not in the symbolic function of paternity (or maternity), but in the institutions of publication and critical debate central to eighteenth-century republicanism.

FEMINISM AND MALE MASOCHISM

Kant is alone neither in his republican insistence on maintaining an opposition between rationality and embodiment, nor in his recognition of its political implications. The same opposition pervades the writings of the Enlightenment feminists who were Kant's contemporaries. As Nina Baym has suggested, such writers are distinguishable by their "refusal to see mind as affected by its connection with a gendered body." While this opposition of mind and body would be attacked by later feminists who mobilized a logic of embodiment in order to defend and privilege women's difference from men, the same opposition was defended by Enlightenment feminists who sought access to rational public discourse by deploying a universalist ideal of rationality. Such authors continued to write, in Baym's words, "as women, but like men, thereby implicitly claiming language and rationality as constituents of their humanity."[29] At its extreme, this tension within the self-abstracting demands of republican rationality could structure the career of a writer like Brown's contemporary Judith Sargent Murray. In the concluding essay of the *Gleaner* series ("The Gleaner Unmasked"), Murray explains that her use of a gender-neutral pseudonym ("The Gleaner") was necessitated by her ambition of "being considered *independent as a writer*." Well aware that many men would argue, like Rousseau, that a woman could only "*ostensibly* wield the pen," Murray adopts a gender-neutral "mask" in public as both a defensive strategy and a theoretical counterargument.[30] By disembodying reason through a logic of self-abstraction, Enlightenment feminists did more than privatize bodily difference in order to access a still masculine public discourse. They also theorized a republicanism in which such access would not rely on any logic of embodiment, sexual or otherwise.

At times in his career, Brown pens a similar argument. In *Alcuin*, a feminist dialogue published three years before *Clara Howard*, Brown's female interlocutor (Mrs. Carter) echoes Murray when she demands social and political equality due to the sexes' shared rationality: "Men and women are partakers of the same nature. They are rational beings, and, as such, the same principles of truth and equity must be applicable to both." As the dialogue continues, Brown pursues the implications of this opposition between rationality and embodiment. In the second half of *Alcuin* (published posthumously in 1815), Brown's previously skeptical male interlocutor (Alcuin) tells Mrs. Carter of his conversion to her principles—a conversion that results from his journey, between the two halves of the dialogue, to a utopian "paradise of women." Alcuin's account of that journey begins as he reports his native guide's confusion when asked about his society's social and political principles with respect to sexual difference. Himself a political philosopher, Alcuin's guide pleads ignorance, referring Alcuin to the "anatomist, or to the hall where he publicly communicates his doctrines." When Alcuin later repeats his query, his guide responds that "a diversity of sex cannot possibly make any essential difference in the claims and duties of reasonable beings." By the end of the dialogue, all of Alcuin's beliefs in sexual difference as a logic of embodiment that determines such principles have been exploded. Neither dress, nor education, nor employment can be rationally linked to sex. Even marriage, Alcuin tells the now skeptical Mrs. Carter, is nothing more than an arbitrary "custom" that "regulate[s] sexual intercourse."[31]

That Brown locates Alcuin's "paradise of women" in a clearly utopian space—"The region, indeed is far distant, but a twinkling is sufficient for the longest of journeys"[32]—may indicate that the dialogue is itself a satire, a reductio ad absurdum of Enlightenment feminist arguments which model, in Wollstonecraft's words, a "world *where there is neither marrying,* nor giving in marriage."[33] Taken seriously, however, *Alcuin* suggests that Brown's initial understanding of the relation between sex (or, more precisely, embodiment) and republican citizenship is as progressive as those of his Enlightenment contemporaries. At the very least, *Alcuin* evinces Brown's awareness of the democratic potential inscribed within the disembodying logic of republican self-abstraction. In contrast, Brown's configuring of the relations among sex, embodiment, and citizenship becomes reactionary in *Clara Howard*. Faced with the possibility of a republic governed without regard to sexual difference, Brown reacts by mobilizing a logic of embodiment that assumes the centrality of sexual difference to any republic. No longer gender-neutral terms, reason and sentiment are gendered in the figures of Clara and Edward. That this arrangement inverts the emerging normative association of reason with masculinity and sentiment with femininity makes little difference in this context. Confronted with either logic of embodiment, Enlightenment principles produce a battle of the sexes. Here, Clara's reason disciplines Edward's sentiments. Elsewhere, the republican attack on "Masculine systems" leads, in John Adams's words, to a "Despotism of the Pet[t]icoat" against which "General Washington and all our brave heroes would fight."[34]

There is an element of truth in Adams's hyperbole. The logic of republican self-abstraction does open the possibility that women, among others, will ascend to positions of political and social power. Even in domestic affairs, Wollstonecraft reasons in her *Vindication of the Rights of Woman*, "many individuals have more sense than their male relatives; and . . . some women govern their husbands without degrading themselves, because intellect will always govern."[35] As indicated by the displacement of the specific referent "women" by the abstract referent "individuals," Wollstonecraft's insistence in this passage that "intellect" ought to govern suggests that the governing individuals may be women as well as men. In a scenario familiar from the ERA battles of the 1970s, both Adams and Brown react to this possibility by mobilizing a logic of embodiment that transforms a democratic call for social and political equality into a masochistic contract for sexual domination. What is most radical and threatening about the rational Clara is, in this sense, neither her characterization as a woman, nor her homosocial identification with Mary, but rather her penchant for rendering moral judgments without regard to any logic of embodiment, including sex. Like Judith Sargent Murray, whose gender-neutral "mask" ensures her "independence as a writer," Clara mobilizes a disembodying logic of self-abstraction in order to ensure her independence as a moral subject and judge. Clara's reason remains as indifferent to gender as the republican polity it ideally regulates.

At the level of plot, Clara's mobilization of this logic places her in direct opposition to the men in the novel not simply as men, but as individuals who threaten her independence. Throughout *Clara Howard*, Edward searches for a strategy that will allow him to fulfill his introductory pledge to narrate the story of his acquisition of both wealth and "that most exquisite of all blessings, a wife." Initially, this narrative of Edward's ascent to full masculine subjectivity seems realizable through the agency of Mr. Howard who, despite his republican principles, offers Clara to Edward. "This heiress of opulence and splendor," Edward exclaims, "this child of fortune, and appropriator of elegance and grace, and beauty, was proffered to me as a wife!" (54). That Clara resists her father's positioning of her as an object of exogamous exchange is inevitable. In her marriage choice, Mr. Howard acknowledges, Clara "will forget ancestry and patrimony, and think only of the morals and understanding of the object" (51). Forced to abandon Mr. Howard's increasingly anachronistic logic of patriarchal exchange, Edward's second recourse is to what we might call an emerging erotics of heterosexual embodiment. As Niklas Luhmann suggests in *Love as Passion*, this erotics is typical of a liberalism in which the concept of "love could no longer be connected to a theory of state or economics; rather the concept correspond[s] precisely to what was to be expected in terms of the other's love."[36] While Mary inspires in Edward a "sentiment, very different from love," Clara provides him with an experience of "passion." Divorced from all social and political logics except gender, this passion takes the form not of a "boundless esteem," but of an unmediatable and, Edward hopes, fully reciprocal relation between (male) self and (female) other (43). For Edward, in short, sex ideally expresses itself in that form of sensuality that many modern readers would recognize (and naturalize) as heterosexuality.[37]

It is Clara's resistance to this second, specifically heterosexual (or heterosensual) strategy that draws the harshest criticism from both Edward and the critics who align themselves with him. Unwilling to differentiate "passion" from the social and political codes within which it operates, Clara applies the same ratio-nalist logic to Edward's romanticism as she does to her father's paternalism. "Per-haps esteem is not the only requisite to marriage," Clara writes in her first letter to Edward. "Of that I am not certain; but I know that it is an indispensable requisite to love. I cannot love in you anything but excellence" (20). Later, Clara reaffirms this logic: "I love you, Edward, as I ought to love you. I love your happiness; your virtue" (109). Clara's insistence on subordinating passionate love to moral ration-ality may mark her as cold, but it is crucial to recognize the source of that cold-ness. Despite her father's benevolence, his offer of Clara to Edward positions her as an object of exchange in a plot hatched between two men. Despite Edward's offer to give her control of any marriage gift from her father (89), his very need to make this offer indicates an economic asymmetry inscribed within the institution of marriage. In either case, the completion of Edward's bildungsroman plot entails the loss of Clara's independence—her translation, in legal terminology, from a *feme sole* to a *feme covert*. In relation to both her father and Edward, Clara resists the engendering logics of embodiment that would mediate her relation to Edward by transforming her, as a woman, into the "possession" of either a hus-band or a father. Clara affirms and reaffirms what could be called, for lack of a better term, a hetero-critical republicanism—a republicanism that resists the engendering logics common to the heteronormative plots of both Edward and Mr. Howard.

In its very extremity, then, Brown's characterization of Clara's republicanism reveals not only the overt gender asymmetry inscribed in Mr. Howard's benevo-lent paternalism, but also the covert asymmetry inscribed in Edward's romantic liberalism. The logic of self-abstraction that empowers Clara is the same logic that undermines each of Edward's (contradictory) beliefs concerning romantic love: that love consists of a reciprocal passion between selves and others that are implicitly gendered as male and female and that such a passion ought to be unmediated by any impersonal concerns. At times, Clara seems to agree with Edward's romantic belief in unmediated passion. Fearful that her rigorous adher-ence to her "duty" has led Edward to abandon her, Clara envisions a post-Enlightenment world in which "conscience" and "heart"—reason and senti-ment—are in perfect accord. "Has it come to this!" she writes to Edward:

> now, that the impediment has vanished, that my feelings may be indulged at the cost
> of no one's peace; now that the duty which once so sternly forbad me to be yours,
> not only permits, but enjoins me to link together our fates; that the sweet voice of an
> approving conscience is ready to sanction and applaud every impulse of my heart,
> and make the offices of tenderness not only free from guilt, but coincident with
> every duty; that now. . . . (141)

This passage's concluding ellipsis points toward the romantic fulfillment of both Edward and Clara as complementary subjects, but it is important to note that even here Clara justifies her love for Edward through reference to an abstract and impersonal duty—both its absence in relation to Mary and its presence in relation to Edward. Since duty continues to mediate desire, Clara's reason continues to regulate Edward's sentiments. This injection of an impersonal logic into interpersonal relations implies that the antinomy of reason and sentiment dominating the novel remains unresolvable. More importantly, it remains unresolvable not because a logic of embodiment results in a gender difference which is itself unresolvable, but because a logic of self-abstraction insists on the rational mediation of even the most sentimental of personalities. The first logic promises to transform Clara into Edward's "possession." Only the second legitimates her political, moral, and erotic independence as a citizen within the republic.

THE MALE COMPLAINT

To the end, the Enlightenment feminism of Clara Howard, the character, prevents the romantic completion of *Clara Howard*, the novel. Because it remains separate from her heart, Clara's hand remains that of a writer, not that of a wife. Historically, of course, the logic of self-abstraction that structures the eighteenth-century republic of letters gave way to the logic of embodiment that structures the nineteenth-century empire of the mother. As social historian Mary P. Ryan points out, the very stability of this logic of embodiment produced a tension within the seat of women's supposed power, the domestic sphere:

> The cult of domesticity celebrated a logical and practical impossibility. It bred male and female into dichotomous roles and temperaments, then venerated their union and required their independence within an isolated home. The heterosexual tension was lodged at the very center of the domestic mode of social reproduction, and it casts a shadow over the empire of the mother.[38]

One resolution of this tension lay in the ideological coding of social and political space as itself gendered. As in the writings of Ann Douglas, the public sphere of disinterested rationality could be figured as male, while the private sphere of interested sentimentality could be figured as female. Or, as in *Clara Howard*, the "wilderness" of the West could be male, while the "civilization" of the East could be female. Even as astute a critic of gender relations as Margaret Fuller could reproduce this heterosexist ideology. Though she claims in "The Great Lawsuit" that there is "no wholly masculine man, no purely feminine woman," her rhetoric nevertheless divides society into male and female as "the two sides of the great radical dualism."[39] "The Great Lawsuit" may begin by linking feminism and abolitionism through a critique of both engendering and racializing logics of embodiment, yet it concludes by collapsing all difference into sexual difference through the figure of the Virgin Mother.[40]

The reductiveness of the engendering hermeneutic produced by this logic of embodiment is surpassed only by its persistence. As Nina Baym pointed out in 1981, the United States literary and literary-critical canons are themselves constituted through a logic of embodiment which engenders both the content and the form of that literature. "Melodramas of beset manhood," Baym argues, contrast an androcentric form of literary innovation—narratives that focus on "exploring and taming the wilderness"—to a gynocentric form of literary conventionality— narratives that focus on domestic and social concerns. By privileging the former over the latter, these "melodramas" leave, in Baym's words, "no place for wo-men. . . . [S]he is either to be silent, like nature, or she is the creator of conven-tional works, the spokeswoman of society."[41] Since 1981, Baym's argument has been extended in two directions. On the one hand, critics like Jane Tompkins have inverted the androcentric literary canon by celebrating sentimental writings by women as powerful critiques of prevailing conventions; on the other hand, crit-ics like Gillian Brown have questioned the presumed unconventionality of the same canon by suggesting that male antisentimentalism is merely the ideological antithesis of female sentimentalism.[42] Both of these approaches yield insights into sentimentalism as a cultural project focused, in Shirley Samuels's words, on the "problem of the body and what it embodies," yet neither moves beyond the engendering, nineteenth-century logic of embodiment that associates sentimen-tality with femininity.[43] In accordance with this critical axiom, sentimental litera-ture remains (as it was for Baym in *Women's Fiction*) a literature written "by," if not exclusively "about," women. United States literary history continues to be written as if the author of *Edgar Huntly* either never wrote *Clara Howard*, or did so only reluctantly.

By focusing in this essay on *Clara Howard* as the novel in which Brown investi-gates the relation between sentimentality and masculinity, I have extended Baym's argument in a third direction. An androcentric canon centered upon antisenti-mental writings may afford little space for women, yet Baym's own reasoning implies that it affords no greater space to male sentimentalism. The literary femi-nization of sentiment renders the figure of the male sentimentalist paradoxical, while literary criticism that assumes this feminization renders the male sentimen-talist invisible. By focusing on *Clara Howard* as an exception to this generalization, I do not mean to suggest that Brown escapes the engendering logic that feminizes sentiment. It would be more accurate to read Brown's inversion of that logic as producing a "male" version of the rhetorical form which Lauren Berlant refers to as the "female complaint." The "female complaint," as Berlant defines it, origi-nated in the late eighteenth century as a "mode of public discourse that demon-strates women's contested value in the patriarchal public sphere by providing commentary from a generically 'feminine' point of view."[44] As such, the com-plaint's criticisms of social and political relations are circumscribed in two ways. First, they reduce all difference to sexual difference. By the end of *Clara Howard*, for example, the class (Clara / Mary) and ethnic (European / Native American) antagonisms that structure the novel's opening letters are resolved through the (contested) ideal of sexual complementarity. Second, the criticisms are circum-scribed by their rhetorical commitment to the emerging ideology of sexual dimorphism—the "heterosexual matrix," to use Judith Butler's term—which divides society into male and female.[45] By inverting male and female, Brown's masochistic "male complaint" both resists and reinscribes that logic of embodiment. If, to paraphrase Barbara Stanwyck in *The Lady Eve,* Clara needs Edward like the axe needs the turkey, then Edward needs Clara like the turkey needs the axe.

Nor do I mean to construct a symmetry between the genres of the female and the male complaint. Fanny Fern's parody of generic masculinity in *Ruth Hall* does parallel Mark Twain's parody of generic femininity in *The Adventures of Huckleberry Finn,*[46] but a criticism unable to distinguish between the rhetorical strategies and political motivations of, say, the women's and the men's movements is impoverished at best. As elsewhere within the letters of the republic, the false symmetry produced by the ideology of sexual difference masks power asymmetries. Edward's narrative ascent (and assent) to full masculine subjectivity promises to secure for him economic and political privilege, while Clara's descent (and dissent) within that same narrative results from her prospective loss of that privilege. What I do mean to suggest is that a critique of the logic of embodiment that underpins both the female and the male complaint is inscribed within Brown's masochistic melodrama of Edward's sentimental manhood. In the figure of Clara Howard, Brown encodes an Enlightenment feminist attack on the engendering logics of embodiment which, as Monique Wittig succinctly puts it, "systematically heterosexualize that personal dimension which suddenly emerged . . . almost two centuries ago."[47] Wittig's dates may be off by a century or so, but her allusion to a "personal dimension" that became politically significant at the end of the eighteenth-century accurately locates the prehistory of (homo- and hetero-) sexuality within the discourse of sentimentalism. What fades from view in both Edward's engendering narrative in *Clara Howard* and the critical responses to that narrative is the eighteenth-century counterpossibility of ungendered sentimental citizenship—a counterpossibility which appears, within *Clara Howard,* in Clara's republican letters. If such an understanding of citizenship is reemerging today in the fields of feminist and queer theory, then it is doing so only in opposition to the engendering logics that produce both literary and literary critical visions of male sentimentalism as male masochism.[48]

NOTES

1. Hawthorne's well-known damning appears in a letter to William Ticknor of 19 January 1855, in *Centenary Edition of the Works of Nathaniel Hawthorne,* vol. 17 (Columbus: Ohio State University Press, 1987), 304. Howells's less-known submission appears in "The Man of Letters as a Man of Business": "The man of letters must make up his mind that in the United States the fate of the book is in the hands of the women. . . . If they do not always know what is good, they do know what pleases them, and it is useless to quarrel with their decisions, for there is no court of appeal from them. To go from them to the men would be

going from a higher to a lower court" (*Criticism and Fiction and Other Essays* [New York: New York University Press, 1959], 305–6).

2. Leslie A. Fiedler, *Love and Death in the American Novel* (New York: Dell Publishing Co., 1960), 8, 31.

3. Ann Douglas, *The Feminization of American Culture* (New York: Anchor Press, 1988), 124. Read with this in mind, the Douglas-Tompkins debate over the political impact of women's sentimental writings is a debate between two readings of the masochistic potential inscribed within the ideology of republican motherhood: for Douglas, that masochistic potential is never realized; for Tompkins, it is realized through the "sentimental power" of those texts. See Jane Tompkins, *Sensational Designs: The Cultural Work of American Fiction, 1790–1860* (Oxford: Oxford University Press, 1985), 122–85. On the Douglas-Tompkins debate, see Laura Wexler, "Tender Violence: Literary Eavesdropping, Domestic Fiction, and Educational Reform," in *The Culture of Sentiment: Race, Gender and Sentimentality in Nineteenth-Century American Culture*, ed. Shirley Samuels (New York: Oxford University Press, 1992), 9–38.

4. Douglas, *Feminization*, 42.

5. Richard von Krafft-Ebing, *Psychopathia Sexualis*, trans. Franklin S. Klaf (London: Staples Press, 1965), 111.

6. Quoted in William Dunlap, *The Life of Charles Brockden Brown* (Philadelphia: James P. Parke, 1815), 2:100.

7. Bill Christophersen, *The Apparition in the Glass: Charles Brockden Brown's American Gothic* (Athens: University of Georgia Press, 1993), 149.

8. Fielder, *Love and Death*, 89.

9. Norman S. Grabo, *The Coincidental Art of Charles Brockden Brown* (Chapel Hill: University of North Carolina Press, 1983), 129.

10. Paul Witherington's earlier positive appraisal of Brown's late novels seems to me a less significant exception. In contrast to other critics' contempt for *Clara Howard* and *Jane Talbot*, Witherington's New Critical sensibilities allow him to applaud the formal coherence of these "other novels" of Brown's. But his analysis merely repeats the critical commonplace that the novels "show the victories of social normalcy over individuality and of order over eccentricity and indecisiveness" ("Brockden Brown's Other Novels: *Clara Howard* and *Jane Talbot*," *Nineteenth-Century Fiction* 29 [December 1975]: 257–72, quotation from 258). Fritz Fleischmann's synthetic account of Brown's career reaches a similar conclusion. Though Brown never abandoned either his "pursuit of fiction" or his "feminist impulse," his late novels, Fleischmann suggests, are marked by his growing awareness of the "impossibility of making a living as a writer of fiction . . . an unremunerative career as a novelist was no way to satisfy the demands of a family" ("Charles Brockden Brown: Feminism in Fiction," in *American Novelists Revisited: Essays in Feminist Criticism*, ed. Fritz Fleischmann [Boston: G.K. Hall & Company, 1982], 36).

11. Sidney Krause, "*Clara Howard* and *Jane Talbot*: Godwin on Trial," in *Critical Essays on Charles Brockden Brown*, ed. Bernard Rosenthal (Boston: G. K. Hall & Co., 1981), 184–211, quotations from 187, 199, 189, 199.

12. I stress *theoretically* gendered and ungendered because both virtue and reason—key terms of republican and democratic political theory—are *historically* gendered as masculine. At the same time, the historical association of virtue and reason with masculinity can be established only by disavowing the ideal of ungendered democratic citizenship which

informs the republic of letters. On the political history of this disavowal, see Mark Kahn, *On the Man Question: Gender and Civic Virtue in America* (Philadelphia: Temple University Press, 1991).

13. Brown's naming of his protagonist Hartley alludes to MacKenzie's Harley, as well as his own Huntly. *The Man of Feeling* along with Lawrence Sterne's *A Sentimental Journey* provide the two best-known examples of the eighteenth-century "man of feeling." Read straight, they demonstrate the noncontradiction between sentiment and masculinity in the period, at least for middle-class men; read parodically, they still resist the nineteenth-century equation of sentiment and femininity. Even as parodies, they undercut the figure of the sentimental male not by accusing him of gender cross-identification, but by exposing the illicit, unrefined, and erotic sensibility that lies beneath his claims to refinement and moral discernment. A significant turning point in this cultural tradition appears in William Godwin's *Fleetwood: or, The New Man of Feeling*, published four years after *Clara Howard* in 1805. For the best reading of the eighteenth-century male sentimentalist, see G. J. Barker-Benfield, *The Culture of Sensibility: Sex and Society in Eighteenth-Century Britain* (Chicago: University of Chicago Press, 1992), 104–53.

14. Quoted in Jay Fleigelman, *Declaring Independence: Jefferson, Natural Language and the Culture of Performance* (Stanford: Stanford University Press, 1993), 61.

15. Grabo, *Coincidental Art*, 132.

16. Charles Brockden Brown, *Clara Howard; In a Series of Letters* (Kent, Ohio: Kent State University Press, 1986), 43. All further references to *Clara Howard* will appear in parentheses in the text.

17. Fleischmann, "Feminism in Fiction," 32.

18. Margaret Fuller, *Papers on Literature and Art*, excerpted in Rosenthal, *Critical Essays*, 62–4, quotation from 63. In *The Early Sentimental Novel* (1906), Lillie Demming Loshe echoes Fuller when she applauds Clara as "the resolute and reasonable woman directing the gentle and irresolute boy" (*The Early American Novel* [New York: Frederick Unger Publishing Company, 1958], 48).

19. Henry James, *The Bostonians* (New York: Vintage, 1991), 418.

20. Krause convincingly argues that Brown's exploration of the problems of moral decision making in both *Clara Howard* and *Jane Talbot* is directly influenced by Godwin. Indeed, one of the principal characters in the latter novel speaks directly of Godwin's *Political Justice* as a "fascinating book," but one which deploys "the art of the grand deceiver; the fatal art of carrying the worst poison under the name and appearance of wholesome food" (*Jane Talbot: A Novel* [Kent, Ohio: Kent State University Press, 1986], 228). I have no interest in establishing a similarly direct connection between Brown and Kant (though Brown is clearly aware of German Enlightenment and Romantic culture, as evinced in the title of *Wieland*, his attacks in *Ormond* on the "Bavarian Illuminati," etc.). Rather, what I am interested in is Brown's and Kant's shared exploration of the republican principles of self-abstraction—principles that structure the writings of many more authors than Godwin, Brown, and Kant, of course. For a reading of Brown's *Arthur Mervyn* along these lines, see Michael Warner, *The Letters of the Republic: Publication and the Public Sphere in the Eighteenth-Century America* (Harvard: Harvard University Press, 1990), 151–76.

21. Immanuel Kant, *The Critique of Practical Reason*, trans. Lewis White Beck (New York: Macmillan Publishing Company, 1985), 77, 82, 126, 81, 88.

22. I adopt the term "sexual dimorphism" from Gilbert Herdt, who defines it as a belief in "a phylogenetically inherited structure of two types of human and sexual nature,

male and female, present in all human groups" ("Introduction: Third Sexes and Third Genders," in *Third Sex, Third Gender: Beyond Sexual Dimorphism in Culture and History* [New York: Zone Books, 1994], 21–81, quotation from 25). For a fuller discussion of the deployment of this concept—and its political significance—in the context of the early republic, see my *Sentimental Bodies: Sex, Gender, and Citizenship in the Early Republic* (Princeton: Princeton University Press, 1998).

23. Kant, *Critique of Practical Reason*, 156–7.

24. Michael Warner, "The Mass Public and the Mass Subject," in *Habermas and the Public Sphere*, ed. Craig Calhoun (Cambridge: MIT Press, 1992), 377–401, quotations from 382, 383.

25. Kant, *Critique of Practical Reason*, 151–2.

26. Ernst Bloch, *Natural Law and Human Dignity*, trans. Dennis J. Schmidt (Cambridge: MIT Press, 1987), 103, 105.

27. Gilles Deleuze, *Coldness and Cruelty*, in *Masochism*, trans. Jean McNeil (New York: Zone Books, 1989), 9–138, quotation from 63. On Sacher-Masoch's relation to Bachofen, see 47–55.

28. Sigmund Freud, "The Economic Problem of Masochism," in *General Psychological Theory* (New York: Collier Books, 1963), 190–201, quotation from 198. Critics like Kaja Silverman who write within this psychoanalytic tradition suggest that the male masochist resists and fractures the association of law with paternity or, in Silverman's words, "radiates a negativity inimical to the social order" (*Male Subjectivity on the Margins* [New York: Routledge, 1992], 206). My objection to such analyses of male masochism is that their psychoanalytic (Freudian / Lacanian) grounding dictates that the "social order" be divided into male and female. Within such an analysis, any other social antagonisms (race, class, and ethnicity, to name three) vanish, as well as any possibility of a move away from the heterosexist ideology of gender difference. Male masochism may be an example of "male subjectivity at the margins," but it is also evidence of how, as a text, the ideology of gender difference inscribes its own margins. On the complicity between "dominant" and "submissive heterosexual men" in writings of the American Renaissance, see Christopher Newfield, "The Politics of Male Suffering: Masochism and Hegemony in the American Renaissance," *differences: A Journal of Feminist Cultural Studies* 1, no. 3 (1989): 55–87.

29. Nina Baym, "Between Enlightenment and Victorian: Toward a Narrative of American Women Writers Writing History," *Critical Inquiry* 18, no. 1 (Autumn 1991): 22–41, quotations from 38, 41.

30. Judith Sargent Murray, *The Gleaner* (Schenectady, N.Y.: Union College Press, 1992), 805 (emphases added).

31. Charles Brockden Brown, *Alcuin: A Dialogue* (Kent, Ohio: Kent State University Press, 1987), 19, 34, 39, 42, 66; for dress, see 40–2; for education, see 43–6; for employment, see 46–9.

32. Ibid., 34.

33. Mary Wollstonecraft, *Mary: A Fiction*, in *A Mary Wollstonecraft Reader* (New York: Mentor Books, 1983), 81–126. Read in this fashion, *Alcuin* parallels *Venus in Furs* in its rendering of gender equality as a strictly utopian (im)possibility. "For the time being," Sacher-Masoch concludes, "there is only one alternative; to be the hammer or the anvil" (Leopold von Sacher-Masoch, *Venus in Furs*, in *Masochism*, 143–293, quotation from 271). In each case, equality is figured as both desirable and unrealistic through the axiomatic assertion of the reality of gender difference.

34. Abigail Adams and John Adams, *The Book of Abigail and John: Selected Letters of the Adams Family, 1762–1784* (Cambridge: Harvard University Press, 1975), 123.

35. Mary Wollstonecraft, *A Vindication of the Rights of Woman* (New York: Penguin Books, 1982), 84.

36. Niklas Luhmann, *Love as Passion: The Codification of Intimacy,* trans. Jeremy Gaines and Doris L. Jones (Cambridge, Mass.: Polity Press, 1986), 132.

37. Luhmann's incisive analysis fails to account for the logic of gender difference that structures the history of romantic love, and thus reinscribes that logic as nonpolitical. *Love as Passion* could be referred to more accurately as *Love as Heterosexual Passion.*

38. Mary P. Ryan, *The Empire of the Mother: American Writing about Domesticity, 1830–1860* (New York: Harrington Park Press, 1982), 129–30.

39. Margaret Fuller, "The Great Lawsuit," in *The Feminist Papers,* ed. Alice S. Rossi (Boston: Northeastern University Press, 1973), 179.

40. Ibid., 182. On the tension between feminism and abolitionism, see Karen Sánchez-Eppler, "Bodily Bonds: The Intersecting Rhetorics of Feminism and Abolition," in Samuels, *Culture of Sentiment,* 92–114.

41. Nina Baym, "Melodramas of Beset Manhood: How Theories of American Fiction Exclude Women Authors," in *The New Feminist Criticism,* ed. Elaine Showalter (New York: Pantheon Books, 1985), 63–80, quotation from 77.

42. Jane Tompkins, *Sensational Designs,* 122–85. Gillian Brown, *Domestic Individualism: Imagining the Self in Nineteenth-Century America* (Berkeley: University of California Press, 1990), 135–69.

43. Samuels's phrase appears in her introduction to the 1992 collection of essays *The Culture of Sentiment* (3–8, quotation from 6). While Samuels emphasizes an expansive definition of sentimentalism as a "project about the nation's bodies and the national body" (3), and while the essays themselves are concerned with logics of embodiment other than gender, the vast majority of those essays focus on women authors; see the introduction to the present volume for a further discussion of this point.

44. Pursuing this line of argumentation, Berlant writes that the complaint's "sentimental abstraction of the values of 'woman' from the realm of material relations meant that intersections among classes, races and different ethnic groups also appear to dissolve in their translation into sentimental semiosis" ("The Female Woman: Fanny Fern and the Form of Sentiment," in Samuels, *Culture of Sentiment,* 265–81, quotations from 268, 269; see also Berlant, "The Female Complaint," *Social Text* 19 / 20 [Fall 1988]: 237–59). This "dissolve" of racial, class and ethnic identifications into a scene of gender identification also structures the male complaint.

45. Judith Butler, *Gender Trouble: Feminism and the Subversion of Identity* (New York: Routledge, 1990), 12.

46. I am referring specifically to chapter fifty-two of *Ruth Hall,* in which Fern satirizes Mr. Skiddy's desire to escape from his wife's dominance by going West, and to chapter seventeen of *Huck Finn,* in which Twain satirizes Emmeline Grangerford's sentimental poetry (Fanny Fern, *Ruth Hall and Other Writings* [New Brunswick: Rutgers University Press, 1986], 103–9; Mark Twain, *Adventures of Huckleberry Finn* [New York: W. W. Norton & Company, 1977], 79–86).

47. Monique Wittig, "The Straight Mind," in *"The Straight Mind" and Other Essays* (Boston: Beacon Press, 1992), 21–32, quotation from 31. On Wittig's retrieval of Enlightenment categories for feminist theory, see Linda Zerilli, "The Trojan Horse of Universalism: Language as 'War Machine' in the Writings of Monique Wittig," in *The Phantom Public Sphere,* ed. Bruce Robbins (Minneapolis: University of Minnesota Press, 1993), 142–73.

48. For examples of such arguments which focus specifically on a reevaluation of the category of sentimentalism, see James Creech, *Closet Writing / Gay Reading: The Case of Melville's Pierre* (Chicago: University of Chicago Press, 1993), 44–61; Julie Ellison, "The Gender of Transparency: Masculinity and the Conduct of Life," *American Literary History* 4 (1992): 584–606; Glenn Hendler, "Tom Sawyer's Masculinity," *Arizona Quarterly* 49, no. 4 (1993): 33–59; D. A. Miller, *The Novel and the Police* (Berkeley: University of California Press, 1988), 192–220; Eve Kosofsky Sedgwick, *Epistemology of the Closet* (Berkeley: University of California Press, 1990), 131–81.

▥

CHAPTER ELEVEN

Sentimental and Romantic Masculinities in *Moby-Dick* and *Pierre*

Tara Penry

[B]y and by, grown up to man's estate, [the toddler] shall leave the very mother that bore it, and the father that begot it, and cross the seas, perhaps. . . . Now cruel father and mother have both let go his hand, and the little soul-toddler, now you shall hear his shriek and his wail, and often his fall.

PIERRE

And still deeper the meaning of that story of Narcissus, who because he could not grasp the tormenting, mild image he saw in the fountain, plunged into it and was drowned. But that same image, we ourselves see in all rivers and oceans. It is the image of the ungraspable phantom of life.

MOBY-DICK

In the two novels often placed at the extreme Romantic and sentimental poles of the Melville canon, images of the questing Narcissus and the wailing toddler appear to reinforce dualist interpretations of Melville's literary modes. As "Romantic" as the Narcissus figure appears in *Moby-Dick* (1851), with its emphasis on symbol, self-scrutiny, and the reflection of the individual in nature, so too does the "wail[ing]," abandoned toddler image in *Pierre* (1852) seem deeply sentimental.[1] But these consecutively published novels work jointly to navigate the channel between affect and isolation in the maturation of "soul-toddlers" such as Ahab, Ishmael, and Pierre. Against a seductive but ultimately destructive vision of Romantic and competitive masculine power, Melville seeks in both novels a model of manhood that will replace both the withdrawn parental hands and the "ungraspable phantom of life" with palpable, practicable human relationships.

The "soul-toddler" metaphor introduced in the middle of *Pierre* represents the conventional sentimental predicament of abandonment against which the male heroes of both novels must define themselves. Describing this a priori state, Melville begins: "Watch yon little toddler, how long it is learning to stand by itself! First it shrieks and implores, and will not try to stand at all, unless both father and mother uphold it; then a little more bold, it must, at least, feel one parental hand, else again the cry and the tremble" (*P* 296). Like the paradigmatic male and female orphans of Susan Warner's *The Wide, Wide World* (1850), E. D. E. N. Southworth's *Ishmael* novels (1876), and other sentimental fiction, Melville's heroes must make their way alone in the "wide world," "without any support" from the absent parents (*P* 270, 296).[2] Pierre estranges himself from his paternal estate and his aristocratic mother after vowing to "protect" (with a pseudomarriage) the attractive woman who claims to be his illegitimate half sister. When his cousin, Glendinning Stanley, the only other bearer of the family surname, fails to acknowledge him, Pierre is, as he elsewhere laments, "cast out" of his family (*P* 198). His mother finalizes his abandonment when she dies without leaving him any of the family property. In *Moby-Dick*, Ishmael, Ahab, and Pip share Pierre's dilemma of abandoned orphanhood. Left to the "awful lonesomeness" of the "heartless immensity" of the ocean, Pip loses his mind in the discovery of the "indifferent . . . God," and Ishmael foreshadows in "The Castaway" his own "like abandonment" at the end of the novel whose last word is "orphan" (*MD* 414, 573). These motherless, fatherless characters, abandoned by their gods, are left to make their own "lay" or living (*MD* 6, 76–8) and to buoy their own souls. To survive, the maturing soul-toddler must elude the temptation of obsessive, self-reliant competition for power. He must find a way to outsmart Narcissus, to "grasp" the hand of his likeness—other males—instead of drowning in his own reflection.

‖

The Romantic model of masculinity in these novels has the toddler shouting defiantly back to the abandoning parents. *Moby-Dick* opens with Ishmael's socially defiant impulse to "knock . . . people's hats off" (*MD* 3). Not yet as angry as Ahab or Pierre, he indulges his antisocial impulses by reflectively going to sea. Ahab's defiance has advanced much further: in "The Candles," for example, he shouts to the godly corposants, "Oh, thou clear spirit, of thy fire thou madest me, and like a true child of fire, I breathe it back to thee" (*MD* 507).[3] As Richard H. Brodhead points out, the defiance of Ahab in *Moby-Dick* springs from the sort of disillusionment that gets dramatized in *Pierre*. *Pierre*, says Brodhead, studies "the origin and development of [the hero's] condition of aggressive estrangement."[4] In defiance, Pierre burns his father's portrait and declares, "Henceforth, cast-out Pierre hath no paternity" (*P* 198). Likewise, after learning that his mother has disowned him, Pierre "[a]t last . . . dismissed his mother's memory into that same profound vault where hitherto had reposed the swooned form of his [former fiancée] Lucy" (*P*

286). Finally orphaned and disinherited, rejected by publishers, and sentenced to death for murder, he echoes Ahab when he declares to no particular offender, "Well, be it hell. I will mold a trumpet of the flames, and, with my breath of flame, breathe back my defiance!" (*P* 360). In the hell of his rejection, the soul-toddler shapes his breath, his voice, around syllables of defiance.

The defiant soul-toddler seeks to refashion himself in isolation, and he begins his self-fashioning with a name. Ahab's mother named him prophetically after a "wicked" and doomed king, but Captain Peleg warns Ishmael never to refer to the prophecy in Ahab's presence. Effectively, Ahab is not to be reminded of his mother's act of naming. Further, Ishmael and the reader learn that Ahab is an orphan: his "widowed mother" died in his infancy, and if his father left him a surname, Ahab does not use it. By his own labor and charisma, "Captain Ahab" has earned a powerful title, which obscures the influence of his earthly father or "crazy" mother (*MD* 79). Ishmael, too, attempts to control his identity through the vehicle of the name. By declaring "Call me Ishmael" in the first line of the novel, he eliminates a surname and assumes the power of creating himself, godlike, from scratch. Mother and father both disappear from the history of his naming. Pierre Glendinning extinguishes his paternal name by embarking on a suicidal quest for self-sufficiency in the city, and by murdering his cousin Glen. The novel reinforces his act of figurative patricide by leaving Pierre's surname out of the title. Like the American Renaissance authors (Emerson, Thoreau, Hawthorne, Whitman, Melville) whose self-naming acts, according to David Leverenz, "imply a self-conscious mixture of alienation, self-assertion, and dependence" and set them in an "arm's-length relationship to social expectations," Melville's soul-toddler heroes betray their consciousness of the "absent father" in their rejections of inherited names and inherited norms.[5]

While Ahab's explosive monologue in "The Candles" offers several of his most defiant declarations, the same passage illustrates the close relationship between abandonment, defiance, and the soul-toddler's yearning for sympathy. Ahab's speech is full of exclamation points and such paradoxes as "defyingly I worship thee!" (*MD* 508)—a violent outcry prompted by the violence of nature, which Ahab interprets as the action of his father-creator-god. The Romantic, powerful hero who announces himself in this chapter struggles in vain for autonomy, finding himself bound sentence after sentence to the fire that "madest me." Ahab declares, for example, "I own thy speechless, placeless power; but . . . will dispute"; "In the midst of the . . . impersonal, a personality"; "of thy fire thou madest me, and . . . I breathe it back" (*MD* 507). The pattern continues: sentences begin with Ahab's observation of metaphysical power trying to dominate him, then, after a semicolon or other syntactic break, end with his defiant "breath[ing] back." Similarly, in the action of the scene, he uses "one blast of his breath" to extinguish the burning harpoon, symbol of the at once phallic and castrating power of the lightning god that struck the harpoon where it "projected" from its "conspicuous crotch" in the bow of the whaleboat (*MD* 508). Ahab's self-assertive breaths respond to (and cannot exist without) the creative / destructive power of the metaphysical father figure. Defiance is not an isolated act, but an act performed by an angry individual in relation to the threatening, yet pitiable, paternal deity. Like Ahab, the "omnipotent" "foundling fire" also lacks a father and therefore suffers and storms in "unparticipated grief" (*MD* 508). For Ahab, Pierre, and even Ahab's corposant divinity, defiance constitutes a perpetual reminder of abandonment, for the violent words of the soul-toddler merely reproduce the prior violence of parental rejection.

In the complex symbolic structures of *Moby-Dick* and *Pierre*, the sexual and socioeconomic potency of the father figure simultaneously engenders and emasculates, creates and castrates, the abandoned son. By striking the harpoon, the corposant "flame" does violence to Ahab's masculinity even while investing it with power and life, figured as fire. Then, in competition with the engendering god, Ahab exerts his greatest power by paradoxically following a threat of symbolic rape with an act of symbolic self-emasculation: he strikes fear among the men by waving his "fiery dart" and "swearing to transfix with it the first sailor that but cast loose a rope's end [in mutiny]," then scatters them by blowing out the flame, thereby extinguishing the source of his masculine power (this flaming phallic symbol is, after all, "Ahab's harpoon" [*MD* 508]). Ahab's defiant competition with his father-god at once creates and compromises his masculine potency.

Pierre too joins in the competitive chain of his sires' masculinity even as he tries to escape it. Growing up on land that his paternal ancestors usurped from native inhabitants and defended in war (*P* 5–6), he understands masculinity to consist of a genteel marriage based on an exchange of love-words with a "pure" woman, and "a monopoly of glory in capping the fame-column, whose tall shaft had been erected by his noble sires" (*P* 8). Pierre inherits money and land, but no affection, from deceased Glendinnings. In giving him life and wealth, his grandfathers have also set for him a standard of sexual potency and economic competitiveness that he must live up to. Caught in a double bind, he must either leave the ancestral estate and try to be "his own Alpha and Omega," to earn a living by his pen without the "ancestral sword and shield" or the inherited fortune of his grandfather (*P* 261), or stay on the estate in a life of ease and thereby fail to live up to his glorious male legacy. The men who gave him his being have left him impossible ideals of chivalry and glory, but no tools for achieving them. They brought a boy into the world pre-emasculated by their successes, doomed to fail in his own aspiration to outdo them. Both Ahab and Pierre discover that their "manmaker" fathers create, like the *Pequod's* carpenter, with "chisel, file, and sand-paper." Any man who wishes to make himself over must also create by destroying, or by getting "a crucible, and into it, and dissolv[ing] myself down to one small, compendious vertebra" (*MD* 472). No matter who the "manmaker" or progenitor, godliness and fatherhood are as destructive as they are creative.

The defiant self-fashioning of these "godlike" (yet abandoned, alienated) Romantic males leaves them gazing into their own reflections for identities they cannot derive from parents or other external sources. After oedipally rejecting the absent, threatening father, the lone male attempts to "become reborn, with a new self, a new identity which would owe nothing to the parental heritage."[6] Melville figures the rebirth as a journey. Pierre literally departs his ancestral estate after burning his father's portrait and declaring himself "disinherited" of the past (*P* 199). In the soul-toddler passage, the narrator of *Pierre* imagines "man's estate" as a voyage across the sea or into "far Oregon lands" (*P* 296); once the parental hands have let go, the hero cannot stay to inherit a patriarchal "estate" such as Saddle Meadows. In *Moby-Dick*, Ishmael adds that the disinherited hero's journey involves self-scrutiny and reflection. He banters, "Let the most absent-minded of men be plunged in his deepest reveries—stand that man on his legs, set his feet a-going, and he will infallibly lead you to water," because "as every one knows, meditation and water are wedded for ever" (*MD* 4). At the end of a sequence of water-seeking images, Ishmael introduces "Narcissus" as "the key to it all": the boy or man who "[can] not grasp the tormenting, mild image he [sees] in the fountain" will drown in his pursuit of identity. The self-seeking waterlust of every "robust healthy boy" is thus fraught with hazard. To survive the self-defining quest "across the seas," the soul-toddler must find a way to "grasp" his likeness—a tactile pun at the root of Melville's complex vision of masculine dangers and masculine possibilities.[7]

In *Moby-Dick*, Narcissus, Ishmael, and Ahab all drown or come close to drowning by staring at their reflections in the water ("Loomings," "The Mast-Head," "Symphony"). But such reflections, or "Descartian vortices" of self-scrutiny, are "ungraspable": Ahab's "shadow in the water sank and sank to his gaze, the more and the more that he strove to pierce the profundity" (*MD* 159, 5, 543). Whereas the abstract "Platonist" thinks he will assert and define himself by leaning toward his reflection—or by reaching for the "half-seen, gliding, beautiful thing that eludes him" in the water—Melville concludes in "The Mast-Head" that such a philosopher "loses his identity" and even his "life" with his misguided "reverie" (*MD* 159). The abandoned soul-toddler will not answer the riddle of his identity by chasing his reflection; only in a masturbatory suicide leap like Ahab's can the self-absorbed male "pierce the profundity" of his own likeness. To prevent drowning and solipsism, a man must find a palpable Other to "grasp."

Pierre's tragedy, like Ahab's, involves two such leaps into his own reflection. First, he projects his own ideal of masculinity onto his relationship with Isabel. According to the narrator, Pierre fantasized about a sister before ever hearing of Isabel: "So perfect to Pierre had long seemed the illuminated scroll of his life thus far, that only one hiatus was discoverable by him in that sweetly-writ manuscript. A sister had been omitted from the text. He mourned that so delicious a feeling as fraternal love had been denied him." In the incestuous confusion that many observe in this text, Pierre thinks that "much that goes to make up the deliciousness of a wife, already lies in the sister." He dreams chivalrously of loving, protecting, and "engag[ing] in a mortal quarrel on a sweet sister's behalf" (*P* 7). This early sister-fantasy is fulfilled in Isabel, whom he claims as a mock wife, and whom he offers to "protect" by the self-imperilling marriage ruse. Isabel, then, emerges as a projection of Pierre's chivalric fantasy of masculinity. Notably, the narrator never provides conclusive evidence that Isabel *is* Pierre's sister, but Pierre nonetheless allows his imagined duty to her to override his preestablished obligations to other women. In this mysterious, ambiguous novel, all that narcissistic Pierre requires is a woman onto whom he can project his sister-fantasies in a manner convincing to his own sense of manhood.[8]

Just as Isabel embodies Pierre's desires, the toilsome book Pierre is trying to write reflects his "appallingly vacant and vast" soul (*P* 285). Since Pierre owes his language, his values, and his own existence to his father, by killing off the memory of his father-god in a "mortal quarrel on [Isabel's] behalf" he has nullified both himself and his ability to write. Speaking unwittingly of the productive capacity of a fatherless soul, Pierre warns, "From nothing proceeds nothing"; all he can assert, as he prepares to write his "gospel" of truth, is that "I am Pierre" (*P* 274). The "vast" book lacks "any confirmed form or conclusion" (*P* 338) because it is the self-projection of a "vacant" soul with no surname and no clear self to project. Without a father, the son cannot be born. By surrounding himself with the vacant mirrors of (supposed) sister and book, Pierre commits Ahab's folly: excessive Romantic self-scrutiny as the accompaniment to defiance. His chief obsessions, Isabel and the book, reflect his own fantasies of protective and literary masculinity, fantasies he has had to fashion on his own in lieu of a mother's or father's guiding hands, and in lieu of any adult hands extended in sentimental fellowship.

ı'ı

The sentimental, tactile, redemptive model of masculinity, which Melville contrasts with the Romantic model, is made possible for the heroes of both novels through the agency of minor characters. The best known of such sentimental pairings is the relationship between Queequeg and Ishmael. With unintentional reference to the sentimental orphan tradition, Lewis Mumford calls this friendship "the first and almost the last *touch of affection* in the whole story: a compact *between two strays and outcasts.*" While Mumford asserts that "Heaven and Hell," eternity, and "the universe" take precedence over Queequeg's role in this novel and that "friendship is a small thing,"[9] in fact the homoerotic "marriage" staged at the Spouter Inn is quite important. As Robert K. Martin explains, this scene represents Ishmael's "discovery of the body as a source of pleasure" apart from the "utility" of the whaling ship, and it also offers a way for Ishmael to "overcome [the] isolation" of his biblical namesake "by joining self and other."[10] Fulfilling the sentimental vision of what Joanne Dobson terms the "self-in-relation," the "affectional bond" between Ishmael and Queequeg takes infinite forms.[11] While bound to Queequeg by the "monkey-rope," Ishmael imagines himself and the harpooneer as business partners at the whaling trade, their "individualit[ies] . . . merged in a joint stock company of two"; they are also "wedded" by the monkey-rope "for better or worse," as at the Spouter Inn, when they awake in a "bride-groom clasp"; and they are "inseparable twin brother[s]," united by an "elongated Siamese ligature." The variety of relations imagined in the monkey-rope scene makes this "hempen bond" a symbol of "the precise situation of every mortal that breathes" (*MD* 320). The image of "entangled" threads connecting individuals remains in Melville's imagination from the monkey-rope scene in *Moby-Dick* to the acknowledgement, in *Pierre,* of the "infinite entanglements of all social things, which forbid that one thread should fly the general fabric, on some new line of duty, without tearing itself and tearing others" (*P* 191). Unlike Pierre, Ishmael is able to enjoy his perilous bond with Queequeg; instead of suicidally and murderously defying the bond, he reflects on the "uncommon advantage" of viewing his partner at work "in the Highland costume—a shirt and socks" (*MD* 320). The masculine "self-in-relation" is, in *Moby-Dick,* partly the sexual self that Martin documents, but also a "self" whose isolation is broken in a number of ways by "infinite entanglements" that the hero can relish.

Recurring alongside the "entangled" thread image in Melville's vision of sentimental masculinity is the image of the outstretched hand, replacing the lost divine or "parental hand" of the soul-toddler. Ishmael, as the protagonist most open to sentimental masculinity in these two novels, is most obsessed with hand-holding. In "The Counterpane," he remembers being sent to his room as a child, where, lonely and abandoned by his punishing stepmother, he felt a "supernatural hand . . . placed in mine." The hand provokes fear for young Ishmael, since the only parental hand he has known is that used by his stepmother to give him a "whipping" or to "drag" him "by the legs out of the chimney" (*MD* 25–6). Ishmael connects supernatural hands with a scene of abandonment after Pip's second jump from a whaleboat, when he reflects, "we are all in the hands of the Gods" (*MD* 413). The impalpable hand again proves the divine parent "heartless"; only "[b]y the merest chance" does the ship recover the castaway, and even then Pip has already surrendered "his soul" to the maddening sea (*MD* 414). But Queequeg's arm, "thrown over [Ishmael] in the most loving and affectionate manner," replaces the withdrawn and terrifying parental hands and initiates the relationship that will restore one character, at least, to a social community. Finally, Ishmael revels in the "squeeze of the hand" of his "co-laborers" at the task of squeezing sperm. As the hyperbole and sentimental diction mount, he fancies saying to the others: "Oh! my dear fellow beings . . . let us squeeze hands all round; nay, let us all squeeze ourselves into each other; let us squeeze ourselves universally into the very milk and sperm of kindness" (*MD* 416). Though the fantasy frankly suggests group masturbation,[12] it becomes dissociated from gender in Ishmael's imagination. Kindness is "universal," represented by both "milk and sperm." Androgynous in nature, the hands of sentimental fellowship are capable of replacing the lost support of both mother and father and restoring the soul-toddler to a community purified of gendered imperatives.[13]

Other relationships between protagonists and minor characters, particularly between Ahab and Pip in *Moby-Dick* and between the title character and a child-hood friend in *Pierre*, also use the motif of the human hand to represent the offer of sentimental masculinity for a questing "soul-toddler." Unfortunately, the hands of misfortune catch up with Pierre before the sentimental hand of fellowship is offered. Though his childhood friend Charlie Millthorpe (fatherless like Pierre) offers to renew their old friendship when they meet in the city, Pierre hangs back in the interest of preserving the secrecy of his false marriage to Isabel. He seeks the friendship of his cousin, representative of the patriarchal family and inherited wealth, rather than the affection of a fellow orphan who also makes his way without financial backing. Only in the closing paragraphs of the novel does Millthorpe's offer of friendship become palpable like Queequeg's, as well as ver-bal; and only after taking physical form does the offer succeed. In place of the "thousand contending hands" that had descended upon Pierre in an earlier scene (*P* 360), Millthorpe takes Pierre, his "school-mate—playmate—friend!" by the "unresponsive hand," and after delivering a short sympathetic monologue to Pierre, feels "one speechless clasp" (*P* 362). This deeply sentimental parting scene resembles a similar scene between Pip and Ahab, as Pip proclaims his last pledge of constancy. First, in a stage direction, Pip "catches [Ahab] by the hand" to keep him from going on deck (*MD* 534); before Ahab leaves, he accepts a handshake with approval, saying, "Thy hand!—Met! True art thou, lad, as the circumference to its centre" (*MP* 535). But feeling himself at the "centre," Ahab leaves the cabin to carry out his "monistic" or "monomaniac" quest.[14] Pip extends to Ahab the sentimental masculine alternative of accepting an outstretched hand, but Ahab turns him down, in pursuit of Romantic fantasy. Faced with the dilemma of aban-donment—left alone in the sea like Pip, disinherited like Pierre, ignorant of his parents like Ahab, or shut up alone in a room like Ishmael—only Ishmael among these novels' soul-toddlers accepts an adult set of handclasps from a fellow orphan / outcast in time to save his life from the alternative form of masculinity: suicidal, Romantic self-absorption.

Sympathy of the eye—signified by tears, by the spectacle of the sufferer, or by an exchanged glance—is secondary in these novels to sympathy of the hand.[15] Occasionally, the two tropes merge, as when Ishmael squeezes whale sperm with his shipmates, "continually squeezing their hands, and looking up into their eyes sentimentally" (*MD* 416). At such times, sentimental masculinity approximates a paradise for the soul-toddler. But the eye alone is an unreliable judge of fellowship in these novels. In Melville's skeptical sentimentalism, tears may be either false (the product of one's education in propriety) or sincere. *Pierre* in particular records the tension between sentimental "kitsch," which Eve Kosofsky Sedgwick calls "the most damning sense . . . of 'sentimental,' " and spectacles that invite identification.[16] Only in combination with physical touches do tears and affective spectacles possess the redemptive power typical of the sentimental tradition.

Even Ahab recognizes that combined visual and tactile expressions of feeling wield more power than anything he can conjure or sustain through defiance. In their parting scene in "The Cabin," framed by handclasps, Ahab silences Pip, whose fidelity and tears combine to jeopardize Ahab's "purpose." "Weep so, and I will murder thee!" warns Ahab, so threatening is Pip's expression of sentiment to his self-seeking quest. Accompanied by the touch of a hand, Pip's tears are incompatible with the Romantic hero's pursuit of social destruction (*MD* 534–5). In "The Symphony," Ahab's ability to look Starbuck in the eye and shed his own tear signifies his temptation to abandon his obsessive quest and return "home." In this dense and pivotal chapter, Romantic and sentimental masculinities vie for the tottering soul of the superficially "untottering Ahab" (*MD* 543). The "human eye" of homeloving Starbuck serves as a "magic glass" through which Ahab can see his wife and child and "the far away home" (*MD* 544). Domesticity and tears alone, however, lack the power that the soul-toddler requires. As though willing to sample the affectional, homoerotic masculinity that beguiles Ishmael, Ahab commands, "Close! stand close to me, Starbuck; let me look into a human eye" (*MD* 544); but Starbuck upholds the proprieties of heterosexuality and nautical rank. Unlike outcast Pip, who has nothing to lose, Starbuck is "[c]areful not to touch [Ahab]," and when the captain notices him and calls him by name, Starbuck answers formally, "Sir" (*MD* 543). Under the influence of the "mild looking sky," Ahab seeks an alternative to "the masoned, walled-town of a Captain's exclusiveness, which admits but small entrance to any sympathy from the green country without," but Starbuck, continuing to call Ahab by the precariously intimate yet formal "my Captain," offers only the sympathy of his eye, not his touch. Thus when "Ahab's glance [is] averted," the contact is broken, and Ahab's anger returns at the sight of a murderous fish leaping out of the quiet sea (*MD* 544–5). The "Mate" who steals away from the deck has failed to offer Ahab a palpable alternative to the abstract self-image he seeks; he must continue to pursue the "hidden lord and master" in the "unsounded sea" (*MD* 545).

In *Pierre*, Melville parodies the tearful tradition that *Moby-Dick* invokes, not to dismiss sentimentality as a model for masculinity but rather to distinguish between genuine affect and spurious, self-serving forms of propriety. The impalpable tears of sentimental authorship belong to the latter kind of sentiment—Sedgwick's "kitsch"—the kind that allows a reader / spectator "to misrepresent the quality or locus of her or his implicit participation in a scene—to misrepresent, for example, desire as pity."[17] The letter that Isabel writes to Pierre in "tearmingled ink" is a sentimental spectacle itself, upon which Pierre builds a fantasy of false feeling. The "tragic sight" of the red-stained letter "move[s Pierre's] inmost soul," as Isabel hoped she might move him by offering: "could'st thou take out my heart, and look at it in thy hand, then thou would'st find it all over written, this way and that, and crossed again, and yet again, with continual lines of longings, that found no end but in suddenly calling thee" (*P* 158–9). Isabel's visible tears give Pierre the opportunity to pity her, instead of recognizing himself under the influence of the same sensual "longings." His vehemence belies his motive: he insists, "that part of the world which knows me, shall acknowledge thee; or by heaven I will crush the disdainful world down on its knees to thee, my sweet Isabel!" (*P* 160). Not only does Isabel fulfill Pierre's chivalric sister-fantasy, she also allows him to give voice to his feelings of masculine competition and egotistic power. Upon reading Isabel's letter, Pierre's soul "moved" not toward affection, but toward desire and defiance, veiled beneath sentimental forms. Sentimental masculinity—a matter of handholding and eyegazing and glorying in the "grand old heart" (*MD* 544)—is carefully distinguished from the merely rhetorical sentimentality of "young America in literature" (see *P* 244–56), which is merely a veil for narcissistic, self-serving fantasies such as Pierre's competitive self-assertion or the desires of publishers and illustrators to capitalize on the fame of authors they have helped to enshrine. Only feelings substantiated by handclasps pass the test of genuine sympathy in *Pierre* and *Moby-Dick*. Disembodied sentiments, like "breaths" of defiance, are merely words without meaning, incapable of providing the soul-toddler with an identity.

⁙

Between the two available masculine responses to the soul's a priori orphan state—defiant Romanticism or tactile sentimentality—Melville chooses sentimental (relational, affectional) masculinity in both novels as the most sustainable model, but he does so with some ambivalence. Not only does sentimental Ishmael survive while defiant Ahab and Pierre perish with all the drama of their passionate natures, but Melville's sentimental motifs—such as the bereaved or abandoned woman and the redemptive death and funeral token—continue the critique of the "overextended Romantic self"[18] and cement the case for sympathy. However, it is still uncertain whether Ishmael's androgynous fantasies of affection will be of any use to him in the gendered world to which he most likely must return.

Besides the wives of Starbuck and Ahab, who are widowed by Ahab's quest, *Moby-Dick* makes reference to many other women whose sole purpose is to mourn the loss of a man—and thus implicitly to critique Romantic masculinity. Although some of these figures do provide a conventionally feminized "alternative to cathartic grief," which Neal L. Tolchin contrasts with Ahab's grieving rage, most mourn "offstage" or out of the reader's sight, and thus the novel seems to emphasize not their method or ritual of mourning but the mere fact of their bereavement.[19] Very early, Melville undercuts the myth of American success—symbolized by the rich dowries and "perennial . . . bloom" of "sailor sweethearts"—with a "scattered congregation of sailors, and sailors' wives and widows" in the New Bedford chapel (*MD* 50–1).[20] Not only do the wives and children of sailors lose their husbands and fathers when ships founder, but other "widows and orphans," investors in the voyage, also lose when men like Ahab forget their social "entanglements" (*MD* 77). In prophetic anticipation of the threat that Ahab's quest poses to women and society, Ishmael narrates the story of the *Jeroboam*. Crewman Macey was swept out of his whaleboat in pursuit of Moby-Dick, but the prophecy for Ahab's own death is not the end of the story: the *Pequod* also carries a letter for Macey in "a woman's pinny hand,—[from] the man's wife, I'll wager" (*MD* 318), which reminds the reader of the social consequences of Macey's insistent pursuit and anticipates the entangled consequences of Ahab's. In *Moby-Dick,* male self-assertion casts many women into mourning and poverty; these women represent the painful social consequences of the defiant quest.

Some of the women in *Pierre* serve a similar function. While this novel is frequently cited as an example of what Nina Baym calls "melodramas of beset manhood,"[21] there is ample evidence that women suffer in consequence of a man's narcissistic quest at least as much as men suffer from feminized propriety. The narrator takes Mrs. Glendinning's cause of death to be Pierre's elopement, for example: although Pierre's fantasy of masculine responsibility leads him to believe that silence would be best for her, his unexplained flight ends her life. The same action also sends Lucy into a deep illness from which no one expects her to recover. Lucy's illness, in turn, infects her sympathetic aunt, who also takes to her sickbed. With one act, Pierre manages to kill or injure three women. Later, after taking up residence with Isabel, he fails her, too, by "transfigur[ing]" her in his imagination "out of the realms of mortalness" (*P* 142). Thus, the narrator informs us, the mortal Isabel must visit the Millthorpes for the simple requirement of human company. In both novels, the Romantic male quest imperils a human community, represented by some of the women in the texts.

Two other stock features of sentimental novels, the highly wrought death scene and its associated "token," appear in both Melville novels. For Jane Tompkins, the conventional sentimental death scene marks a triumph, not a failure. Death is an "access to power" for the departed soul, and sentimental tokens, standing in for the lost loved one, collaborate with death to "redeem the unregenerate." So, for example, Little Eva's lock of hair redeems the unruly slave girl Topsy for Christianity and affection in *Uncle Tom's Cabin.*[22] But, like Isabel's tearful letter, the deaths and tokens of *Pierre* are pointedly unredemptive, until the ambivalent closing scene. Defying the convention of a protracted demise, Mrs. Glendinning's death comes as a four-word report in a short list of "tidings from the Meadows" (*P* 285). Pierre sheds "tears like acid" for the parent "whose eyes had been closed by unrelated hands that were hired; but whose heart had been broken, and whose very reason been ruined, by the related hands of her son" (*P* 285–6). The requisite tears appear, but there is no redemption when someone else's hands have performed the final acts of care. Pierre's most sentimental death token, carefully preserved until the beginning of the novel, is his father's portrait. But he opts to replace the token from the deceased parent with a look-alike, supposed daughter. At the same time, he disowns his sentimental past, lamenting, "Hitherto I have . . .

been a worshiper of all heir-looms; a fond filer away of letters, locks of hair, bits of ribbon, flowers, and the thousand-and-one minutenesses which love and memory think they sanctify:—but it is forever over now!" (*P* 197). These scenes are bitter, not redemptive, in their emotional extravagance. Instead of responding to abandonment (death scenes) with authentic, redemptive sentiment, Pierre "mold[s] a trumpet of the flames [of his hell], and . . . breathe[s] back [his] defiance" (*P* 360). But when the dying Pierre responds to Charlie Millthorpe's fraternal handclasp, he reverses his mother's death scene, for now there is a caring friend to hold the hand of the dying. Unfortunately, in this case the character who needs to be redeemed is the one who does the dying.

Adapting the same sentimental motif of redemptive deaths and tokens, the conclusion to *Moby-Dick* portrays a character more convincingly "redeemed" by another's death. Queequeg's coffin is often cited as the final symbol of redemptive "fraternity" in *Moby-Dick,* and this suggests a relation to the contemporaneous literary trope of death tokens. Though the coffin is not a deliberate gift from Queequeg, it does "[shoot] lengthwise from the sea, [fall] over, and float . . . by [Ishmael's] side," as though delivered to Ishmael from the sea where Queequeg has just disappeared. At the timely moment of loss, the coffin reminds Ishmael and the reader of the affection that Queequeg has represented in the novel. As the coffin literally saves Ishmael's life, the affection it represents in Queequeg saves Ishmael from the narcissistic influence of Ahab, redeeming him for human society aboard the *Rachel* and on land. Not just any piece of flotsam, this "life-buoy" replaces the extended arm of Queequeg as a link for Ishmael to the social world that he relishes so "sentimentally" in the sperm-squeezing scene. The coffin / life-buoy also charms the waters around Ishmael so that "[t]he unharming sharks . . . glided by as if with padlocks on their mouths; the savage sea-hawks sailed with sheathed beaks" (*MD* 573). The padlocked mouths of the "masculine murderous sharks," whose feeding frenzy had represented "rapacious competition" earlier in the novel, suggest that Ishmael is doubly protected from competitive, egotistic masculinity at the end of the novel: he survives Ahab's quest for the white whale, and competitive masculinity gives way before the power of the sentimental death-token.[23] Like tears, deaths and tokens in these novels are redemptive for the man who has managed to "grasp" the fraternal hand that Narcissus missed.

And what does the male look forward to if he survives the illusory temptation of defiant, competitive power? *Pierre* does not give its hero a chance to ask the question. Of *Moby-Dick,* Susan K. Harris claims,

> Ishmael is redeemed for ordinary domesticity (which critics of this male text tend to refer to as the human community); that is, in Melville's words, Ishmael learns to lower his "conceit of attainable felicity," and settle for "the wife, the heart, the bed, the table, the saddle, the fire-side, the country."[24]

Indeed, *Moby-Dick* does idealize domesticity and fertility in several scenes, including Ishmael's marriage fantasy with Queequeg at the Spouter Inn, the sperm-squeezing scene, and Queequeg's rescue of Tashtego from a whale's head (a form of "midwifery"), in which vital male-male relationships are overlaid with male-female imagery. In all of these scenes, the combination of heterosexual imagery and overt homoeroticism leaves it unclear whether the *Pequod* is a "paradise of bachelors" or a school for men, teaching lessons that apply in a heterosexual world.[25] The chapter entitled "The Grand Armada" tilts the scales—but only slightly—in the latter direction, depicting heterosexuality as both a "delight" and a danger.

While Ishmael's language in "The Grand Armada" suggests a claustrophobic fear of the womb as a metaphor for social entrapment ("We must watch for a breach in the living wall that hemmed us in; the wall that had only admitted us in order to shut us up" [*MD* 387]), he is fascinated by the "enchanted calm which they say lurks at the heart of every commotion." He learns that what "they say" is true: after "the jerking harpoon" that led the whaleboat into the womblike, fertile center of the pod "drew out," the men in Ishmael's boat witness scenes of "dalliance and delight" to which the competitive mandate of their gender usually prohibits them access. (Other males, human and "Leviathan," continue their "tumults" at the periphery of the pod.) In this postcoital Eden of fertility, pregnant and nursing whales are "beset" by the assertion of an adult male who has been losing the competition of the whale hunt. "[T]ormented to madness" by the spade that turns his attention selfishly inward, a lone whale tears through the "lake" of calm and disrupts the whole pod into motion (*MD* 389–90). The aggression of the male hunt, and the self-absorption of the lone whale preoccupied with the sting of the spade (an inward evil), are the adverse forces in this scene of domestic tranquillity, which is offered as a human paradigm by repeated figures of "human infants," "bridal-chambers and nurseries," and even human consumption of a whale mother's milk (*MD* 388, 389, 388 n.). In this chapter, the rage of the whale, like the obsessive defiance of Ahab, threatens not only the peacefully domestic whale community, but even the whaleboat stalled in its midst. The whale's violence is not figured in heterosexual or rapacious terms, but in the imagery of battle: he is "the lone mounted desperado Arnold, at the battle of Saratoga," "wounding and murdering his own comrades" (*MD* 389). The whale hunt, then, a competition between human and leviathan motivated by economic competition among humans on shore and by narcissistic quests like Ahab's, is much more dangerous than the fleeting heterosexual act, which allows for a world of "enchanted calm" from which men are barred access only if they are engaged in the competition of the hunt. In "The Grand Armada," Ishmael learns that heterosexual fertility itself inflicts much less violence than competitive male rage; heterosexuality, unlike obsessive monomania, also offers a "calm" and "delight[ful]" reward of fertility.

Nonetheless, the men in the whaleboat witness these delights only by suspending their masculinity. Only Queequeg, unfettered by gender constraints, enjoys his usual tactile ease here, patting the foreheads of the "domesticated" whales near the boat. Starbuck, on the other hand, must restrain his heterosexual impulses. He "scratched their backs with his lance; but fearful of the consequences, for the time refrained from darting it" (*MD* 387). That interruption, "for the time," reminds the reader that this party of men, after all, defines itself sexually and economically by its harpoons and lances. As a man and the first mate of a whale ship, Starbuck will inevitably have to cast his harpoon. Men can enjoy the tactile and visual delights of the whale bower, it seems, only if they leave their sexual impulses and their economic professions elsewhere. (But the paradox: without sex, there are no births; and in the human realm, at least, domesticity needs cash support.) Furthermore, as Ishmael gazes into the transparent depths, he sees the farthest thing from a flattering, godlike reflection. The nursing whale calves look "up towards us, but not at us, as if we were but a bit of Gulf-weed in their new-born sight" (*MD* 388). Stripped of power and sexuality, a man is reduced to a spectator in the mystery of fertility. Ishmael identifies androgynously with the "calm" lagoon: "deep down and deep inland" in his own spirit he recognizes "eternal mildness of joy" like that which he witnesses in the "lake" (*MD* 389). If masculinity is competition, godliness, or a phallic "dart," then the whale bower emasculates; but Ishmael finds "delight" there, suggesting that he, like Queequeg, can accommodate an androgynous renunciation of power. This chapter suggests the problem, then, of masculinity in the novel: affection and sympathetic touch turn out to be just as emasculating as defiance. In order for a boy to mature and survive, he must give up the dream of becoming a "man" in favor of a powerless but strangely delightful androgyny, for which his fathers and his gods offer no model.

ιʰι

In *Hero, Captain, and Stranger: Male Friendship, Social Critique, and Literary Form in the Sea Novels of Herman Melville*, Robert K. Martin argues that Melville engaged in "a lifelong search for a way to repudiate the power-lust of Western man," and that his novels as a whole offer a "subversive form of love that could counteract power."[26] Indeed, Melville turns against the self-absorbed, power-hungry masculinity of the defiant toddler, but not wholeheartedly. While composing *Moby-Dick*, he wrote to Nathaniel Hawthorne of a hypothetical, fearless man, "the man who, like Russia or the British Empire, declares himself a sovereign nature (in himself) amid the powers of heaven, hell, and earth. He may perish; but so long as he exists he insists upon treating with all Powers upon an equal basis." Melville glides from the hypothetical third person into the first person within the same paragraph, adding, "If any of those other Powers choose to withhold certain secrets, let them; that does not impair my sovereignty in myself; that does not make me tributary."[27] Like his Romantic heroes, Melville dreamed of power and self-contained "sovereignty"; in apparent self-contradiction, however, he also sought the affection of other men.

Melville's friendships and his motives for authorship owe as much to sentimental ideals of affection as to Romantic ideals of autonomous power. The Melville who wrote to Hawthorne about his sovereign nature could also call his friend "my dear fellow mortal" (*C* 192), and call Evert Duyckinck "Beloved" (*C* 167). As a renegade in search of "the powers of heaven, hell, and earth," he lamented to Hawthorne, "Try to get a living by the Truth—and go to the Soup Societies" (*C* 191). Yet to Richard Henry Dana he professed a sentimental motive for authorship, seeking—after money—only sympathy. In 1850, not long before he would draft the "Monkey-rope" chapter of *Moby-Dick*, he wrote,

> I am specially delighted at the thought, that those strange, congenial feelings, with which after my first voyage, I for the first time read "Two Years Before the Mast", and while so engaged was, as it were, tied & welded to you by a sort of Siamese link of affectionate sympathy— —that these feelings should be reciprocated by you, in your turn. . . . In fact, My Dear Dana, did I not write these books of mine almost entirely for "lucre" . . . I almost think, I should hereafter—in the case of a sea book—get my M.S.S. neatly & legibly copied by a scrivener—send you that one copy—& deem such a procedure the best publication. (*C* 160)

A sovereign Romantic and an unapologetic sentimentalist, Melville wished to write for "Truth" *and* "affectionate sympathy." Preventing him from accomplishing either to his satisfaction was his masculine obligation to earn money.

Like Melville, the soul-toddler heroes of *Moby-Dick* and *Pierre* are trapped by the ideology of masculinity itself. Although Ishmael survives the doom of defiant, competitive narcissism, his novel does not address how he will express his sexuality on land without reverting to systems of domination, nor does it leave him with any money. As androgyne, he will depend on the charity of the *Rachel* (and perhaps others) until he can attach himself to another ship and become a productive man again. In the capitalist world that launched the *Pequod* and gave birth to Pierre, Anglo–American men must fight Indians, they must wrest sperm from whales, they must do battle with other men in order to earn money and a name, and they must violate the "enchanted calm" of a woman's womb in order to make more men. In a world of differentiated genders and capitalist competition—in which power attracts even men like Melville who wish to repudiate it—the "subversive form of love that could counteract power" (in Martin's phrase) only exists in a hesitant subjunctive case. Melville dreamed to Dana, "*did I not* write these books of mine almost entirely for 'lucre' . . . I *almost* think, I *should* hereafter . . . send you that one copy" (emphasis added). But of course, as a husband and a father, Melville had to write for money. Dana's sympathy and the sovereign soul's "Truth" were dream motives. Unlike Ishmael, Melville in the 1850s had already committed himself to being a "man," and despite fantasy masculinities of defiance and affection (both of which turn out to castrate as they create—to constitute no masculinity at all), Melville, if not his characters, had joined the cycle that his society prepared for men: the cycle of competing for money to provide for sons who, in turn, could try to outstrip him, the "heartless," "foundling" father-god.

NOTES

1. References are to the following editions: Herman Melville, *Moby-Dick: or The Whale*, ed. Harrison Hayford, Hershel Parker, and G. Thomas Tanselle (Evanston: Northwestern University Press and Newberry Library, 1988), hereafter cited as *MD*, and Melville, *Pierre; or The Ambiguities*, ed. Harrison Hayford, Hershel Parker, and G. Thomas Tanselle (Evanston: Northwestern University Press and Newberry Library, 1971), hereafter cited as *P*. My epigraphs are from *P* 296 and *MD* 5.

2. Susan Warner, *The Wide, Wide World* (New York: Feminist Press, 1987); E. D. E. N. Southworth, *Ishmael; or In the Depths* (New York: Hurst & Company, n.d.), and *Self-Raised; or Out of the Depths* (Chicago: M. A. Donohue & Company, n.d.). In *Mourning, Gender, and Creativity in the Art of Herman Melville* (New Haven: Yale University Press, 1988), Neal L. Tolchin associates Melville's Ishmael with "a standard character in the sentimental novel, 'another orphan' " (137).

3. For other discussions of Ahab's well-documented defiance toward the paternal deity, see Lawrance Thompson, *Melville's Quarrel with God* (Princeton: Princeton University Press, 1952); T. Walter Herbert, Jr., *Moby Dick and Calvinism: A World Dismantled* (New Brunswick: Rutgers University Press, 1977); Philip Young, " 'These Be Thy Gods, O Ahab!' " in *Studies in the American Renaissance 1990*, ed. Joel Myerson (Charlottesville: University Press of Virginia, 1990), 329–40.

4. Richard H. Brodhead, *Hawthorne, Melville, and the Novel* (Chicago: University of Chicago Press, 1976), 166.

5. David Leverenz, *Manhood and the American Renaissance* (Ithaca: Cornell University Press, 1989), 9–10.

6. Regis Durand, " 'The Captive King': The Absent Father in Melville's Text," in *The Fictional Father: Lacanian Readings of the Text*, ed. Robert Con Davis (Amherst: University of Massachusetts Press, 1981), 48–72, quotation from 64.

7. Hereafter, Romantic "narcissism" will be differentiated from sentimental homoeroticism, following Melville's distinction in these novels between the impossible quest for one's own impalpable reflection, and the alternate quest for human contact, represented most often by the touch of other men. This is opposed to Freud's equation of narcissism with homoeroticism, for a recent discussion of which see Michael Warner, "Homo-Narcissism; or, Heterosexuality," in *Engendering Men: The Question of Male Feminist Criticism*, ed. Joseph A. Boone and Michael Cadden (New York and London: Routledge, 1990), 190–206, especially 192–3.

8. For other readings of Isabel as a projection of Pierre's "self-made-word" or narcissism, see Sacvan Bercovitch, "How to Read Melville's *Pierre*," in *Herman Melville: A Collection of Critical Essays*, ed. Myra Jehlen (Englewood Cliffs, N.J.: Prentice-Hall, 1994), 116–25, especially 120; and Edgar A. Dryden, "The Entangled Text: Melville's *Pierre* and the Problem of Reading," 100–15 in the same collection, especially 102.

9. Lewis Mumford, *Herman Melville* (New York: Harcourt, Brace & Company, 1929), 160–1, emphasis added.

10. Robert K. Martin, *Hero, Captain, and Stranger: Male Friendship, Social Critique, and Literary Form in the Sea Novels of Herman Melville* (Chapel Hill: University of North Carolina Press, 1986), 73–4.

11. Joanne Dobson, "The American Renaissance Reenvisioned," in *The (Other) American Traditions: Nineteenth-Century Women Writers*, ed. Joyce W. Warren (New Brunswick, N.J.: Rutgers University Press, 1993), 164–82, quotation from 170.

12. See Martin, *Hero, Captain, Stranger*, 82.

13. This is not to suggest that Melville's vision of sentimental fellowship extends to any *real* women in *Moby-Dick*. While his use of feminine imagery (other examples are discussed later in this essay) suggests an ideal gender-free community, he is unable to render such a community among male and female characters.

14. Ishmael calls Ahab a "monomaniac" (*MD* 463). In "The Despotic Victim: Gender and Imagination in *Pierre*," *ATQ: American Transcendental Quarterly* 4 (March 1990): 67–76, quotation from 71, Kris Lackey introduces the term "monistic" to characterize Pierre's similarly self-centered and linear action. I am here applying Lackey's description of Pierre's linear self-absorption to Ahab, his literary double.

15. On the importance of tears to the sentimental mode, see E. Douglas Branch, *The Sentimental Years, 1836–1860* (New York: D. Appleton-Century Company, 1934), 131; Jane Tompkins, *Sensational Designs: The Cultural Work of American Fiction, 1790–1860* (New York: Oxford University Press, 1985), 131; Judith Fetterley, ed., *Provisions: A Reader from Nineteenth-Century Women* (Bloomington: Indiana University Press, 1985), 25; and Dobson, "American Renaissance Reenvisioned," 170.

16. Eve Kosofsky Sedgwick, *Epistemology of the Closet* (Berkeley: University of California Press, 1990), 150–1. On the sentimental "tableau" or "spectacle intéressant" and the fantasy of viewer or reader identification, see David Denby, *Sentimental Narrative and the Social Order in France, 1760–1820* (Cambridge: Cambridge University Press, 1994), 76.

17. Sedgwick, *Epistemology of the Closet*, 151.

18. For further discussion of the problem of Romantic masculinity, see Jeffrey Steele, *The Representation of Self in the American Renaissance* (Chapel Hill: University of North Carolina Press, 1987), quotation from 89.

19. See Tolchin, *Mourning, Gender, and Creativity*, 137.

20. Ann Douglas cites the "unceasing grief" of the New Bedford chapel women to support her assertion that in *Moby-Dick* "women are the mourners and the losers: they have no other role" (*The Feminization of American Culture* [New York: Alfred A. Knopf, 1977], 304). This conclusion does not account for many of the novel's women (e.g., the "squaw Tistig" [*MD* 79], the mother and stepmother of Ahab and Ishmael) or most of the feminized imagery, but it does at least single out an important motif in the novel's sentimental value scheme.

21. Nicholas Canaday, for example, blames Mrs. Glendinning and Pierre's feminized upbringing for the youth's ignorance of masculine norms (396), his "arrested sexuality" (399–400), and his authorial failure in "Pierre in the Domestic Circle," *Studies in the Novel* 18 (1986): 395–402; Cynthia S. Jordan calls the feminine forces in *Pierre* the "greatest threat" to the hero and to narrative form in *Second Stories: The Politics of Language, Form, and Gender in Early American Fictions* (Chapel Hill: University of North Carolina Press, 1989), 180, 190. See also Nina Baym, "Melodramas of Beset Manhood: How Theories of American Fiction Exclude Women Authors," *American Quarterly* 33 (1981): 123–39.

22. See Tompkins, *Sensational Designs*, 127–8.

23. On the competitive masculinity of Melville's sharks, I quote Henry Nash Smith, "The Image of Society in *"Moby-Dick,"*" in *"Moby-Dick": Centennial Essays*, intro. by Tyrus Hillway and Luther S. Mansfield (Dallas: Southern Methodist University Press, 1953), 59–75, quotations from 72.

24. Susan K. Harris, *19th-Century American Women's Novels: Interpretative Strategies* (Cambridge: Cambridge University Press, 1990), 20.

25. I allude to Melville's 1855 pair of sketches, "The Paradise of Bachelors and the Tartarus of Maids," which criticizes the privileged realm of homoeroticized male fellowship by exposing its exploitation of "maids." In the paper factory of Tartarus, an allegoric womb, the "maids" devote their dull lives to a nine–minute paper–making machine so that bachelors such as the narrator—a distributor of seeds—can conduct their businesses.

26. Martin, *Hero, Captain, Stranger,* 126.

27. Melville, *Correspondence,* ed. Lynn Horth (Evanston: Northwestern University Press and Newberry Library, 1993), 186 (hereafter cited as *C*).

[Ⓜ]

CHAPTER TWELVE

Sentimental Realism
in Thomas Eakins's Late Portraits

Martin A. Berger

He was the most consistent of American realists, and throughout the forty-five
years of his artistic career his point of view remained practically the same. . . .
The purpose of his work seems at times akin to that of a scientist—of a natural
historian who sets down the salient traits of the subject that he is studying.

When the curator of Thomas Eakins's memorial exhibition wrote these words in
1917, no American painter was more securely linked to realism than Eakins
(1844–1916).[1] From his first exhibition in 1871 until the present, both nineteenth-
and twentieth-century critics have consistently remarked on his unswerving alle-
giance to the realist tradition.

The realism that Victorian audiences found in Eakins's work was, of course,
not formed in a vacuum, but rather in relation to pre-existing styles of painting.
Romantic, sentimental, and later impressionist canvases offered foils that allowed
Eakins's contemporaries to classify his work. Of all these styles, sentimentality was
perhaps the most consequential in defining Eakins's realism, for few modes of
painting enjoyed greater critical acceptance or commercial success during the second half of the nineteenth century.

During much of the twentieth century, sentimentality has been disparaged for
its emphasis on exaggerated and false emotion.[2] But as scholars in recent years
have pointed out, sentimentality's links to artificiality are relatively new. First
appearing in England during the middle of the eighteenth century, "sentimental"
meant simply that which is "characterized by or exhibit[s] refined and elevated
feeling,"[3] and from its inception the term possessed generally positive associations.
It was only from the middle of the nineteenth century onward, after sentimental

thought achieved a measure of hegemony, that sentimentality came to be seen as the antithesis of the real and authentic.[4]

Even among those critics sympathetic to sentimentality, definitions of the term are notoriously supple. In part, this equivocality is explained by the fact that scholars have interpreted the cultural work of the sentimental so broadly. In the past fifteen years, scholars of nineteenth-century culture have pointed to the importance of sentimental ideology in the abolitionist and feminist movements, as well as in middle class formation, gender constructions, and nationalism.[5] During most of the nineteenth century—but especially between 1830 and 1860—sentimentality was much less a literary or painterly style than a way of ordering one's relation to the social world.

Despite the fluidity with which sentimentality has been defined, it is possible to generalize about the commonalities of those American canvases customarily called sentimental.[6] Unlike much of the midcentury's fiction, which Nathaniel Hawthorne derided because it was created by a "d——d mob of scribbling women,"[7] sentimental paintings and prints were produced largely by men for both male and female patrons. The majority of these images feature formulaic scenes of domestic life, often concentrating on women and children; most importantly, they illustrate scenes in which "emotion" commands a central place in the narrative. Rather than merely depicting emotional scenes, or prompting viewers' own emotional responses—though both of these ingredients are essential—sentimental art illustrates emotion as the ordering system of life.

Unlike Romantic texts (which similarly privilege emotion), sentimental works concern themselves less with spiritual transcendence than with the corporeal concerns of the body. In sentimental art, the body acts as conduit for emotions to pass between characters and readers. As Karen Sánchez-Eppler has noted, the corporeal signs offered by characters—their tears, wounds, and scars—communicate the depth of their feelings and so engender a corresponding physical response on the reader's part. For Sánchez-Eppler, what matters is the physicality involved in reading sentimental texts—the flesh and blood reader's experience of a fictional character's emotions, not clever rhetorical strategies or logical arguments—for this physicality "radically contracts the distance between narrated events and the moment of their reading, as the feelings in the story are made tangibly present in the flesh of the reader."[8] As long as sentimentality retained its associations with authentic feelings, the text's emotionality helped make the narrative seem real.

American sentimental painters, much like their literary peers, drew heavily from British prototypes, adapting the genre to fit the tastes of local markets. Whereas popular British painters such as Frank Holl (1845–1888) were able to sell many dark and brooding images of family life, including his 1875 *Doubtful Hope* (fig. 6), their American contemporaries built markets for more optimistic images.[9] The English immigrant painters John George Brown (1831–1913) and Seymour Joseph Guy (1824–1910) enjoyed great popularity in the United States, dominating

Figure 6. Frank Holl, *Doubtful Hope*, 1875. Forbes Magazine Collection, New York, N.Y.

Figure 7. John George Brown, *The Lost Child*, 1881. James F. Scott, Greenwood, Va.

Figure 8. Thomas Eakins, *The Gross Clinic*, 1875. Jefferson Medical College of Thomas Jefferson University, Philadelphia, Pa.

the American market with their hopeful scenes of domestic life. If Holl's sorrowful image of mother and child at the apothecary suggests sickness and the possibility of death, Brown's 1881 *The Lost Child* (fig. 7), with its depiction of a manageable and comparatively minor problem, is more typical of the types of sanguine paintings that American sentimentalists produced.

It was into this context of sentimental genre paintings that Eakins cast his early realist works. Paintings such as his 1875 *The Gross Clinic* (fig. 8) offered audiences a virtual manifesto of Eakins's artistic creed, presenting a graphic depiction of modern life. With his spotlit brow, Doctor Samuel Gross steps back from his operation to explain a technical point to the students arrayed around him in the amphitheater. Gross's controlled, thoughtful pose is contrasted with the evident alarm of the patient's mother, who sits to the doctor's right. With clenched hands shielding her face, the terrified figure recoils from the scene that the surgeon calmly surveys. In juxtaposing the famous surgeon with the anonymous mother—thus suggesting the triumph of masculine intellect over feminine emotion—the painting helps clarify Eakins's own artistic hierarchy.

Whereas Holl's painting foregrounds the anxious mother and places the men of science at the rear of the scene, Eakins's image reverses the equation by both highlighting the surgeons and relegating the grief-stricken mother to the margin of the canvas. In contrast with *Doubtful Hope, The Gross Clinic* asks its viewers to identify not with the patient's mother and her fears, but rather with the doctors, their knowledge, and their practised skills. If Holl's painting leaves viewers to ponder the child's fate, Eakins's canvas seems confidently to proclaim the mastery of Gross over the weakness and sickness of the body. Shunning sentimentality's focus on our emotional experience of life, Eakins's early canvases represent a world in which emotions are restrained by rational thought.

In a basic way, Eakins's painting attempts to separate the artist and his works from the culture of sentimentality that proliferated in painting during the second half of the nineteenth century. Responding to what were, from midcentury on, increasingly vigorous calls for a more "masculine" culture, Eakins presents us with a composition in which emotions, romance, and the notion of idealized art have no place next to the towering figure of Gross and the calm, calculated reason that he represents.[10] If "the masculine tone [was] passing out of the world," as Basil Ransom declares in Henry James's *The Bostonians* (1886), we get little sign of it in Eakins's canvas.[11]

Eakins's efforts to suppress *The Gross Clinic*'s sentimental strains ultimately point to the impossibility of creating art that is "purely" realist. *The Gross Clinic*'s realism rests heavily on the inclusion of the "hysterical" mother who offers a foil against which Gross and his operation might be defined. But even the operation itself—arguably the most "realist" passage of the canvas—aroused in Victorian audiences physical and emotional sensations more typically associated with sentimental texts. As a critic noted in 1876, the painting was "a picture that even strong men find difficult to look at long."[12] For many Victorians, viewing the canvas meant experiencing the very emotions that the work's narrative rails against.

Despite such ideological fissures, *The Gross Clinic* works hard to stress the divisions between realism and sentimentality. Confident in both his abilities and his chosen mode of representation, the artist reveled in his distinctiveness, deviating markedly from prevailing commercial styles.[13] Yet, within a decade of *The Gross Clinic*'s debut, Eakins's paintings expressed a more complicated relationship toward sentimental ideology, as commercial and critical success continued to elude him. If his paintings from the 1870s downplay ties to sentimental culture, many of Eakins's portraits from the late 1880s through the early 1900s work consciously to reinscribe stereotypically "sentimental" tropes into "realist" canvases for the express purpose of making the paintings appear more real and more masculine.

While Eakins is best known today for his two monumental paintings of surgical scenes and for his images of rowers on the Schuylkill River in Philadelphia, portraits comprise the vast majority of his artistic output. During the latter decades of his career, Eakins created hundreds of bust- and torso-sized portraits, unlike any others previously produced in America (figs. 9, 10). In these depictions, Eakins usually rendered his sitters in three-quarter profile with deep lines of shadow falling across their faces. Almost all the figures are dressed in old and worn clothing and placed against a shallow, blank background, with few or no props. But what makes these portraits unique is the artist's concern with imbuing his sitters with conspicuous emotions.

Eakins's persistence in dressing his sitters in casual clothing was unusual but not unprecedented in American art. John Singleton Copley (1738–1815), one of Eakins's naturalistic forebears, painted Paul Revere in his workaday silversmith clothing in the process of engraving a tea pot. Dismayed with what they perceived as too informal a depiction, Revere's descendants rolled up Copley's canvas and stored it out of sight.[14] From the colonial period through the close of the Victorian era, such casual dress suggested that viewers were catching the sitter in an intimate and personal moment.

While Victorian portraits were often crowded with identifiable props as clear emblems of the sitter's social status or profession, Eakins's late portraits are generally spare. Not only does Eastman Johnson's 1859 *portrait d'apparat* of Genio Scott (fig. 11) place the sitter in a recognizable room, but the stack of books to his right and the fishing pole to his left point to Scott's profession as a publisher and to his favorite pastime. Having eliminated both props and setting in most of his portraits, Eakins compelled viewers to comprehend the sitters based solely on his depiction of their worn clothing, physical features, and expressions.

Whether painted or photographed, nineteenth-century portraits rarely showed their sitters' feelings, and the depictions never displayed overt sadness. Yet almost all of Eakins's late portraits feature worn, haggard faces, many of them misty eyed, and some doubtless on the verge of tears. The obvious emotionality of Eakins's portraits was not lost on Victorian audiences. If many sitters refused to pick up their portraits, or later returned them, or simply had them destroyed, they frequently claimed that Eakins got the "expression" wrong. "Not a good likeness," "entirely too severe," or "too old," were frequent complaints voiced by Eakins's would-be patrons. Upset with how the artist had rendered her head, one sitter recalled that "Thomas Eakins was not interested in my face—I have always felt a sense of being decapitated." Even when Eakins's portraits were accepted, the sitters' families tried hard to explain away the obvious emotions by claiming that, "Mother was sick when this was painted," or "Father was very tired," or "having business troubles."[15] Whether driving patrons to reject the portraits outright, or

Figure 9. Thomas Eakins, *William H. Macdowell*, ca. 1904. Memorial Art Gallery of the University of Rochester, Rochester, N.Y. Marion Stratton Gould Fund.

compelling viewers to explain the sitters' unusual emotionality, the corporeal quality of Eakins's portraits engendered strong emotional reactions on the part of Victorian audiences.

The canvases' overt emotionalism, however, never dissuaded Victorian critics from proclaiming Eakins's realist credentials. Despite the fact that his portraits depict figures that were commonly held to be uncharacteristically worn and emotional, Eakins's contemporaries were never shaken from their belief that the painter was a realist. In commenting on the head of a typically haggard portrait,

Figure 10. Thomas Eakins, *Mrs. Edith Mahon*, 1904. Smith College Museum of Art, Northampton, Mass.

a reporter for the *New York Times* wrote that "the face and attitude are realism itself."[16] But all of this merely begs the questions of why Eakins would have employed such a potentially feminized style, and how critics could have ignored what seems—from our present-day vantage point—to be Eakins's obvious debts to the sentimental.

For Eakins, sentimentality would have been both alluring and frightening. The allure stemmed from the highly commercial qualities of the genre: craving sales, yet unable to sell more than a handful of his realist canvases, Eakins would have

Figure 11. Eastman Johnson, *Genio Scott*, 1859. The Cleveland Museum of Art, Cleveland, Ohio.

been aware that sentimental paintings enjoyed a substantial share of the art market. Sales were very important for the artist's self-esteem, for in many ways Eakins had failed to live up to the masculine standards of his middle-class Victorian peers. Unable to earn a livelihood, long unmarried, living with his parents, having bought his way out of Civil War service, and working in a profession that had long held feminine associations, Eakins possessed what might best be termed an awkward masculine subject position.[17] Of all these, Eakins's inability to support himself was surely the most significant to both the artist and his contemporaries, for increasingly over the second half of the nineteenth century, nothing defined manhood as forcefully as a man's success or failure at work.[18] Thus by the late 1880s, after suffering a series of personal and professional setbacks—not least a forced resignation from his teaching position at the prestigious Pennsylvania Academy of the Fine Arts, and the resulting financial insecurity—Eakins concentrated almost exclusively on portrait painting.[19] Given that American artists had long relied on portraits to earn their livelihoods, even as they craved commissions for loftier historical or religious scenes, it is only logical that the artist would have turned his attention to the most commercial genre of painting in an effort both to support himself and to reaffirm his manhood.

But despite the obvious commercial allure of sentimental art, Eakins had to be careful about how he appropriated sentimentality, for Victorians generally allied it with the feminine. Given that his masculine position was already problematic, the painter could hardly have wished to encourage additional links between himself and feminine culture. Eakins's late portraits managed to avoid sentimentality's feminine resonances only because his reputation as a realist had been so firmly established by early paintings such as *The Gross Clinic,* and because of the particular ways in which he and the Victorian press promoted his links to realism. Instead of imagining his realism as a function of either his subject matter or the mimetic precision of individual canvases, critics have long assumed it to be grounded in the artist's peculiarly scientific working methods.

During both the nineteenth and twentieth centuries, commentators have explained Eakins's realism as a function of his obsessive use of trigonometric equations, perspective sketches, stop-action photographs, wax figurines, nude studies, and dissections.[20] This assumed relation between production technique and style has tended to downplay nuances in the paintings themselves by elevating process over content. Not only has this structuralist production-model tended to de-emphasize narrative and stylistic developments in Eakins's work, but it has also masked attributes of the paintings that do not neatly fit into the realist camp. Because Eakins's realist affiliation was formed through a process that relegated analysis of style and subject matter—and hence ideology—to secondary importance, the sentimental strains of many of his later canvases have long remained buried.

It is because the "realism" of these works was largely preestablished by their means of production that scholars have usually rationalized the paintings' appearances with "masculine" as opposed to "feminine" explanations. In other words, since the realism of the canvases was taken for granted, it was easier for critics to tie the paintings' meanings to the masculinity of science than to the femininity of emotions, given realism's largely masculine associations by the 1880s.[21] Beginning in the late nineteenth century, Eakins's emotion-laden portraits were singled out for their creator's facility in illuminating the "psychology" (rather than the feelings) of his sitters. Many viewers assumed that his portraits revealed worn and sad individuals because the artist was able to penetrate their public personas, so presenting their true selves. Reviewing the 1885 Annual Exhibition at the Pennsylvania Academy of the Fine Arts, a commentator claimed that

> with Mr. Eakins portraiture is realism. . . . He has manifestly a way of getting at the very psychology of his model through its external characteristics, which strikes me as almost uncanny. . . . The sitter may have done his best; he has certainly been unable to circumvent Mr. Eakins'[s] fatal penetration.[22]

Explaining his reticence to sit for a portrait by Eakins, the painter Edwin Austin Abbey claimed that "he would bring out all those traits of my character that I have been trying to conceal from the public for years."[23]

By the start of the twentieth century, the cliché of Eakins as a psychological portraitist was so firmly entrenched that articles and monographs on the artist invariably made reference to his psychological penetration. John Wilmerding, for example, writes of "the disturbing insights into private truths confronting us in Eakins'[s] portraits."[24] Likewise, William Homer claims that Eakins's "profound knowledge of the human head and body provided a foundation for his unusual skill in penetrating surface appearances to reveal the psychological traits of . . . subjects."[25] By cloaking these works under a psychological mantle, both nineteenth- and twentieth-century critics have downplayed the canvases' emotional qualities, implying that Eakins's vision goes much deeper.

Eakins's works may be psychological, but certainly not in the Freudian terms that late-twentieth-century audiences typically assume. Eakins's brand of psychology more closely approximates that of the Paris-based neurologist Jean Martin Charcot, who popularised the study of the mind during the late 1860s while the painter trained in France. Now almost completely forgotten outside of academic circles, Charcot and his Salpêtrière School developed a modern, clinical approach for the study of hysterics, even as his methods retained strong ties to older positivist traditions. Credited with teaching Freud about the importance of symptoms for studying mental illness, Charcot's own work nonetheless relied on physiognomical studies that purported to reveal essential qualities of mind and character based on an individual's external characteristics. During Eakins's lifetime, the battle fought by Freudian theorists against the belief that our internal, mental workings are manifest merely in our physical appearance was far from won.

Many twentieth-century critics have used Eakins's portraits to "psychoanalyze" his sitters, implicitly assured that the painter's realism elevated their projects above those of mere physiognomists.[26] While it is true that Freud himself attempted to analyze Leonardo da Vinci through his art and writings, Freud would never have considered using a portrait to psychoanalyze its sitter.[27] Critics' desire to perform such analyses relates much more closely to Charcot's own idiosyncratic project of diagnosing hysterics retrospectively from portraits than it corresponds to anything resembling modern psychological practice.[28] A number of contemporary scholars, as well as some of Eakins's peers, may have believed that the portraits provided them a glimpse into the internal, mental workings of the sitter, but given that the "evidence" they were offered was nothing more than a naturalistic look at the external, physical manifestation of the sitter's visage, we must question how such knowledge could be possible in modern psychological terms.[29]

To be sure, naturalistic portraits depicting a sitter's interiority have existed at least since the Renaissance, but interiority should not be confused with a psychological self. That, in the end, is one of the strongest arguments against the existence of a naturalistic psychological portraiture, since many of the portraits by Franz Hals, Rembrandt, and Diego de Velázquez—produced long before the concept of the psychological existed—"look" as psychological as anything Eakins created in turn-of-the-century America. Precisely because Freudian psychology shuns physiognomic readings as the ultimate proof of an individual's mental condition, psychological portraiture—in any modern sense—was not a possibility prior to the abstract portraits by artists such as Constantin Brancusi and Pablo Picasso.

For twentieth-century audiences, then, the label "psychological" is highly misleading. Rather than accentuating the bodily nature of the portraits—their obvious corporeality and emotionality—the label effectively severs the sitters from their bodies by coupling them to a more modern conception of psychology. In the process, viewers have lost the portraits' historical connections to physiognomical and phrenological theories, thus further distancing the works from sentimental associations.[30] Whether they are aware of it or not, viewers of Eakins's portraits, readers of sentimental fiction, and physiognomists share much in common, with each searching expectantly for internal meaning in the external signs of the body.[31]

But the question remains as to why Eakins embraced sentimentality decades after its eclipse by realism. Its allure for Eakins at the century's close was not, I believe, radically different from what first captured American interest in the sentimental. Karen Halttunen has explained the development in antebellum America of a sentimental typology, which held that forms of dress and behaviour should stand as outward signs of an individual's authentic, inner character. Developed originally to counteract the "false" dictates of fashion, this typology self-destructed when its success led to the establishment of new rituals that became as stylish and as institutionalized as any of the "artificial" fashions that they replaced. According to Halttunen, the very ubiquity of sentimentality at midcentury led increasingly, during the 1860s and 1870s, to the perception that sentimentality itself was artificial and its dictates arbitrary.[32] Sentimentality, of course, never completely faded from American culture, but by the late 1880s, when Eakins began to incorporate sentimental tropes into his canvases, its authenticity in literature, social customs, and at times genre paintings was questioned by Victorian audiences. In portraiture, however, Eakins was able to give his sitters "authentic" emotions with sentimental conceits precisely because of the era's paucity of sentimental portrait images. Just as sentimentality was understood as real when it was introduced into social rituals in the 1830s, so it was real again when Eakins recycled it into his late-century portraits. Because emotions were so infrequently depicted in portraiture, his standard sentimental tropes were construed by both nineteenth- and twentieth-century audiences as "real." Emotions were more real—and hence more masculine—because of a context in which they were so rare.

Eakins's project was not consciously political. He certainly had little desire to problematize artistic or cultural categories for the purpose of expanding the sphere of feminine culture in Victorian America. What interested him was the creation of a portrait style that was at the same time both more masculine and more commercial than that of his earlier canvases. If Eakins never hit on a profitable formula that might have challenged the popularity of fashionable portraitists, then he at least crafted a distinct genre of portraiture that reinforced his metaphoric ties to male culture. The portraits are ultimately interesting less for the means by which twentieth-century revisionists may interpret their sentimentality, than for the fact that such strains have remained buried for more than a century. Given the paintings' strong visual connections to sentimentality, they offer a clear testament to the powerful cultural desire of nineteenth- and twentieth-century audiences to guard realism from what they perceive as the corrupting, feminine influences of the sentimental.

NOTES

1. Bryson Burroughs, *Loan Exhibition of the Works of Thomas Eakins* (New York: Metropolitan Museum of Art, 1917), vi. The catalogue for Eakins's memorial exhibition in Philadelphia voiced much the same opinion, claiming that the artist was "destined to become the greatest of all modern realists" (Gilbert Sunderland Parker, *Memorial Exhibition of the Works of the Late Thomas Eakins* [Philadelphia: Pennsylvania Academy of the Fine Arts, 1917], 7).

2. For twentieth-century studies critical of sentimentality, see for example Herbert Ross Brown, *The Sentimental Novel in America, 1789–1860* (Durham: Duke University Press, 1940); Ann Douglas, *The Feminization of American Culture* (New York: Knopf, 1977); and Howard W. Fulweiler, *"Here a Captive Heart Busted": Studies in the Sentimental Journey of Modern Literature* (New York: Fordham University Press, 1993). See also the discussion in the introduction to the present volume.

3. Oxford English Dictionary, 2d ed., s.v. "sentimental."

4. For a detailed discussion of the evolving meanings of sentimentality, see Fred Kaplan, *Sacred Tears: Sentimentality in Victorian Literature* (Princeton: Princeton University Press, 1987), 11–20.

5. For an especially varied collection of essays examining the cultural work of sentimentality, see Shirley Samuels, ed., *The Culture of Sentiment: Race, Gender, and Sentimentality in Nineteenth-Century America* (Oxford: Oxford University Press, 1992). This collection and related works are also discussed in the introduction to the present volume.

6. For a discussion of sentimental subject matter in American art, see Lee M. Edwards, *Domestic Bliss: Family Life in American Painting, 1840–1910* (New York: The Hudson River Museum, 1986). For studies that examine the function of sentimentality in American art, see Joy S. Kasson, *Marble Queens and Captives: Women in Nineteenth-Century American Sculpture* (New Haven: Yale University Press, 1990) and David M. Lubin, "Lilly Martin Spencer's Domestic Genre Painting in Antebellum America," in David C. Miller, ed., *American Iconology: New Approaches to Nineteenth-Century Art and Literature* (New Haven: Yale University Press, 1993), 135–62.

7. Hawthorne to William D. Ticknor, 19 January 1855, in *The Centenary Edition of the Works of Nathaniel Hawthorne*, vol. 17, ed. Thomas Woodson, James A. Rubino, L. Neal Smith, and Norman Holmes Pearson (Columbus: Ohio State University Press, 1987), 304.

8. Karen Sánchez-Eppler, *Touching Liberty: Abolition, Feminism, and the Politics of the Body* (Berkeley: University of California Press, 1993), 26–7.

9. For more on English sentimental painting, see Julian Treuherz, *Hard Times: Social Realism in Victorian Art* (Manchester: Manchester City Art Galleries, 1987).

10. David E. Shi, *Facing Facts: Realism in American Thought and Culture, 1850–1920* (Oxford: Oxford University Press, 1995), 26–9.

11. Henry James, *The Bostonians* (New York: Macmillan and Company, 1886), 333.

12. "The Society of American Artists Second Annual Exhibition," *New York Daily Tribune,* 22 March 1879, 6. For sentimentality's investment in the body, see Ann Cvetkovich, *Mixed Feelings: Feminism, Mass Culture, and Victorian Sensationalism* (New Brunswick, N.J.: Rutgers University Press, 1992), 27; see also Sánchez-Eppler, *Touching Liberty,* 14–49.

13. As late as 1904, Eakins was still proud of his distinctive painting style, writing in a letter of its "divergent character" and its "novel" qualities (quoted in Lloyd Goodrich, *Thomas Eakins* [Cambridge: Harvard University Press, 1982], 2:230).

14. Carrie Rebora, Paul Staiti, Erica E. Hirshler, Theodore Stebbins Jr., and Carol Troyen, *John Singleton Copley in America* (New York: Harry N. Abrams, 1995), 248–9.

15. Quoted in Goodrich, *Thomas Eakins,* 2:78, 231, 234, 78, 242, 78.

16. *New York Times,* 1 January 1905, quoted in Gordon Hendricks, *The Life and Work of Thomas Eakins* (New York: Grossman, 1974), 250.

17. For more on Eakins's failure to be manly, see Martin A. Berger, "Painting Victorian Manhood," in Helen Cooper, ed., *Thomas Eakins: The Rowing Pictures* (New Haven: Yale University Art Gallery and Yale University Press, 1996), 102–23, especially 104–6.

18. See E. Anthony Rotundo, *American Manhood: Transformations in Masculinity from the Revolution to the Modern Era* (New York: Basic Books, 1993), 167–9, 178–93; Robert L. Griswold, *Fatherhood in America: A History* (New York: Basic Books, 1993), 13–4.

19. For more on the scandal surrounding Eakins's resignation, see Kathleen A. Foster and Cheryl Leibold, *Writing About Eakins: The Manuscripts in Charles Bregler's Thomas Eakins Collection* (Philadelphia: University of Pennsylvania Press, 1989), 69–79, 214–8, 235–9.

20. Such a link between the artist's realism and his scientific production techniques was first articulated by William C. Brownell ("The Art Schools of Philadelphia," *Scribner's Monthly Illustrated Magazine* 20 [May 1880]: 1–15), but it has been picked up by every subsequent study devoting serious attention to Eakins. For recent twentieth-century examples, see Goodrich, *Thomas Eakins;* Elizabeth Johns, *Thomas Eakins: The Heroism of Modern Life* (Princeton: Princeton University Press, 1983); and William Innes Homer, *Thomas Eakins: His Life and Art* (New York: Abbeville Press, 1992). For a work that complicates understandings of Eakins's realism, see Michael Fried, *Realism, Writing, Disfiguration: on Thomas Eakins and Stephen Crane* (Chicago: University of Chicago Press, 1987).

21. Naomi Schor, *Reading in Detail: Aesthetics and the Feminine* (New York: Methuen, 1987), 4, 42–7; Shi, *Facing Facts,* 7–9, 34–6.

22. "Academy Exhibition—Second Notice," *The Press,* 31 October 1885.

23. Quoted in Goodrich, *Thomas Eakins,* 2:77.

24. John Wilmerding, "The Tensions of Biography and Art in Thomas Eakins," in John Wilmerding, ed., *Thomas Eakins (1844–1916) and the Heart of American Life* (London: National Portrait Gallery, 1993), 16–35, quotation from 34.

25. Homer, *Thomas Eakins,* 7.

26. For examples of this kind of "analysis" in recent Eakins scholarship, see the entries on *Amelia Van Buren, Maud Cook, Louis N. Kenton,* and *Alice Kurtz,* in Wilmerding, *Thomas Eakins,* 120–1, 124–5, 148–9, 158–9.

27. Sigmund Freud, *Leonardo da Vinci and a Memory of his Childhood,* trans. Alan Tyson (New York: W. W. Norton & Company, 1964).

28. The scientific and artistic interests of Charcot and Eakins overlap in many important ways. Not only did Eakins depict medical themes in painting, but he was convinced that dissections and anatomical study of the human body were essential for the creation of art. Charcot, for his part, founded two journals, *Iconographie de la Salpêtrière* and *Nouvelle Iconographie de la Salpêtrière,* both of which combined discussions of art and medicine. See Ludy T. Benjamin, Jr., *A History of Psychology: Original Sources and Contemporary Research* (New York: McGraw-Hill, 1988), 140. For Charcot's efforts to diagnose hysteria from portraits, see Jean-Martin Charcot, *Les Démoniaques Dans L'Art* (Paris: Delahaye & Lecrosnier, 1887).

29. David M. Lubin has recently argued that Eakins's late portraits might have actually contributed to the development of the concept of the psychological ("Thomas Eakins and the Rhetoric of Dejection," in *Inventing the Psychological: Toward a Cultural History of Emotional Life in America,* ed. Joel Pfister and Nancy Schnog [New Haven: Yale University Press, 1997], 133–66).

30. At least two Eakins scholars have linked the artist's portraits to physiognomical traditions, but their discussions have focused on Eakins's interest in average types; see Kate Kernan Rubin, "Thomas Eakins, *The Veteran,*" *Yale University Art Gallery Bulletin* 39 (Winter 1984): 20–4, and Nicolai Cicovsky, Jr., "*The Art Student (Portrait of an Artist),*" in *American Paintings from the Manoogian Collection* (Washington: National Gallery of Art, 1989), 126–31. I believe that physiognomic discourses were of interest to Eakins precisely for their ability to portray distinct individuals. For more on physiognomy's potential for individuating faces, see Alan Sekula, "The Body and the Archive," *October* 39 (Winter 1986): 3–64.

31. Karen Sánchez-Eppler first drew my attention to this connection by linking readers of sentimental fiction to phrenologists, who occupy a subcategory of the physiognomic tradition (Sánchez-Eppler, *Touching Liberty,* 29). For more on physiognomical thought, see Christopher Rivers, *Face Value: Physiognomical Thought and the Legible Body in Marivaux, Lavater, Balzac, Gautier, and Zola* (Madison: University of Wisconsin Press, 1994); for physiognomy in art, see Mary Cowling, *The Artist as Anthropologist: The Representation of Type and Character in Victorian Art* (Cambridge: Cambridge University Press, 1989).

32. Karen Halttunen, *Confidence Men and Painted Ladies: A Study of Middle-Class Culture in America, 1830–1870* (New Haven: Yale University Press, 1982), 188–90.

CHAPTER THIRTEEN

M

Sentimental Tentacles

Frank Norris's The Octopus

Francesca Sawaya

"A Plea for Romantic Fiction" (1901), Frank Norris's famous manifesto for what he called "Romantic" or "naturalistic" writing,[1] begins with a dramatic expulsion of sentimentalism from the topic of analysis:

> Let us at the start make a distinction. Observe that one speaks of Romanticism and not of sentimentalism. One claims that the latter is as distinct from the former as is that other form of art which is called Realism. Romance has been often put upon and overburdened by being forced to bear the onus of abuse that by right should fall to sentiment; but the two should be kept very distinct, for a very high and illustrious place will be claimed for Romance, while sentiment will be handed down the scullery stairs. (*LC* 75)

Realism, Norris makes clear, "is very excellent as far as it goes" (*LC* 76), and can be combined with Romance to create great art, but sentimentalism—in one of the numerous and inconsistent personifications of genre in the essay—is apparently the scullery maid who must be hustled out the back stairs. Sentimentalism's crime seems to be that it has not only been *linked* to Romance, but also that this linking has allowed it to escape the abuse that it deserves and that Romance has instead received. There is something rather Christ-like in the imagery associated with Romance, which has been "forced to bear" critical abuse for the sins of sentimentality.

This image of Christ is one I shall discuss later. What I want to focus on here is the way analyses of Norris's writing and of naturalism have followed his advice on handing sentimentalism "down the scullery stairs." Norris's essay suggests that there is a relation between naturalism and sentimentalism, albeit a scandalous upstairs / downstairs relation that must be hidden; however, critics who follow Norris have simply ignored it. In traditional versions of American literary history, critics narrate a story in which only two serious genres compete at the turn of the century—realism and naturalism. As the story goes, realism's "optimistic" view of man's ability to act and think freely evolved in the late nineteenth century into naturalism's "pessimistic" view that man is predetermined to act in certain ways.[2] While realism's optimism and naturalism's pessimism have been problematized,[3] the pairing of the two genres has remained constant. A discussion of each genre has entailed and continues to entail a discussion of the other. Meanwhile, the scullery maid of sentimentalism tends to appear only as a figure of those unfortunate lapses in judgment to which even the greatest authors (and genres) are prone.[4]

There are many good reasons why realism and naturalism have been paired in American literary studies, not least of which is, as the case of Norris suggests, that realist and naturalist authors defined their works in relation to each other. But surely one must ask why it was important for American naturalists always to position their writing in relation to realist writing. Why were the two categories of realism and naturalism continuously explored in their works, while sentimentalism disappeared from the field of analysis? And relatedly, why have critics followed in these writers' footsteps? Besides the tendency of literary histories to narrate a seamless progression from one movement to the next, there is a politics of classification at work here that is worth exploring.

Mark Seltzer's brilliant analysis of the links between scientific theories of sexual difference and the development of the naturalist novel helps us begin to explore this politics of classification. The naturalist novel, he argues, "registers . . . a displaced competition between rival sexual forces, between what Norris, for instance, calls the 'two world-forces, the elemental Male and Female' " (*BM* 27). These "world-forces," Seltzer says, are figured in the naturalist novel as the machine and the mother, respectively. The discourse of the machine in naturalism works to "displace . . . the colossal mother," and to "place . . . power back into the hands of the immortal and autonomous male technology of generation" (*BM* 31). Seltzer demonstrates the way naturalism constructed itself through "scientific," abstract accounts of force and generation as "an emphatically 'male' genre" (*BM* 29), and the way that sexual difference is deployed in the naturalist novel so that it reproduces the antinomies it constructs. Although Seltzer ends by once again exploring the question of naturalism's relation to realism, his work provides us with an important clue as to why sentimentalism disappeared from analyses of naturalism. If, as Seltzer convincingly argues, the biological mother is displaced in naturalism, then the thematics and aesthetics indissociably linked to her in nineteenth-century sentimentalism must also have been displaced.

This essay relies on Seltzer's conclusions about how science was used in the naturalist narrative to explain and justify "gender inequalities" (*BM* 41) in society. But I want to return to the thematics and aesthetics associated with the figure of the mother, a figure who Seltzer has shown is crucial to naturalism's self-construction. While I assume the social factors that Seltzer describes are at work, I focus instead on how they are, as Pierre Bourdieu would say, "retranslated into the specific logic" of the "literary field" at the turn of the century, where "entirely specific struggles" occur, "notably [struggles] concerning the question of knowing who is part of the [literary field], who is a real writer and who is not."[5]

At the same time that gender inequality was being given a biological basis, and naturalism was using that biology to construct its thematics and aesthetics, literary study in the United States was becoming professionalized. In this essay, I argue that, in order to construct itself as a serious genre, worthy of scrutiny by the new literary professionals, naturalism worked at distancing itself from any association with femininity, or the genre perceived as feminine—sentimentalism. By pairing realism and naturalism, writers at the turn of the century could bypass the possibility that the sentimentalism of the "feminine fifties" had had an effect on these serious genres, defined as worthy of serious, academic study. Specifically, I argue that naturalism's construction of itself as a serious genre results in a dependence on the sentimentalism against which it defines itself. An analysis of Frank Norris's naturalist novel *The Octopus* (1901) helps solidify this claim.

ı'ı

Between 1890 and 1915, as Gerald Graff has demonstrated, modern literary study in the United States—which before that time had been indissociably associated with women's colleges—sought to efface its "reputation for effeminacy."[6] Not coincidentally, the university at large was at the same time seeking to refashion itself as a professional and scientific institution.[7] Frank Norris's critical writings perhaps best exemplify the coordination between the defeminization and professionalization of academic literary study, and the development of naturalism. Despite his claims to the contrary, Norris was an academically trained writer, studying literature first at the University of California, Berkeley (1890–4), and then at Harvard (1894–5),[8] and Norris's writings compulsively seek to prove that serious (i.e., naturalist) literature is necessarily masculine. Just as compulsively, however, he demonstrates the fragility of this masculinity, which in his writings is always threatened by women and women's culture. The threat posed by women, therefore, shapes his definition of professional (masculine) authorship.

The importance of gender in Norris's understanding of authorship is most evident in his discussions of training. In order to construct authorship as professional work, Norris argues consistently throughout his critical essays that being a poet is "a question of training" (*LC* 15), and that the notion that " 'poets are born not made' . . . is sheer nonsense" (*LC* 14). But while such a notion of training may seem gender neutral, Norris makes clear in a variety of places why it is not. For example, in "Why Women Should Write the Best Novels: And Why They Don't" (1901), Norris argues that while women have the "leisure, . . . education, . . . [and] temperament" to become writers, "[i]t is, of course, a conceded fact that . . . the producers of the best fiction are men and not women" (*LC* 35). Such a "fact" is explained as being social in its roots: because "the majority of women still lead, in comparison with men, secluded lives" (*LC* 36), their writing is shaped by "literature" and not "life" (*LC* 35), hence their writing fails.[9]

But because this argument leaves open the possibility that women could, in the future, become "producers of the best fiction," Norris concludes his essay by using the argument for inborn genius, the very argument which he had previously described as "sheer nonsense." Besides their lack of "experience," Norris writes, women have "more specialized" brains than men (*LC* 36). They therefore "try to do too much, to polish too highly, to develop more perfectly," and are finally reduced to "hysteria" (*LC* 36). And, Norris asks, "who shall say how many good, even great, novels have remained half written, to be burned in the end, because their women authors mistook lack of physical strength for lack of genuine ability?" (*LC* 36).

This curious conclusion, which imagines women novelists burning their too polished, too perfect drafts, seems to satisfy Norris. Nonetheless, it raises the question of how any woman could have "genuine ability," given women's lack of experience and their "specialized" brains. The answer can be found in Norris's claim that authorial ability is simply a question of training, and that such training should include academic work:

> From almost the very first the young man studies with an eye to business, or to a profession. . . . But what girls' seminary does not prescribe the study of literature through all its three or four years, making of this study a matter of all importance? And while the courses of literature do not, by any manner of means, make a novelist, they familiarize the student with style and the means by which words are put together. The more one reads, the easier one writes. (*LC* 34)[10]

Despite their secluded lives and specialized brains, some women have "genuine" literary ability because they have been trained in college to read and understand literature.

In fact, it is women college students and the academic writing they produce that seems to worry Norris the most, and it is these women for whom he reserves his greatest spleen.[11] To indict the literary training he received at Berkeley, for example, Norris argues that it is women and effeminate men who are most productive under this method of training:

> The "co-eds" take to the "classification" method even better than the young men. They thrive and fatten intellectually on the regime. They consider themselves literary. They write articles on the "Philosophy of Dante" for the college weekly, and after graduation they "read papers" to literary "circles" composed of post-graduate "co-eds," the professors' wives and daughters and a very few pale young men in spectacles and black cutaway coats. After the reading of the "paper" follows the "discussion," aided and abetted by cake and lemonade. This is literature! Isn't it admirable! (*LC* 7)

This description obviously registers a competitive anxiety about these greedy consumers and excessive producers of literature and lemonade, who are attempting to assume the mantle of professionalism. But it is also self-reflective. If co-eds fatten on classification, Norris does as well, for it is through classification that he is able to expel co-eds from the literary field, if only figuratively, since the literal co-eds were apparently not burning their papers to the degree that their novelist sisters were. Remember that his manifesto for naturalism, "A Plea for Romantic Fiction," begins in the best classificatory fashion: "Let us at the start make a distinction." And that distinction, which erases sentimental women's writing, is repeated in all his discussions of naturalism.

Expelling women and women's writing from the literary field in order to define serious, professional (i.e., naturalist) literature as masculine became a gesture embedded in the study of American literature. The Harvard philosopher George Santayana's essay "The Genteel Tradition in American Philosophy" (1911), an essay crucial to the development of professional American literary studies,[12] enacts the same expulsion. First delivered as a talk at Norris's California alma mater, "The Genteel Tradition" has generally been read as Santayana's critique of the timidity of American intellectual traditions (particularly New England's intellectual traditions) in face of the supposed creativity of American business life;[13] however, this dichotomy is worked out in the essay as a specifically gendered one. In his famous description of America's exuberant business life and its derivative aesthetic traditions, Santayana writes that this bifurcation

> may be found symbolised in American architecture: a neat reproduction of the colonial mansion—with some modern comforts introduced surreptitiously—stands beside the sky-scraper. The American Will inhabits the sky-scraper; the American Intellect inhabits the colonial mansion. The one is the sphere of the American man; the other, at least predominantly, of the American woman. The one is all aggressive enterprise; the other is all genteel tradition. (*SA* 38)

Santayana's use of the language of separate spheres—the public, modern building versus the private, historical home—clearly refers to sentimentality, and thus associates America's bankrupt and derivative American intellectual traditions, "at least predominantly," with women and sentimentalism. He concludes his talk with a paean not only to the redemptive powers of nature but to the redemptive powers of philosophical naturalism. Philosophical naturalism, exercised on the frontier, creates a democratic revolution in aesthetics that will overthrow the "genteel tradition":

> This revolution, I should think, might well find an echo among you [Californians], who live in a thriving society, and in the presence of a virgin and prodigious world. When you transform nature to your uses, when you experiment with her forces, and reduce them to industrial agents, you cannot feel that nature was made by you or for you, for then these adjustments would have been pre-established. . . . [I]t is the yoke of this genteel tradition itself that these primeval solitudes lift from your shoulders. (*SA* 54–6)

What my brief history of the relation of literary professionalization to naturalism suggests is that naturalism created itself, in part, by insisting on its masculinity and its relation to other "masculine" genres (like realism), and by opposing itself to femininity and the "feminine" genre of sentimentalism. At the same time, however, to prove its value and virtue, writers depicted naturalism as a threatened and suffering masculine genre beset by women sentimentalists. These women sentimentalists, in their colonial mansions, never venturing out into the "primeval solitudes," are protected from the criticism they rightfully deserve. Worse yet, they sit in their mansions, reading their work to each other, imagining *incorrectly* that "This is literature!" (*LC* 7). Meanwhile, male naturalists, with no inherited rights or property, do daily battle with "primeval solitudes," for which they are crucified by the very criticism that should rightfully apply to the protected sentimentalists. Adapting Nina Baym's formulation, one could say that these naturalist writers narrate sentimental stories of beset professional manhood.

Eve Kosofsky Sedgwick has suggested in her extraordinary rereading of sentimentalism that sentimentalism may really be at the core of the self-pitying struggles over "masculine identity" from the 1880s to World War I, during which time

> the exemplary instance of the sentimental ceases to be a woman per se, but instead becomes the body of a man who . . . physically dramatizes, *embodies* for an audience that both desires and cathartically identifies with him, a struggle of masculine identity with emotions or physical stigmata stereotyped as feminine.

Specifically, she argues, male sentimentalism is worked out "in the explicit context of the displayed body of Jesus."[14] Such an analysis works for both Norris and Santayana, who metaphorically link a masculine naturalism to Christ: naturalism wrongfully bears the sins of the "genteel tradition" even as it works to escape that tradition's "yoke." The cases of Norris and Santayana further suggest that sentimentalism is at the core of struggles over the identity of professional literary studies in the United States at this time. Norris's *The Octopus* exemplifies these literary struggles, both in its explicit critiques of sentimentalism and in its seemingly unconscious use and appropriation of it.

᛫᛫᛫

The Octopus depicts the primary problem with sentimentalism through the figure of the mother. Against the personal, individual, and domestic power of the sentimental mother, Norris poses a universe governed by abstract and impersonal force. The moment the familiar and personal power accorded to the sentimental mother is invoked in *The Octopus,* then, it must be negated by a "factual" account of naturalist force.[15] The best example of this critique through negation occurs in the depiction of Hilma Tree, at first the sentimental girl and later, more crucially, the sentimental mother *par excellence.*

In the tradition of sentimentalism, Hilma Tree morally creates Annixter when she marries him. Annixter describes her effect on him to the poet Presley: "she's made a man of me. . . . [A]s soon as I woke up to the fact that I really loved her, why, it was glory hallelujah all in a minute, and, in a way, I kind of loved everybody then."[16] When Hilma becomes pregnant, her influence expands: at a picnic, sitting on a rise above everyone, "as on a throne, raised above the rest, the radiance of the unseen crown of motherhood glowing from her forehead," her status as mother leads the rough ranchers around her to bare their heads in honor of her and to refrain from using foul language (*O* 504). Meanwhile, Annixter, "living in this influence of a wife, who was also a mother," is described in true sentimental fashion as "trembling on the verge of a mighty transformation" (*O* 497). To negate this version of "sentimental power," Norris has the abstract force of Nature (embodied by the railroad) kill Annixter and the rancher whom Hilma has influenced immediately following the picnic, while Hilma herself miscarries her child.[17]

This direct attack on sentimental accounts of the mother's personal power is echoed most dramatically by the novel's infamous ending. After most of the novel's main characters have been killed, Presley reflects on the greater good that is done despite "the welter of blood":

> But the WHEAT remained. Untouched, unassailable, undefiled, that mighty world-force . . . moved onward in its appointed grooves. . . . Falseness dies; injustice and oppression in the end of everything fade and vanish away. Greed, cruelty, selfishness, and inhumanity are short-lived; the individual suffers, but the race goes on. Annixter dies, but in a far distant corner of the world a thousand lives are saved. (*O* 651–2)

Force wins out not only over "the Mother" (*O* 496), but also over the personalized narrative form of sentimentalism.

But this ending, which has received so much criticism, could be read in a different way. In these last two paragraphs of the novel, thousands of lives "are saved," while "Annixter dies." Why this invocation of one specific individual, namely Annixter, at the moment when abstract impersonal force triumphs? Annixter is being figured here in the same way that naturalism is in "A Plea for Romantic Fiction," as Christ, though Annixter is specifically sacrificed in order to save the people Cedarquist describes as the "hungry Hindoo" (*O* 648). While the "white man's burden" is a crucial part of *The Octopus*'s ending, I want instead to focus on why Presley—the novel's poet—juxtaposes Annixter's individual death to the larger abstract force of nature.

Before as well as after his marriage to Hilma, Annixter has a special relationship with Presley. They are "the best of friends" and "never me[e]t without a mutual pleasure, taking a genuine interest in each other's affairs, and often putting themselves to great inconvenience to be of trifling service to help one another" (*O* 27). In addition, both men are described *in relation* to each other as being college educated: Presley "had graduated and post-graduated with high honours from an Eastern college, where he had devoted himself to a passionate study of literature" (*O* 9), while Annixter "like [Presley] . . . was a college graduate" (*O* 24). Annixter and Presley's college educations mark them, like Vanamee (the third main character whom Norris develops), as men "of wide reading and great intelligence" (*O*

35). Despite Norris's continual attacks on academic study as opposed to "life," he nonetheless imagines a college education as crucial in forming men's most profound intellectual and emotional ties.[18]

Annixter's death enforces and renders more poignant these college men's close relation. When Annixter dies on the verge of his "mighty transformation," the novel posits that it is Presley's, not Hilma's, duty to memorialize him and his development. Norris makes this point first by depicting Presley as switching places with Annixter—"When [Hilma] spoke [to Presley], it was with the old-time velvety huskiness of voice that Annixter had learned to love so well" (*O* 628)—then by describing Presley as being "made" into a man by Hilma, just as Annixter was. What is noticeable about this "making," however, is that Hilma is not involved in it:

> Then suddenly all the tired heart of him went out towards her. A longing to give the best that was in him to *the memory of her* . . . leaped all at once within him, leaped and stood firm, hardening to a resolve stronger than any he had ever known. (*O* 629–30, emphasis added)

Presley is "hardening" into manhood, but it is through a "memory," a memory of the "old-time," obsolete, sentimental mother. So, despite the erotics of the scene, Norris does not suggest that Presley will marry Hilma. Instead, Presley says to her, "I am going away and it is quite possible I shall never see you again" (*O* 631).

Just as Presley becomes Annixter (though an Annixter for whom Hilma is a "memory"), so too is the dead Annixter transformed into Hilma—into the sentimental, maternal man. Presley sees Hilma as "strengthened and infinitely ennobled by his [Annixter's] death" (*O* 629), and advises her that her sorrow for Annixter "will only be a great help to you. It will make you more noble, a truer woman, more generous" (*O* 630). In other words, Annixter's influence now "makes" Hilma, and by implication it will "make" Presley, and even the "hungry Hindoo." Like any number of sentimental heroines, Annixter's influence works from beyond the grave. Hilma, of course, says she does "not understand" (*O* 631) Presley's vision of Annixter's sentimental power. But she does understand why he is memorializing Annixter thus: "I do not know why you should want to be so kind [to me], unless—yes, of course—you were my husband's dearest friend" (*O* 631). It is Presley's job to memorialize Annixter, not Hilma's, for Presley, not Annixter's mother / wife, was his "dearest friend."

So in this scene of memorializing, Presley assumes Annixter's place, and Annixter assumes Hilma's place. Presley becomes a man, and Annixter becomes a kind of sentimental man / mother, the memory of him influencing others for good from beyond the grave. Presley and Annixter become more closely tied to each other through bonds of love, while Hilma disappears except as a marker for a certain kind of obsolete rhetoric. Sentimentalism is thus negated and then refigured, refigured not as the man's bond with the wife or "the Mother," but as his bond with another man.

With this in mind, the ending of the novel seems less incoherent. The novel argues that the specific case does not matter; only abstract force and the whole matters. But, in fact, the novel only knows how to make this point through the specific, personal, and sentimental. For example, if Vanamee can preach the greater good of force by the end of the novel, it is only because his dead lover is replaced by a personal, reborn lover, who murmurs to him "I love you, I love you" (O 639). Similarly, Presley's understanding of the greater good, which Vanamee has explained to him, comes when he can memorialize Annixter in terms of the sacrifice necessary to save the "hungry Hindoo," himself, and Hilma.[19] The personal and the sentimental have not been deleted from the text; rather, the representation merely changes from a suffering woman to a suffering man. More importantly, control over sentimental representation has moved from a woman and mother (the unprofessional), to a man and poet (the professional). The professional struggle of naturalist writers against sentimentalism is being worked out here through the opposition between the figures of the mother and the poet.

This leads us into *The Octopus*'s second main critique of sentimentalism, specifically of its (unprofessional) aesthetics, through the figure of the leisured, cultivated, and well-educated woman. In Norris's view, sentimentalism imagines itself as working in an aesthetic and moral realm outside of capitalism. But, Norris argues, sentimental aesthetics are actually deeply implicated in creating and reproducing the exploitative relations of capitalist production, an argument that has also been explored by contemporary critics like Ann Douglas and Nancy Armstrong.

Norris's attack on sentimental aesthetics is articulated most clearly in his satirical account of society ladies in San Francisco. These ladies are first described as "a file of hens" invading the sanctuary of a male club on "Ladies' Day" (O 309). This invasion of hens into a "masculine haunt" (O 309) disrupts the conversation that the men are having about strategies to outmaneuver the railroad (O 305–7). Specifically, the ladies disrupt the men's political conversation in order to view a painting of "a girl in a pink dress and white sunbonnet" standing against the Contra Costa foothills: "The ladies and young girls examined the production with little murmurs of admiration, hazarding remembered phrases . . . expressing their opinions in the mild technicalities of the Art Books and painting classes" (O 311).

Because these women disrupt the work of life with their educated *and* dilettantish aestheticism, the book depicts them as enabling the railroad's oppression of the people. They embody the city itself, "a Midway Plaisance" in Cedarquist's description, where art lulls the public into "indifference," allowing the railroad to crush its opposition (O 303). But equally bad, in Norris's account, is these women's conviction that they have the education to define what is good art. Through his displacement of the sentimental girl / mother, Hilma, as well as through the men's discussion of the railroad, Norris has shown that "a girl in a pink dress and a white sunbonnet" (O 311) has nothing to do with the "real" story of California. Nor does she have anything to do with the stylistics of "naked" (O 60) naturalist force. It is not simply art that distracts the public from the struggle with the railroad, but *bad* art, of the kind admired by educated women.

In the novel's most outraged scene, in fact, Norris depicts these educated, society ladies' desire for what is "tasteful" as coterminous with the murderous desire and force of the railroad. At some level, the ladies become the railroad. Presley is invited to an elaborate dinner where tasteful art and tasty delicacies are the only topics of discussion. He finds himself comparing the ladies at this dinner to the recently dead "Harran, Annixter, Osterman, Broderson, Hooven," imagining that "all these fine ladies with their small fingers and slender necks suddenly were transfigured into harpies tearing human flesh" (*O* 608). Norris upholds Presley's vision of these ladies by juxtaposing them and their chatter about taste with Mrs. Hooven's death by starvation on the streets of San Francisco (*O* 592–603). The juxtaposition suggests that the insatiable desire of dainty women for what they think are tasteful and tasty objects fuels and disguises the market forces which crush the masses.

Despite this understandable critique of sentimentalism, however, the novel concludes that social reality *is* in fact divorced from aesthetics. At the end of the novel, when Presley meets Shelgrim, the railroad's titan, he finds not "a brute, a terrible man of blood and iron . . . [but] *instead* . . . a sentimentalist and an art critic" (*O* 574, emphasis added). The opposition between the "brute" and the "art critic" is Presley's, but in the discussion of aesthetics that follows between Presley and Shelgrim, the narrator again upholds Presley's view. Shelgrim does not criticize Presley's poem "The Toilers" because of its socialist protest against the railroad; rather, he criticizes the poem for being derivative, inspired by art rather than life. Says Shelgrim, "I like the picture [of "The Toilers"] better than the poem. . . . There's only one best way to say anything. And what has made the picture of 'The Toilers' great is that the artist said in it the *best* that could be said on the subject" (*O* 574). To Shelgrim, art is good or bad depending on whether or not it is original or derivative, whether or not it is expressed well or badly. Aesthetics is one question; social reality is an entirely different one. Specifically, laissez-faire capitalism is a different question. Presley is depicted as progressively converted, first by Shelgrim's analysis of aesthetics and *then* by his discussion of laissez-faire capitalism. Shelgrim is right about each and right about their separation.

Presley and the narrator's views are confirmed by the trajectory of the book as a whole. At the beginning of the novel, the railroad, driving its way forcefully into the lives of the ranchers, is meant to embody a narrative refusal to separate personal emotions, private life, and aesthetics from social reality (*O* 49–51); by the end of the novel, however, the railroad is itself sentimentalized, a market force envisioned as transhistorical and transcendent, separated from mere humdrum social reality.

Like Norris's critical essays, then, *The Octopus* enacts the competition between rival narrative forms which took place as the field of literary studies was being professionalized. In order to distance itself from the "unprofessional" feminine genre of sentimentalism, the naturalist novel seeks to erase a literary history that enabled its own self-production. But, as we have seen, such an attempt does not erase sentimentalism from the naturalist narrative. Instead, it simply shifts the object of representation, and the authority to represent and to critique, from women to men, from the "unprofessional" female writer to the "professional" male writer.

ı^ıı

If this paper has argued that one must read the "emphatically 'male' genre of naturalism" (*BM* 29) with the emphatically "female" genre of sentimentalism, I want to conclude by suggesting that the struggles in the "literary field" at the turn of the century over the gender of genre have implications not only for our understanding of the literary field, but also for our understanding of the construction of men and women's social roles. Elsewhere I have argued that women intellectuals at the turn of the century created new, more public vocations for themselves by combining domestic ideology and sentimentalism with notions of the transcendent value of culture.[20] By contrast, this essay argues that male intellectuals at the turn of the century imagined their vocations through a denial of sentimentality and domesticity and an appeal to life over culture. The constructed sexual differences of genre, that is, have implications for understanding how social identities are formulated in various historical moments. In the case of naturalism, we see particularly how the gendering of genres shaped professional identity as it worked to create itself at the turn of the century.

NOTES

I would like to thank Joshua Piker, Jean Gregorek, and Jeremy Telman for their invaluable help in writing this essay.

1. Norris often used the terms romanticism and naturalism indistinguishably in order to define them against realism, as is the case here. For his use of these three terms, see *The Literary Criticism of Frank Norris*, ed. Donald Pizer (Austin: University of Texas Press, 1964), 69–70, hereafter cited parenthetically in the text and abbreviated *LC*.

2. For different variations of this basic narrative, see John C. Conder, *Naturalism in American Fiction: The Classic Phase* (Lexington: University of Kentucky Press, 1984); Alfred Habegger, *Gender, Fantasy, and Realism in American Literature* (New York: Columbia University Press, 1982); Lee Clark Mitchell, *Determined Fictions: American Literary Naturalism* (New York: Columbia University Press, 1991); and Charles Walcutt, *American Literary Naturalism: A Divided Stream* (Minneapolis: University of Minnesota Press, 1956). Habegger does include sentimentalism in his version of the basic narrative, but the trajectory remains the same: realism is the "crucial middle m[a]n" (65) between sentimentalism and naturalism, enabling the birth of the serious "masculine" (65) genre of naturalism. The important relation is that between the serious genres of realism and naturalism.

3. For different critiques of the basic narrative, see Donna M. Campbell, *Resisting Regionalism* (Athens: Ohio University Press, 1997); Philip Fisher, *Hard Facts: Setting and Form in the American Novel* (New York: Oxford University Press, 1985); June Howard, *Form and History in American Literary Naturalism* (Chapel Hill: University of North Carolina Press, 1985); Amy Kaplan, *The Social Construction of American Realism* (Chicago: University of Chicago Press, 1988); Walter Benn Michaels, *The Gold Standard and the Logic of Naturalism* (Berkeley: University of California Press, 1987); Donald Pizer, *The Theory and Practice of American Literary Naturalism* (Carbondale: Southern Illinois University Press, 1993); and Mark Seltzer, *Bodies and Machines* (New York: Routledge, 1992), hereafter cited parenthetically in the text and abbreviated as *BM*.

4. Sentimental elements have been identified in individual naturalist texts; however, critics generally do not focus on the relationship between the two genres in and of themselves. Fisher is an exception: in *Hard Facts*, he directly and systematically links sentimentalism to naturalism. Fisher's emphasis, however, is the opposite of mine. He argues that sentimentalism is a precursor to naturalism, that it has "an awareness" (126) of " 'forces'— climate, inheritance, and economic system" (125) that is "unmatched in American literature until Naturalism fifty years later" (126). By contrast, I argue that sentimentalism is crucial to naturalism's oppositional self-definition, though I would agree with Fisher that there are more similarities between the two genres than we might expect. See also Howard's discussion in *Form and History* of the ways naturalists used sentimentalism to open up disruptive fissures in their texts, and Campbell's analysis of naturalists' critique and use of women's local color writing in *Resisting Regionalism*.

5. Pierre Bourdieu, *The Field of Cultural Production*, ed. Randal Johnson (New York: Columbia University Press, 1993), 163–4.

6. Gerald Graff, *Professing Literature: An Institutional History* (Chicago: University of Chicago Press, 1989), 38.

7. Ibid., 62.

8. Norris's novel *Vandover and the Brute* (1914) is, in fact, dedicated to a professor at Harvard, Lewis Gates, whose literary criticism helped shape Norris's views (*LC* xvii). It is also important to note that Norris's literary studies were preceded by his study of painting from 1887–88, in Paris at the Académie Julian. The professionalism of the academicians who taught Norris, William B. Dillingham argues convincingly, had a major impact on Norris's work (*Frank Norris: Instinct & Art* [Lincoln: University of Nebraska Press, 1969], 14–24).

9. Ironically, Norris got this idea about the importance of "life" over "literature" from his literature teacher at Harvard, Lewis Gates (*LC* xvii).

10. For an almost exact repetition of this idea, see "Novelists to Order—While You Wait" (*LC* 15).

11. Elaine Showalter similarly argues that in the English context male authors' anxiety about women's increasing political power and about strong female precursors led to the orchestrated displacement of "Queen Realism" (George Eliot) by "King Romance" (Haggard, Conrad, Kipling) (*Sexual Anarchy: Gender and Culture at the Fin de Siecle* [New York: Viking, 1990], chapter 5). It is important to note that Norris was deeply influenced by the authors Showalter lists under the heading of "King Romance," particularly by Kipling and the misogynistic aesthetics expressed in his *The Light that Failed* (*LC* 20–4). See also Dillingham's excellent chapter "The Philosophy of Masculinity," in *Instinct & Art*.

12. For an extensive list of U.S. writers and critics who were influenced by Santayana, see Robert Dawidoff, *The Genteel Tradition and the Sacred Rage* (Chapel Hill: University of

North Carolina Press, 1992), 151. It is particularly through Vernon Louis Parrington's Santayana-inspired *Main Currents in American Thought* (3 vols. [New York: Harcourt, Brace and Co., 1927–30]) that this influence can be traced in literary studies (see Graff, *Professing Literature*, 215–6).

13. See Richard Colton Lyon, introduction to George Santayana, *Santayana on America; essays, notes, and letters on American life, literature, & philosophy* (New York: Harcourt, Brace & World, 1968), xxvii. Hereafter cited parenthetically in the text and abbreviated *SA;* "The Genteel Tradition" is on 36–56.

14. Eve Kosofsky Sedgwick, *Epistemology of the Closet* (Berkeley: University of California Press, 1990), 145, 148.

15. Critics who have traced the way in which abstract issues become personalized and domesticated in the sentimental novel include Nancy Armstrong (*Desire and Domestic Fiction: A Political History of the Novel* [New York: Oxford University Press, 1987]), Ann Douglas (*The Feminization of American Culture* [New York: Doubleday, 1988]), Mary P. Ryan (*The Empire of the Mother: American Writing about Domesticity, 1830–1880* [New York: Harrington Park, 1985]), and Jane Tompkins (*Sensational Designs: The Cultural Work of American Fiction, 1790–1860* [New York: Oxford University Press, 1985]). Similarly, critics who have traced the workings of force in the naturalist novel include Fisher, Howard, Mitchell, Pizer, Seltzer, and Walcutt, cited in notes 2 and 3 above.

16. Frank Norris, *The Octopus* (New York: Penguin, 1986), 467. Hereafter cited parenthetically in the text and abbreviated *O.*

17. I am indebted to Seltzer's reading of this scene (*BM* 25–44), though I am focusing on the topic of sentimentalism while he focuses on the mother's replacement by the machine.

18. That Norris believes a college education is crucial in forming *men's* most profound intellectual and emotional ties, and that co-eds just cannot be included, is proven by the case of Annie Derrick. Specifically described as college educated, Annie Derrick wishes to be friends with Presley (*O* 61). Her education, however, renders her unfit for true intellectual and emotional camaraderie, for it has provided her not with naturalist, but with sentimental aesthetics: "Her taste was of the delicacy of point lace. . . . She read . . . the little toy magazines, full of the flaccid banalities of the 'Minor Poets' " (*O* 61). Therefore, Presley rightly ignores her tentative gestures towards friendship.

19. S. Behrman's death is also intensely sentimental in the way it enacts "revenge" upon an individual, but Norris tries to explain this away by locating the sentimentality in Behrman, not in the narrative. Because Behrman becomes "sentiment[al]" (*O* 639) about the wheat he has obtained, he can be killed off, whereas before that, as Presley points out, he is impervious to death.

20. Francesca Sawaya, "Domesticity, Cultivation, and Vocation in Jane Addams and Sarah Orne Jewett," *Nineteenth-Century Literature* 48 (1994): 507–28.

NOTES ON CONTRIBUTORS

MARTIN A. BERGER recently completed a Ph.D. in American Studies at Yale University. He is an Assistant Professor of Art History at SUNY, Buffalo, and has published a number of articles on nineteenth-century American art and culture. His book, *Man Made: Thomas Eakins and the Construction of Gilded Age Manhood,* is being published in 1999 by the University of California Press.

VINCENT J. BERTOLINI recently completed his dissertation, "Constitutional Bodies: Practising National Subjectivity in Antebellum Writing," in the Department of English at the University of Chicago. He has also published a translation of Dacia Maraini's *Searching for Emma: Gustave Flaubert and Madame Bovary* with the University of Chicago Press.

BRUCE BURGETT is an Associate Professor of American Studies at the University of Washington, Bothell. He is the author of *Sentimental Bodies: Sex, Gender, and Citizenship in the Early Republic* and is currently working on a study of antebellum sexual reform cultures.

MARY CHAPMAN, Assistant Professor of English at the University of British Columbia, has published essays on American literature and culture in *Legacy, Wide Angle, Studies in American Indian Literatures,* and *Canadian Review of American Studies.* She has edited a paperback edition of Charles Brockden Brown's *Ormond* for Broadview Press, and is currently completing a book on *tableaux vivants* in nineteenth-century American literature and culture.

CASSANDRA CLEGHORN is at work on a manuscript, *Seeing Through Doing Good,* based on her 1995 Ph.D. dissertation in American Studies from Yale University,

"Bartleby's Benefactors: Toward a Literary History of Charity in Antebellum America." She teaches English and American Studies at Williams College.

P. GABRIELLE FOREMAN teaches English and American Studies at Occidental College in Los Angeles. Her essays on African American representation and literature have been published in *New Essays on Harriet Jacobs, Callaloo, Representations, Feminist Studies, The Yale Journal of Criticism,* and elsewhere.

PHILIP GOULD, William A. Dyer Jr. Assistant Professor in the Humanities at Brown University, is the author of *Covenant and Republic: Historical Romance and the Politics of Puritanism.* He has published on various topics on the Early Republic, as well as the writings of Sedgwick, Belknap, and Ellison, in *New England Quarterly, American Literature, a / b: Auto / Biography Studies, Arizona Quarterly, American Literary History, Early American Literature,* and *William and Mary Quarterly.*

KIRSTEN SILVA GRUESZ is Assistant Professor of English at the University of California at Santa Cruz, where she teaches nineteenth- and twentieth-century literature of the Americas, including Chicano / Latino literature. She has published essays on Longfellow and his Latin American translators, on the Argentine poet Esteban Echeverria, and on Walt Whitman, and is completing a book entitled *Ambassadors of Culture: Poetry and Identity Across the Americas, 1823–1898.*

GLENN HENDLER has published essays on Twain, Alger, and Alcott in *Arizona Quarterly, American Quarterly,* and *American Literary History,* and is currently completing a book entitled *Public Sentiments: Fictions of the Public Sphere in Nineteenth-Century America.* He is Assistant Professor of English at the University of Notre Dame.

TARA PENRY is an Assistant Professor of English at the University of Maine at Presque Isle. In addition to Melville and sentimentalism, her other research interests include American regional literature, small-press magazines of the nineteenth century, and American ethnic newspapers. She received her Ph.D. from Fordham University in February 1998.

JOHN SAILLANT teaches in the departments of English and History at Western Michigan University, as well as handling interactive computer resources for the Omohundro Institute of Early American History and Culture. His essays on eighteenth- and early-nineteenth-century religion, political philosophy, and notions of race and slavery have appeared in journals such as the *Journal of American Studies, Plantation Society in the Americas, Eighteenth-Century Studies, New England Quarterly, Early American Literature,* and *Journal of the Early Republic.*

KAREN SÁNCHEZ-EPPLER, Associate Professor of English and American Studies at Amherst College, is the author of *Touching Liberty: Abolition, Feminism, and the Politics of the Body.* She is presently completing a book on the cultural uses of childhood in nineteenth-century America. Her essay here is part of that project, as are recent essays in *American Quarterly* and *American Literary History* on temperance literature and Sunday school fiction.

SCOTT A. SANDAGE is Assistant Professor of History at Carnegie Mellon University and is completing a cultural history of failure in nineteenth-century America for Harvard University Press. He is the coeditor, with Peter Karsten, of a forthcoming reader in American cultural history, to be published by New York University Press. His 1993 article "A Marble House Divided: The Lincoln Memorial, the Civil Rights Movement, and the Politics of Memory, 1939–1963" (*Journal of American History*) won prizes from the Eugene V. Debs Foundation and the Organization of American Historians.

FRANCESCA SAWAYA, Assistant Professor of English and American Studies at Portland State University, is at work on a book about women writers and professional discourse.

INDEX

Designer: Barbara Jellow
Compositor: Impressions Book and Journal Services, Inc.
Text: 10/12 Baskerville
Display: Baskerville
Printer and binder: Edwards Bros., Inc.